TAX TACTICS
HANDBOOK

TAX TACTICS HANDBOOK

*The Aggressive Tax Planner's Guide
to IRS Audit Techniques,
Audit Triggers,
and Tax Savings Opportunities*

Ralph L. Guyette

Prentice-Hall, Inc.   Englewood Cliffs, New Jersey

Prentice-Hall International, Inc., *London*
Prentice-Hall of Australia, Pty. Ltd., *Sydney*
Prentice-Hall Canada, *Toronto*
Prentice-Hall of India Private Ltd., *New Delhi*
Prentice-Hall of Japan, Inc., *Tokyo*
Prentice-Hall of Southeast Asia Pte. Ltd., *Singapore*
Whitehall Books, Ltd., *Wellington, New Zealand*
Editora Prentice-Hall do Brazil Ltda., *Rio de Janeiro*

© 1983 by

Ralph L. Guyette

"This publication is designed to provide accurate and authoritative information in regard to the subject matter covered. It is sold with the
understanding that the publisher is not engaged in rendering legal,
accounting, or other professional service. If legal advice or other expert
assistance is required, the services of a competent professional person
should be sought."

—*From the Declaration of Principles jointly adopted by a Committee of the
American Bar Association and a committee of Publishers and
Associations.*

Library of Congress Cataloging in Publication Data

Guyette, Ralph L.
    Tax tactics handbook.

    Includes index.
    1. Tax auditing—United States. 2. United States.
Internal Revenue Service. 3. Tax administration and
Procedure—United States. 4. Tax planning—United
States. I. Title.
KF6314.G89 1983   343.7304'2   83-9456
ISBN 0-13-886754-2

Printed in the United States of America

About the Author

Ralph Guyette is a tax and financial consultant and former comptroller of Green Mountain College at Poultney, Vermont. His career in taxation and business spans more than 40 years. Starting as an internal auditor, he progressed through various corporate accounting offices to the Internal Revenue Service, where he worked his way through all three IRS income tax divisions, and spent 20 years as a special agent in the Intelligence Division (now Criminal Investigation Division).

While in the IRS, Mr. Guyette directed the dissection of the records of hundreds of businesses, both large and small, or performed such operations personally. He has been a tax instructor at the college level, a free-lance writer and a Director of Personnel.

He was a principal in a certified public accounting firm and is presently on the board of directors of several corporations.

Mr. Guyette is the author of the *Complete Guide to a Successful Small Client Tax Practice* published by Prentice-Hall.

What This Book Will Do for You

Tax Tactics Handbook is a one-stop reference guide designed to help you tackle most of the frequently met tax problems which you are likely to encounter in professional practice. It takes the "search" out of research by bringing together in one place the information you need to exploit tax-saving opportunities, prepare tax returns that stand up to IRS scrutiny, and emerge victorious from an audit.

Here's how *Tax Tactics Handbook* provides research shortcuts and helps save you valuable time:

■ It zeroes in on specific problem areas you are likely to encounter with each of 30 vital tax issues.

■ It reveals how the IRS sees each issue and what it does in terms of enforcement. The *Tax Tactics Handbook* is fully integrated with actual IRS audit procedures and you'll find valuable "inside information" taken directly from IRS Audit Manuals and special project studies.

■ It untangles and interprets complicated regulations—and gives you pertinent references to Code sections, revenue rulings, court cases, and more.

■ It helps you prepare almost "audit-proof" tax returns by showing you how the IRS thinks . . . what entries raise red flags for audit classifiers and computers . . . why various methods of preparing a tax return fail—and why others will not.

■ It shows you how to handle the audit, and which steps and regulations will lead you to a successful defense of your tax position. Also included are successful taxpayer defenses of actual audits.

■ It gives you inside tips and tactics that save tax dollars for your client . . . alerts you to potential pitfalls . . . makes your contacts with IRS personnel less trying and more profitable . . . and enhances your chances of victory at examination time.

HOW THE "TOP 30" WERE CHOSEN

The 30 critical tax issues covered in the *Tax Tactics Handbook* were selected on the basis of extensive research and consultation with key tax professionals. A detailed analysis of all IRS manuals—focusing particularly on tax issues which bear the strongest government emphasis—laid the groundwork for this volume. The IRS Prime Issues List was also searched and utilized. Former members of the IRS, now legal or CPA tax practitioners, were consulted as this handbook was prepared.

Finally, the author, Ralph L. Guyette, called upon his own 42 years of experience both as a tax practitioner and as an IRS agent. The end result is an invaluable reference source covering the key tax issues you are most likely to encounter in professional practice.

How This Book Can Help You

A glance at a single succinct chapter from the *Tax Tactics Handbook* will quickly demonstrate its value as a research tool. Suppose, as in Chapter 1 on Hobby Losses, that the government has decided that your client's loss operation is "not entered into for profit" and that such a deficit, therefore, is not deductible. This chapter will quickly acquaint you with the problem, outline the key points at issue, and help you fully understand both sides of the question. You'll discover, for example,

- The reasons for the IRS objection.
- Nine tests which the government will utilize in deciding whether a hobby loss has occurred.
- When the burden of proving a "profit motive" shifts from the taxpayer to the IRS. (Such knowledge can be extremely important at negotiation time.)
- How to make use of ten fully explained strategies which will aid in avoiding a tax audit for the subject activity.
- How to postpone the hobby-loss determination to a more favorable date.
- How to defend your original position—that losses from the particular activity were indeed deductible and not hobby losses.
- Which Code sections or tax-service references will serve you best under the conditions.
- Which court cases and Revenue Rulings will lend the most strength to your position—or will damage it in any way. (Both pros and cons are supplied.)
- What the IRS Audit Manuals have to say about specific audit techniques in this much-contested area of taxation.

Multiply this kind of practical help by 30 and you'll see why *Tax Tactics* will fast become an indispensable aid to quick, complete research. For your thorniest tax problems, you'll have at your fingertips the answers to such questions as:

- Is the government correct in its presumption?
- What strong points does its case possess? What weak ones?
- What IRS points can be rebutted with a good chance of success?
- Is the case worth contesting?

As a time saver, educator, troubleshooter, tax planner, and practice builder, the *Tax Tactics Handbook* will serve you well.

Ralph L. Guyette

ACKNOWLEDGMENTS

To my wife, Louise, a thousand thanks for her encouragement and for the many hours of effort which she expended in the production of this manuscript.

Many thanks also to my son Andrew E. Guyette, CPA, for his invaluable technical assistance.

CONTENTS

WHAT THIS BOOK WILL DO FOR YOU _____ **5**

HOW THIS BOOK CAN HELP YOU _____ **7**

1

HOBBY LOSSES _____ **21**
(Section 183)

1.1 Identifying the Problem ____ 21
1.2 How the IRS Sees the Issue ____ 21
1.3 Factors Which the IRS Considers When Making Its Audit Decision ____ 22
1.4 Considerations When Preparing the Return ____ 24
1.5 Handling the Audit ____ 25
1.6 Pertinent Court Decisions–Pro and Con ____ 25
1.7 Relevant Code and Regulation Sections ____ 27
1.8 Applicable IRS Manual References ____ 28

2

REPAIRS VS. CAPITAL EXPENDITURES _____ **29**
(Sections 162, 190, 212, 263)

2.1 Identifying the Problem ____ 29
2.2 How the IRS Sees the Issue ____ 30
2.3 Factors Which the IRS Considers When Making Its Audit Decision ____ 30
2.4 Considerations When Preparing the Return ____ 32
2.5 Handling the Audit ____ 34
2.6 Pertinent Court Decisions–Pro and Con ____ 35
2.7 Relevant Code and Regulation Sections ____ 37
2.8 Applicable IRS Manual References (Investigative Techniques) ____ 37

3

EMPLOYEE OR INDEPENDENT CONTRACTOR _____ **39**
(Section 3401)

3.1 Identifying the Problem ____ 39
3.2 How the IRS Sees the Issue ____ 42
3.3 Factors Which the IRS Considers When Making Its Audit Decision ____ 44
3.4 Considerations When Preparing the Return ____ 48
3.5 Handling the Audit ____ 49

3.6 Pertinent Court Decisions–Pro and Con —— 50
3.7 Relevant Code and Regulation Sections —— 52
3.8 Applicable IRS Manual References (Investigative Techniques) —— 52

4

CASUALTY LOSSES —————————————————————————— 53
(Section 165)

4.1 Identifying the Problem —— 53
4.2 How the IRS Sees the Issue —— 54
4.3 Factors Which the IRS Considers When Making Its Audit Decision —— 55
4.4 Considerations When Preparing the Return —— 58
4.5 Handling the Audit —— 61
4.6 Pertinent Court Decisions–Pro and Con —— 62
4.7 Relevant Code and Regulation Sections and IRS Publications —— 64
4.8 Applicable IRS Manual References (Investigative Techniques) —— 65

5

DEALERS VS. INVESTORS ———————————————————————— 67
(Sections 64 and 1202)

5.1 Identifying the Problem —— 67
5.2 How the IRS Sees the Issue —— 69
5.3 Factors Which the IRS Considers When Making Its Audit Decision —— 71
5.4 Considerations When Preparing the Return —— 74
5.5 Handling the Audit —— 78
5.6 Pertinent Court Decisions–Pro and Con —— 80
5.7 Relevant Code and Regulation Sections —— 82
5.8 Applicable IRS Manual References (Investigative Techniques) —— 83

6

MEDICAL AND DENTAL DEDUCTIONS —————————————————— 85
(Section 213)

6.1 Identifying the Problem —— 85
6.2 How the IRS Sees the Issue —— 85
6.3 Factors Which the IRS Considers When Making Its Audit Decision —— 86
6.4 Considerations When Preparing the Return —— 87
6.5 Handling the Audit —— 92
6.6 Pertinent Court Decisions–Pro and Con —— 94
6.7 Relevant Code and Regulation Sections, plus Publications —— 95
6.8 Applicable IRS Manual References (Investigative Techniques) —— 95

7

VACATION HOMES AND OTHER DWELLING UNITS ———————————— 97
(Section 280A)

7.1 Identifying the Problem —— 97
7.2 How the IRS Sees the Issue —— 98
7.3 Factors Which the IRS Considers When Making Its Audit Decision —— 98

7.4 Considerations When Preparing the Return —— 99

7.5 Handling the Audit —— 101

7.6 Pertinent Court Decisions–Pro and Con —— 102

7.7 Relevant Code Sections —— 103

7.8 Applicable IRS Manual References —— 103

8

HOME OFFICE _____ 105
(Section 280A)

8.1 Identifying the Problem —— 105

8.2 How the IRS Sees the Issue —— 106

8.3 Factors Which the IRS Considers When Making Its Audit Decision —— 107

8.4 Considerations When Preparing the Return —— 107

8.5 Handling the Audit —— 109

8.6 Pertinent Court Decisions–Pro and Con —— 111

8.7 Relevant Code and Regulation Sections and IRS Publications —— 112

8.8 Applicable IRS Manual References (Investigative Techniques) —— 112

9

CHARITABLE CONTRIBUTIONS _____ 115
(Section 170)

9.1 Identifying the Problem —— 115

9.2 How the IRS Sees the Issue —— 116

9.3 Factors Which the IRS Considers When Making Its Audit Decision —— 117

9.4 Considerations When Preparing the Return —— 118

9.5 Handling the Audit —— 125

9.6 Pertinent Court Decisions–Pro and Con —— 126

9.7 Relevant Code and Regulation Sections, plus Publications —— 128

9.8 Applicable IRS Manual References (Investigative Techniques) —— 128

10

MOVING EXPENSES _____ 129
(Section 217)

10.1 Identifying the Problem —— 129

10.2 How the IRS Sees the Issue —— 130

10.3 Factors Which the IRS Considers When Making Its Audit Decision —— 130

10.4 Considerations When Preparing the Return —— 130

10.5 Handling the Audit —— 134

10.6 Pertinent Court Decisions–Pro and Con —— 137

10.7 Relevant Code and Regulation Sections, plus Publication —— 138

10.8 Applicable IRS Manual References (Investigative Techniques) —— 138

11

CHILD AND DISABLED DEPENDENT CARE _____ 139
(Section 44A)

11.1 Identifying the Problem —— 139

11.2 How the IRS Sees the Issue —— 142

11.3 Factors Which the IRS Considers When Making Its Audit Decision —— 143
11.4 Considerations When Preparing the Return —— 144
11.5 Handling the Audit —— 148
11.6 Pertinent Court Decisions–Pro and Con —— 149
11.7 Relevant Code and Regulation Sections, plus Publication and Form —— 150
11.8 Applicable IRS Manual References (Investigative Techniques) —— 150

12

SALE OF A RESIDENCE ——————————————————————— 153
(Sections 1034 and 121)

12.1 Identifying the Problem —— 153
12.2 How the IRS Sees the Issue —— 155
12.3 Factors Which the IRS Considers When Making Its Audit Decision —— 155
12.4 Considerations When Preparing the Return —— 157
12.5 Handling the Audit —— 160
12.6 Pertinent Court Decisions–Pro and Con —— 163
12.7 Relevant Code and Regulation Sections, plus Publications —— 164
12.8 Applicable IRS Manual References (Investigative Techniques) —— 165

13

BRIBES, ILLEGAL PAYMENTS, AND KICKBACKS ———————————— 167
(Section 162(c))

13.1 Identifying the Problem —— 167
13.2 How the IRS Sees the Issue —— 169
13.3 Factors Which the IRS Considers When Making Its Audit Decision —— 171
13.4 Considerations When Preparing the Return —— 173
13.5 Handling the Audit —— 174
13.6 Pertinent Court Decisions–Pro and Con —— 177
13.7 Relevant Code and Regulation Sections —— 178
13.8 Applicable IRS Manual References (Investigative Techniques) —— 179

14

EDUCATIONAL EXPENSES ———————————————————————— 181
(Section 162–Regulation 1.162-5)

14.1 Identifying the Problem —— 181
14.2 How the IRS Sees the Issue —— 182
14.3 Factors Which the IRS Considers When Making Its Audit Decision —— 183
14.4 Considerations When Preparing the Return —— 183
14.5 Handling the Audit —— 186
14.6 Pertinent Court Decisions–Pro and Con —— 187
14.7 Relevant Code and Regulation Sections, plus Publications —— 188
14.8 Applicable IRS Manual References (Investigative Techniques) —— 188

15

EXEMPTIONS AND DEPENDENTS ————————————————— 189
(Sections 151 and 152)

15.1 Identifying the Problem —— 189
15.2 How the IRS Sees the Issue —— 189
15.3 Factors Which the IRS Considers When Making Its Audit Decison —— 192
15.4 Considerations When Preparing the Return —— 195
15.5 Handling the Audit —— 198
15.6 Pertinent Court Decisions–Pro and Con —— 199
15.7 Relevant Code and Regulation Sections, plus Publications —— 202
15.8 Applicable IRS Manual References (Investigative Techniques) —— 203

16

BAD DEBTS ———————————————————————— 205
(Section 166)

16.1 Identifying the Problem —— 205
16.2 How the IRS Sees the Issue —— 206
16.3 Factors Which the IRS Considers When Making Its Audit Decision —— 207
16.4 Considerations When Preparing the Return —— 208
16.5 Handling the Audit —— 213
16.6 Pertinent Court Decisions–Pro and Con —— 214
16.7 Relevant Code and Regulation Sections, plus Publication —— 215
16.8 Applicable IRS Manual References (Investigative Techniques) —— 215

17

INADEQUATE BOOKS AND RECORDS ———————————————— 217
(Section 6001)

17.1 Identifying the Problem —— 217
17.2 How the IRS Sees the Issue —— 218
17.3 Factors Which the IRS Considers When Making Its Audit Decision —— 219
17.4 Considerations When Preparing the Return —— 222
17.5 Handling the Audit —— 223
17.6 Pertinent Court Decisions–Pro and Con —— 228
17.7 Relevant Code and Regulation Sections, plus Publication —— 229
17.8 Applicable IRS Manual References (Investigative Techniques) —— 230

18

TRAVEL AND ENTERTAINMENT EXPENSES ——————————————— 231
(Sections 162, 212, 274)

18.1 Identifying the Problem —— 231
18.2 How the IRS Sees the Issue —— 232
18.3 Factors Which the IRS Considers When Making Its Audit Decision —— 233

18.4 Considerations When Preparing the Return ___ 233
18.5 Handling the Audit ___ 239
18.6 Pertinent Court Decisions–Pro and Con ___ 241
18.7 Relevant Code and Regulation Sections, plus Publication ___ 242
18.8 Applicable Manual References (Investigative Techniques) ___ 243

19

ABANDONMENT AND DEMOLITION LOSSES _____ 245
(Sections 165, 167, 280B)

19.1 Identifying the Problem ___ 245
19.2 How the IRS Sees the Issue ___ 246
19.3 Factors Which the IRS Considers When Making Its Audit Decision ___ 246
19.4 Considerations When Preparing the Return ___ 247
19.5 Handling the Audit ___ 251
19.6 Pertinent Court Decisions–Pro and Con ___ 252
19.7 Relevant Code and Regulation Secions, plus Applicable Publication ___ 253
19.8 Applicable IRS Manual References (Investigative Techniques) ___ 254

20

DIVORCE AND ALIMONY _____ 255
(Sections 71 and 215)

20.1 Identifying the Problem ___ 255
20.2 How the IRS Sees the Issue ___ 256
20.3 Factors Which the IRS Considers When Making Its Audit Decision ___ 257
20.4 Considerations When Preparing the Return ___ 258
20.5 Handling the Audit ___ 262
20.6 Pertinent Court Decisions–Pro and Con ___ 263
20.7 Relevant Code and Regulation Sections, plus Publication ___ 264
20.8 Applicable IRS Manual References (Investigative Techniques ___ 264

21

BARTERING _____ 265
(Section 61)

21.1 Identifying the Problem ___ 265
21.2 How the IRS Sees the Issue ___ 265
21.3 Factors Which the IRS Considers When Making Its Audit Decision ___ 266
21.4 Considerations When Preparing the Return ___ 267
21.5 Handling the Audit ___ 269
21.6 Pertinent Court Decisions–Pro and Con ___ 271
21.7 Relevant Code and Regulation Sections, plus Publication ___ 271
21.8 Applicable IRS Manual References (Investigative Techniques) ___ 271

22

COMPENSATION, EXCESSIVE OR NOT _____ 273
(Section 162)

22.1 Identifying the Problem ___ 273
22.2 How the IRS Sees the Issue ___ 274

22.3 Factors Which the IRS Considers When Making Its Audit Decision —— 274
22.4 Considerations When Preparing the Return —— 275
22.5 Handling the Audit —— 277
22.6 Pertinent Court Decisions–Pro and Con —— 278
22.7 Relevant Code and Regulation Sections, plus Publication —— 279
22.8 Applicable IRS Manual References (Investigative Techniques) —— 279

23

LEGAL AND PROFESSIONAL FEES —————————————————————— 281
(Sections 162 and 212)

23.1 Identifying the Problem —— 281
23.2 How the IRS Sees the Issue —— 282
23.3 Factors Which the IRS Considers When Making Its Audit Decisions —— 282
23.4 Considerations When Preparing the Return —— 283
23.5 Handling the Audit —— 287
23.6 Pertinent Court Decisions–Pro and Con —— 288
23.7 Relevant Code and Regulation Sections, plus Publication —— 289
23.8 Applicable IRS Manual References (Investigative Techniques) —— 289

24

EVASION OR AVOIDANCE —————————————————————————— 291
(Sections 6653 and 7201)

24.1 Identifying the Problem —— 291
24.2 How the IRS Sees the Issue —— 292
24.3 Factors Which the IRS Considers When Making Its Audit Decision —— 293
24.4 Considerations When Preparing the Return —— 295
24.5 Handling the Audit —— 297
24.6 Pertinent Court Decisions–Pro and Con —— 299
24.7 Relevant Code and Regulation Sections —— 300
24.8 Applicable IRS Manual References (Investigative Techniques) —— 301

25

INTEREST EXPENSE ————————————————————————————— 303
(Section 163)

25.1 Identifying the Problem —— 303
25.2 How the IRS Sees the Issue —— 304
25.3 Factors Which the IRS Considers When Making Its Audit Decision —— 304
25.4 Considerations When Preparing the Return —— 306
25.5 Handling the Audit —— 310
25.6 Pertinent Court Decisions–Pro and Con —— 311
25.7 Relevant Code and Regulation Sections, plus Publication —— 312
25.8 Applicable IRS Manual References (Investigative Techniques) —— 313

26

CAPITAL GAINS AND LOSSES ——————————————————————— 315
(Section 1202)

26.1 Identifying the Problem —— 315
26.2 How the IRS Sees the Issue —— 315

26.3 Factors Which the IRS Considers When Making Its Audit Decision ____ 316
26.4 Considerations When Preparing the Return ____ 317
26.5 Handling the Audit ____ 321
26.6 Pertinent Court Decisions–Pro and Con ____ 322
26.7 Relevant Code and Regulation Sections, plus Publications ____ 323
26.8 Applicable IRS Manual References (Investigative Techniques) ____ 324

27

THE BUSINESS AUTOMOBILE _____ 325
(Sections 162 and 212)

27.1 Identifying the Problem ____ 325
27.2 How the IRS Sees the Issue ____ 326
27.3 Factors Which the IRS Considers When Making Its Audit Decision ____ 326
27.4 Considerations When Preparing the Return ____ 327
27.5 Handling the Audit ____ 331
27.6 Pertinent Court Decisions–Pro and Con ____ 333
27.7 Relevant Code and Regulation Sections ____ 334
27.8 Applicable IRS Manual References (Investigative Techniques) ____ 334

28

RESIDENTIAL RENTAL PROPERTY _____ 335
(Sections 61 and 212)

28.1 Identifying the Problem ____ 335
28.2 How the IRS Sees the Issue ____ 336
28.3 Factors Which the IRS Considers When Making Its Audit Decision ____ 336
28.4 Considerations When Preparing the Return ____ 337
28.5 Handling the Audit ____ 339
28.6 Pertinent Court Decisions–Pro and Con ____ 340
28.7 Relevant Code and Regulation Sections, plus IRS Publications ____ 341
28.8 Applicable IRS Manual References (Investigative Techniques) ____ 342

29

DEDUCTIONS FOR TAXES _____ 343
(Section 164)

29.1 Identifying the Problem ____ 343
29.2 How the IRS Sees the Issue ____ 344
29.3 Factors Which the IRS Considers When Making Its Audit Decision ____ 345
29.4 Considerations When Preparing the Return ____ 345
29.5 Handling the Audit ____ 348
29.6 Pertinent Court Decisions–Pro and Con ____ 350
29.7 Relevant Code and Regulation Sections, plus Publications ____ 351
29.8 Applicable IRS Manual References (Investigative Techniques) ____ 351

30

SICK PAY AND DISABILITY INCOME _____ **353**
   (Sections 104 and 105)

   30.1 Identifying the Problem _____ 353
   30.2 How the IRS Sees the Issue _____ 353
   30.3 Factors Which the IRS Considers When Making Its Audit Decision _____ 354
   30.4 Considerations When Preparing the Return _____ 355
   30.5 Handling the Audit _____ 358
   30.6 Pertinent Court Decisions–Pro and Con _____ 359
   30.7 Relevant Code and Regulation Sections, plus Publications _____ 360
   30.8 Applicable IRS Manual References (Investigative Techniques) _____ 361

APPENDIX _____ **363**

INDEX _____ **371**

Hobby Losses
(Section 183)

1

1.1 IDENTIFYING THE PROBLEM

When a taxpayer engages in an activity that regularly produces operating losses, the IRS becomes suspicious and claims that the operation is an "activity not engaged in for profit" (Code Section 183), thereby causing such so-called hobby losses to become nondeductible. In effect, this move by the government disallows expenses that would ordinarily be permitted under Section 162 (Trade or Business) or Section 212 (Expenses for the Production of Income).

1.2 HOW THE IRS SEES THE ISSUE

Generally the issue arises in situations where the taxpayer is either wealthy or is running a highly profitable business in addition to a loss operation. The government particularly objects when large tax benefits result from an activity that appears to generate personal pleasure or recreational opportunities. See Regulation 1.183-2(b)(8) reproduced below:

> (8) *The financial status of the taxpayer.* The fact that the taxpayer does not have substantial income or capital from sources other than the activity may indicate that an activity is engaged in for profit. Substantial income from sources other than the activity (particularly if the losses from the activity generate substantial tax benefits) may indicate that the activity is not engaged in for profit especially if there are personal or recreational elements involved.

Conversely, people with little capital or other income—and few tax benefits—usually have little difficulty with the IRS.

NOTE:

Regulation 1.183-2(c) illustrates three examples of farm losses. Two concern wealthy persons who may be classed as "gentlemen farmers." Their profit motive is denied. The third person, with a small amount of income, is deemed to have a profit motive. It is apparent, therefore, that most government challenges will appear in instances where the taxpayer is wealthy or enjoys substantial other income.

1.3 FACTORS WHICH THE IRS CONSIDERS WHEN MAKING ITS AUDIT DECISION

As in much tax law, each case must be judged on its own particular merits ... hobby losses even more so than others. Using Regulation 1.183-2, government auditors will consider the following factors:

1. *Manner in which the taxpayer carries on the activity.*
   A taxpayer in a hobby-suspect operation should make certain that he functions as would any prudent businessperson—maintaining and periodically analyzing good financial records—operating the activity in much the same fashion as a successful comparable venture—using new operational techniques—discarding those that prove to be outmoded—maintaining equipment and buildings in good functional condition—using any and all steps that might prove an intention toward profit making.

2. *Expertise of the taxpayer or his advisors.*
   While it may not be necessary for taxpayers to be thoroughly experienced in the operation of their loss activities, they should nevertheless be able to prove that they attempted to become knowledgeable, either through extensive study or through consultation with others.

   Courts have accepted acquisition of knowledge as "previous experience," but have not treated taxpayers kindly where they: (1) have not made positive efforts to overcome or avoid losses, (2) have not studied the market potential before beginning the activity, (3) have not advertised in situations that clearly called for such a move, (4) have not devoted any appreciable amount of time to bettering the hobby-suspect business.

3. *Time and effort expended by the taxpayer in carrying on the activity.*
   The won-lost farm case history in this category strongly favors those taxpayers who have either employed competent workers under their immediate supervision or who have performed all of the work themselves or with their families. Judges appear to give much weight to the amount of personal effort expended by the taxpayer.

4. *Expectation that assets used in the activity may appreciate in value.*
   According to Regulation 1.183-2(b)(4):

   The term 'profit' encompasses appreciation in the value of assets, such as land, used in the activity. Thus, the taxpayer may intend to derive a profit from the operation of the activity and may also intend that, even if no profit from current operations is derived, an overall profit will result when appreciation in the value of the land used in the activity is realized, since income from the activity together with the appreciation of land will exceed expenses of operation.

IMPORTANT:
   At first glance, this fourth criterion for judging a hobby loss would seem to be an excellent escape route for those with farm operations. Not so—not unless the farm activity, with all of its appreciable assets, is considered *one* activity.

   Land purchased primarily as an investment—but also farmed—would be considered as two activities, thereby negating any use of this section in the justification of a profit motive.

5. *Success of taxpayer in carrying on other similar or dissimilar activities.*
   Meeting this category will definitely be a plus. Failure to meet it will not necessarily be fatal.

6. *Taxpayer's history of income or losses with respect to the activity.*

Regulation 1.183-2(b)(6) clearly states that: A series of losses during the initial or start-up stage of an activity may not be necessarily be an indication that the activity is not engaged in for profit.

Circumstances beyond the control of the taxpayer will be considered—drought, disease, fire, theft, weather damage, depressed market conditions, and involuntary conversions. Continued losses are not necessarily fatal.

A bank executive suffered steady losses over a twelve-year period in the operation of a Vermont ski lodge. The IRS disallowed the losses but the tax court did not, recognizing that the taxpayer had studied the skiing industry before building the lodge—operated it in a businesslike manner—advertised his rentals with real estate brokers and newspapers. Adverse conditions such as an influx of other investors and a lack of snow legitimized the losses. The tax court recognized no elements of personal pleasure in the rental operation, since neither the taxpayer nor his family utilized the lodge except to stay overnight in connection with management duties. (Truett E. Allen (1917) 72 TC No. 3)

7. *Amount of occasional profits, if any, which are earned.*

Here's how the IRS sees this criterion when attempting to arrive at a taxpayer's intent:

A. It considers the amount of profits in relation to the amount of losses—and in relation to the amount of the taxpayer's investment and the value of the assets used in the activity. In other words, an occasional small profit from an activity generating large losses—or from an activity in which the taxpayer has made a large investment—would not generally indicate a profit motive.

B. A substantial profit, even though occasional, would be indicative that a business is engaged in for profit, particularly where the investment, or losses, are comparatively small.

C. Furthermore, an opportunity to earn ultimately solid profits in a highly speculative venture would ordinarily be sufficient to indicate a profit intention.

8. *Financial status of the taxpayer.*

This one is quite obvious. Individuals without substantial income or capital from sources outside the Section 183 activity generally have nothing to fear from the IRS. Taxpayers with substantial income from outside sources become suspect, particularly if they realize large tax benefits from the hobby-suspect activity—and even more so if there are personal or recreational elements involved.

9. *Elements of personal pleasure or recreation.*

This regulation, 1.183-2(b)(9), clearly states that it is not necessary that an activity be engaged in with the exclusive intention of deriving a profit or with the intention of maximizing profits.

If elements of personal pleasure or recreation are present, however, it does cause the operation to become suspect. It would appear foolhardy, for example, to equip a dairy farm with a swimming pool, riding horses, and a putting green—unless, of course, they were for rent to the general public.

Seemingly, a complete lack of any appeal other than potential profits would strongly indicate a money-making intent.

Even though the IRS lists these nine as "Relevant Factors," it freely admits that *all* facts and circumstances are taken into account and that no one factor is determinative—not even "History of Profits and Losses," which would seem to be all important.

Burden of Proof. In hobby-loss situations the burden of proving that a "profit motive" exists rests with the taxpayer. It shifts to the IRS, however, if a profit appears in any of two or more taxable years in a period of five consecutive years (2 out of 7 years for the breeding, training, showing, or racing of horses). See Code Section 183(d).

In the latter situation a presumption arises that the activity *was* engaged in for profit unless the Treasury establishes to the contrary. This it may do by showing obvious manipulations of income and deductions so as to cause the "manufacturing" of profits.

IMPORTANT:

No inference as to lack of profit motive can be drawn from the fact that the 2 in 5 (or 7) year test is not met (Regulation 1.183-4).

1.4 CONSIDERATIONS WHEN PREPARING THE RETURN

If you are on the scene *before* Section 183 problems arise, there is much that you and your clients can do to avoid IRS difficulties. Suggest that they take the following steps:

■ Establish the operation in a businesslike fashion:

• Install a good set of records; maintain them in an efficient manner.

• Establish a separate checking account. (The courts have many times criticized the lack of one.)

• Take all of the normal steps that might be expected of a prudent businessperson.

• Employ capable, proven employees where necessary.

• Purchase operational reading material that is designed to improve the type of activity in question.

■ Acquire knowledge through study or consultation so that they are in a position to prove a certain amount of expertise.

■ Keep a record of all attempts to better the operation—and of all plans for future improvement.

■ In a legitimate sense, time the receipt of income and payment of expenses to provide a favorable result for any given year.

■ Make prudent efforts to show profits in at least two of the consecutive-year periods.

■ Use conservative but realistic depreciation and salvage provisions.

■ Capitalize or not (where allowable) so that the election will produce desirable results.

■ When selling capital assets, use timely installment methods to swing gains so as to produce a couple of years' profits.

■ Make all moves that would normally be expected of business people in their activity. (If they have a cattle-breeding operation, for example, they should maintain a good herd book.)

■ Expend as much personal effort as possible and do not be concerned whether they enjoy what they are doing or not.

NOTE:

The courts have remarked that taxpayers need not dislike what they are doing in order to have profit motives.

Once established, a base such as the one presented above should insure success in most audit situations. However, should you inherit a client who has ignored Section 183 dangers, proceed as follows:

1.5 HANDLING THE AUDIT

Your objective will be simple: show a profit motive. Before all else, carefully review with your client the defense possibilities inherent in the nine "Relevant Factors" as listed in Regulation 1.183-2. Proceed then to develop as much strength as possible from items listed in the previous section, "Considerations When Preparing the Return."

Remember that the burden of proving a profit motive rests with your client unless profits appeared in 2 out of 5 (or 7) years. If they did not, all is still not lost. You may postpone the "Hobby Loss" determination for 5 to 7 years, as the case may be.

You should also closely interrogate your client. Isolate each point which might possibly indicate a profit motive; then attempt to exploit all such situations by strengthening them with a regulation or court decision. "Hobby losses" are indeed a gray area of taxation. Pros and cons abound. Don't just study the cases in your favor. Examine the others as well. They many times contain excellent material which can be used to impress the IRS examiner.

Postponement of the "Hobby Loss" determination. If the 2-5 (or 7) presumption rule is followed to the letter, a taxpayer would be precluded from using it to his advantage if he showed a loss at the end of the first year of his activity. He would be without profits from the "consecutive 5 (or 7) year period."

Section 183(e) corrects this situation by allowing a taxpayer to postpone a determination whether the presumption exists until the close of the 4th taxable year (6th for horses) following the tax year in which he first engages in the activity.

If such an election is desired, Form 5213 (Election to Postpone Determination) should be filed. This form may be utilized within three years after filing a return, or within 60 days after an IRS notice of disallowance of loss.

WARNING:

Such filing extends the statute of limitations for assessing deficiencies attributable to Section 183 for a period of two years.

1.6 PERTINENT COURT DECISIONS — PRO AND CON

Pro
Sebastian DeGrazia and Anna Maria DeGrazia
(TC Memo 1962-296)

Findings of Fact

Petitioners filed a joint income tax return for 1957. The hobby-loss issue applies only to Anna Maria, who identified herself on the return as an "artist."

She was born in Switzerland but spent most of her life in Italy until she came to the United States in 1952, married Sebastian, and became an American citizen.

The taxpayer became seriously interested in painting in 1940 and sold one painting. Most of her early work was destroyed during the war. She originally painted with her right hand but, because of a polio condition, was forced to learn all over again with her left.

In 1942 her paintings won several prizes. After receiving attestations from three professional artists that she was a professional, she was allowed to join the Italian painters' union. By 1957 she had studied under three famous artists and had achieved recognition in Italy as an artist in her own right.

From 1948 through 1956 her career was spotty, as she alternately painted and stopped several times during this period. Subsequent to 1957 she exhibited in one-person shows in three Italian cities. After these shows and the resultant good publicity, she obtained a $500 commission to do a portrait. From this time forward she continued to study and exhibit and learn the business aspects of being an artist. Although she realized no sales in 1957 because she was attempting to build up an inventory, her painting income increased gradually during the years 1958 through 1961.

Opinion

In this case, the judge relied on Edwin S. George, 22BTA 189, to state:

> Although it is not necessarily determinative, the intent of the taxpayer is very important in deciding whether certain activities constitute a trade or business.

After hearing the taxpayer's testimony and noting Anna Maria's strong efforts to overcome adversity and learn her profession, the court said that it was well satisfied that her intent was to seek profit rather than to indulge in mere recreation. In closing, the judge highlighted an important consideration in the hobby-loss controversy for artists and for those engaged in other activities that require a long period of time for fruition:

> It is well recognized that profits may not be immediately forthcoming in the creative art field. Examples are legion of the increase in value of a painter's works after he receives public acclaim. Many artists have to struggle in their early years. This does not mean that serious artists do not intend to profit from their activities. It only means that their lot is a difficult one.

Con
Norman R. and Caroline W. Pickering
(TC Memo 1979-243)

Findings of Fact

Petitioners Norman and Caroline Pickering purchased 183 acres of land in 1961 but did not work or live on it until 1969, at which time they began sharecropping their tobacco allotment and raising some hay for a small number of beef cattle and five horses.

Norman, an airline pilot, earned upward of $50,000 a year at his profession. Neither he nor any member of his family had any appreciable amount of farm experience.

Since Norman was absent from ten to sixteen days a month, the farm was operated mostly by the wife and children. From 1969 through 1973 the farm was gradually improved but always showed losses. Five horses were maintained—one to run cattle; the others were show horses in which wife Caroline and daughter Norma were greatly interested. Caroline, in fact, was an active member of the United States Pony Club.

Petitioners began their beef cattle herd in 1969 with ten cows and their calves. By adding a bull and six more cows, they built their herd to approximately thirty head by the end of 1973. Their only farm plan was to utilize the "natural increase method" of herd development. Witnesses testified that it would take ten years to build a profitable herd in this manner.

The Pickerings did not hire any help except for some odd jobs. To reduce their workload they sharecropped tobacco and received some assistance from neighbors. They did not participate in any government agricultural programs, nor did they maintain a separate checking account for the farm operation.

Two neighbors with smaller acreage and no major sources of additional income were making profits from their farm activities.

Opinion

The court, in using the "Nine Relevant Factors," had this to say in ruling for the Commissioner:

The farm was not operated in a businesslike manner.

Reliable records were not maintained.

A separate checking account was not utilized.

The taxpayers were not able to provide the court with an exact number of cattle held at the end of 1973.

No records of herd changes were maintained.

No development plan had been prepared.

Neighbors operated smaller farm at a profit.

Farm experience was lacking, yet taxpayers did not employ knowledgeable help.

Norman spent from one-third to one-half of each month away from the farm.

The farm land and livestock did appreciate, but such appreciation was attributable as much to general price increases as to the farm operation.

Petitioners made no showing of prior farming success or failures.

Portions of taxpayer's income of well over $50,000 a year could have been used to acquire a productive herd and to hire experienced help..

An element of personal pleasure existed in maintenance of the show horses.

1.7 RELEVANT CODE AND REGULATION SECTIONS

Code

Section 162	Trade or business expenses
165(c)(2)	Losses incurred in any transaction entered into for profit, though not connected with a trade or business
183	Activities not engaged in for profit
183(d)	Presumption that an activity was engaged in for profit
183(e)	Special rule concerning presumption
212	Expenses for the production of income

Regulations

Section 1.183-1	Activity not engaged in for profit	
1.183-2	Activity not engaged in for profit, defined in general	

1.8 APPLICABLE IRS MANUAL REFERENCES

Audit Technique Handbook

MT 4231	Section 233.2	Some Items to Verify on Form 1040 with Business and Farm Schedules
MT 4231	690	Farmers

Standard Explanations Handbook

MT 428(11)14	Section 45	Losses

The *Standard Explanations Handbook* contains a master list of standard explanations to be used on all automated Examination Writing Systems. These explanations were compiled basically from a *frequency use study* which is invaluable to you and me, because it tells us *just where the IRS believes the golden eggs lie.*

Audit—General

Manual Supplement	40RDD-81	Activities Not Engaged in For Profit

This manual supplement provides instructions for the operation of a special IRS project designed to ferret out loss revenues through "hobby losses." Its existence indicates the importance the Service applies to this issue.

NOTE:

Copies of Internal Revenue Audit Manuals may be obtained from
Freedom of Information Reading Room
Internal Revenue Service
1111 Constitution Avenue NW
Washington DC 20224

The charge is small. A copy of *Tax Audit Guidelines For Internal Revenue Examiners* (IRM 4231) may also be obtained from Prentice-Hall, Inc., Englewood Cliffs, N.J. 07632.

Repairs vs. Capital Expenditures (Sections 162, 190, 212, 263)

2

2.1 IDENTIFYING THE PROBLEM

Since the Economic Recovery Tax Act of 1981 the repairs vs. capital expenditures problem is not as acute as it once was. It is expected, nevertheless, that it will remain an important area of IRS inquiry. The Service will continue to look for expenses that can be disallowed as deductions—and capitalized. Implementation of this simple goal, however, is not easy as the scores of judicial actions attest.

The Code itself does not deal specifically with repairs, except indirectly through Section 162(a) which states that:

> There shall be allowed as a deduction all ordinary and necessary expenses paid or incurred during the taxable year in carrying on any trade or business.

...and through Section 212 which says substantially the same, but:

> in the case of an individual for the production of income.

Only the regulations, in Section 1.162-4, directly approach repairs and then but briefly through a short paragraph, which is reproduced below:

> The cost of incidental repairs which neither materially add to the value of the property nor appreciably prolong its life, but keep it in an ordinarily efficient operating condition, may be deducted as an expense, provided the cost of acquisition or production or the gain or loss basis of the taxpayer's plant, equipment, or other property, as the case may be, is not increased by the amount of such expenditures. Repairs in the nature of replacements, to the extent that they arrest deterioration and appreciably prolong the life of the property shall either be capitalized and depreciated in accordance with Section 167, or charged against the depreciation reserve if such an account is kept.

It can readily be seen, therefore, why this is such a gray area of federal taxation.

2.2 HOW THE IRS SEES THE ISSUE

In order to make the distinction between repairs and improvements, the government utilizes guidelines that are clearly epitomized by an old Board of Tax Appeals case, *Illinois Merchants Trust Company* (Ex. 4BTA 103):

> A repair is an expenditure for the purpose of keeping property in an ordinarily efficient operating condition. It does not add to the value of the property, nor does it appreciably prolong its life. It merely keeps the property in an operating condition over its probable useful life for the uses for which it was acquired. Expenditures for the purpose are distinguishable from those for replacements, alterations, improvements, or additions which prolong the life of the property, increase its value, or make it adaptable to a different use. The one is a maintenance charge, while the others are additions to capital investment which should not be applied against current earnings.

Patching a roof, for example, is a repair; installing a new roof is a capital improvement. Fixing the carburetor on a business vehicle is a repair; installing a new motor is not.

The IRS is fully aware that, in these days of expensive money and high taxes, a taxpayer would much rather repair existing assets—and take a full and immediate deduction—than invest cash or borrowed funds in property that would return only small depreciation deductions over many years.

Its object, then, is to make certain that evidence suppports the former. From the myriad of pro and con court decisions, it is evident that each case must stand on its own merits—and triumph or fall in direct relation to the manner in which the proof *exists and is presented.*

2.3 FACTORS WHICH THE IRS CONSIDERS WHEN MAKING ITS AUDIT DECISION

In attempting to locate additional revenue through the repairs-improvement vehicle, the IRS takes a shotgun approach. It doesn't just examine each large repair item; it goes down many additional paths.

If, for example, a business performs its maintenance program through use of its own personnel, might it not make improvements that were expensed through payrolls, operating supplies, repairs, etc.? Certainly.

The agents examine job sheets, work orders, or other records that might indicate what Peter the plumber and Charlie the carpenter were doing all year. Maybe the elements of labor, materials, freight, and some overhead should be assembled, removed from their various expense accounts, and depreciated.

To uncover this possibility, an agent might request a tour of the plant or inquire as to whether any new construction had occurred. If the investigator does so, his or her reasoning will be obvious.

Page 4231-74 of the *Audit Technique Handbook for Internal Revenue Agents* reads:

On occasion the taxpayer or, in the case of a corporation, an officer will invite an agent to inspect the plant or a particular repair job which is being questioned. The agent should accept such invitations in a gracious manner ...

Page 4233-17 reads:

Refer to notes taken on inspection of plant which relate to apparent new construction, equipment, etc., and determine if such items have been properly capitalized.

Small repair accounts are even suspect, the theory being that if a taxpayer owns substantial fixed assets, the small repair total may be indicative of the practice of charging repairs to other accounts which are less likely to be checked.

Other Key Audit Techniques

In addition to initially examining repair and maintenance accounts for obvious capital expenditures, the IRS at the same time and for other reasons:

1. Searches for duplicate invoices.
2. Tries to identify transactions between related parties.
3. Looks for personal expense items.
4. Compares deductions claimed with those of prior years. (If the increase is substantial, the agent will want to know why.)
5. Searches for expenditures for new assets with a useful life of more than one year.
6. Is alert to the existence of general improvement or reconditioning projects. (Possibly expenditures that would be deductible as repairs if incurred separately can be turned into capital costs when incident to an overall betterment.)
7. Watches closely for addresses on invoices. (Deliveries made to a corporate officer's residence, or that of an individual taxpayer, give strong indication that the expense was personal in nature.)
8. Becomes concerned when extensive, otherwise legitimate repairs are made shortly after acquisition of a property—and will want to treat such expenditures as part of the cost of the asset.
9. Looks for items that may be turned from repair costs to nondeductible replacements.
10. In situations where the property is used for both residence and business, examines repair expenses for correct allocations.
11. For documentation, will want to see both cancelled checks *and invoices*. (The latter will many times become the deciding factor as to just what was purchased, what other components there might be, where the item was installed, etc.)
12. As represented by some astute agents, might examine parallel accounts such as freight and insurance—plus corporation minutes—to locate major equipment purchases or substantial rehabilitation projects.

The IRS asks for a reasonable approach from its agents in two particular circumstances:

1. That they recognize the question of degree. (What is material to a small business may not be for a larger one.)

2. That they give consideration to taxpayers who utilize a conservative depreciation policy. (Under such circumstances there should be good grounds for giving more leeway on repair items.)

2.4 CONSIDERATIONS WHEN PREPARING THE RETURN

Keep in mind that repairs merely maintain a property in good operating condition. They do not:

1. Change its use.
2. Increase its value.
3. Lengthen its life.

Capital expenditures may do all or some of these things. Since the law on the issue is unclear and subject to varied interpretations, taxpayers have much leeway in shaping expenses to their advantage. This does not mean, however, that benefits always lie in the taking of an immediate and full deduction.

When Repair Deductions Are Not Beneficial

Possibly a business is new and growing and does not need immediate tax relief—but will later. Then its expenditures possibly should be shaped into capital improvements so that they can be recovered gradually over future years as depreciation.

NOTE:

This consideration has become particularly important in light of the accelerated depreciation possibilities provided by the Economic Recovery Tax Act of 1981.

Since repairs to a personal residence are not deductible in any sense, it would be good tax planning to include them with major improvements wherever possible so that such costs would increase the basis of the dwelling and thus reduce taxable gain, if the property should be sold.

In the case of Section 38 property (available for investment credit), it may suit the taxpayer's purpose, for example, to capitalize the cost of rebuilding machinery or automotive equipment—so that he or she can take the maximum investment credit—rather than deduct such expenses as a one-shot benefit.

If circumstances are right, such a move carries an obvious advantage which the IRS doesn't like, but can do nothing about. Capitalizing the expense will not only generate an investment credit but will allow quick recovery of the entire cost as well.

Major Areas of Repair Controversies

Key Timing Points for Simultaneous Repairs and Improvements

In this situation the IRS will not allow deductions for repairs unless records or circumstances clearly differentiate between them and improvements. Timing, therefore, can be of great importance.

Wherever possible:

1. The two projects should be accomplished at different times.

2. They should not be attempted in the same contract.

3. If segregation is not practical, careful records should be maintained to document each type of work.

4. Suppliers and contractors should be asked to present segregated billings. A plumber, for example, should separate his charges for repairing a leaking pipe on the second floor from the installation of a new furnace in the basement.

5. Where maintenance and improvement projects are performed by employees, work orders, time sheets, or other labor control records should clearly identify their accomplishments, i.e., "Painting floor of payroll office," or "Repairing brickwork of main entrance facade."

General plan of improvement. Repairs that might normally constitute deductible expenses will usually be disallowed if performed under a general plan of permanent rehabilitation and betterment. It is imperative, therefore, as in the section above, that all such work be segregated, clearly identified and performed, if possible, at different times.

Restoration of rundown property. Where property is purchased in a dilapidated condition, the IRS will usually require that the cost of restoration be capitalized.

Courts, however, have frequently allowed substantial rebuilding of *owned* property where such construction did not add to value or life of the asset.

For example, in National Weeklies, Inc., the replacement of a building wall by an iron beam supported by iron posts imbedded in cement was allowed, because the construction only placed the building in its previous condition—before use of heavy machinery had weakened it.

Replacement of worn equipment (Regulation 1.162-4) In general, wherever a piece of machinery or other operating equipment is replaced by another having a useful life of more than one year, the cost must be capitalized. Repairs to the extent that they arrest deterioration and appreciably prolong the life of the asset must also be depreciated or charged against the depreciation reserve, if one exists.

Replacement of small parts or normal maintenance costs will normally be allowed.

Expenses of removing architectural and transportation barriers for the handicapped and elderly. Such costs would normally be classed as improvements. Under Code Section 190, however, a taxpayer may elect to deduct the first $25,000 of such qualifying expenditures for calendar years which began after December 31, 1976, and ended before January 1, 1983. Regulation 1.190-2 reads:

> The term "architectural and transportation barrier removal expenses" means expenditures for the purpose of making any facility, or public transportation vehicle, owned or leased by the taxpayer for use in connection with his trade or business more accessible to, or usable by, handicapped individuals or elderly individuals.

A qualifying expense may be an architectural change, such as the installation of a ramp leading to a store entrance. Amounts expended in excess of the $25,000 limit must be capitalized.

A word of caution: Regulation 1.190-2(b) states that qualifying expenses do not include any part of any expense paid or incurred in connection with the construction or comprehensive renovation of a facility or public transportation vehicle or the normal replacement of depreciable property.

Write-Offs Under ACRS

The accelerated cost recovery system (ACRS), as generated by the Economic Recovery Tax Act of 1981, has provided for new, fast write-offs for business equipment and for depreciable business and investment realty—as placed in service after 1980. This new system will practically eliminate controversy over the useful life of a property but will probably not make the repair-capital expenditure issue disappear.

ACRS does not require that a taxpayer use the shorter useful life route, or accelerated depreciation options, but merely make them available.

WARNING:

Look twice before jumping on this wagon. For nonresidential real estate—upon disposition—the gain, up to the amount of depreciation taken, will be ordinary income. Any excess will be capital gain.

For residential property, the gain will be recaptured as ordinary income only to the extent that depreciation under the accelerated method exceeds that which would have been allowed if the straight-line method had been used over the 15-year period.

For both types of realty, where the straight-line method had been used, any gain will be capital.

New "expensing" rules, which apply to the purchase of qualified property acquired after 1981, allow for writing off up to $5,000 a year of such costs in 1982 and 1983 (for marrieds—$2,500 for singles). This dollar limitation continues to rise until it reaches $10,000 in 1986. BUT, should such property subsequently be sold, the entire amount of such "expensing" allowance must be recaptured as ordinary income.

Good records are important. Since the line between repairs and capital improvement is so often vague, it is imperative that good records be maintained to clearly establish the purpose of the expenditure. Taxpayers have many times failed because costs were not segregated. Remember, the burden of proof is upon the taxpayer.

2.5 HANDLING THE AUDIT

If an audit should arrive, practitioners will find that they are either:

1. Well-prepared because they looked forward to the possibility of an IRS visit and readied their workpapers and documentation to meet such an eventuality, or
2. Not prepared because, when doing the return, they entered the taxpayer's figures without question or explanation, or
3. Not prepared because they did not put together the original return.

Presuming the latter two situations, practitioners should first of all completely analyze the various repair and labor accounts which might be involved, review corporate minutes where applicable, examine asset accounts for indications of capital improvements, and then closely question the taxpayer. Become fully knowledgeable, in other words.

After all data is laid out and segregated, clearly capital items should be at least mentally set aside as ultimately becoming nondeductible. Calling an obvious improvement a repair will not make it so but will only upset the revenue agent and cause him or her to lose confidence in the balance of a presentation.

Having cleared the deck, so to speak, the practitioner should set about building evidence to support the remaining repair deductions—not with words but with documentation, contracts, invoices, cancelled checks, proof of unusual circumstances, for example:

> An expenditure that might clearly be classed as a leasehold improvement might actually be a repair under the right circumstances.

> Suppose that the taxpayer had only one year remaining on his lease—and had been notified in writing that the lease would not be renewed—and suppose that the taxpayer believed that a certain improvement would pay for itself and more within the 12-month period; then he could honestly deduct such an expenditure, since its useful life was one year or less.

Favorable court decisions should also be collected.

The practitioner should bear in mind that a determination, as made by the IRS, is always presumptively correct (Bishoff v. Com. (CCA-3, 1928) 27 F. 2d 91, 6 AFTR 7870).

To overcome this presumption, the burden is on the taxpayer to prove that the expenditure was:

- Actually made or incurred
- A repair expense, not a capital expenditure
- A business expense, not a personal one
- Deducted in the proper accounting period

Certainly a good presentation will greatly increase a practitioner's chance for success.

In any case, where the repair-improvement controversy exists, it is difficult for any taxpayer to come up entirely empty-handed. Should the expenditure be disallowed for the year in question, and capitalized, the taxpayer loses currently but recovers his entire cost eventually as depreciation—and possibly even in situations where his tax bracket has greatly increased.

IMPORTANT:

Under these conditions, taxpayers should always decide any questionable repair/ improvement uncertainty in their favor—calling the item either one, as best suits their purpose.

2.6 PERTINENT COURT DECISIONS—PRO AND CON

Pro
Oklahoma Transportation Company vs. U.S.
(DC Okla 1966) 19 AFTR2d 1538, 272 F. Supp 729

Findings of Fact

Among other adjustments, the Commissioner disallowed a deduction of some $3,000 as an ordinary and necessary business expense in accomplishing certain roof repairs, contending that such an expenditure must be capitalized.

Opinion

The Court found for plaintiff and stated that:

> The evidence is to the effect that this money was spent to replace deteriorated roof decking which involved a part of the roof of one building and which condition was detected when other repairs were being made to the roof by reason of a storm.

> The Court finds that from the nature of this work it constituted the repair of deteriorated parts of the building and such did not appreciably prolong the original useful life of the property.

Con
Herman Barron and Ann Barron
(TC Memo 1963-315)

Findings of Fact

Petitioners, who were husband and wife, had been engaged for approximately 20 years in the business of buying run-down real estate which they would remodel and sell. In October of 1958 they purchased a 24-unit apartment building with its corresponding land for $83,000. The structure was run-down and unrentable.

The taxpayers moved into one apartment and began a general renovation of the building. During the balance of 1958 and all of the year 1959 they installed a new boiler and water line, new roof, steel fire escapes, six new bathrooms, etc., spending $9,495 in the former year and $11,855 in the latter, all of which they capitalized.

In addition, they deducted as repairs $3,900 in 1958 and $8,500 in 1959—for papering, painting, sanding and finishing floors, new linoleum, window shades, electrical work and plumbing, and general repair work, relying on Regulation 1.162-4 which allows a deduction for incidental repairs.

The IRS objected, claiming that these deducted amounts were actually spent as part of a renovating and remodeling program and should be capitalized.

Opinion

Evidence indicated that the repairs were more than incidental. When the building was purchased in 1958 it was in an unrentable condition. By the date of trial in 1963 more than $50,000 had been spent in repairs—and even then, only about one-third of the necessary work had been completed. Clearly the petitioners were engaged in a program of renovating and remodeling.

The judge cited Joseph Merrick Jones, 24 T.C. 563 (1955) affd. 242 F 2d 616 (50 AFTR 2040) C.A. 5, 1957) and noted that this taxpayer had attempted to expense similar repairs by relying on the predecessor of Regulation 1.162-4. "We held there," he said,

> that the expenditures were not for "incidental repairs" but were part of an overall plan for the general rehabilitation, restoration, and improvement of an old building which had lost its commercial usefulness due to extreme deterioration. The building had passed beyond "an ordinarily efficient operating condition," and expenditures were to restore it to, rather than to "keep it in," operating condition***

> The purpose and effect of the expenditures***were not ordinary maintenance expenses and cannot be separated from the general plan and purpose.***

"It is true," continued the judge, "that if a particular item of repair were considered by itself it might be considered a deductible expense, when, as here, there is a general plan of renovation, all items are a part of that plan and must be capitalized."

2.7 RELEVANT CODE AND REGULATION SECTIONS

Code

Section 162(a)	Trade or Business Expenses—in General
190	Expenditures to Remove Architectural and Transportation Barriers to the Handicapped and Elderly
212	Expenses for the Production of Income
263	Capital Expenditures

Regulations

Section 1.162.1	Business Expenses—in general
1.162-4	Business Expenses—repairs
1.167(a)-11 (d)(2)(ii)	Election of repair allowance (CLADR)
1.190-2(a)	Definition, Architectural and Transportation Barrier Removal Expense

2.8 APPLICABLE IRS MANUAL REFERENCES (INVESTIGATIVE TECHNIQUES)

Audit Technique Handbook

MT 4231	Section 233.2	Some Items to Verify
	233.2(d)	Disproportionate Repairs to Depreciable Assets
	675	Repairs

Employee or Independent Contractor

3

(Section 3401)

3.1 IDENTIFYING THE PROBLEM

Difficulties encountered in the Employee/Independent Contractor controversy are easily recognizable:

1. The cost of payroll taxes has escalated—and will continue to escalate—to a point where they will become true financial, operational hazards—particularly as to Social Security. Assuming the proposed 1987 FICA rate to 7.15 percent with a wage base of $42,600, the total FICA business expense for one employee will exceed $3,000. In the same year, the self-employment rate will increase to $4,260.

2. As a consequence, the business community wants to class every worker possible as an independent contractor, one who is not subject to federal and state employment levies, withholding or unemployment insurance taxes, or wage and hour laws.

3. The IRS, on its part, does not appreciate this trend and has markedly stepped up its enforcement efforts.

Since Social Security taxes are by far the largest costs involved, this chapter will be primarily concerned with their application.

Who Is an Employee Subject to FICA Taxes?

Basically, workers are employees and their wages subject to FICA if they fall into one of the following three categories as set forth in Section 3121(d), reproduced as Figure 3-1:

1. Officers of a corporation.
2. Common law employees.
3. Employees engaged in certain activities such as delivery and sales persons and certain home workers—but see last paragraph of Section 3121(d) for exceptions.

(d) Employee.—For purposes of this chapter, the term "employee" means—

(1) any officer of a corporation; or

(2) any individual who, under the usual common law rules applicable in determining the employer-employee relationship, has the status of an employee; or

(3) any individual (other than an individual who is an employee under paragraph (1) or (2)) who performs services for remuneration for any person—

(A) as an agent-driver or commission-driver engaged in distributing meat products, vegetable products, fruit products, bakery products, beverages (other than milk), or laundry or dry-cleaning services, for his principal;

(B) as a full-time life insurance salesman;

(C) as a home worker performing work, according to specifications furnished by the person for whom the services are performed, on materials or goods furnished by such person which are required to be returned to such person or a person designated by him; or

(D) as a traveling or city salesman, other than as an agent-driver or commission-driver, engaged upon a full-time basis in the solicitation on behalf of, and the transmission to, his principal (except for side-line sales activities on behalf of some other person) of orders from wholesalers, retailers, contractors, or operators of hotels, restuarants, or other similar establishments for merchandise for resale or supplies for use in their business operations;

if the contract of service contemplates that substantially all of such services are to be performed personally by such individual; except that an individual shall not be included in the term "employee" under the provisions of this paragraph if such individual has a substantial investment in facilities used in connection with the performance of such services (other than in facilities for transportation), or if the services are in the nature of a single transaction not part of a continuing relationship with the person whom the services are performed.

Last amendment.—Sec. 3121(d) appears above as amended by Sec. 206(a) of Public Law 761, Sept. 1, 1954 (qualified effective date rule in Sec. 206(b) of PL761).

Implied amendment of Sec. 3121(d) was made by Sec. 530(a) of P.L. 95-600, Nov. 6, 1978, amended by Sec. 9(d)(1) of P.L. 96-167, Dec. 29, 1979 and Sec. 1(a) of P.L. 96-541, Dec. 17, 1980.

Reproduced from the *Prentice-Hall Federal Taxes* service (1983 edition) with the permission of the publisher.

Figure 3-1

Causing most of the controversy is (2)—defining a "common-law" employee.

The Common Law Rule

Every individual who performs services subject to the will and control of an employer, both as to what shall be done and how it shall be done, is an employee for purposes of all federal payroll taxes. It doesn't matter that the employer permits the employee considerable discretion and freedom of action, so long as the employer has the legal right to control both the method and result of the services. For more details, see Regulation 31.3401(c)-1, Figure 3-2.

This rule, at first glance, appears clear enough; yet, in its interpretation, literally hundreds of IRS/taxpayers confrontations, Revenue Rulings, and judicial proceedings have failed to set forth a clear definition of a "common law employee."

A following section will present the criteria which the IRS uses in arriving at *its* definition. Additional IRS criteria will undoubtedly evolve as a result of the Tax Equity and

0—§31.3401(c)-1 (T.D. 6259, filed 10-25-57; republished in T.D. 6516, filed 12-19-60; amended by T.D. 7068, filed 11-10-70.) **Employee**

(a) The term "employee" includes every individual performing services if the relationship between him and the person for whom he performs such services is the legal relationship of employer and employee. The term includes officers and employees, whether elected or appointed, of the United States, a State, Territory, Puerto Rico, or any political subdivision thereof, of the District of Columbia, or any agency of instrumentality of any one or more of the foregoing.

(b) Generally the relationship of employer and employee exists when the person for whom services are performed has the right to control and direct the individual who performs the services, not only as to the result to be accomplished by the work but also as to the details and means by which that result is accomplished. That is, an employee is subject to the will and control of the employer not only as to what shall be done but how it shall be done. In this connection, it is not necessary that the employer actually direct or control the manner in which the services are performed; it is sufficient if he has the right to do so. The right to discharge is also an important factor indicating that the person possessing that right is an employer. Other factors characteristic of an employer, but not necessarily present in every case, are the furnishing of tools and the furnishing of a place to work to the individual who performs the services. In general, if an individual is subject to the control or direction of another merely as to the result to be accomplished by the work and not as to the means and methods for accomplishing the result, he is not an employee.

(c) Generally, physicians, lawyers, dentists, veterinarians, contractors, subcontractors, public stenographers, auctioneers, and others who follow an independent trade, business, or profession, in which they offer their services to the public, are not employees.

(d) Whether the relationship of employer and employee exists will in doubtful cases be determined upon an examination of the particular facts of each case.

(e) If the relationship of employer and employee exists, the designation or description of the relationship by the parties as anything other than that of employer and employee is immaterial. Thus, if such relationship exists, it is of no consequence that the employee is designated as a partner, coadventurer, agent, independent contractor, or the like.

(f) All classes or grades of employees are included within the relationship of employer and employee. Thus, superintendents, managers, and other supervisory personnel are employees. Generally, an officer of a corporation is an employee of the corporation. However, an officer of a corporation who as such does not perform any services or performs only minor services and who neither receives nor is entitled to receive, directly or indirectly, any remuneration is not considered to be an employee of the corporation. A director of a corporation in his capacity as such is not an employee of the corporation.

(g) The term "employee" includes every individual who receives a supplemental unemployment compensation benefit which is treated under paragraph (b) (14) of §31.3401 (a)-1 as if it were wages.

(h) Although an individual may be an employee under this section, his services may be of such a nature, or performed under such circumstances, that the remuneration paid for such services does not constitute wages within the meaning of section 3401(a).

Figure 3-2

Fiscal Responsibility Act of 1982 (TEFRA).

TEFRA has classified two types of self-employed individuals as definite independent contractors, but conditionally. Real estate agents and direct sellers can escape the employee stigma. However, two conditions must be met:

1. Substantially all of their income from services must be directly related to sales or other output.
2. Their services must be performed under a written contract that provides that they will not be treated as employees for federal tax purposes.

NOTE:

A direct seller is described in Code Section 3508 as a person who is engaged— ... in the trade or business of selling (or soliciting the sale of) consumer products to any buyer on a buy-sell basis, a deposit-commission basis, or any similar basis which the Secretary prescribes by regulations, for sale (by the buyer or any other person) in the home or otherwise than in a permanent retail establishment ...

Who Is an Employer?

Generally, an employer is any individual, corporation, partnership, trust, group, or entity for whom an individual performs or performed any service, of whatever nature, *as an employee*. For details see regulation 31.3401(d)-1, Figure 3-3.

O—§31.3401(d)-1 (T.D. 6259, filed 10-25-57; republished in T.D. 6516, filed 12-19-60; amended by T.D. 7068, filed 11-10-70.)**Employer.**

(a) The term "employer" means any person for whom an individual performs or performed any service, of whatever nature, as the employee of such person.

(b) It is not necessary that the services be continuing at the time the wages are paid in order that the status of employer exist. Thus, for purposes of withholding, a person for whom an individual has performed past services for which he is still receiving wages from such person is an "employer."

(c) An employer may be an individual, a corporation, a partnership, a trust, an estate, a joint-stock company, an association, or a syndicate, group, pool, joint venture, or other unincorporated organization, group, or entity. A trust or estate, rather than the fiduciary acting for or on behalf of the trust or estate, is generally the employer.

(d) The term "employer" embraces not only individuals and organizations engaged in trade or business, but organizations exempt from income tax, such as religious and charitable organizations, educational institutions, clubs, social organizations and societies, as well as the governments of the United States, the States, Territories, Puerto Rico, and the District of Columbia, including their agencies, instrumentalities, and political subdivisions.

(e) The term "employer" also means (except for the purposes of the definition of "wages") any person paying wages on behalf of a nonresident alien individual, foreign partnership, or foreign corporation, not engaged in trade or business within the United States (including Puerto Rico as if a part of the United States).

(f) If the person for whom the services are or were performed does not have legal control of the payment of the wages for such services, the term "employer" means (except for the purpose of the definition of "wages") the person having such control. For example, where wages, such as certain types of pensions or retired pay, are paid by a trust and the person for whom the services were performed has no legal control over the payment of such wages, the trust is the "employer."

(g) The term "employer" also means a person making a payment of a supplemental unemployment compensation benefit which is treated under paragraph (b) (14) of §31.3401 (a)-1 as if it were wages. For example, if supplemental unemployment compensation benefits are paid from a trust which was created under the terms of a collective bargaining agreement, the trust shall generally be deemed to be the employer. However, if the person making such payment is acting solely as an agent for another person, the term "employer" shall mean such other person and not the person actually making the payment.

(h) It is a basic purpose to centralize in the employer the responsibility for withholding, returning, and paying the tax, and for furnishing the statements required under section 6051 and §31.6051-1. The special definitions of the term "employer" in paragraphs (e), (f), and (g) of this section are designed solely to meet special or unusual situations. They are not intended as a departure from the basic purpose.

Figure 3-3

3.2 HOW THE IRS SEES THE ISSUE

The Internal Revenue Service, after conducting a study of 7,000 cases involving the Employee/Independent Contractor issue, found that at least 47 percent of the contractors involved did not report any of their self-employment earnings for income tax purposes and 62 percent did not pay any of the self-employment taxes that were required.

This taxpayer noncompliance, according to the study, cost the national revenue an estimated one billion dollars. It is not surprising, therefore, that the requirement for Form 1099 NEC was born.

Statements for Recipients of Nonemployee Compensation (Form 1099 NEC)

In an attempt to plug these independent-contractor loss-revenue holes, the government established a reporting requirement (Code Section 6041). This laws requires the filing of Form 1099 NEC for all organizations which pay more than $600 to individuals in compensation as identified below:

> All fees, commissions, prizes, awards, or any other compensation paid to (or on behalf of) any individual for services rendered in the course of a trade or business when that individual is not treated as an employee.

Such 1099s must be transmitted to required Service Centers through use of Forms 1096 (Annual Summary and Transmittal of U.S. Information Returns). Section 6041 has since been enlarged upon by TEFRA.

TEFRA tightened up this information-reporting system by adding Section 6041A which requires, in addition to the above, a filing of Forms 1099 for "direct sales" individuals as previously defined. As a general rule, a direct selling business need report only gross purchases if the buyer purchases $5,000 or more of goods in one year.

Government Reaction to Results of Noncompliance Study

With at least a billion dollars to work with, the IRS knows that this area of taxation will be lucrative in an "enforcement dollar spent" — "enforcement collar earned" comparison.

HOWEVER, it has been prevented by Congress from an all-out compliance drive because of the continuing chaos in arriving at a clear definition of a common law employee.

Safe Haven Laws

With the enactment of Section 530 of the Revenue Act of 1978 (P.L. 95-600) the Legislature provided temporary relief for taxpayers until such time as it could enact clarifying legislation.

It prohibited the IRS from reclassifying any individual from independent contractor to employee status through 1979—in instances where the taxpayer utilized a reasonable basis in determining the worker's employment status. Since then, Congress has continued to extend this "Safe Haven" law until TEFRA finally extended the moratorium indefinitely. This TEFRA extension, however, does not apply to real estate dealers and direct sales people.

Reasonable Basis Defined

"Reasonable basis" is defined as reliance on:

1. Past IRS audit practice with respect to the taxpayer.
2. Published rulings or judicial precedent.
3. Recognized practice in the taxpayer's industry.
4. Technical advice or a letter ruling given to taxpayer.

In addition, all required information returns must have been filed by the taxpayer for the periods after December 31, 1978—and no other worker with substantially the same position may have been treated as an employee.

NOTE:

Taxpayers involved in administrative or judicial action may use these Safe Haven tests, as may those who wish to file claims for refunds or credits, unless barred by the statute of limitations.

3.3 FACTORS WHICH THE IRS CONSIDERS WHEN MAKING ITS AUDIT DECISION

The Service's approach to the employer-employee relationship—and its determination as to whether a worker is a common law employee or not—cannot better be stated than by reproduction of its own guidelines. See Figure 3-4, therefore, which is a reproduction of excerpts from an IRS training bulletin pp. 44-48.

Employment Tax Procedures   **8463**

Exhibit 4640-1

Excerpts from Training 3142-01 (Rev. 5-71)

Chapter 2—Part 1
Employer-Employee Relationship
2.01
Introduction
For FICA, FUTA, and income tax withholding purposes the term "employee" (Secs. 3121(d), 3306(i), and 3401(c)) includes any individual who, under the usual common law rules applicable in determining the employer-employee relationship, has the status of an employee.
2.02
The Common Law Rules—Factors
Under the common law test, a worker is an employee if the person for whom he works has the right to direct and control him in the way he works both as to the final results and as to the details of when, where, and how the work is to be done. The employer need not actually exercise control. It is sufficient that he has the right to do so.

If the relationship of employer and employee exists, it is of no consequence whether the employee is designated as a partner, coadventurer, agent, independent contractor, or the like. Furthermore, all classes or grades of employees are included within the relationship of employer and employee. Thus, superintendents, managers, and other supervisory personnel are employees.

The factors or elements that show control are described below in the following 20 items. Any single fact or small group of facts is not conclusive evidence of the presence or absence of control.

These common law factors are not always present in every case. Some factors do not apply to certain occupations. The weight to be given each factor is not always constant. The degree of importance of each factor may vary depending on the occupation and the reason for existence. Therefore, in each case the agent will have two things to consider: First, does the factor exist; and second, what is the reason for or importance of its existence or nonexistence.

Instructions. A person who is required to comply with instructions about when, where, and how he is to work is ordinarily an employee. Some employees may work without receiving instructions because they are highly proficient and conscientious workers. However, the control factor is present if the employer has the right to require compliance with the instructions. The instructions which show how to reach the desired result may be oral or written (manuals or procedures).

Training. Training a person by an experienced employee working with him, by correspondence, by required attendance at meetings, and by other methods indicates that the employer wants the services performed in a particular method or manner. This is especially true if the training is given periodically or at frequent intervals. An independent contractor ordinarily uses his own methods and receives no training from the purchaser of his services. In fact, it is usually his methods which bring him to the attention of the purchaser.

Integration. Integration of the person's services into the business operations generally shows that he is subject to direction and control. In applying the integration test, first determine the scope and function of the business and then whether the services of the individual are merged into it. When the success or continuation of a business depends to an appreciable degree upon the performance of certain services, the people who perform those services must necessarily be subject to a certain amount of control by the owner of the business.

Services Rendered Personally. If the services must be rendered personally, presumably the employer is interested in the methods as well as the results. He is interested in not only the result but also the worker.

Hiring, Supervising, and Paying Assistants. Hiring, supervising, and paying assistants by the employer generally shows control over the men on the job. sometimes one worker may hire, supervise, and pay the other workmen. He may do so as the result of a contract under which he agrees to provide materials and labor and under which he is responsible for only the attainment of a result. In this case he is an independent contractor. On the other hand, if he hires, supervises, and pays workmen at the direction of the employer, he may be an employee acting in the capac-

ity of a foreman for or representative of the employer (Rev. Rul. 70-440, 1970-2 C.B. 209).

Continuing Relationship. A continuing relationship between an individual and the person for whom he performs services is a factor which indicates that an employer-employee relationship exists. Continuing services may include work performed at frequently recurring though somewhat irregular intervals either on call of the employer or whenever the work is available. If the arrangement contemplates continuing or recurring work, the relationship is considered permanent even if the services are part-time, seasonal, or of short duration.

MT 4600-23

Internal Revenue Manual

8463-2   Part IV—Audit

Exhibit 4640-1 Cont. (1)

Excerpts from Training 3142-01 (Rev. 5-71)

Set Hours of Work. The establishment of set hours of work by the employer is a factor indicating control. This condition bars the worker from being master of his own time, which is the right of the independent contractor. If the nature of the occupation makes fixed hours impractical, a requirement that the worker work at certain times is an element of control.

Full Time Required. If the worker must devote his full time to the business of the employer, the employer has control over the amount of time the worker spends working and impliedly restricts him from doing other gainful work. An independent contractor, on the other hand, is free to work when and for whom he chooses. Full time does not necessarily mean an 8-hour day or a 5- or 6-day week. Its meaning may vary with the intent of the parties, the nature of the occupation, and customs in the locality. These conditions should be considered in defining "full time."

Full-time services may be required even though not specified in writing or orally. For example, to produce a required minimum volume of business may compel a person to devote all of his working time to that business; or he may not be permitted to work for anyone else, and to earn a living he necessarily must work full time.

Doing Work on Employer's Premises. Doing the work on the employer's premises in itself is not control. However, it does imply that the employer has control, especially when the work is the kind that could be done elsewhere. A person working in the employer's place of business is physically within the employer's direction and supervision. The use of desk space and telephone and stenographic services provided by an employer places the worker within the employer's direction and supervision. Work done off the premises indicates some freedom from

control. However, this fact by itself does not mean that the worker is not an employee. Control over the place of work is indicated when the employer has the right to compel a person to travel a designated route, to canvass a territory within a certain time, or to work at specific places as required. In some occupations services must be performed away from the premises of the employer; for example, employees of construction contractors or taxicab drivers.

Order or Sequence Set. If a person must perform services in the order or sequence set for him by the employer, it shows that the worker is not free to follow his own pattern of work but must follow the established routines and schedules of the employer. Often, because of the nature of an occupation, the employer either does not set the order of the services or sets them infrequently. It is sufficient to show control, however, if he retains the right to do so. The outside commission salesman for example, usually is permitted latitude in mapping out his activities and may work "on his own" to a considerable degree. In many cases, however, at the direction of the employer he must report to the office at specified times, follow up on leads, and perform certain tasks at certain times. Such directions interfere with and take preference over the salesman's own routines or plans; this fact indicates control.

Oral or Written Reports. Another element of control is the requirement of submitting regular oral or written reports to the employer. This action shows that the person is compelled to account for his actions. Such reports are useful to the employer for present controls or future supervision; that is, they enable him to determine whether his instructions are being followed or, if the person has been "on his own," whether instructions should be issued.

Payment by Hour, Week, Month. Payment by the hour, week, or month generally points to an employer-employee relationship, provided that this method of payment is not just a convenient way of paying a lump sum agreed upon as the cost of doing a job. The payment by a firm of regular amounts at stated intervals to a worker strongly indicates an employer-employee relationship. (The fact that payments are received from a third party, e.g. tips or fees, is irrelevant in determining whether an employment relationship exists.) The firm assumes the hazard that the services of the worker will be proportionate to the regular payments. This action warrants the assumption that, to protect its investment, the firm has the right to direct and control the performance of the worker. It is also assumed in absence of evidence to the contrary that the worker, by accepting payment upon such basis, has agreed that the firm shall have such right of control. Obviously, the firm expects the worker to give a day's work for a day's pay. Generally, a person is an employee if he is guaranteed a minimum salary or is given a drawing account of a specified amount at stated intervals and is not required to repay any excess drawn over commissions earned.

MT 4600-23

Commerce Clearing House

Employment Tax Procedures   8463-3

Exhibit 4640-1 Cont. (2)

Excerpts from Training 3142-01 (Rev. 5-71)

Payment made by the job or on a straight commission generally indicates that the person is an independent contractor. Payment by the job includes a lump sum computed by the number of hours required to do the job at a fixed rate per hour. Such a payment should not be confused with payment by the hour.

Payment of Business and/or Traveling Expense. If the employer pays the person's business and/or traveling expenses, the person is ordinarily an employee. The employer, to be able to control expenses, must retain the right to regulate and direct the person's business activities.

Conversely, a person who is paid on a job basis and who has to take care of all incidental expenses is generally an independent contractor. Since he is accountable only to himself for his expenses, he is free to work according to his own methods and means.

Furnishing of Tools, Materials. The fact that an employer furnishes tools, materials, etc., tends to show the existence of an employer-employee relationship. Such an employer can determine which tools the person is to use and, to some extent, in what order and how they shall be used.

An independent contractor ordinarily furnishes his own tools. However, in some occupational fields, e.g., skilled workmen, workers customarily furnish their own tools. They are usually small hand tools. Such a practice does not necessarily indicate a lack of control over the services of the worker.

Significant Investment. Investment by a person in facilities he uses in performing services for another is a factor which tends to establish an independent contractor status. On the other hand, lack of investment indicates dependence on the employer for such facilities and, accordingly, the existence of an employer-employee relationship.

In general, facilities include equipment or premises necessary for the work, such as office furniture, machinery, etc. This term does not include tools, instruments, clothing, etc., commonly provided by employees in their trade, nor does it include education, experience, or training.

In order for an investment to be a significant factor in establishing that an employer-employee relationship does not exist, it must be real, it must be essential, and it must be adequate.

Is investment real? Little weight can be accorded to a worker's investment in equipment if he buys it on time from the person for whom he does the work and if his equity in the equipment is small. The same is true if the worker purchases equipment from his employer on a time basis but the employer retains title to the equipment, has the option of retaining legal ownership by paying the worker the amount of his equity in the equipment at any time before the equipment is fully paid for, requires its exclusive use in the operation of his business, and directs the worker in its use. Such investments are not "real."

Is investment essential? An investment in equipment or premises not required to perform the services in question is not essential. For example, a photographer's model may have a large investment in a wardrobe; however, if she poses for a photographer who ordinarily requires that his models wear clothing he furnishes, her investment is not essential even though the photographer lets her use her own wardrobe as a matter of indulgence. The photographer hires her only for her photogenic qualities and her ability to pose; it is not required that she furnish her own wardrobe.

Is investment adequate? Ownership by an individual of facilities adequate for the work and independent of the facilities of another points to an independent contractor relationship. Ownership of such facilities is an influential factor in letting the contract of service. The important point is the value of the investment compared to the total value of all the facilities for doing the work. An investment in facilities is not adequate if the worker must rely appreciably on the facilities of others to perform the services. For instance, an individual who is engaged to perform a machine operation on his own premises and who furnishes his own equipment of substantial value may be a self-employed subcontractor instead of an employee of the manufacturer.

Significant in determining the weight of the investment factor is ascertaining who has the right to control the facilities. Ownership of equipment or premises points toward an independent contractor status because it is inferred that the owner has the right to control their use. However, if the owner, as part of the agreement, surrenders complete dominion over the equipment or premises

and the right to decide how they shall be used, "ownership" loses its significance.

Suppose an individual who owns a truck is hired by a trucking company to deliver goods and materials to business firms. The fact that he uses his own truck to perform these services is not significant if, in general, the firm uses it like its own trucks. For example, the firm sets the order and time of deliveries; pays for all upkeep and repair of the individual's truck while used in its business or otherwise compensates the individual for these costs; restricts him from using the truck to perform services for others, etc.

MT 4600-23

Internal Revenue Manual

8463-4

Exhibit 4640-1 Cont. (3)

Part IV—Audit

Excerpts from Training 3142-01 (Rev. 5-71)

Realization of Profit or Loss. The man who can realize a profit or suffer a loss as a result of his services is generally an independent contractor, but the individual who cannot is an employee.

"Profit or loss" implies the use of capital by the individual in an independent business of his own. Thus, opportunity for higher earnings, such as from pay on a piecework basis or the possibility of gain or loss from a commission arrangement, is not considered profit or loss.

Whether a profit is realized or loss suffered generally depends upon management decisions; that is, the one responsible for a profit or loss can use his own ingenuity, initiative, and judgment in conducting his business or enterprise. Opportunity for profit or loss may be established by one or more of a variety of circumstances, e.g.:

1. The individual hires, directs, and pays assistants.

2. He has his own office, equipment, materials, or other work facilities.

3. He has continuing and recurring liabilities or obligations, and his success or failure depends on the relation of his receipts to his expenditures.

4. He agrees to perform specific jobs for prices agreed upon in advance and pay expenses incurred in connection with the work.

5. His services and/or those of his assistants establish or affect his business reputation and not the reputation of those who purchase the services.

Working for More Than One Firm at a Time. A person who works for a number of persons or firms at the same time is generally an independent contractor because he is usually free from control by any of the firms. It is possible, however, for a person to work for a number of people or firms and be an employee of one or all of them.

Making Service Available to General Public. The fact that a person makes his services available to the general public usually indicates an independent contractor relationship. An individual may hold his services out to the public in a number of ways: he may have his own office and assistants; he may hang out a "shingle" in front of his home or office; he may hold business licenses; he may be listed in business directories or maintain business listings in telephone directories; or he may advertise in newspapers, trade journals, magazines, etc.

Right to Discharge. The right to discharge is an important factor in indicating that the person possessing the right is an employer. He exercises control through the ever-present threat of dismissal, which causes the worker to obey his instructions. An independent contractor, on the other hand, cannot be fired so long as he produces a result which meets his contract specifications.

Right to Terminate. An employee has the right to end his relationship with his employer at any time he wishes without incurring liability. An independent contractor usually agrees to complete a specific job; he is responsible for its satisfactory completion or legally obligated to make good for failure to complete the job.

We have now covered the 20 factors; i.e., does the factor exist? We will now consider the second point: what is the reason for or importance of its existence or nonexistence?

All facts must be weighed, and the conclusion must be based on a careful evaluation of all the facts, IRS published rulings, and the presence or absence of factors which point to an employer-employee relationship or to an independent contractor status.

Take the example of a barbershop. The shop owner may say that he does not control the hours, fix the amount charged for a haircut, or control the barber's cleanliness. However, in determining the weight of each of these factors, the agent should consider the reason for their nonexistence. He may find that the union in effect controls the hours and sets the price for haircuts and that the State Barber Board of Examiners controls the cleanliness of the shop. He correctly concludes, then, that the weight to be given each of these three factors is nothing.

In the case of salesmen, it might be found that the employer does not control the hours of work because, to make a sale, the salesman may have to arrange his hours to fit the customers' hours, such as calling in the evening when the husband and wife are at home. This may be true of other occupations. The important thing is to weigh any factor being considered according to its reason for existence or nonexistence.

2.03

FICA Statutory Employee Rules

In addition to common law employees, the FICA provides for statutory employees, which include (1) agent drivers and commission drivers, (2) full-time life insurance salesmen, (3) home workers, and (4) traveling or city salesmen.

MT 4600-23

Commerce Clearing House, Inc

Figure 3-4

3.4 CONSIDERATIONS WHEN PREPARING THE RETURN

Know that all classes of Internal Revenue Agents will be interested in **payroll taxes**—regular revenue agents, revenue agents who are employment tax specialists, tax auditors. All will probably want to examine and inquire into the preparation of all employment tax returns from Forms W-2 to Forms 941 and 1099.

In addition to normal audit inquiries such as: were the returns filed, were they accurate, did they agree with the records, the agents will have other not-so-obvious reasons for their examinations. Paramount among these will be the identification of employees disguised as independent contractors.

They will most certainly examine a **taxpayer's cash disbursements journal** for reoccurring payments to an individual who is not on the payroll. If such a person is located, they will want to know why the individual was considered to be an independent contractor and whether or not a 1099 was filed for such a worker.

The agents will also probably ask for a **breakdown of "Labor" or other such accounts** not included in payroll. Their purpose: to locate common law employees. They may review "Repair," "Miscellaneous," and other expense accounts and supporting invoices in an effort to locate individuals (for whom Forms 1099 should have been filed) who were hiding under the guise of a trade name, i.e.: William Part Plumbing Company—actually only William Part, a lone plumber.

It follows, then, that practitioners should make all of these inquiries themselves while preparing a return and touch all of the bases that the IRS will. Nothing will succeed to a greater degree at audit time than good preparation for such an eventuality.

Tax Return Preparation Checklist

As concerns the Employee/Independent Contractor question and employment taxes in general, it is suggested that a checklist somewhat like the one following be used during the preparation of each return so as to insure that all possible IRS points of inquiry will be covered:

■ Are copies of Forms W-4 (Employee's Withholding Allowance Certificate) on hand?

- Were W-4 regulations correctly followed?
- Are copies of Forms W-2 (Wage and Tax Statement) on hand?
- Does the Form W-3 (Transmittal of Income and Tax Statements) correctly reflect W-2 totals?
- Were all Forms 941 (Employer's Quarterly Federal Tax Return) filed?
- Were Federal Tax Deposit 501s for withheld income and social security taxes properly and timely filed and tax paid?
- Was the Form 940 (Employer's Annual Federal Unemployment Tax Return) filed?
- Were Federal Tax Deposit 508s for unemployment taxes properly and timely filed with payments?
- Were all required Forms 1099 and 1096 properly filed?
- Was taxpayer questioned and were cash disbursement journals examined for employees disguised as independent contractors?
- Were all "Outside Labor" accounts analyzed for common law employee possibilities?

Employer Classification of a Worker, Not Governing

Only facts in each case carry weight. The IRS cares not what the worker is called but is concerned only with how the individual compares with its points of consideration as embodied in Figure 3-4.

Securing an IRS Employee/Independent Contractor Decision

By filing a Form SS-8 (Information for Use in Determining Whether a Worker Is an Employee for Purposes of Federal Employment Taxes and Income Tax Withholding) a taxpayer can eliminate all doubt as to which category governs for any employee or group of employees.

CAUTION:

Only photostatic copies of supporting contracts and other documents should be supplied, since this material will not be returned.

3.5 HANDLING THE AUDIT

If the tax preparer in this instance has followed the procedures as outlined in the previous paragraphs, he or she should have no difficulty with an audit. If not, then it becomes a matter of *wait and see* and hope.

Before the audit—and after notification that it is coming, the preparer should run through the Return Preparation Checklist as shown above and put his or her house in order—or at least in as good order as possible.

Possibly the agent, with other matters pending, will check only to determine that all employment tax returns were filed. Very likely, though, he or she will at least scan the cash disbursements journal with an eye toward large expenditures that might reflect nondeductible items. In so doing, reoccurring payments to an individual may come to light.

If this happens, and the practitioner has noted the guidelines which the IRS uses in deciding whether an individual is a common law employee, he or she will have an opportunity to correlate the facts and adjust them so as to possibly satisfy the IRS criteria. Certainly, evidence should not be altered or manufactured but put into correct perspective for greater effectiveness. Employment contracts, invoices, bills of lading—anything that might prove independent contractor status, should be collected and used to substantiate the taxpayer's position. Mere words will serve little purpose.

If you feel that your position is sound, all Appeal Steps should be taken.

NOTE:

The Tax Court does not have jurisdiction over Employment Tax Cases. Ordinarily, the taxpayer must pay the IRS assessment for at least one quarter, then sue for a refund in either a District Court or a Court of Claims.

Section 4633 of the Internal Revenue Manual reads in part:

There are no provisions in the Code whereby employment taxes may be appealed to the United States Tax Court.

WARNING:

In all cases where a knowledge of rules of evidence, constitutional law, civil and criminal tax fraud, appeals procedures, and other such legal matters are required— and you do not possess this knowledge—by all means, employ a knowledgeable tax attorney who does.

Not to at least make such a recommendation to your client under the above circumstances can be catastrophic—and very damaging indeed to your E&A insurance coverage.

3.6 PERTINENT COURT DECISIONS–PRO AND CON

Pro
Jerry M. Drake v U.S.
(DC Northern Dist of Texas) CA-3-7241-D. 1975

Findings of Fact

Mr. Drake, an independent contractor during the years 1969 and 1970, was engaged in the business of applying siding to residences. He employed salesmen and siding applicators as independent contractors. The government considered those in both categories to be employees.

Evidence before the court indicated that the taxpayer could control:

1. The number and frequency of work breaks

2. The manner in which the siding was sold and applied

3. The details of the sales techniques used

4. The kind of tools and equipment used

5. The working schedule

The judge explained in detail to the jury all facts which they should consider such as: whether the workers provided their own tools, whether they had an opportunity to make a profit or the risk of taking a loss, whether Mr. Drake had the right to assign territories, etc.

Opinion

The jury's verdict: Both salesmen and siding applicators were independent contractors.

Con
Arthur R. Klingler, dba Klingler Construction
v U.S. (DC Northern Dist of Iowa) C 77-22, 1978

Findings of Fact

The taxpayer, a carpentry contractor during the period 1972 through 1974, considered all of his workers to be independent contractors. The IRS objected. Evidence indicated the following.

1. Plaintiff had been a carpentry contractor in the Cedar Rapids, Iowa, area for 30 years; his business generally involved residential construction.

2. Following a tax audit for the years 1972-1974 the IRS determined plaintiff owed $7,150.91 in employment taxes, interest, and penalties because his workers were employees, not independent contractors.

3. In January 1977 plaintiff paid $194.66 of the assessment and sued for a refund.

4. Defendant counterclaimed for the remaining taxes in the sum of $6,956.25.

5. Plaintiff had hired workers on the oral understanding that they were to pay their own taxes.

6. Plaintiff generally hired workers by advertising in the newspapers. He generally paid them by the hour, though on some occasions workers were paid by the job and they did not profit from managerial skills.

7. Plaintiff provided major power tools, ladders, and scaffolding at work sites. Workers provided their own hand tools.

8. Plaintiff could suggest methods for doing particular jobs. He trained inexperienced workers and supervised the general appearance of the work site.

9. Even plaintiff's most experienced workers generally acquiesced to plaintiff's suggested methods.

10. Plaintiff could and did move workers from job to job.

11. If workers were ineffective at one job, plaintiff would try them at another.

12. Plaintiff had the power to hire and fire.

13. Generally, full-time workers didn't attempt to find other work or hold themselves out as contractors while working for plaintiff.

14. Generally, when one job was completed, workers expected to be and were taken to the next job.

15. One worker, Ira Mann, had his own carpentry business and occasionally worked for plaintiff. He worked on his own time.

16. Plaintiff had liability insurance to cover carpenters.

Opinion

One employee, Ira Mann, was an independent contractor. The others were employees, since they worked under the supervision and control of plaintiff. The taxpayer could and sometimes did dictate the manner in which a job was accomplished, supplied major tools and equipment, and had the power to hire and fire.

3.7 RELEVANT CODE AND REGULATION SECTIONS

Code

Section 3401(a)	Definition of Wages
3401(c)	Definition of an Employee
3401(d)	Definition of an Employer
6041(a)	Information at Source—Payments of $600 or more

Regulations

Section 1-61.2(a)	Compensation for Services, including fees, commissions, and similar items—in General
31.3401(c)-1	Definition of an Employee
31.3401(d)-1	Definition of an Employer

3.8 APPLICABLE IRS MANUAL REFERENCES (INVESTIGATIVE TECHNIQUES)

Probably because of the Safe Haven Rules, the IRS in its Topical Index—to Part IV of its Audit Manual does not mention "Independent Contractors" or "Nonemployees" as such, meaning that they have not as yet specifically zeroed in on the employee/independent contractor issue.

Only in *Manual Supplement 40 RDD-79, 9-22-80, "1099 Non-employer Compensation (NEC) Study—Tax Year 1979,"* is the subject approached—and then only to give operational instructions for the study, opening with:

> This Supplement implements the 1099 Study for TY 1979 and places responsibility for timely completion and quality control upon appropriate regional service center and district office.

Manual Section 4600 (Employment Tax Procedures) does, however, encompass the issue in its instructions for employment tax audits. This manual was prepared before enactment of Section 530 of the Revenue Act of 1978. These criteria are still in use today and will continue to be after removal of the Safe Haven provisions.

Casualty Losses
(Section 165)

4

4.1 IDENTIFYING THE PROBLEM

The basic law, as represented by the Code and Regulations, is stingy when defining a casualty loss, particularly as to "other casualties."

The Code in Section 165 simply states that "an individual may deduct—as to property not connected with a trade or business—losses in excess of $100 that arise from fire, storm, shipwreck, or other casualty." The Regulations produce little more in the way of an actual definition.

IRS Publication 547 (Tax Information on Disasters, Casualties and Thefts), however, does expand somewhat on the meaning of the law:

> A casualty is the damage, destruction, or loss of property resulting from an identifiable event that is sudden, unexpected, or unusual.

> A *sudden* event is one that is swift, not gradual or progressive. An *unexpected* event is one that is ordinarily unanticipated and one that you do not intend. An *unusual* event is one that is not a day-to-day occurrence and one that is not typical of the activity in which you were engaged

With this enlargement of the meaning of "other casualty," the courts extended the deduction to include even the loss of a wife's diamond ring because her husband slammed a car door on her hand. (John P. White, 48TC 430; Acq., Rev. Rul. 77-592, 1972-2 CB101)

Even this apparent leniency has not caused the controversy to disappear. In fact, the difficulty in arriving at a consistent approach to the definition of a casualty has become so impossible that the Comptroller General of the U. S. has suggested:

■ Outright repeal of the deduction, or

■ Replacement with a deduction for casualty and theft insurance premiums, or

■ Elimination of the deduction unless it exceeds 10% of adjusted gross income.

Regulation 1.165-1(b) hasn't helped the situation any. This section only adds another hurdle:

Nature of loss allowable. To be allowed as a deduction under Section 165(a) a loss must be evidenced by closed and completed transactions, fixed by identifiable events, and except as otherwise provided in Section 165(h) and 1.165-11, relating to disaster losses, actually sustained during the taxable year ...

(A qualified disaster loss may be deducted in the year immediately preceding the year of the casualty.)

In many instances, disagreement with the IRS arises over the point in time when the loss became "closed and completed."

These problems and others, as follows, all make this issue a difficult area of federal taxation:

■ Who may take the deduction?

■ How can the necessary valuations be accomplished to everyone's satisfaction?

■ What is the special election for "disaster losses?"

■ How can gain on an involuntary conversion be deferred?

■ How do Tenants by the Entirety handle the casualty loss deduction?

■ And on and on!

AND THEN CAME:

The Tax Equity and Fiscal Responsibility Act of 1982 (TEFRA). Beginning in 1983, the new law applies a 10 percent-of-adjusted gross income (AGI) floor on the deduction of personal casualty and theft losses. It also retained the $100 limitation.

CAREFUL:

If you think that '83 losses can be carried back to '82, you are correct BUT Congress thought of this loophole, too. TEFRA requires that such a carryback also be subjected to the new 10 percent of AGI floor.

The remainder of this chapter will help to remove most of the clouds and bring into sharp focus correct methods of handling casualty losses.

4.2 HOW THE IRS SEES THE ISSUE

Internal Revenue persons will, in a general sense, be primarily concerned with proof of six main categories:

1. That a casualty loss occurred—and carried with it the following three characteristics:
   a. Was identifiable.
   b. Was damaging.
   c. Came about as the result of a sudded, unexpected, or unusual happening such as fire, storm, shipwreck, or other casualty. (Not through normal deterioration.)
2. That the loss deduction was the lesser of:
   a. The decrease in the FMV of the property as a result of the casualty, or
   b. The adjusted basis of the property.
3. That the loss occurred in year deduction was taken, except in the case of farming losses (Regulation 1.165-6)-qualifying disaster losses (Regulation 1.165-11)—or in cases where damages could not be ascertained because of insurance claims (Regulation 1.165-1(d)(2).

4. That insurance recoveries were properly considered.

5. That the taxpayer was the owner of the property.

6. That the personal deduction limitation of $100 was considered.

7. That the TEFRA "10% of AGI" rule was followed.

The government will also be interested in whether the possibility of *arson* exists. If it does, an "in-depth" examination will begin. (See last section of this chapter for more details.)

In addition, agents will want to determine whether gains from an involuntary conversion (destruction by fire, for example) were correctly handled—and whether any of the damaged assets were located in a foreign country.

Inherent in these major areas of IRS interest are most of the specific points of evidence which auditors will ask to review.

4.3 FACTORS WHICH THE IRS CONSIDERS WHEN MAKING ITS AUDIT DECISION

Identification of the alleged casualty loss. Direct damage by storm or shipwreck easily passes muster. Identification of "other casualties" does not. To qualify, the accident must be swift, precipitous, unexpected, and unusual such as those caused by:

- An auto accident (unless triggered by the owner's willful negligence)
- Earthquake
- Lightning
- Freezing rain, ice, & snow
- Drought
- Explosion
- Sonic booms
- Vandalism

IMPORTANT:

The fact that the loss was foreseeable will not eliminate its deductibility.

Examiners will be particularly inquisitive if the decrease in value of the asset appears to have occurred because of normal deterioration such as in the case of the freezing and thawing of a road or gradual dry rot of building beams.

Valuation determination. Where property is totally destroyed, amount of the loss is easily computed. It is either:

■ The fair market value, or

■ The adjusted basis (usually cost to an individual) before the casualty.

Difficulties arise, however, where a property is only partially destroyed. In this situation, a taxpayer will usually utilize the "cost-of-repairs" method which is allowed by the IRS, provided the work was necessary to restore the property to precasualty condition.

Failing to use this method, the taxpayer must prove fair market values before and after the casualty. This usually involves appraisal expenses—and can result in much controversy with the IRS. As to this valuation issue, auditors may also wish to inquire:

1. If the "cost-of-repairs" approach was used, did the resultant expenses restore the property *only* to its original value, or did it *increase* its value? (If it did, the allowable deduction will be reduced accordingly.)

2. Was the cost of repairs excessive? Regulation 1.165-7(a)(2) says that it cannot be. (What is "excessive?" Well, it's just another taxpayer obstacle, since he or she must prove it is not.)

3. Were losses involving both realty and improvements (residence and shrubbery) evaluated as a single loss? (They should have been. The deduction is measured by the decrease in value of the entire property, not separately.)

4. Were sentimental values considered in determining the loss? (They should not have been.)

5. Were clean-up costs included as part of the evaluation loss? (The IRS says they should not be but should be used like repairs as a measure of loss. The Tax Court and two Circuit Courts, on the other hand, say that the reduction in value *and* the clean-up costs constitute the deduction.)

6. Was a willing seller-willing buyer approach taken in establishing the value of personal property? The IRS and the Court in Gay (TC Memo 1980-19) say that it must be. The Tax Court, however, in Cornelius (56TC 976) says that a taxpayer may use cost less depreciation.

Calculation of loss deduction. A good illustration is contained in IRS Publication 547 (Tax Information on Disasters, Casualties and Thefts) and reproduced as Figure 4-1. Beginning in 1983 an additional computation will be required to determine the 10 percent of AGI floor.

Real property. In figuring a loss to real estate that you own for personal use, all improvements, such as building and ornamental trees, are considered together. The amount of the loss is either the decrease in the fair market value of the entire property or its basis, whichever is less. From this amount you must subtract the insurance and other reimbursement you receive or expect to receive. The amount remaining that is more than $100 is your personal casualty loss deduction.

Example 1. Your lakeside cottage, which cost you $13,600 (including $1,600 for the land) several years ago, was partially destroyed by fire in July. The value of the property immediately before the fire was $16,000 ($14,000 for the building and $2,000 for the land), and the value immediately after the fire was $12,000. You collected $3,050 from the insurance company. Your deduction for the casualty loss is $850, figured in the following manner:

1) Value of entire property before fire	$16,000
2) Value of entire property after fire	12,000
3) Decrease in fair market value of entire property	$ 4,000
4) Basis (cost in this case)	$13,600

5) Amount of loss (lesser of 3 or 4)	$ 4,000
6) Minus: Insurance	3,500
7) Loss after reimbursement	$ 950
8) Minus: $100	100
9) **Casualty loss deduction**	$ 850

Example 2. A few years ago you bought a house, which you then lived in as your home. You paid $6,000 for the land and $30,000 for the house itself. You also paid $2,000 for landscaping. In 1980 your home was totally destroyed by fire. The fire also damaged the shrubbery and trees in your yard. Competent appraisers said that the property as a whole had a fair market value immediately before the fire of $44,000, but that its value was only $10,000 after the fire. Shortly after the fire, the insurance company paid you $30,000 for the loss. Your casualty loss deduction is figured as follows:

1) Value of entire property before fire	$44,000
2) Value of entire property after fire	10,000
3) Decrease in fair market value of entire property	$34,000
4) Basis of the entire property (cost of land, building, and landscaping)	$38,000

5) Amount of loss (lesser of 3 or 4)	$34,000
6) Minus: Insurance	30,000
7) Loss after reimbursement	$ 4,000
8) Minus: $100	100
9) **Casualty loss deduction**	$ 3,900

Personal property. Personal property is generally any property that is not real estate. If your personal property is stolen or is damaged or destroyed by a casualty, you must figure your loss separately for each individual item of property.

Example 1. Your pleasure boat, which cost you $4,500 was destroyed by a storm. Its value immediately before the storm was $2,300. You had no insurance, but were able to salvage the motor of the boat and sell it for $200. Your casualty loss deduction is $2,000, figured as follows:

1) Value before storm	$2,300
2) Value after storm	200
3) Decrease in value	$2,100
4) Basis (cost in this case)	$4,500
5) Amount of loss (lesser of 3 or 4)	$2,100
6) Minus: Insurance	none
7) Loss after reimbursement	$2,100
8) Minus: $100	100
9) **Casualty loss deduction**	$2,000

Example 2. A fire in your home damaged an upholstered chair and completely destroyed a rug and antique table. You did not have fire insurance to cover your loss. The chair had cost you $150, and you established that it had a fair market value of $75 just before the fire and $10 just afterwards. The rug had cost you $200 and had a value of $50 just before the fire. You had bought the table at an auction for $15 before discovering it was a valuable antique. It had been appraised at $350 before the fire. Your loss on each of these items is figured as follows:

	Chair	Rug	Table
1) Basis (Cost)	$150	$200	$ 15
2) Value before fire	$ 75	$ 50	$350
3) Value after fire	10	-0-	-0-
4) Decrease in value	$ 65	$ 50	$350
5) Loss (lesser of 1 or 4)	$ 65	$ 50	$ 15
6) Total loss			$130
7) Minus: $100			100
8) **Casualty loss deduction**			$ 30

Figure 4-1

The IRS, on its part, will not only wish to determine that you followed this formula but will want also to delve into other facets of this computation:

1. Were any deductions taken for living expenses or for personal-injury care, or for moving or other costs, not directly connected to the casualty? (If so, they should not have been.)

2. Were computations of personal property losses (except a personal residence) accomplished separately? (They should have been—then added together to comprise the loss deduction. See *Disaster Loss Workbook,* IRS Publication 584.)

3. Were rehabilitation payments from disaster relief agencies—for use in repairing or replacing the taxpayer's damaged property—used to reduce the deduction? (They should have been.)

4. Was the cost of the insurance premium included in the loss? (It should not have been.)

5. If no insurance recovery was involved, did the taxpayer carry insurance—and, if so, was a claim filed with the carrier? (If not, the casualty loss will not be allowed even though recent court decisions have gone against the IRS in this respect.)

6. Were costs of photographs and appraisal fees included in the loss? (They should not have been, but they can be deducted as an itemized deduction.)

7. If an automobile casualty, was the damage caused by willfulness on the part of the owner? (If so, no deduction will be allowed.)

Establishing the owner. Generally, only the outright owner of a property may take the casualty-loss deduction. Others however, with lesser interests, may qualify. The IRS will want to make sure that the taxpayer is at least one of these:

- A tenant who has invested in leasehold improvements. (This person may take a deduction to the extent that such improvements are damaged.)
- A remainderman. (He or she may deduct the pro rata share of the loss to the remainder interest.)
- An estate. (This fiduciary can take the loss on either the Form 706 (Estate Tax Return) or Form 1041 (Fiduciary Income Tax Return.)
- Property in the possession of minor children who are the taxpayer's dependents. (Taxpayers are considered owners.)
- Joint owners. (Each may take a deduction which is limited to the extent of his or her interest. Spouses, however, are treated as one taxpayer when they file joint returns.)

NOTE:

For joint owners, other than spouses who file joint returns, the $100 limitation will be applied on a per owner basis.

- Tenants by entirety. (Where spouses own property in this fashion and file separately, each may take one-half of the deduction.)

Proper year for the deduction. The rule in Regulation 1.165-1(d) seems very clear:

Year of deduction. (1) a loss shall be allowed as a deduction under 165(a) only for the taxable year in which the loss is sustained ...

But then the rule goes on for hundreds of words to make exceptions. Despite this smoke screen of verbosity, government agents will want the taxpayer to show why the loss was taken in the year in question.

1. If an insurance settlement had not yet been made, how was the amount of the loss arrived at? (Supposedly, the deduction can amount to only the difference between the loss and *expected* insurance recovery.)
2. If the loss deduction was taken in a year subsequent to the casualty, why? Here, the taxpayer must show that a situation existed whereby he or she could not possibly have determined a "closed and completed transaction" because, for example:
   a. A prolonged, abnormally hard ice storm occurred on December 30 and 31. Damage to trees and shrubs did not become apparent until May, or
   b. Difficulties with the insurance carrier made an estimate of loss impossible, or
   c. Damage to a beach home because of hurricane, winds, and attendant waves didn't show up until two years after the storm.
3. If the loss was taken in the year prior to the casualty, can the taxpayer prove the existence of a qualified disaster loss? (Such a deduction is allowable under Section 165(h) where the casualty was incurred in a Presidentially declared disaster area. More on this subject in section 4.4.)

4.4 CONSIDERATIONS WHEN PREPARING THE RETURN

It would be my strong suggestion that every facet of a casualty-loss deduction be thoroughly explored before entry on a tax return—most certainly if the deduction is of any size. As you have probably already noticed, this area of federal taxation is replete with traps. Here are some additional ideas which will help in avoiding them.

Computing the Casualty Loss

For a sample calculation, see Figure 4-1 under previous heading, "Calculation of Loss Deduction," in Section 4.3 of this chapter.

In the case of individuals the loss deduction can be entered directly onto Form 1040 (Schedule A) if the following circumstances exist:

■ The casualty or theft resulted in a loss.

■ You had only one loss during the year.

■ Only one item was lost or damaged from this loss.

■ The loss was to property that was not used in a trade or business, or for income-producing purposes.

Otherwise, Form 4684 (Casualties and Thefts) must be completed—along with Form 4797 (Supplemental Schedule of Gains and Losses) wherever Section 1231 enters the picture. It involves property used in a trade or business or an involuntary conversion.

Allocating insurance recoveries. If the insurance company breaks down its payment, use its figures. If not, make an allocation on the basis of the FMV of damaged items.

Reimbursed casualty-induced living expenses do not decrease or increase the loss deduction, but they can produce additional gross income. It works this way:

> The portion of the reimbursement which equals normal cost of living must be reported as income. The excess expenses, incurred because of the casualty, are tax free. (Code Section 123)

Attorney and court costs. Litigating costs in settling the insurance claim are treated as a reduction of the insurance recovery, thus in effect increasing the loss deduction in the settlement year.

Insurance recovery in year following casualty. Normally, the deduction should be taken in the year of the casualty and theoretically should be the amount of the *expected* loss. Suppose, therefore, that fire damage amounted to $20,000 and the taxpayer filed an insurance claim for $18,000. The loss deduction in the year of the fire would be $2,000, less the $100 limitation.

However, the claim was settled in the following year for only $16,000. This generated another loss deduction of $2,000 but without the necessity of subtracting the $100. Such a limitation applies only to each casualty.

Insurance recovery which produced a profit. In the above situation, suppose that the taxpayer had recovered the entire $20,000 in the year after the casualty. The $1,900 as previously deducted could properly be reported as ordinary income under Section 111 (Recovery of amounts previously deducted). An amended return would not be required for the prior year.

Postponement of gain. The Code treats casualty losses as involuntary conversions. If a gain results, it can be postponed through the involuntary conversion provisions of Section 1033 which allows for reinvestment in like property. The replacement should be purchased within two years.

If the conversion is directly to similar property, the basis of the new asset is the basis of the old, less any money received but not expended on the replacement, plus any gain recognized.

If the conversion was to money and then to like property, the basis of the new property will be its cost, less any gain not recognized.

THE $125,000 EXCLUSION:

Under Section 121, destruction of a personal residence is considered an "involuntary sale" and as such is eligible for the once-in-a-lifetime $125,000 exclusion. What is more—and this can be a very important consideration—if a taxpayer qualifies and does elect the Section 121 option, the loss is removed from the requirements of Section 1231. This is like escaping from a nest of barbed wire unscathed.

The monkey wrench that is Section 1231 (Property Used in the Trade or Business and Involuntary Conversions). This statute requires the application of Sections 1033, 1245, and 1250 and must be considered in the case of all recognized involuntary conversions (casualty losses in this instance.) It flip flops gains and losses so that different combinations produce varied results—some beneficial, some not.

EXAMPLE:

Casualties generally produce *ordinary* losses but, if there are larger 1231 gains in the picture, then these losses may be converted into *capital* losses, particularly if the damaged or destroyed property had been held for a period of more than one year.

If the net of Section 1231 transactions results in a gain, then all the gains and losses shall be treated as long-term capital gains and losses. If the Section 1231 net is a loss, then all the gains are ordinary income and all the losses are ordinary losses.

Section 1231 rules apply to gains or losses from the sale, exchange, or involuntary conversion of depreciable business property (including business realty) and capital assets (whether held for investment or personal use) provided such properties have been held for more than one year.

IMPORTANT:

It therefore becomes important—if circumstances permit—to consider carefully whether 1231 property should be sold or exchanged in the same taxable year that a casualty loss has occurred.

Business and income-producing property. Unlike nonbusiness assets, damage to these properties are deductible whether or not they qualify as casualty losses. There are, however, some important differences in the computation:

- There is no $100 limitation or TEFRA consideration.
- Loss, because business items were stolen or totally destroyed, is measured by the adjusted basis, not by the difference in FMV.
- In the case of a partial loss, the deduction is computed under regular rules, as previously set forth (excepting a personal residence) through use of a separate computation for each item, e.g., building, shrubbery, office equipment, machinery, etc.
- Attaching an explanatory statement, setting forth all salient features of the casualty, can frequently eliminate the necessity for an audit.
- In the case of income-producing properties, loss deductions are computed in the aggregate as for personal-use property.

- Because of this separate-components rule, should an insurance recovery exceed the adjusted basis of a particular asset, the excess cannot be sheltered against other losses but must become a taxable gain.

"Disaster Area" Losses Produce Special Election

Section 165(h) permits the taking of casualty loss deduction in the year prior to the disaster. To qualify, the region in which the casualty occurred must have been declared a disaster area by the President and made eligible for federal relief under the Disaster Relief Act of 1974.

An election may be made by filing it in writing on or before the later of:

1. The due date for filing the return for the year in which the disaster occurred (without regard to extensions), or

2. The due date (including extensions) for filing for the immediately preceding tax year.

The election must specify the date of the disaster and the city, town, county, and state in which the damaged property was located when the casualty occurred. It may be revoked within 90 days from the date of filing.

TIME-SAVING SUGGESTION:

To speed up the rebate processes and secure a "Quickie Refund," label the top of each Form 1040 or 1040X, as the case may be, DISASTER AREA LOSS-REFUND.

Disaster Loss Workbook (Pub. 584). This booklet can be extremely helpful in establishing the amount of loss sustained in the destruction, or partial destruction, of a residence or automotive equipment. It provides an excellent set of work papers.

More Key Points to Consider:

- Disaster relief, such as food and medical supplies, does not reduce the casualty loss.

- Costs incurred to protect against future damage are not deductible as casualty losses.

- Cash gifts from friends or neighbors to help with disaster expenses are not taxable income and do not reduce the casualty-loss deduction, unless restricted for use in restoration of the damaged property.

- Loss is decided by FMV before and after the casualty—not by the cost of repairs. It is, therefore, possible for a taxpayer to restore a damaged property himself—and still maintain a deduction in excess of repair costs.

- Be sure that photos are taken as quickly after the disaster as possible and that newspaper clippings are retained.

4.5 HANDLING THE AUDIT

In any meeting with IRS personnel, nothing beats preparation—no amount of talk will succeed more surely than documentation and a showing that you cared and made an honest attempt to meet the requirements of the code. This of course will have occurred if you or your client completed the *Disaster Loss Workbook,* Pub. 584. If not, attempt to do so before meeting with the auditor.

Primarily, the IRS will expect substantiation:

- As to ownership of the damaged or destroyed property.

- As to the nature and date of casualty.

■ That the loss resulted from the casualty.

■ To prove basis of the property, together with cost of improvements.

■ As to the amount of insurance received.

■ As to depreciation involved, if any.

■ As to opinions of value before and after the casualty.

Otherwise, any of the situations that have been mentioned in this chapter can arise. All can require negative or positive *proof,* as the case may be. Photographs, for example, can be an important aid in proving that the casualty occurred—newspaper clippings, too. If you don't possess the latter, go to any of the newspaper morgues in the locale where the disaster took place and ask for help. You will generally get it without difficulty.

The best evidence in the case of personal property, of course, is cancelled checks and invoices. Failing to possess these, try locating riders on insurance policies. Many taxpayers insure valuable items separately—and secure appraisals of each at the time of doing so.

Companies where major items, such as refrigerators and washing machines, were purchased can many times come up with the cost.

Once costs are obtained, the government probably will allow a taxpayer to arrive at FMVs through application of normal depreciation rates—in much the same fashion as an insurance adjuster would.

In the case of a personal residence, the cost is generally easily established either through the mortgage or bank or through the attorney's office where the purchase transaction took place. If the structure was built, the building contractor can probably name the cost. Appraisers, bankers, city assessors, insurance brokers and adjusters, and fire departments are all good sources of FMV information after the casualty.

For solidifying a specific casualty position, use the Code and Regulations as listed in the following section. Search out court decisions that lean your way. The pros and cons in deciding the casualty-loss deduction jump every which way. Catch the ones that do you the most good.

DON'T OVERLOOK THIS IMPORTANT STRATEGY:

If the IRS auditor declines to allow the casualty loss because the property involved was covered by insurance—and because no claim was filed—object, and appeal the issue if necessary.

In a series of recent decisions, the Tax Court has recognized the legitimacy of not filing claims under circumstances where increased premiums or loss of coverage might result.

4.6 PERTINENT COURT DECISIONS–PRO AND CON

Pro
John P. and Agnes S. White (48TC42)

Findings of Fact

In 1950 John purchased a 1.38 carat diamond ring for his wife Agnes at a cost of $1,200. Appraisal value at time of loss was proved to be not less than the purchase price.

On a windy day in October of 1963 John drove his wife home from a shopping trip and opened the door for her. She got out of the car, then reached back in to retrieve something left on the seat. At the same time John, whose attention had been diverted by one of their children, closed the door forcefully to overcome the strong wind that was then blowing. The door impacted Agnes's hand directly on the ring.

Agnes, crying with pain, quickly withdrew her injured hand, shaking it vigorously. Two of the four metal flanges which had held the stone in place had been broken by the mishap, allowing the diamond to fly free.

An intensive search, which continued for weeks, failed to locate the diamond. It was uninsured at the time; so the taxpayers claimed a casualty-loss deduction on their 1963 return in the amount of $1,200. They used Section 165(c)(3) "Other casualty" as their authority, along with William H. Carpenter (TC Memo 1966-228 C.A. 6, Apr 3, 1967) which had allowed a deduction for the loss of a ring ground up by a disposal.

The IRS objected, saying that the loss was caused by an ordinary, everyday, domestic, household mishap.

In disagreeing with the respondent, the court raised several interesting points that we believe are of sufficient importance to reproduce here:

> With respect to the presence of accepted and essential casualty attributes, we find little to distinguish the situation now confronting us from other cases in which loss deductions arising from "other" casualties have been allowed. The events giving rise to the undisputed loss here were sudden, unexpected, violent and not due to deliberate or willful actions by petitioners or either of them. These events involved the application of considerable destructive force to the subject ring and as an immediate, direct and proximate result thereof Agnes lost the diamond from her solitaire. The relative presence of these characteristics has long been deemed controlling in determining whether a loss may qualify as "other casualty."

> Respondent urges that in order to be embraced by the term "other casualty," an occurrence must be cataclysmic in character. He relies upon Heyn, supra, wherein we held that an earthslide constituted a casualty under section 165(c)(3). We find respondent's reliance upon Heyn for this proposition totally misplaced. In Heyn, we merely observed that the physical characteristics of the landslide in question were those normally associated with a casualty and stated that the landslide "involved a sudden and violent movement of a large mass of earth that was cataclysmic in character, and was similar in nature to a fire, storm, or shipwreck." Heyn, supra at 307, 308. Nowhere in Heyn did we hold or suggest that a loss must be in the nature of a cataclysm to qualify as a casualty. We simply took notice that the landslide in question was cataclysmic in character. To hold that a loss must be cataclysmic in order to qualify as some "other casualty" under section 165(c)(3) would be to limit the availability of the casualty loss deduction to circumstances which are virtually catastrophic in character.

> We think it clear that the magnitude of the casualty is not and should not be the controlling factor in determining whether a questioned event qualifies for casualty loss deduction treatment....

> Mere negligence on the part of the owner-taxpayer has long been held not to necessitate the holding that an occurrence falls outside the ambit of "other casualty." Shearer v. Anderson, supra at 996; Harry Heyn, supra at 308. Needless to say, the taxpayer may not knowingly or willfully sit back and allow himself to be damaged in his property or willfully

damage the property himself. In the instant case, while one or both of the petitioners may have acted negligently, certainly it cannot be said that either petitioner acted willfully or in a grossly negligent manner. The forceful slamming of the automobile door on a blustery fall day upon Agnes' hand and ring was clearly an unexpected accident. We hold that the resulting loss was a casualty within the meaning of the code.

Con
Harvey and Florence Pulvers, 48 TC 245, Aff'd
(9 Cir, 1969) 23 AFTR 2d 69-678, 407 F2d 838

Findings of Fact

Taxpayers claimed a deduction for "other casualty loss" when, as a consequence of a nearby landslide that ruined three nearby homes—but did no physical damage to theirs—the value of their property dropped because of fear that their home might be next. Access to and egress from their residence were not impaired.

Opinion.

In denying the appeal, the court noted that no actual loss was incurred, only a hypothetical loss or a mere fluctuation in value. It also made an interesting point. To quote:

> We think their loss is one that the Congress could not have intended to include in Section 165(c)(3). The specific losses named are fire, storm, shipwreck, and theft. Each of those surely involves physical damage or loss of the physical property. Thus, we read "or other casualty," in para materia, meaning "something like those specifically mentioned." The first things that one thinks of as "other casualty losses" are earthquakes and automobile collision losses, both involving physical damage losses.

> One trouble with the construction of taxpayers on "other casualty" is that the consequences are limitless. Think of the thousands of claims that could be made for loss of value because of shift of highways, but still involving no lack of ingress.

> If one is over the San Andreas fault in California, an authentic report (if one could be had) that it is about to slip would depreciate one's property value before the event. A notorious gangster buying the house next door would depreciate the value of one's property.

4.7 RELEVANT CODE AND REGULATION SECTIONS AND IRS PUBLICATIONS

Code

Section 111	Recovery of Bad Debts, Prior Taxes and Delinquency Amounts
121	One-time Exclusion of Gain from Sale of Principal Residency by Individual Who Has Attained Age 55
123	Amounts Received Under Insurance Contracts for Certain Living Expenses
165	Losses
165(a)	Losses—General Rule
165(c)	Limitation on Losses of Individual

165(h)	Special Election Rules
1033	Involuntary Conversions
1231	Property Used in the Trade or Business and Involuntary Conversions
1245	Gain from Disposition of Certain Depreciable Property
1250	Gain from Disposition of Certain Depreciable Realty

Regulations

Section 1.165-1	Losses
1.165-1(a)	Allowance of Deduction
1.165-1(b)	Nature of Loss Allowable
1.165-1(d)	Amount Deductible
1.165-1(d)	Year of Deduction
1.165-1(e)	Limitation of Losses on Individuals
1.165-6	Farming Losses
1.165-7(a)(1)	Casualty Losses—in General—Allowance Deduction
1.165-7(a)(2)	Method of Valuation
1.165-11	Election in Respect of Losses Attributable to a Disaster
1.1011-1	Adjusted Basis
1.1012-1	Basis of Property

IRS Publications

| 547 | Tax Information on Disasters, Casualties, and Thefts |
| 584 | Disaster Loss Workbook |

4.8 APPLICABLE IRS MANUAL REFERENCES (INVESTIGATIVE TECHNIQUES)

Audit Guidelines for Examiners

| MT 4231-47 | Section 575 | Casualty and Theft Losses |

Standard Explanations Handbook

| MT 428-11 | Section 33 | Casualty and Theft Losses |

Dealers vs. Investors
(Sections 64 and 1202)

5

5.1 IDENTIFYING THE PROBLEM

The question, at least, is simple. In the sale of real property or securities, is the taxpayer a "dealer" (whose gain must be reported as ordinary income) or an "investor" (who may take advantage of Section 202 to report his or her profit as capital gain)?

The court in Thompson vs Commissioner referred to this dilemma as an "old, familiar, recurring, vexing, and oftimes elusive problem." Most Circuits, however, have been able to agree as to which factors should be considered in making the capital gains decision. They are:

1. Nature of acquisition and length of ownership.
2. Extent and nature of taxpayer's efforts to sell.
3. The number, extent, continuity, and substantiality of the sales.
4. Amount of improving, developing, and advertising to increase sales.
5. Use of a business office for sales efforts.
6. Type and degree of supervision over any representative selling the property.
7. Time and effort habitually devoted by the taxpayer to sales efforts.

Clear enough, but difficulties arise when human beings atttempt to weigh one factor against another to arrive at a final decision. In 1954 Congress tried to help. It enacted Section 1221 which was supposed to have defined a "capital asset." (See Figure 5-1).

Part III—General Rules for Determining Capital Gains and Losses

Sec. 1221. Capital asset defined.
Sec. 1222. Other items relating to capital gains and losses.
Sec. 1223. Holding period of property.

SEC. 1221. CAPITAL ASSET DEFINED.

For purposes of this subtitle, the term "capital asset," means property held by the taxpayer (whether or not connected with his trade or business), but does not include—

---

(1) stock in trade of the taxpayer or other property of a kind which would properly be included in the inventory of the taxpayer if on hand at the close of the taxable year, or property held by the taxpayer primarily for sale to customers in the ordinary course of his trade or business;

(2) property, used in his trade or buisness, of a character which is subject to the allowance for depreciation provided in section 167, or real property used in his trade or business;

(3) a copyright, a literary, musical, or artistic composition, a letter or memorandum, or similar property, held by—

(A) a taxpayer whose personal efforts created such property.

(B) in the case of a letter, memorandum, or similar property, a taxpayer for whom such property was prepared or produced, or

(C) a taxpayer in whose hands the basis of such property is determined, for purposes of determining gain from a sale or exchange, in whole or part by reference to the basis of such property in the hands of a taxpayer described in subparagraph (A) or (B);

Last amendment.—Sec. 1221(3) appears above as amended by Sec. 514(a) of Public Law 91-172, Dec. 30, 1969, effective (Sec. 514(c) of P.L. 91-172) to sales and other dispositions occurring after July 25, 1969. Sec. 1221(3) as it read before this amendment is in P-H Cumulative Changes.

(4) accounts or notes receivable acquired in the ordinary course of trade or business for services rendered or from the sale of property described in paragraph (1);

Last amendment—Sec. 1221(4) appears above as amended by Sec. 2132(a) of Public Law 94-455, Oct. 4, 1976, effective (Sec. 2132(b) of P.L. 94-455) for sales, exchanges and contributions made after Oct. 4, 1976. Sec. 1221(4) as it read before this amendment is in P-H Cumulative Changes.

(5) [Repealed]

Repealer.—Sec. 1221(5) was repealed by Sec. 505(a) of Public Law 97-34, Aug. 13, 1981, effective (Sec. 508(a), (c) of P.L. 97-34) generally for property acquired and positions established by the taxpayer after June 23, 1981, in taxable years ending after such date.

25,845 *(I.R.C.)*　　　　　Code § 1221(5)　　　　　1-20-83

Prior amendment.—Former Sec. 1221(5), was previously amended by Sec. 2132(a) of Public Law 94-455, Oct. 4, 1976, effective (Sec. 2132(b) of P.L. 94-455) for sales, exchanges, and contributions made after Oct. 4, 1976. Former Sec. 1221(5) as so amended is in P-H Cumulative Changes.

(5) a publication of the United States Government (including the Congressional Record) which is received from the United States Government or any agency thereof, other than by purchase at the price at which it is offered for sale to the public, and which is held by—

(A) a taxpayer who so received such publication, or

(B) a taxpayer in whose hands the basis of such publication is determined, for purposes of determining gain from a sale or exchange, in whole or in part by reference to the basis of such publication in the hands of a taxpayer described in subparagraph (A).

Last amendment.—Sec. 1221(5) (formerly (6)) appears above as redesignated by Sec. 505(a), (c) of Public Law 97-34, Aug. 13, 1981, effective (Sec. 508(a) of P.L. 97-34) generally for property acquired and positions established by the taxpayer after June 23, 1981, in taxable years ending after such date. Sec. 1221(5) (formerly (6)) as it read before this amendment is in P-H Cumulative Changes.

Addition.—Sec. 1221(5) (formerly (6)) was added by Sec. 2132(a) of Public Law 94-455, Oct. 4, 1976, effective (Sec. 2132(b) of P.L. 94-455) for sales, exchanges, and contributions made after Oct. 4, 1976.

Deadwood changes.—Sec. 1221 was amended by Title XIX, P.L. 94-455, 10-4-76.

Reproduced from the *Prentice-Hall Federal Taxes* service (1983 edition) with the permission of the publisher.

Figure 5-1

This added statute seems to have helped very little, since the dealer/investor controversy continues undiminished. Regulations Section 1.1221(a) tries to explain but seems to make matters worse. It says:

> The term "capital assets" includes all classes of property not specifically excluded by Sec. 1221. In determining whether property is a "capital asset" the period for which held is immaterial.

This last sentence evidently means nothing to Circuit Courts for, as previously noted, one of their criteria in making the dealer/investor decision is "length of ownership."

The very large taxpayer advantage between after-tax profits reported as capital gains and those reported as ordinary income is extremely tempting and causes the public frequently to adopt a "let's-go-for-it" attitude.

This chapter will deal generally with the subjects of real estate and securities (which contain principles that may apply equally to other types of property) and will attempt to provide methods of structuring such transactions so as to arrive at the most favorable tax results.

5.2 HOW THE IRS SEES THE ISSUE

Simply put, the IRS feels strongly that the taxpaying public is going too far in using Section 1221 to avoid the "ordinary income" stigma—that too many transactions have no business purpose other than tax avoidance.

Government thinking along these lines is clearly stated in its *Audit Manual*, Section 525 of MT 4232, which deals with capital gains vs. ordinary income as concerns real estate transactions:

Capital Gains vs. Ordinary Income

(1) Capital gains vs. ordinary income is perhaps the most troublesome area in the real estate industry. Taxpayers employ various methods in an effort to convert ordinary income into capital gains. The validity of these transactions must be determined from the facts and circumstances in each individual case. Some of the various methods employed to secure capital gain treatment are:

(a) The shareholder of a controlled real estate developing corporation may purchase land and sell it to the corporation at a large profit. The corporation has a stepped-up basis, and the shareholder sometimes treats the profit as a long-term capital gain. In most cases the purchase by the stockholder will have had no business purpose other than tax avoidance.

(b) Some taxpayers will report sales as capital gains and contend that they, as individuals, are "investors" rather than "dealers." Generally, sales by an investor give rise to capital gains or losses, while sales by a dealer are ordinary gains or losses. A person who buys and sells property as his/her principal business is clearly a "dealer." It is equally clear that one who makes only isolated or occasional sales is not a dealer. Between these extremes are many possibilities. The determination is usually based on the presence or absence of the following factors:
1. Frequency and continuity of sales
2. Purpose for which property was acquired and held

3. Improving and developing activities
4. Sales activities
5. Rental activities
6. Accounting treatment of such property

(c) Taxpayers who are in the subdividing and developing business will often rent houses for periods ranging from six months to two years and then report the sales as capital gains. The mere renting of a house does not convert it to an IRC 1221 or 1231 asset.

(d) Old houses are sometimes traded in on the sale of a new house. Many times these old houses are undervalued and are rented for a period of time or transferred to stockholders or related companies at the undervalued basis. When these houses are subsequently sold, the sale is sometimes erroneously treated as a sale of an IRC 1231 asset.

(e) Gains realized on the repossession and resale of a house may be reported erroneously as a capital gain in many instances.

(f) It is a common practice among developers to subdivide a portion of a large tract of land and hold back choice commercial plots. These plots are subsequently sold after their values have appreciated as a result of the other development that has taken place. The gain resulting from these sales should normally be treated as ordinary income.

(g) Some builders will build a house or a commercial building and lease it with an option to purchase at a stated price within a specific period of time. The amount of the rent received during the leased period will approximate interest on the stated sales price. Transactions of this nature should be closely scrutinized to determine the proper method of handling them.

NOTE:

"The mere renting of a house does not convert it to IRC 1221 or 1231 asset." Many practitioners have long believed that it does.

In the case of securities we can get some IRS compliance ideas from *Audit Manual* Section 131 of MT 4232.5:

Dealer vs. Trader

(1) A stock broker is a person or organization who regularly buys and sells securities for another and receives a commission for rendering this service.

(2) He/she must be prepared at all times to accept delivery and pay cash for securities purchased and to deliver and collect cash for securities sold.

(3) The broker acts as an agent for the customer when he/she buys securities for the customer from another broker. This type of transaction is referred to as a commission transaction.

(4) If the broker sells his/her own securities he/she then acts as a principal. Acting as a principal, the broker may buy securities on his/her own account for resale to customers in the ordinary course of buisness. In this instance he/she is a dealer in securities. The broker may also, acting as a principal, buy securities on his/her own account for investment. In this instance he/she is a trader or investor. Thus, a broker may be an agent in one transaction and a principal in the next.

(5) Therefore, securities held by dealers may be classified as follows.

    (a) *Dealer securities* (also referred to as trading securities) are those held primarily for sale to customers, which result in ordinary income to the dealer when sold.

(b) *Investment securities* are those which result in a capital gain or loss to the dealer when sold.

(6) Dealer securities represent stock in trade and may be inventoried, while investment securities are just the opposite. Part of your audit responsibilities will be to distinguish between the two different types of securities and the related activities of the brokers. We will cover this phase of your audit in subsequent sections.

(7) At this point, to further understand this delineation you may wish to research the following items.

(a) Dealer in securities vs. trader in securities—
  1. Regs. 1.471-5;
  2. Schafer v. Helvering, 299 U.S. 171, 57S. Ct. 148.

5.3 FACTORS WHICH THE IRS CONSIDERS WHEN MAKING ITS AUDIT DECISION

Real Estate

In categorizing real estate operations the IRS considers the following points:

a. *A Broker* is a special type of agent who acts as an intermediary between buyers and sellers for a commission or fee. This individual does not take title to property but acts as an agent. EARNINGS ARE ORDINARY INCOME.

b. *A Dealer* is one who is in the business of buying and selling real estate. The property which this operation purchases—and possibly also subdivides and develops—is stock in trade, even though such holdings cannot be inventoried (Rev. Rul. 69-536, 1969-2 CB 109). PROFITS ARE STOCK IN TRADE.

c. *Investors* are taxpayers who buy properties with the *intention of holding them for long periods of time so as to realize gains—or who invest in real estate with rental expectations over a **substantial period of time. These operators are passive buyers or sellers who realize infrequent transactions. PROFITS ARE TREATED AS CAPITAL GAINS.

CAUTION:

*Notice this word "intention." The courts generally give it much consideration. In Malat v Riddell 66-1 USTC 9317, 383 U.S. 569, the Supreme Court held that where a taxpayer has a "primary" intent of holding the property for sale to customers, such taxpayer has acquired dealer status.

Section 1221(1) contains the word "primarily" and the high court defines it as being "of first importance or principally." The tax court in George T. Hicks (37 TCM 1540, 1978) listed some of the considerations which it uses in deciding the issue of whether property is held "primarily for sale to customers in the ordinary course of business." Those that do not duplicate the Circuit Court criteria, as previously listed, are shown below:

1. The purpose for which the property was purchased and subsequently held
2. Extent to which the property was improved
3. The ordinary business of the taxpayer
4. The listing of property with real estate brokers
5. The purpose for which the property was held at the time of sale

Courts have many times noted that none of the above factors is conclusive by itself but rather all of the factors, taken as a whole, should govern.

NOTE:

**Remember the previous reference whereby some taxpayers believe that renting a property for a short period of time will change its character to that of a capital asset. Not so. The rental period must be "substantial."

d. *Subdividers* purchase raw or improved land and divide it into sections or lots for resale. They are distinguished from developers in that the land becomes a salable commodity (stock in trade) after such division and without the necessity for improvements thereon. SALES ARE REPORTABLE AS ORDINARY INCOME.

(A portion of Section 5.4 will illustrate circumstances under which income of some subdividers can be considered Capital Gains.)

e. *Developers* are taxpayers who improve undeveloped properties usually by grading, installing streets, curbs, sidewalks, sewers, and water systems. They may even erect a few model homes to interest the public in the project. SALES ARE REPORTABLE AS ORDINARY INCOME.

f. *Speculative Builders* construct homes or other buildings to sell. THEY ARE CONSIDERED DEALERS.

g. *Operative Builders* construct buildings on contract. THEY ARE CONSIDERED DEALERS.

h. *Investor Builders* usually build to specifications for a particular entity, then lease the property to it with an option to buy. Such options may be granted to the lessee or the lessee's nominee. Because the leases usually require lessees to hold the property for a period of time before the options can be exercised, builders will report income from options which are exercised as long-term capital gains. If this pattern is repeated frequently, the IRS will claim that such income is ORDINARY.

The IRS also sees the taxpayer as a real estate dealer where the following situations exist:

■ Investment property is not identified as such in books and records, nor is it segregated from stock-in-trade holdings.

■ Profits from realty sales regularly exceed income from other sources.

■ Occupation, as stated on return, is that of "real estate dealer."

■ Real estate holdings are substantial and sales are frequent.

■ Advertising by taxpayer or his agent is extensive.

■ Subdivided property is heavily improved and offered for sale.

Securities. In making the securities dealer/investor decision the IRS uses Regulation 1.1236-1 (Figure 5-2).

Section 471 (Inventories by dealers in securities), as mentioned in Figure 5-2, defines a dealer in securities:

For the purposes of this section, a dealer in securities is a merchant of securities, whether an individual, partnership, or corporation, with an established place of business, regularly engaged in the purchase of securities and their resale to customers; that is, one who as a merchant buys securities and sells them to customers with a view to the gains and profits that may be derived therefrom. If such business is simply a branch of the activities carried on by such person, the securities inventoried as provided in this section may include only those held for purposes of resale and not for investment. Taxpayers who buy and sell or hold securities for investment or speculation, irrespective of whether such buying or selling constitutes the carrying on of a trade or business, and officers of corporations and members of partnerships who in their individual capacities buy and sell securities, are not dealers in securities within the meaning of this section.

The IRS, therefore, will make its decision based generally on the weight carried by each of the following considerations:

O— § 1.1236 **Statutory provisions; dealers in securities.**[Sec. 1236, IRC]

O— § 1.1236-1(T.D. 6253, filed 9-25-57; republished in T.D. 6500, filed 11-25-60; amended by T.D. 6726, filed 4-28-64.) **Dealers in securities.**

(a) *Capital gains.* Section 1236(a) provides that gain realized by a dealer in securities from the sale or exchange of a security (as defined in paragraph (c) of this section), shall not be considered as gain from the sale or exchange of a capital asset unless—

(1) The security is, before the expiration of the thirtieth day after the date of its acquisition, clearly identified in the dealer's records as a security held for investment, or if acquired before October 20, 1951, was so identified before November 20, 1951; and

(2) The security is not held by the dealer primarily for sale to customers in the ordinary course of his trade or business at any time after the identification referred to in subparagraph (1) of this paragraph has been made.

Unless both of these requirements are met, the gain is considered as gain from the sale of assets held by the dealer primarily for sale to customers in the course of his business.

(b) *Ordinary losses.* Section 1236(b) provides that a loss sustained by a dealer in securities from the sale or exchange of a security shall not be considered a loss from the sale or exchange of property which is not a capital asset if at any time after November 19, 1951, the security has been clearly identified in the dealer's records as a security held for investment. Once a security has been identified after November 19, 1951, as being held by the dealer for investment, it shall retain that character for purposes of determining loss on its ultimate disposition, even though at the time of its disposition the dealer holds it primarily for sale to his customers in the ordinary course of his business. However, section 1236 has no application to the extent that section 582(c) applies to losses of banks.

(c) *Definitions—(1) Security.* For the purpose of this section, the term "security" means any share of stock in any corporation, any certificate of stock or interest in any corporation, any note, bond, debenture, or other evidence of indebtedness, or any evidence of any interest in, or right to subscribe to or purchase any of the foregoing.

(2) *Dealer in securities.* For definition of a "dealer in securities," see the regulations under section 471.

(d) *Identification of security in dealer's records.* (1) A security is clearly identified in the dealer's records as a security held for investment when there is an accounting separation of the security from other securities, as by making appropriate entries in the dealer's books of account to distinguish the security from inventories and to designate it as an investment, and by (i) indicating with such entries, to the extent feasible, the individual serial number of, or other characteristic symbol imprinted upon, the individual security, or (ii) adopting any other method of identification satisfactory to the Commissioner.

(2) In computing the 30-day period prescribed by section 1236(a), the first day of the period is the day following the date of acquisition. Thus, in the case of a security acquired on March 18, 1957, the 30-day period expires at midnight on April 17, 1957.

Figure 5-2

---

1. Was the security, within *30 days after date of acquisition, clearly identified in the dealer's records as one held for investment?

2. Was the security ever held for sale to customers in the ordinary course of buisness—after the above procedure had been followed? (If the answer to (1) is "No" and to (2) "Yes," then no capital gain will be allowed.)

3. For purposes of determining loss, has the taxpayer attempted to change the status of the security from capital asset to stock in trade? (This cannot be done.)

4. Was the security investment clearly labeled in the taxpayer's records by use of serial number or other characteristic symbol printed on the security? (It should have been.)

5. In computing the 30 days as mentioned in (1), was the first day of the period considered to have been the day following the date of acquisition? (It should have been.)

6. Does an established place of business exist from whence securities are bought and sold? (If so, dealer status exists.)

7. Were securities in question ever inventoried? (If so, upon sale, gain will be ordinary.)

8. Is the taxpayer primarily engaged in an activity unrelated to securities? (If so, this helps in establishing investor status.)

9. Was there an investment risk at time of purchase? (If not, there is an indication of dealership.)

10. Was the volume of turnover large and were turnovers rapid? (This situation might lead to ordinary income treatment.)

NOTE:

*The Economic Recovery Tax Act of 1981 eliminates this 30-day grace period and requires that dealers in securities identify a security as held for investment by the close of business on the day of acquisition (effective as of 8-13-81).

5.4 CONSIDERATIONS WHEN PREPARING THE RETURN

Keeping in mind all that has gone before, specific areas of this dealer/investor issue are important enough to carry a need for additional clarity.

Held Primarily for Sale to Customers

This phrase causes much of the difficulty which evolves from the dealer/investor controversy. The Supreme Court in Malet v Riddell (as previously mentioned) defines "primarily" as "of first importance" or "principally." Some factors used in deciding whether the evidence meets this definition follow.

Selling activity of the taxpayer. Frequent and consistent property sales are perhaps the most important indication of dealer status, particularly as to real estate. They are, at least, the flag which usually starts the IRS audit machine in motion. Substantial subdivision and improvement of a tract of land is also a strong indication of the taxpayer's intent to hold property for sale in the course of a business. (This latter situation will be covered in detail in a following section.)

Solicitation and advertising. Vigorous sales campaigns usually bring forth negative responses from courts. Taxpayers who sell without solicitation usually do well.

Selling activity of taxpayer's agent is usually imputed to the taxpayer. However, where independent agents have been given wide latitude and broad discretion in the disposition of the property, capital gains have been allowed.

Purpose and manner of acquisition. If it can be proved that the property was obtained for investment purposes (possibly through the broker who sold it)—or if it was acquired by inheritance, gift, corporate liquidation, or the like, and passively liquidated—capital gains may be allowed.

Change of holding purpose. Property bought with investment intent, but later changed to a highly developed subdivision, will bring ordinary income. Intent at time of sale governs.

Should the reverse happen—and property purchased for sale to customers become investment property—courts have given heavy consideration to the reason for such a change. In Lomas V. Nettleton Financial Corporation vs. U.S., for example, the court noted that (1) a series of events made it impossible to continue with the original development plan; (2) the gain was attributable to natural accretion in the land's value over a period of time; (3) all but 70 of 1100 acres were sold in three transactions, one of which had no consequences. The court held that the gain was capital in nature.

Reason and method of sale Certain sales in themselves give indication of capital gains:

- Single isolated transactions
- Sale under threat of condemnation
- Sale to raise needed cash
- Disposal of property because it no longer meets the requirements for which purchased
- Property held for a long period of time

Real Estate Held by a Dealer

This can be a tough one but certainly not insurmountable. Most of the previously mentioned points apply except that in this instance *segregation of holdings is paramount.* An occasional sale should not bring on dealer status for the taxpayer's true investments. Here's how court decisions have evolved:

- Dealer segregated his investments, holding them in his own name and placing the rest in the names of a partnership and a corporation. HELD TO BE CAPITAL GAINS.
- Broker's extensive investments in real estate were not segregated from those held for sale to customers. HELD TO BE ORDINARY INCOME.
- Handling of parcels was inconsistent with their designation in records as investments or stocks in trade. HELD SALES TO BE ORDINARY INCOME.
- Dealer's frequent and continuous buying and selling of lots. RULED TO BE ORDINARY INCOME.

Real Property Subdivided for Sale

Normally, real estate held for sale to customers in the ordinary course of business is not a capital or Section 1231 asset. There is, however, in the case of an individual (and certain corporations) an exception which is allowed under Section 1237 (Figure 5-3).

With care, this statute can be made to work well. Here, in summary, are the tests that must be met for qualification under its rules.

Section 1237 tests. To qualify under this section taxpayers must show that they:

1. Haven't previously held the tract (or any lot or parcel thereof) for sale to customers in the ordinary course of a trade or business.
2. Did not in year of sale hold any other real estate for sale to customers as a dealer.
3. Have held the property for five years (not necessary if property was acquired by inheritance).

4. Did not make substantial improvements *(nor were deemed to have made them) which markedly enhanced the value of the property sold, while they held the property.

5. Did not make substantial improvements enhancing the value of the property sold nor did the buyer, under a contract of sale.

NOTE:

Improvements are imputed to the taxpayer if made under conditions contained in Regulation 1.1237-1(c)(2) (Figure 5-3).

SEC. 1237. REAL PROPERTY SUBDIVIDED FOR SALE.

(a) **General.**—Any lot or parcel which is part of a tract of real property in the hands of a taxpayer, other than a corporation shall not be deemed to be held primarily for sale to customers in the ordinary course of trade or business at the time of sale solely because of the taxpayer having subdivided such tract for purposes of sale or because of any activity incident to such subdivision or sale, if—

(1) such tract, or any lot or parcel thereof, had not previously been held by such taxpayer primarily for sale to customers in the ordinary course of trade or business (unless such tract at such previous time would have been covered by this section) and, in the same taxable year in which the sale occurs, such taxpayer does not so hold any other real property; and

(2) no substantial improvement that substantially enhances the value of the lot or parcel sold is made by the taxpayer on such tract while held by the taxpayer or is made pursuant to a contract of sale entered into between the taxpayer and the buyer. For purposes of this paragraph, an improvement shall be deemed to be made by the taxpayer if such improvement was made by—

(A) the taxpayer or members of his family (as defined in section 267(c)(4)), by a corporation controlled by the taxpayer, or by a partnership which included the taxpayer as a partner; or

(B) a lessee, but only if the improvement constitutes income to the taxpayer; or

(C) Federal, State, or local government, or political subdivision thereof, but only if the improvement constitutes an addition to basis for the taxpayer; and

(3) such lot or parcel, except in the case of real property acquired by inheritance or devise, is held by the taxpayer for a period of 5 years

Last amendment.—Sec. 1237(a) appears above as amended by Sec. 2(a)(1) of Public Law 91-686, Jan. 12, 1971, effective (Sec. 2(b) of P.L. 91-686) with respect to taxable years beginning after Jan. 12, 1971.

Prior amendments.— Sec. 1237(a) was previously amended by the following:

Sec. 55 of Public Law 85-866, Sept. 2, 1958 (qualified effective date rule in Sec. 1(c)(1) of P.L. 85-866.)*

Sec. [1] of Public Law 495, Apr. 27, 1956, effective (Sec. 3 of P.L. 495) for taxable years beginning after Dec. 31, 1954.*

---

*Sec. 1237(a) as so amended is in P-H Cumulative Changes.

25,862 *(I.R.C.)*   Code § 1237(b)   **1-20-83**

(b) **Special Rules for Application of Section.**—

(1) **Gains.**—If more than 5 lots or parcels contained in the same tract of real property are sold or exchanged, gain from any sale or exchange (which occurs in or after the taxable year in which

the sixth lot or parcel is sold or exchanged) of any lot or parcel which comes within the provisions of paragraphs (1), (2) and (3) of subsection (a) of this section shall be deemed to be gain from the sale of property held primarily for sale to customers in the ordinary course of the trade or business to the extent of 5 percent of the selling price.

(2) Expenditures of Sale.—For the purpose of computing gain under paragraph (1) of this subsection, expenditures incurred in connection with the sale or exchange of any lot or parcel shall neither be allowed as a deduction in computing taxable income, nor treated as reducing the amount realized on such sale or exchange; but so much of such expenditures as does not exceed the portion of gain deemed under paragraph (1) of this subsection to be gain from the sale of property held primarily for sale to customers in the ordinary course of trade or business shall be so allowed as a deduction, and the remainder, if any, shall be treated as reducing the amount realized on such sale or exchange.

(3) Necessary improvements.—No improvement shall be deemed a substantial improvement for purposes of subsection (a) if the lot or parcel is held by the taxpayer for a period of 10 years and if—

(A) such improvement is the building or installation of water, sewer, or drainage facilities or roads (if such improvement would except for this paragraph constitute a substantial improvement);

(B) it is shown to the satisfaction of the Secretary that the lot or parcel, the value of which was substantially enhanced by such improvement, would not have been marketable at the prevailing local price for similar building sites without such improvement; and

(C) the taxpayer elects, in accordance with regulations prescribed by the Secretary, to make no adjustment to basis of the lot or parcel, or of any other property owned by the taxpayer, on account of the expenditures for such improvements. Such election shall not make any item deductible which would not otherwise be deductible.

Last amendment.—Sec. 1237(b)(3) appears above as amended by Sec. 2(a)(2) of Public Law 91-686, Jan. 12, 1971, effective (Sec. 2(b) of P.L. 91-686) with respect to taxable years beginning after Jan. 12, 1971.

Prior amendment.—Sec. 1237(b)(3) was previously amended by Sec. 2 of Public Law 495, Apr. 27, 1956, effective (Sec. 3 of P.L. 495) for taxable years beginning after Dec. 31, 1954, Sec. 1237(b)(3) as so amended is in P-H Cumulative Changes.

(c) Tract Defined.—For purposes of this section, the term "tract of real property" means a single piece of real property, except that 2 or more pieces of real property shall be considered a tract if at any time they were contiguous in the hands of the taxpayer or if they would be contiguous except for the interposition of a road, street, railroad, stream, or similar property. If, following the sale or exchange of any lot or parcel from a tract of real property, no further sales or exchanges of any other lots or parcels from the remainder of such tract are made for a period of 5 years, such remainder shall be deemed a tract.

Deadwood changes.—Sec. 1237 was amended by Title XIX, P.L. 94-455, 10-4-76.

Reproduced from the *Prentice-Hall Federal Taxes* service (1983 edition) with the permission of the publisher.

Figure 5-3

Substantial improvements—general rule, under Regulation 1.1237-1 (b)(c) Section 1237, will not apply if the taxpayer or certain others make improvements on the tract which are substantial and which substantially increase the value of the lot sold. Certain improvements are not substantial within the meaning of Section 1237(a)(2) if they are necessary to make the lot marketable at the prevailing local price and meet the other conditions of Section 1237(b)(3).

Capital Gain Limitations

Having met all of the provisions of 1237, the taxpayer still is not home free. Part of gain on sale may be taxable as ordinary income.

Five-lot rule. If not more than five parcels were sold during the taxable year, the gain would be capital in nature. Sales of two or more contiguous lots to a single buyer would constitute the sale of one parcel.

Five percent rule. If more than five lots were sold in the taxable year, the gain on all sales in that year would have to be allocated. The gain, up to five percent of the selling price, would be ordinary income and the balance capital gain. However, if five lots were sold in the taxable year and another in the next year, the five percent rule would apply only to the sale in the following year. But see the five-year rule below.

Five-year rule. Should a taxpayer fail to make additional sales (after the last one is consummated) for a period of five years, the five percent rule does not apply until he has again sold five lots.

Selling expenses are deductible in full against ordinary income. The remainder, if any, reduces capital gain. Such expenses cannot be deducted as business costs against other income.

NOTE:

Under this possibility, application of the five percent rule may not be as damaging as it might appear. Brokers' fees, transfer taxes, legal fees, and the like may eat up most of the five percent, leaving the balance for capital gain treatment.

More Key Points to Keep in Mind When Preparing the Return

There are a few additional points to be remembered when preparing the return:

1. Realize that the IRS (on audit) will scrutinize both the preceding and the following years in an attempt to establish a pattern.
2. Do not identify the taxpayer's occupation as "real estate dealer" or "stock broker," or the like, if such classification can possibly be legally avoided.
3. Do all possible to clearly establish intent at time of purchase and sale.
4. Above all else, make certain that properties sold and for sale are correctly segregated in the records.
5. Be careful how you present facts. Suppose a dentist owns rental property and he deducts as a "business" expense "Auto (40%) $800." Unless this item is explained as necessary to rent collections, it might trigger an audit or come back to haunt the taxpayer should he sell some real estate. The IRS may use the "business auto expense" nomenclature as a level in proving that the doctor was a real estate dealer.

5.5 HANDLING THE AUDIT

Dealing successfully with the IRS on this issue can best be accomplished by advance planning. Illustration: Your client, in a dealer/investor position has been with you for many years. You understand his or her financial aspirations. You know that the taxpayer is somewhat of an entrepreneur who will make money wherever possible. Sit down with this person now and thoroughly review this chapter. Explain the importance of consultations *before* deals are made. Shape and legally arrange facts to fit your goal. Do some tax planning; structure the dealings so that they won't encounter this controversy. After the fact, happenings cannot be changed, but the future is yours to deal with.

Checklist outlining what to do if the audit has arrived unexpectedly to a new client or to an old one—and you are unprepared

The following few basic suggestions can be applied to any audit situation but are particularly appropriate here:

- You learn the controlling facts for a given problem—the governing points of law—the shades of meaning best suited to your purpose.
- You listen to your client's story.
- Make certain that he or she understands enough law to recognize the important facts.
- Cross-examine client in minute detail.
- Be sure to secure *all facts* and documents to support your position.
- Carefully interpret what you have discovered. Be alert for the fact that will swing the decision your way.
- Structure a meaningful and professional presentation. The manner in which facts are put together is as important as the facts themselves. Know that advocacy in itself is an important part of your profession.

Handling Documentation

Having assimilated all available facts—and educated yourself as to points of law—choose your strongest area of defense, then set about to exploit it with documentation.

Let's presume that your client operates an ice cream dealership in corporate form. She has time on her hands and dabbles in real estate—legally, as an investor—but she canot resist taking a profit when the opportunity arises. Her returns show two real estate transactions per year for a three-year period—corporate salaries $25,000 per year—average capital gains from real estate dealings $40,000. The IRS claims dealer status because of frequency and continuity of transactions.

Facts to exploit. You analyze each purchase and sale and determine from the taxpayer, and your workpapers, the following:

- Total holdings of taxpayer after the six sales, two rental properties—hardly a dealer inventory. You document these with closing statements and warranty deeds that show holding periods of four and six years respectively.
- As to the six transactions which have already occurred, you learn that:
  Property 1 was acquired through gift from taxpayer's mother and disposed of as not being worthy of an investment holding. Produce gift tax return.

  Property 2 was acquired as a protective device when it was learned that a leather tannery which would be odoriferous was planned for the site which was next door to rental property No. 8. Secure application for tannery operation from Zoning Board. Property was sold under restrictive clause which allowed continuance of only a two-family dwelling on the site. Produce sales agreement.

Property 3 was purchased inexpensively as an investment and sold 14 months later for use as a parking lot by a new retail store. Taxpayer did not advertise or in any way attempt to sell the property. Show written offer by store and a note in your workpapers to the effect that client mentioned sale of securities "to obtain funds for a good real estate buy which couldn't lose if held long enough."

Property 4 was heavily advertised for sale and listed with a real estate broker. Taxpayer needed cash for education of her son. This in itself should remove the transaction from dealer status, but you locate several court decisions which indicate that intent at time of sale is governing and that the motive here was not profit as such.

Property 5 held for six months resulted in short-term gain but did give indication of dealer status. You learn that it was sold at a large profit because a condominium complex next door had to have the acreage for use as a leach field for its septic system—or it wouldn't have been able to build. Taxpayer was approached by buyer. You claim a passive sale.

Property 6 was bought and sold within 13 months, clearly as a money-making venture. You claim an isolated transaction and prove that such does not remove investor status by producing several court cases to that effect.

More Key Suggestions in "After-the-Fact" Situations

Your work papers are extremely important. Be sure to review them for hepful notations that you may have forgotten. Make use of realtors, appraisers, bankers, local assessors, and zoning boards who might have knowledge of your client's purchase intent and reason for sale.

A showing that ownership was unintentional—and disposition passive—will do wonders. Scores of court cases abound on both sides of issues. Locate those that seem to support your position then *read them in their entirety.* Do not depend upon short summaries as found in tax services. Read the adverse decisions as well. There might be something in them that you can use.

Examine all sales agreements, real estate listings, and deeds in a search for documentation of your point of view. Review client's records, including check stubs, for evidence. Possibly you will find a forgotten notation that will prove intent at time of purchase. Maybe something like: "Clark Street investment."

Taken by themselves, the results of such efforts might mean little but, together, as a developing pattern, they can accomplish much.

5.6 PERTINENT COURT DECISIONS—PRO AND CON

Pro
Bradford v U.S. (1971) 28 AFTR 2d
71-5228 195 Ct Cl 500, 444 F2d 1133

Findings of Fact

J. C. Bradford and Company was a partnership engaged in the business of acting as a dealer in securities, broker, and investment banker.

The securities which the company held in the ordinary course of business were carried in a general trading account. On occasion, the partners of the company, either alone or in a joint venture with others, purchased securities with a view toward capital gains. Such purchases were segregated from the trading account and placed in separate investment accounts.

In the latter part of 1956 the plaintiffs learned of an opportunity to buy and sell 55,348 shares of Knights Life Stock. They discussed the possibility of a long-term capital gain and eventually structured both ends of the transaction toward this end. They arranged to borrow up to $4,000,000 for purchase money.

Eventually, the stock was bought and designated on the J. C. Bradford and Company books as held for investment. This was done before expiration of the 30-day rule. The stock was sold to the American General Insurance Company on August 1, 1957. The company claimed a capital gain. The government said no.

Opinion

In holding for the plaintiff, the court said:

> An examination of the facts. ... indicates that the company was acting as a trader on its own account with respect to the Knights Life Stock here in issue. Company performed no merchandising functions on those shares; it was not acting as a middleman bringing together buyer and seller, nor did it perform the usual services of retailer or wholesaler of goods. Company's status as to the source of supply of the stock was in no way different from that of American General. There is nothing in the record to indicate that the shares were not as easily accessible to American General as to Company. Company performed no services for which it would have been compensated by a mark-up of the price of the Knights Life shares. Rather, Company's profit was solely dependent on an advantageous purchase which enabled it to sell to American General at a price in excess of cost. Furthermore, Company did not hold the shares in Knights Life as stock in trade but clearly segregated those shares from the general trading account and identified them as held for investment.

Con
Gault v Comm. (2 Cir; 1964) 13 AFTR 2d 1571,
332 F2d aff'g.

Findings of Fact

The petitioner is president of L. H. Gault & Co., Inc., which operates a prosperous fuel oil, cement, and sand gravel business in Westport, Connecticut. In January of 1950 he purchased 167 acres of undeveloped land in Westport for $50,000, and shortly thereafter named the tract Gault Park. He began gradually to improve the property by surveying lots, installing roads, water mains, etc. From 1950 to 1958 the petitioner sold 68.5 lots for substantial sums and spent more than $52,000 to improve the tract.

Mr. Gault's sales efforts were passive. Buyers were not solicited. Neither did the taxpayer advertise or hire salesmen. The property was not listed with any real estate broker, nor did the plaintiff hold himself out as a broker. He had a full-time job managing his corporation, devoting only two or three hours a week to his real estate venture. In 1957 and 1958 his income from the sale of lots was about 35 percent of total receipts.

The IRS disallowed capital gain treatment.

Opinion

Before giving his decision, the judge had this to say about the dealer/investor issue:

Because there is a good deal of overlapping between business and investment property in this area, the cases are legion. Indeed, the case law has grown to a jungle-like abundance accompanied by much of the welter and impenetrability which such fertility produces.

In the end, he upheld the decision of the Tax Court, saying:

Sales began within seven months after the date of purchase. More than $52,000 was spent in improving the property from 1950 to 1958. Petitioner had it surveyed and platted, built roads, and installed mains and fire hydrants. Substantial amounts were realized from more or less continuous sales over the eight-year period. During the two tax years in question, 20½ lots were sold for more than $67,000. The petitioner took an active interest in the development of the tract, rejecting proposed houses he considered too modern, and in general sought to ensure that Gault Park would develop into an exclusive residential area. While petitioner's motive in purchasing the tract is not too clear, his own testimony reveals that he regarded Gault Park as more than just an investment:

(1) We think the record amply supports the Tax Court's inference that this property was being held primarily for sale to customers, and that the petitioner's sales and other activities with regard to this tract were sufficiently frequent and continuous to categorize the petitioner as a dealer in real estate.

5.7 RELEVANT CODE AND REGULATION SECTIONS
Code

Section 64	Ordinary Income Defined
454(b)	Short Term Obligations Issued on Discount Basis
471	General Rule for Inventories
1091	Wash Sales
1202	Deduction for Capital Gains
1221	Capital Asset Defined
1231	Property Used in the Trade or Business and Involuntary Conversions
1236	Dealers in Securities
1237	Real Property Subdivided for Sale
1237(b)(3)	Necessary Improvements

Regulations

Section 1.471-5	Inventories by Dealers in Securities
1.1221	Capital Assets Defined
1.1221(a)	Meaning of Terms
1.1236.1(a)	Dealers in Securities
1.1237.1	Real Property Subdivided for Sale
1.1237-1(b)(c)	Substantial Improvements—General Rule

1.1237-1(c)(2)   Improvements Made or Deemed to Be Made by the Taxpayer

1.1237-1(e)(2)(iii)(G) Definition of Tract

1.1237-1(c)(5)   Special Rules Relating to Substantial Improvements

5.8 APPLICABLE IRS MANUAL REFERENCES (INVESTIGATIVE TECHNIQUES)

Audit Guidelines for Examiners

MT 4231-46   Section 6(15)0   Real Estate Brokers

Specialized Industries Audit Guidelines

MT 4232.5-1   Section 300   Techniques for Verification of Dealers' Security Transactions

                 Section 310   Techniques for Verifying Compliance With IRC *1236

                 Section 312   Audit Techniques

   *Dealers in Securities

Medical and Dental Deductions
(Section 213)

6

6.1 IDENTIFYING THE PROBLEM

Aside from the usual difficulties of substantiation, problems frequently arise in the following areas of medical and dental deductions:

1. Whether Section 213 (Medical, Dental, etc.) Expenses are personal in nature under Section 262 and deductible as itemized deductions—or business expenses deductible in their entirety under Section 162 (Trade or Business) Expenses. For example, is an actor's facelift medical in nature or a necessary business expense?

2. Whether the involved expenses meet the Section 213(e)(1)(A) definition of "Medical Care"—amounts paid: "for the diagnosis, cure, mitigation, treatment, or prevention of disease, or for the purpose of affecting any structure of the body."

3. Whether a medical deduction involving capital expenditures has been properly handled.

4. Whether travel expenses, deducted as medical expenses, meet the requirements of 213(e)(1)(B): "for transportation primarily for and essential to medical care referred to in subparagraph (A) ..."

5. Whether expenses concerning institutional care or education can properly be deducted as medical expenses.

6. Whether various indirect costs, such as child care when mother is ill, can become medical deductions.

6.2 HOW THE IRS SEES THE ISSUE

The Service sees every substantial *medical and dental expense* deduction as a potentially lucrative pocket for its search mission. Buried in the myriad of deduction possibilities are dozens of fine points that can be exploited by the IRS to produce additional taxes. All of the above six areas, of course, are included, plus all sorts of questionable items within the six, such as:

■ The employment of a practical nurse. (What portion of her wages, if any, can be deducted?)

■ The cost of meals and lodging. (When can they be included with medical transportation deductions?)

■ The cost of accident and health insurance. (Is it deductible in its entirety as medical insurance?)

Since the burden of proof rests with the taxpayer—and since this area of taxation provides such latitude for error—the government feels secure in its belief that hunting here will generally prove profitable.

6.3 FACTORS WHICH THE IRS CONSIDERS WHEN MAKING ITS AUDIT DECISION

In the verification of medical expenditures, the IRS asks its examiners to be alert for the existence of:

■ *Double deductions* by accepting an unreceipted invoice as proof of a qualified expenditure. For example, a hospital might issue a bill in the amount of $450. Insurance covered $300 but the taxpayer deducted the entire $450, not the $150 which he or she actually paid. If the examiner asks for the receipted bill, the "error" will be uncovered.

■ *Double deductions* which result when a taxpayer pays the bill and is then reimbursed for all or part of it by an insurance company. Inquiry must be made of the taxpayer to determine the existence of insurance and any recoveries which might have resulted.

■ *Large claims for drugs and prescriptions.* If such amounts appear unreasonable, the agents are asked to connect them to specific illnesses by minutely examining hospital bills and by thoroughly questioning the taxpayer.

■ *Pharmaceutical charges which appear on hospital invoices.* These will be removed and subjected to the 1 percent limitation. (TEFRA aside—covered later in a separate section.)

■ *Medicine and drugs* will be analyzed carefully with an eye to removing toiletries and other such nondeductible items.

■ *If a deduction is taken for hospitalization insurance,* the IRS person is asked to review the coverage to make sure that:

"Medicare A" premiums are deducted only in situations where the taxpayer is 65 or older and not entitled to social security benefits.

"Medicare A" premiums have not been deducted if they were paid as part of the taxpayer's social security tax.

Premiums were not deducted if paid for life insurance or accidental loss of life, limb, or sight—or for loss of earnings—or for a policy which guaranteed a specified amount each week (for a specified number of weeks) while taxpayer was hospitalized.

In combined policies, such as accident and health, the auditor is asked to satisfy himself or herself that the portion of premium allocated to medical care is not unreasonably large. (If it is, it will be disallowed.)

The auditor is also cautioned to make certain that insurance premiums were paid in their entirety by the taxpayer, and not by his or her employer.

In addition, examiners are requested to determine whether costs of transportation include amounts expended for board and lodging—and whether dependency qualifications have been correctly applied.

Unusual expenditures must be traced and analyzed—items such as:

■ The cost of Braille books and magazines. (Only the excess of cost over regular publications is deductible.)

■ The cost of keeping a mentally retarded person in a special home.

■ The cost of a weight reduction program or a program to stop smoking. (Not deductible.)

The law concerning all of these points and others will be presented in the following section.

6.4 CONSIDERATIONS WHEN PREPARING THE RETURN

The courts have interpreted Section 213 (Medical, Dental, etc. Expenses) in a truly broad sense. Each potential medical deduction, therefore, should be carefully scrutinized. All sorts of unusual expenditures have been allowed, or are actual law:

■ Advance payments to a private institution for lifetime care, treatment, and training of a physically or mentally handicapped dependent, if taxpayer should die or become unable to care for his or her dependent, are deductible. The payments must be a condition for the institution's future acceptance of the dependent and must not be refundable.

■ The tax court allowed a medical deduction for part of the cost of building an attached garage (the difference between the cost of the garage and the increase in value of the property). The taxpayer was seriously disabled. His original garage was 70 feet from his home and so narrow that he couldn't fully open his car door. The court found a primary medical purpose. (More about capital expenditures later.)

■ A taxpayer may deduct the cost of a facelift, even without a doctor's recommendation. Why? Because the purpose of the operation was to "affect a structure of the body."

■ In Rev. Rul. 58-223, 1958-1 C.B. 156, the IRS ruled that the costs of a tape recorder, special typewriter, a projection lamp to enlarge printed materials, and special lenses to aid in educating a child who was becoming progressively blind were proper medical deductions.

On the medical-deduction issue, both the courts and the IRS seem sympathetic.

TAX-SAVING SUGGESTION:

Don't let a single possibility of this type pass without first doing your best to place it in tax-aid status. Specific points of law follow.

Basic rules. In general, a taxpayer may deduct as itemized deductions all medical and dental expenses, including transportation and hospitalization insurance costs which satisfy the provisions of Section 213 for himself, his or her spouse, and legal dependents with 3 percent and 1 percent exclusions as explained later (TEFRA aside).

Status of spouse must have existed either at the time when medical services were rendered or at the time when such expenses were paid. Section 6013(d) governs.

"Dependents," for purposes of 213, include those for whom the taxpayer contributed more than one-half of their support, despite the fact that the taxpayer cannot claim them as personal exemptions because they had gross income equal to or exceeding the statutory amount allowable for a personal exemption.

Time of payment. Generally the medical or dental expense can be deducted *only* in the year paid, regardless of whether taxpayer was on cash or accrual basis. This rule opens the possibility of moving payments from one year to another of doubling up, so as to exceed the 3 percent and 1 percent limitations (5 percent after '82—no drug limitation after '83) under circumstances where—if paid separately in each of two years—no deduction would result.

Under Regulation 1.213-1(e)(4) insurance premiums paid by a taxpayer who has not reached age 65 (for policies providing medical care after he or she or their dependents reach 65) are deductible as medical expenses if paid on a level payment basis, either for a period of ten years or more, or until the year in which the taxpayer reaches 65 (but in no case for a period of less than 5 years).

Community property states. If married persons in these states file separate returns, they may divide equally any medical expenses paid out of community funds. If such expenses, however, were paid out of separate funds, only the spouse who paid the bills may deduct them.

What is medical care? Once again, let's look at the definition in Section 213(e)(1)(A): The term means amounts paid "for the diagnosis, cure, mitigation, treatment, or prevention of disease, or for the purpose of affecting any structure or function of the body."

Even though this definition is clearly based in health problems, its interpretation covers a wide range of expenditures, all the way from payments made to doctors, dentists, nurses, and hospitals to the cost of installing a specially designed swimming pool.

A checklist for medical expenses, as reproduced from IRS Publication 502 (Medical and Dental Expenses) is included as Fig. 6-1. Taken by categories, the most frequently contested issues are:

**Check List for
Medical Expenses**

The following list is a check for those expenses that generally are deductible or nondeductible.

You May Deduct

Fees for doctors, surgeons, dentists, osteopaths, ophthalmologists, optometrists, chiropractors, chiropodists, podiatrists, psychiatrists, psychologists, and Christian Science practitioners.

Fees for hospital services, therapy, nursing services (including nurse's meals while on duty), ambulance hire, and laboratory, surgical, obstetrical, diagnostic, dental, and X-ray services

Meals and lodging provided by a hospital during medical treatment, and meals and lodging provided by a center during treatment for alcoholism or drug addiction

Medical and hospital insurance premiums

Special equipment, such as a motorized wheelchair, hand controls on a car, and a special telephone for the deaf

Special items, including false teeth, artificial limbs, eyeglasses, hearing aids, crutches, and guide dogs for the blind or deaf

Transportation for needed medical care

All your medicines and drugs

Pills or other birth control items your doctor prescribed

Special foods and drinks your doctor prescribed only for the treatment of an illness

Vitamins, iron, etc., your doctor prescribed

You May Not Deduct
Bottled water

Care of a normal and healthy baby by a nurse	Social activities, such as dancing lessons for the general improvement of your health, even though your doctor advises them
Diaper service	
Funeral and burial expenses	Toothpaste, toiletries, cosmetics, etc.
Health club dues	Trip for general improvement of health
Household help	Vitamins for general health
Illegal operation or treatment	Weight loss program
Maternity clothes	
Program to stop smoking	

Figure 6-1

Nursing and Other Medical Services. It is important to note that this type of medical deduction does not depend on the title or qualifications of the person providing the services. It is the type of care that governs. For example, if a student provides exercise instructions for a child with cerebral palsy, under a doctor's instructions, the cost would constitute a medical deduction, even though the student was not a professional physical therapist.

Employment of a practical nurse, however, might produce ony a partial medical deduction. Only the portion attributable to medical care, such as administering medication, washing the patient, etc., could be deducted, not housecleaning.

NOTE:

Social Security taxes paid by the taxpayer in connection with hired medical services are deductible.

Special Education and Training. Payments to a special school for a mentally or physically handicapped person are deductible as medical expenses, if the *main* reason for attendance is to obtain medical aid for the ailment. Costs of meals, lodging, and ordinary education are also deductible if incidental to the *main* purpose as mentioned. (Regulation 1.213-1(e)(1)(v))

Expenses at a regular school may even qualify. In one instance a taxpayer's son was retarded and needed special attention, but the local school district couldn't supply it. So the taxpayer sent his son to a regular school in a neighboring district that possessed a specially trained staff which could deal with the boy's needs. The IRS allowed not only the tuition but transportation costs as well.

Nursing Homes, Extended Care Units, and Other Such Institutions. Payments made to these organizations can be deducted in their entirety under the same rules as those that apply to "Special Education and Training."

CAUTION:

The principal purpose must be medical in nature. If it is not—and if the patient is in a home for the aged, for example, because of family reasons—then only costs directly related to medical care will be allowed.

Capital expenditures as medical deductions. Payments for special equipment installed in a home, or similar improvements made for medical reasons, are deductible to the extent that such expenditures exceed the increase in the value of the property. (Regulation 1.213-1(e)(1)(iii))

Cost of a home elevator was allowed for an elderly, arthritic taxpayer, even though not prescribed by a physician.

The cost of maintaining or operating a capital asset is also deductible, if primarily for medical purposes, even though none, or only a portion of the asset's original cost, was deductible.

Transportation expenses. These are deductible as expenses for medical care where such travel is essential for proper treatment.

NOTE:

Cost of meals and lodging, however, are not. The Supreme Court in Comm. v. Bilder had this to say:

Deduction denied for cost of lodging of taxpayer while on trip to Florida required for medical reasons. 1954 code Section 213(e)(1)(B) expressly allows deduction for cost of transportation only, thus excluding personal and living expenses.

Taxpayers have been successful, however, in situations where handicapped persons deducted costs of travel, meals, and lodging for assistants who performed services for them while taxpayers were on business trips. Rev. Rul. 75-317 1975-2 CB 57 considers that such costs are medical expenses.

Insurance premiums. Under Regulation 1.213-1(e)(4) the following types of medical insurance are deductible (but see Section 6.3 "Factors Which the IRS Considers When Making Its Audit Decision," for exceptions and limitations):

• Health & Hospitalization
• Surgical
• Major Medical
• Separately stated health portions of accident & health policies
• Monthly premiums paid for doctors' bills under the Medicare program
• Group hospitalization and clinical care
• Membership in an association which furnishes cooperative medical service

Special limitations attach to the deductibility of medical insurance. One-half of the premium (up to $150) is allowed as a deduction and is not subject to the three percent rule. The remaining half, plus the excess over the $150 ceiling, is includible with other medical expenses.

Computing the medical deduction. After computation of the insurance allowance, as above, the cost of medicine and drugs may be deducted only to the extent that they exceed one percent of the adjusted gross—and then only in an amount by which they, plus all other medical expenses, exceed three percent of adjusted gross. Schedule A (Form 1040) presents a format for use in computing this deduction.

IMPORTANT:

Since 1966, all maximum limitations on medical-dental deductions have been removed.

TEFRA changes. Beginning in 1983, the law increases the floor on medical expenses to five percent of adjusted gross income (AGI) and eliminates entirely the separate deduction for half of the premiums paid for medical insurance. Starting in 1984 it removes the one percent floor on drug purchases but limits the definition of drugs to "prescription drugs and insulin." The latter will be considered as regular medical expenses subject to the five percent floor.

Reimbursements from insurance, or other sources, must be deducted from costs in arriving at the medical or dental deduction (Section 213(a)).

■ *If the reimbursement is received in a subsequent year,* this receipt is includible in income for the year received, up to the amount of the previous deduction.

■ *If the reimbursement exceeds the medical-dental expenditures,* an amount equal to the deduction is taken into income. *The excess is not taxable.*

NOTICE:

If a taxpayer uses the standard deduction and then, in the following year, receives medical reimbursement, the government considers that no medical deduction had been allowed and, therefore, no part of the reimbursement need be included in income.

■ *Are permanent injury payments received under an employer-financed accident or health plan taxable and/or considered reimbursement?* Section 105(c), Payments Unrelated to Absence from Work, says that such payments are not includible in gross income. Section 105(f), Rules for Application of Section 213, says that permanent-injury payments are not considered compensation by insurance or otherwise.

■ *Indemnification for loss of earnings under an accident and health policy* is not considered medical reimbursement.

■ *If a taxpayer receives excess reimbursement* from the personal ownership of multiple medical insurance policies and from an employer-financed policy, the portion attributable to the taxpayer's contribution is excludible from income under Section 104(a)(3); the balance is taxable.

Purifying adjusted gross. Since the size of the medical deduction appears in direct relationship to the amount of adjusted gross, you should make certain that the latter will emerge in as low a state as possible.

A search should be made, for example, for items that might appear as miscellaneous itemized deductions but could have been employee business expenses—deductions such as nonreimbursed travel expenses, union dues, and seminar costs. If deducted through use of Form 2106, the total of these expenses would have been deducted from gross in arriving at adjusted gross, thereby reducing the latter and the medical exclusions of one and three percent before TEFRA.

Maybe a Schedule C should have been filed for a person carrying on a trade or business, but wasn't, thus increasing the adjusted gross unnecessarily.

Outside salesman expenses may have all been lumped into miscellaneous itemized deductions.

CAUTION:

Watch for these possibilities. They can make a considerable difference in the medical-dental deduction.

Medical reimbursment plans offer both a tax benefit and a big boost for employee morale. For closely held corporations, or employers of any kind who are searching for ways to aid employee morale, the medical reimbursement plan can be a big boost.

Under such a plan, employers pay employees' medical expenses or reimburse them for such costs. The former realize a full deduction; the latter receive a tax-free fringe benefit.

Also important is the fact that tax losses caused by the one percent medicine and drug and the three percent medical exclusion are both eliminated.

6.5 HANDLING THE AUDIT

IRS persons will be searching all of the previously mentioned nooks and crannies. In meeting their inquiries, three areas are of prime importance:

1. Substantiation of medical expenses
2. Establishment of the "medical" connection
3. Types of insurance coverage

Guidelines for Substantiating Medical Expenses

A practitioner should begin with the first return he or she prepares. If the taxpayer will clearly be purchasing medications on a regular and continuous basis, such as for insulin, the preparer should request that he or she arrange for a charge account at a drug store or use a credit card when making the purchases. This will provide built-in proof at year's end.

Where regular travel is involved, the practitioner should determine the mileage or public transportation costs and ask the client to keep a record of each trip taken. This knowledge will pin down travel expenses. Should the taxpayer fail to keep a record of days traveled, the practitioner can probably obtain them by match-ups with records of drug stores, hospitals, or of doctors' offices visited.

The client should be asked to keep a record of every medical expense paid, including: names and addresses of payees, professions of payees, and amount and dates of payments.

IMPORTANT:
> **Mention to the client, in particular, the importance of paying with a check or securing a receipt. Some medical or dental offices will not offer the latter. Taxpayers should insist that a receipt be furnished.**

Presuming that the above steps were not taken, the taxpayer should begin collecting proof of expenditures such as cancelled checks and receipted bills.

NOTE:
> **Secure also those invoices which have not been receipted. The IRS will occasionally accept a reasonable approximation or estimation of expenses. These invoices, even though not good evidence of payment, still may aid in establishing approximate costs, or in locating other medical deductions.**

Lacking proof of hospital or doctor expenditures, these payees should be contacted for a record of receipts from the taxpayer. Consult with drug store employees. They may be able to supply a statement as to approximate cash purchases of nonprescription drugs, particularly if continuous. Most pharmacists will be able to identify and cost prescription drugs purchased even if paid for with cash.

If a collection agency has been used to collect medical bills from the taxpayer, it will have a record of such receipts, even if it paid the doctor or dentist or other practitioner with one lump-sum check to cover all patients involved.

Search for applications to Blue Cross-Blue Shield or other insurance carriers. If none can be located, write to such companies for copies. Ask your client if he or she maintained appointment notations anywhere. If so, secure such records. Anything that will indicate trips or expenses for medical or dental purposes will help with substantiation.

How to establish the medical connection. Search each expenditure or type of expenditure for the medical purpose. If any of such costs are not obvious, set about clarifying their need. Bear in mind the twice-repeated definition of "Medical Care" under Section 213(e)(1)(A), Figure 6-1.

Written doctors' opinions which require the expenditure of funds for medical purposes are good but not always infallible. In J. Willard Harris, 46 TC 672, despite a doctor's letter to the effect that special foods were necessary for the health of a diabetic, the court ruled that such foods were part of the patient's nutritional needs and not deductible.

This case aside, you should start with the doctor or dentist and ask for a written statement to the effect that the questionable expenditures were necessary for health reasons. Show, if possible, that the doctor's orders were immediately followed.

Past and continuing history of the illness will help. Proof of a recovery or alleviation, because of the controversial expenditure, will help. Letters from nurses or companions to this effect will add good evidence.

HELPFUL HINT:

> **A showing that you have segregated all nondeductible but related items, such as toothpaste, from the pharmacy bill will be evidence of good intent and aid in strengthening weak evidence being used as support for other items. Failure to claim a deduction for meals and lodging, for instance, will make a physician-ordered medical trip more palatable to the IRS examiner.**

Above all else, the medical connection must be made before a deduction can be secure.

Types of insurance coverage, unless they are obvious—as for Blue Cross-Blue Shield— must be identified. This can be done only by reading the policies. Before doing this, however, review Section 6.3 (if a deduction is taken for hospitalization insurance) and Section 6.4 (insurance premiums) of this chapter.

Adhere to what you have read and prepare answers to any questions that you think the IRS examiner might pose. Defenses here are mostly factual. Either the deduction is allowable or it is not. There is little room for compromise.

6.6 PERTINENT COURT DECISIONS - PRO AND CON

Pro
26 CFR 1.213-1: Medical, Dental, etc.
Expenses Rev. Rul. 68-452

Findings of Fact

A taxpayer entered a hospital as a patient for the purpose of a kidney transplant. The donor traveled from a distant city and was entered as a patient at the same hospital for the purpose of donating a kidney to the taxpayer. The taxpayer paid the plane fare and all surgical and hospital expenses incurred by the donor. Were these deductible medical expenses?

Opinion

The surgical and hospital expenses of the donor of the kidney were incurred for the medical care of the taxpayer and are deductible by him for the years in which paid, subject to the limitations prescribed by Section 213 of the Internal Revenue Code of 1954.

Further, the donor's plane fare to and from the hospital qualifies as transportation primarily for and essential to medical care of the taxpayer and is therefore a deductible medical expense.

Con
26 CFR 1.213-1: Medical, Dental, etc
Expenses Rev. Rul. 68-525

Findings of Fact

The taxpayers, a husband and his wife, entered into agreements with a retirement home that is constructing an infirmary and apartment facilities, under which they are entitled to live in one of the apartments and to receive lifetime care. They paid a lump-sum payment that is apportioned between the cost of constructing the infirmary and the apartment, and are to pay a monthly fee for lifetime care.

Opinion

Held, the lump-sum payment does not qualify as a medical expense deductible under Section 213 of the Internal Revenue Code of 1954, since it is attributable to the construction of the infirmary and apartment and is not to provide medical care. Furthermore, in regard to the monthly fee for lifetime care, see Revenue Ruling 67-185, C.B. 1967-1, 70, which holds that where a husband and wife pay a monthly life-care fee to a retirement home, and prove that a specific portion of the fee covers the cost of providing medical care for them, that portion of the fee is deductible as an expense for medical care in the year paid, subject to the limitations prescribed in Section 213 of the Code.

6.7 RELEVANT CODE AND REGULATION SECTIONS, PLUS PUBLICATION

Code

Section 104(a)(3)	Compensation for Injuries or Sickness
105(c)	Payments Unrelated to Absence from Work
105(f)	Rules for Application of Section 213
162	Trade or Business Expenses
213	Medical, Dental, etc., Expenses
213(a)	Allowance of Deduction
213(e)(1)(A)	Definitions—Medical Care
262	Personal, Living, and Family Expenses
6013(d)	Joint Returns of Income Tax by Husband and Wife—Special Rules

Regulations

Section 1.213-1(e)(3)	Status of Spouse or Dependent
1.213-1(e)(4)	Medical Insurance
1.213-1(e)(1)(v)	Definitions—General—in-patient Hospital Care
1.213-1(e)(1)(iii)	Definitions— General—Capital Expenditures

Publication

502	Medical & Dental Expenses

6.8 APPLICABLE IRS MANUAL REFERENCES (INVESTIGATIVE TECHNIQUES)

The *Standard Explanations Handbook* contains a master list of the most frequently discovered adjustments by IRS auditors. This "inside" information is invaluable to a practitioner or taxpayer. The "Medical and Dental" Section 46 has been reproduced in Figure 6-2. Be sure to review this material. It is indeed enlightening.

46. Medical and Dental

46.1 Only the amount of medical expenses that exceeds a certain percentage of your adjusted gross income is deductible. Since your adjusted gross income has been changed, we have adjusted your medical expenses deduction as shown in the accompanying computation.

46.2 Premiums paid for life insurance policies are not deductible as medical expenses.

46.3 Premiums paid for policies which reimburse you for loss of earnings or for the accidental loss of life, limb, sight, etc., are not deductible as medical expenses.

46.4 Premiums paid for policies that guarantee a specified amount each day, week, or month in the event of hospitalization are not deductible as medical expenses.

46.5 Your medical expense deduction is reduced by the reimbursements you actually received.

46.6 Since the medical expense was not paid for yourself, your spouse, or your qualified dependent, the amount is not deductible as a medical expense.

46.7 Payments for personal analysis required as part of your training are not deductible as medical expenses.

46.8 Payments for cosmetics, toiletries, toothpaste, and

like items are not deductible as medical expenses.

46.9 Payments for items that are not generally accepted as medicine or drugs are not deductible as medical expenses.

46.10 The cost of special foods or beverages that you substitute for those you normally consume is not deductible.

46.11 Since medical care is not the primary reason for your being in a nursing home, rest home, or other institution, the cost of meals and lodging is not deductible.

46.12 The cost of meals and lodging while you are traveling for medical care or for the alleviation of a specific condition is not deductible as a medical expense.

46.13 Since your travel to another city for necessary medical treatment was a pesonal choice, the travel expense is not deductible.

46.14 A trip taken to change environment, or generally improve health, is not deductible as a medical expense, even when the trip is made on the advice of a physician.

46.15 Only the amount of the costs of permanent improvements made to property for medical reasons that exceed the increase in the fair market value of the property are deductible.

46.16 Payments to household help are not deductible as medical expenses, even when you are physically unable to perform these duties.

46.17 Funeral and burial expenses are not deductible.

46.18 Since you did not prove that the amount shown was (a) a medical expense, and (b) paid, the amount is not deductible.

46.19 You are allowed an additional deduction for medical expenses.

46.20 Since these medical expenses are deductible only as itemized deductions, and you claimed the standard deduction or used a Tax Table, no deduction is allowed.

46.21 Since the medical expenses were not paid during the year, they are not deductible.

46.22 We have adjusted your medical expense deduction as shown in the accompanying computation.

46.23 We have computed your allowable deduction for automobile travel related to medical care at the standard rate of 7 cents a mile (for years 1974 and after).

46.24 Since you used an unallowable mileage rate to compute your automobile travel expenses, we have computed your deduction for those automobile expenses related to medical care at the standard rate of 7 cents a mile (for years 1974 and after).

46.25 Since many nondeductible items can be purchased at drug stores, canceled checks alone are not considered adequate verification of payment for the drugs and medicines claimed on your return. We have, therefore, reduced the amount you claimed to the expenses you verified as paid for drugs and medicines.

46.26 Since we disallowed the exemption you claimed, you may not deduct the medical expenses you paid for that individual.

Figure 6-2

Vacation Homes and Other Dwelling Units
(Section 280A)

7

7.1 IDENTIFYING THE PROBLEM

The Tax Reform Act of 1976 took all of the fun and (tax) games out of owning a vacation home. Before that, ownership of such real estate was a good hedge against inflation and a reasonably good tax shelter. Now Section 280A (Disallowance of Certain Expenses in Connection with Business Use of a Home, Rental of Vacation Homes, etc.) has put a lid on many of the former tax advantages.

Vacation home rules

Taken in their entirety, the new rules are quite simple. Taxpayers can no longer realize any substantial pleasure out of their vacation homes—and get a tax advantage too—nor can they enjoy a continued rental loss unless they can escape Section 183 (Activities Not Engaged in for Profit).

If a taxpayer owns and rents out a vacation home or other dwelling unit that is also *used as a residence* (for even one day during the tax year), expenses of operation must be prorated between rental and personal use.

A dwelling unit is considered to have been used as a residence during the tax year if it was occupied for *personal purposes*

1. More than 14 days, or
2. More than 10 percent of the number of days during the tax year it is *rented at a fair rental,* whichever is greater.

In making the "personal-purposes" test, any day or part of a day that the dwelling was occupied in the following manner is a "personal-use" day:

1. Used for personal purposes by the taxpayer or by any other person who had an interest in the residential unit—or by a family member (defined later), or

2. Used by anyone under a reciprocal arrangement that enables the taxpayer to use some other dwelling unit, or

3. Used by anyone at less that fair rental value (FRV).

Fair rental value presumably means comparable rents charged for like property in the same general locale. It appears, therefore, that the problem is one of frustration.

NOTE:

Public Law 97-119 (Dec. 29, 1981) altered Sec. 280A so as to allow rental to a family member under the following quoted conditions:

In general—a taxpayer shall not be treated as using a dwelling unit for personal purposes by reason of a rental arrangement for any period if for such period such dwelling unit is rented, at a fair rental, to any person for use as such person's principal residence.

7.2 HOW THE IRS SEES THE ISSUE

The IRS was delighted with the Tax Reform Act of 1976 insofar as it affected the vacation home issue. For far too many years American taxpayers had been using this tax loophole to their avoidance advantage.

The Service now expects complete adherence to Section 280A which brings into play not only all sorts of specific rules, but also an interplay with Section 183 (Activities Not Engaged In For Profit). The IRS believes that it finally has the means to stop this drain on the Treasury and expects to exploit them completely.

7.3 FACTORS WHICH THE IRS CONSIDERS WHEN MAKING ITS AUDIT DECISION

Fortunately, in this area of second homes, the law is relatively clear and basic. Specific periods of time and definite percentages are stated. Adherence, or not, is clear-cut in most instances, except for the "Hobby Loss" issue. However, since it is still possible to secure a deductible loss from recreational property, the IRS will be concerned with these four major questions:

1. Was the home rented for less than 15 days during the taxable year?

If so, no deductions attributable to such rental are allowed, but neither is the income taxable. Interest, taxes, and casualty losses may be deducted as itemized deductions.

2. Did the taxpayer rent the home for 15 days or more and personally use it less than 15 days or, if more, not more than 10 percent of total rental days?

If so, he or she may deduct the portion of expenses attributable to the rental use. For example, if 75 percent of the total use of the house was for rental purposes, then 75 percent of the expenses may be deducted.

3. If the situation in (2) exists and it produced an operating loss, was this an activity entered into for profit?

Should the IRS decide negatively, then such losses would not be allowed. (Answers to this question are set forth in Chapter 1, "Hobby Loss.")

4. Was the home rented for 15 days or more, and did the taxpayer also have personal occupancy for more than 14 days, or for more than 10 percent of the total rental days, whichever is greater?

If so, the deductible expenses are limited in the following fashion:

a. Gross rental income must be reduced by the amount of interest, taxes, and casualty losses which are attributable to the rental period.

b. The remaining income, if any, must then be reduced by the allocated portion (as in (a)) of maintenance and other rental expenses.

c. Allocated depreciation can finally be used to reduce any remaining rental income.

This formula, in effect, eliminates any possibility of losses which might be utilized against other taxable income. The leftover portions of interest, taxes, and casualty losses, however, may be utilized as itemized deductions.

NOTE:

Section 280A(e)(1) places certain deduction limits (as previously mentioned) on a taxpayer who uses a vacation home for more than the greater of 14 days or 10 percent of the number of days the home was rented. When such an excess occurs, Section 280A deductions (for expenses connected with the rental) are required to be limited to the proportion of such expenses *that the number of days the house was rented bears to the number of days it was used.*

In a recent court case (Dorance D. Bolton, 77 T.C. 8) the tax court agreed with the taxpayer and allowed him to allocate interest and property taxes *according to the percentage of the year the house was rented, not according to the percentage of time the house was occupied as decreed by the IRS.*

The property was rented for 91 days. Accordingly, the taxpayer was allowed to deduct 91/365ths of interest and tax expenses. (If applicable, the balance could be used as itemized deductions.)

In computing maintenance costs, the tax court allowed the taxpayer to use a fraction in which the numerator was the number of days the property was rented (121) and the denominator was the number of days the property was used. Thus, 91/121, or about 75 percent of the maintenance expenses, were allowed to be allocable to the rental activity, subject to the further limitation of Section 280A.

The court reasoned that real estate taxes and interest payments should be allocable according to the percentage of the year a house is rented rather than occupied, because these are annual expenses unrelated to usage and deductible in any event. Maintenance and repairs, on the other hand, are closely connected to use and occupancy and should be deducted to the nature and extent of the use.

In making its decision the court characterized the government's findings as "overkill with a vengeance" and "bizarre."

7.4 CONSIDERATIONS WHEN PREPARING THE RETURN

The best way to begin this section is with some definitions:

A taxpayer, for purposes of this chapter, is any individual or electing small business corporation.

A dwelling unit includes a house, apartment, condominium, mobile home, boat, or similar property. It does not include property that is used only as a hotel, motel, inn, or similar establishment.

Any other person who has an interest in the residential unit is defined as a partner, a beneficiary, or a stockholder if the unit is owned by a partnership, estate, trust, or tax-option corporation.

A member of a family includes brothers and sisters (whether whole or half blood), spouse, ancestors (parents, grandparents, etc.), and lineal descendants, children, grand-children, etc.).

Computing Gain or Loss

Your first concerns, of course, should include the four major points which were enumerated under Section 7.3 of this chapter. Example computations of Situations 2 and 4 are presented here so that you will have a clear picture of each.

Situation 2—rental of home 15 days or more with personal use less than 15 days or, if greater, not more than 10 percent of total rental days. Gain or loss is computed as follows:

1. Number of rental days (100) ÷ total number of days used (110) = <u>91%</u>

2. Rental income $3,600

3. Less allocable expenses:

Interest	1800 × .91 = 1638	
Taxes	1200 × .91 = 1092	
Maintenance	900 × .91 = 819	
Depreciation	1000 × .91 = <u>910</u>	<u>4,459</u>
Net rental loss		<u>$ 859</u>

Situation 4—home rented 15 days or more and personal occupancy also exceeded 14 days, or more than 10 percent of total rental days, whichever is greater. Gain or loss is computed as follows:

1. Number of days rented (90) ÷ total number of days used (120) = <u>75%</u>

2. Rental income $4,000

3. Less allocable expenses:

Interest	1800 × .75 = 1350	
Taxes	1200 × .75 = <u>900</u>	<u>2,250</u>

4. Gross rental income that exceeds interest and taxes 1,750

5. Minus:

Maintenance	900 × .75 =	<u>$ 675</u>

6. Gross rental income that exceeds interest, taxes, and operating expenses 1,075

7. Minus depreciation, limited to the portion chargeable to rental use or Line 6, whichever is less:

Depreciation of $1500 × .75 = 1175
Use <u>1,075</u>
Net rental gain or loss <u>$ -0-</u>

Notice that under the last computation a rental loss cannot be realized. The answer to this dilemma, obviously, is to resist personal use—stay within the 14 day/10 percent rule and rejoice in the tax shelter, provided the hobby-loss tag can be ducked. Maybe the rent can be increased and profits shown in two of five years.

See "Bolton, 77 TC-8" Section 7.3 if you are adventuresome.

CONSIDER THIS:

In Herbert B. Copeland (TC Memo 1980-476) the court recognized that "hope of appreciation" was a legitimate factor in carrying on an activity for profit. It rules that taxpayer's rental of a beach cottage was not a "hobby loss" even though it had not shown a profit for eight years.

What Constitutes Personal Use?

Personal occupation of premises while doing repairs does not constitute "personal use" if performed during the normal work day.

Vacation homes occupied by employees, under Section 119 (Meals or Lodging Furnished for the Convenience of the Employer) does not constitute "personal use."

You should, however, be wary of the "entertainment facility" tag of Section 274 (Disallowance of Certain Entertainment, etc., Expenses). A business purpose must be shown.

Interest on collateral loans against other assets, to secure funds for the purchase of a second home, cannot be ignored when making the rental income computation. Such an expense must be considered in the same light as mortgage interest applicable to the second or recreational home.

Qualifying energy-saving credits apply only to a principal residence. They are not credits against a vacation home, even if the latter is considered a personal residence under Section 280A.

Offered for rent—no takers. This claim, if unsubstantiated, will not place the rental in the category of an "activity entered into for profit."

House swapping or time sharing is considered personal-use time. If, for example, a taxpayer swapped one month of an owned ski chalet in Vermont for one month at a villa in France, the length of time involved would be personal use.

Vacation home rules do not apply to principal residences. Originally, under the Tax Reform Act of 1976, they did. This created an unintended problem for persons who rented their personal residence while they were overseas, for example.

The Tax Reform Act of 1978 corrected this situation by installing Section 280A(d)(3) which allows a taxpayer to utilize a dwelling before and after a qualified rental period without acquiring the "personal use" stigma.

7.5 HANDLING THE AUDIT

The IRS in this instance—depending on the history of losses—will be initially interested in the Section 183 issue. (Activities Not Engaged in for Profit). This subject has been well covered in Chapter 1, "Hobby Losses." Study it well. It will quickly become apparent that this problem is not unsolvable.

After Section 183 has been considered and if the issue has been disposed of in favor of the taxpayer, the balance of the audit will be mostly a matter of substantiation:

Proof of occupancy—and by whom. Leases or rental agreements are excellent in this respect. They set rental dates that are incontrovertible.

• Written occupancy schedules with names and dates are acceptable proof.

• Paid plumbing and other such bills give indication as to when a vacation retreat was liveable and when not. These documents can narrow use periods for application of other evidence.

• Statements from neighbors are admissible.

Basis or adjusted basis of property. Depending on method of acquisition, various documents might be required:

• Warranty deeds with closing real estate statements.

• Proof of cost of improvements.

• Gift tax returns.

• Estate tax valuations.

Proof of related expenditures. This goes without saying. All in all, if the losses are modest and appear to be reasonable under the circumstances, the examiner will not make a big deal out of this issue. His or her primary concern will have been with "hobby loss" consideration.

7.6 PERTINENT COURT DECISIONS–PRO AND CON

Pro
(Richard H. Nelson Memo TC 1978-287)

Findings of Fact

During the period 1969 to 1975, petitioner purchased nine parcels of realty in Florida, including a condominium in December 1973.

The condominium was not rented in 1974, was rented for approximately four months in 1975, three months in 1976, and eight months in 1977. A permanent tenant has been renting continuously since 1977.

In 1974, petitioner notified the condominium association that his unit was for rent, hired a real estate agency to manage the rentals for a year, and placed advertisements in *The Wall Street Journal* and a local newspaper.

From 1973 through 1977 petitioner averaged four weeks a year vacation, yet during this period he and his family spent less than four weeks in the unit. Was the condominium purchased and held as an activity engaged in for profit?

Opinion

Based on the record, it was ruled that the petitioner had a bona fide expectation of making a profit and the entire amounts of expenses and depreciation were allowed as deductions.

Con
(Rev. Rul. 75-14 1975-1 CB 90)

Findings of Fact

During 1973 an individual rented a house to his brother and sister-in-law at less than its fair rental value. Total expenses exceeded gross income. Was the loss deductible?

Opinion

The required profit motive was not present and the taxpayer was neither engaged in a trade or business nor holding property for the production of income. Deduction not allowed.

7.7 RELEVANT CODE SECTIONS

Section 183	Activities Not Engaged in for Profit
274	Disallowance of Certain Entertainment, etc., Expenses
280A	Disallowance of Certain Expense in Connection with Business Use of Home, Rental of Vacation Homes, Etc.
280A(a)	General Rule
280A(d)(2)	Personal Use of Unit
280A(d)(3)	Rental of Principal Residence
280A(e)	Expenses Attributable to Rental
280A(f)(1)	Dwelling Unit Defined
280A(g)	Special Rule for Certain Rental Use

7.8 APPLICABLE IRS MANUAL REFERENCES

Most of the instructions which the IRS gives its examiners concerning vacation homes is covered in the "Hobby Loss" chapter. It does, however, give some space to the subject in its *Standard Explanations Handbook*. See Sections 45.1 and 45.19 which are reproduced below:

45. *Losses*

45.1 Since this activity is not engaged in for profit, the income from it is includible on your return. From this income, you may deduct the following expenses in the order shown:

(a) interest, taxes, and other deductible items without regard to the profitability of the activity;

(b) operating expenses, except those in item (c) below (to the extent gross income from the activity exceeds deductions allowable under (a) above); and

(c) depreciation and other basis adjustment items to the extent gross income from the activity exceeds deductions allowable under (a) and (b), above.

45.19 Renting a personal residence temporarily prior to its sale does not convert it to business property. Since information provided indicates that the loss resulted from the sale of a personal residence, we have disallowed it.

NOTE:

This issue is of sufficient importance to be placed on *The National Office List of Prime Issues*.

Home Office
(Section 280A)

8

8.1 IDENTIFYING THE PROBLEM

The Home Office is a first cousin to the Vacation Home in that they are both subject to the same statute—code Section 280A (Disallowance of Certain Expenses In Connection with Business Use of Home, Rental of Vacation Homes, etc.). Like the vacation home, the deduction for home office expenses has come onto hard times.

Before the Tax Reform Act of 1976, which spawned 280A, the Code allowed an employee to deduct a proportionate share of maintenance and depreciation expenses, if work at home was a condition of his or her employment.

The courts went even further. The Second Circuit allowed the deduction when it was *more practical* for an employee to work at home—and the Tax Court ruled for the taxpayer because the home office was *helpful* to work-related functions. The rules, as they evolved through legislation, did indeed become liberal.

Present Position

From this Utopian position, Section 280A(c)(1) caused recession to a point which now allows business use for a portion of a residence only if such space is used *exclusively* on a *regular* basis and is

1. the principal place of business for any trade or business of the taxpayer,
2. a place of business which is used by patients, clients, or customers in meeting or dealing with the taxpayer in the normal course of his trade or business, or
3. in the case of a separate structure which is not attached to the dwelling unit, in connection with the taxpayer's trade or business.

In the case of an employee, the preceding sentence shall apply only if the exclusive use referred to in the preceding sentence is for the convenience of his employer.

To compound the difficulty, the IRS insisted that a deduction was not allowable for a home office which was used for a taxpayer's second business. Thus, if you had a regular position as a corporate employee and also operated a small accounting office as an avocation, you supposedly could not have taken a deduction for a home office.

NOTE HOWEVER:

The tax court's position was contrary to that of the IRS. In Curphey, 73 TC 61, it ruled that the taxpayer could have a separate principal office for a separate business.

AND FINALLY:

H.R. 5159 provides that a home office can qualify as a taxpayer's "principal place of business" even though the activities carried on in the office do not constitute the taxpayer's main business.

8.2 HOW THE IRS SEES THE ISSUE

There are four clearly defined exceptions to Section 280A(a) which states that "an individual or an electing small business corporation may not take a deduction for expenses incurred in the use of a dwelling which is used during the taxable year as a residence."

Four Exceptions to Section 280A

1. Office where patients, clients, or customers meet or deal with taxpayer. The IRS believes that this exception applies only if the use of the dwelling unit for this purpose is substantial and integral to the conduct of the business—not occasional meetings.

2. Use of a separate structure, by government standards, means that the unit must be used exclusively and on a regular basis in connection with the taxpayer's trade or business— not for any personal use such as for a guest house.

3. Use of a storage unit for taxpayer's inventory. Section 280A(c)(2) provides an exception to the general rule of Section 280A(c) for any item to the extent such item is allocable to space within the dwelling unit which is used on a regular basis as a storage space for inventory use in taxpayer's trade or business of selling products at retail or wholesale.

A storage unit includes only the space actually utilized. Thus, if only one corner of a basement was used, only that corner is considered—even if the entire remainder of the basement remains empty.

This exception to Section 280A(c), according to the IRS, applies only if:

a. The dwelling unit is the sole fixed location of that trade or business.

b. The space used is a separately identifiable space suitable for storage.

4. Day care services for children or for individuals who have attained age 65, or for persons who are physically or mentally incapable of caring for themselves, generate allowable deductions if allocable expenses are incurred on a regular basis in the taxpayer's trade or business.

The government allows much latitude in adherence to day care regulations. If, however, the services rendered are primarily educational or instructional in nature, they will not qualify as "day care services"—except in the case of nursery school children and children of kindergarten age—if the instruction is not in lieu of public instruction under a state compulsory education requirement.

In order for a day care center to operate under this exception, it must be acting in accordance with the applicable state law relating to the licensing, certification, registration, or approval of day care centers or family or group care homes.

8.3 FACTORS WHICH THE IRS CONSIDERS WHEN MAKING ITS AUDIT DECISION

In making Section 280A(c) decisions, the IRS depends greatly on the three "facts-and-circumstance" factors, as mentioned previously under *principal place of business*.

If it determines that a taxpayer's activity does adhere to these factors—and does meet the requirements of one of the four exceptions—the Service then looks to the deductions themselves:

- *Are they proper?*
  Unrelated expenses attributable to other portions of the house, such as the kitchen, cannot be deducted. Costs of lawn care or landscaping are also out.

- *Has the limitation rule in Section 280A(c)(5) been considered?*
  The deductions cannot exceed the excess of:
  1. The gross income derived from a trade or business conducted from the home office during the taxable year, over
  2. The deductions allocable to such use which are allowable under this chapter for the taxable year whether or not such unit (or portion thereof) was so used.

- *Were expenditures allocated on a correct basis?*
  Regulations state that any reasonable method may be used—by number of rooms if all are relatively the same size—or by percentage of floor space.

- *If the taxpayer is an employee, was he or she using the home office for the convenience of the employer?*
  Burden of proof will be on the taxpayer.

- *If the taxpayer operated a day care facility, did he/she use the space exclusively for business?*
  If not, was the percentage of buisness use correctly computed?

- *In itemizing deductions, did the taxpayer deduct total amount of mortgage interest and real estate taxes attributable to the residence?*
  Only portions allocable to nonbusiness should have been deducted.

8.4 CONSIDERATIONS WHEN PREPARING THE RETURN

A decision should be made at the outset as to whether deductions for a home office are desirable for a particular taxpayer. They may not be of sufficient consequence to warrant loss of *residence status* for a portion of the dwelling unit.

WATCH:

> *Sale of residence partially used for business.* Under Section 1034 (Rollover of Gain on Sale of Principal Residence) deferral of gain on such sale is allowed—but only as to the portion of the property which is applicable to the principal residence. Gain on sale of the business portion is taxable in year of sale, *whether the home office deduction is successful or not.*

In addition, gain on the business portion will not qualify for any part of the $125,000 one-shot exclusion. IRS Publication 523 contains a good illustration of the computation which should be used in allocating residential and business gain. (See Figure 8-1).

Property partly used as your home. You may use your property partly as your home and partly for business or to produce income. Examples are a working farm on which your house is located, an apartment building in which you live in one unit and rent out the others, or a store building with an upstairs apartment in which you live. If you sell the whole property, you postpone only the tax on the part used as your home. This includes the land and outbuildings, such as a garage for the home, but not those for the business.

You must reinvest in the new home only the part of the selling price for the part used as your home, to have the tax on that part of the gain postponed. If you use only part of the new property as your home, only the cost of that part counts as reinvestment. You should look at the whole transaction as the sale of two properties.

Example. You own a four-unit apartment house. You live in one unit and rent three units. You sell the apartment house, and buy and live in a new home. Your records show.

Apartment house:

Cost	$40,000
Capital improvements	2,000
	$42,000
Minus: Depreciation (on 3 rented units only).	6,000
Adjusted basis	$36,000
Selling price	$80,000

Selling expense .... $ 4,000
New home: Purchase price $35,000

Because one-fourth of the apartment building is your home, you figure the gain on which tax is postponed as follows:

	Personal (1/4)	Rental (3/4)
1) Selling price	$20,000	$60,000
2) Selling expense	1,000	3,000
3) Amount realized (adjusted sales price)	$19,000	$57,000
4) Basis (including improvements)...	$10,500	$31,500
5) Depreciation		6,000
6) Adjusted basis	$10,500	$25,500
7) Gain [(3) minus (6)]	$ 8,500	$31,500
8) Gain not postponed		$31,500
9) Gain postponed	$ 8,500	

The gain of $31,500 on the three-fourths of the building that was rental property is subject to tax in the year of sale. The tax is postponed on the gain on the one-fourth that was your home because the $19,000 adjusted sales price of this one-fourth was less than the $35,000 cost of your new home. The basis of the new home is $26,500 ($35,000 cost minus $8,500 postponed gain).

Figure 8-1

DON'T DESPAIR:

Presume these circumstances: The taxpayer used a portion of his home for business purposes and properly deducted home office expenses under Section 162 (Trade or Business Expenses) until the enactment of Section 280A. At this time (1976) he continued to use a portion of his office as a residence but ceased to deduct applicable expenses.

When he sold his residence in November of 1981, Rev. Rul. 82-26 (IRB 1982-6) stated that he was not required to make any allocation between the prior business portion and the personal portion of the residence.

The ruling explicitly makes this statement: "part of the gain on sale of personal residence that's allocable to part of residence used in taxpayer's trade or business may not be defined under Sec. 1034 if business use met requirements of Sec. 280A(c)(1) in year of sale.

However, no allocation is required if business use of part of residence in year of sale doesn't meet requirements of Sec. 280A(c)(1)." (Emphasis mine)

If the underlined sentence can be taken at face value, then sale of a residence with a proper home office can avoid the allocation requirement if the taxpayer stops using the home office in the year prior to sale.

The exclusive-use and regular-basis clauses cause a great deal of difficulty. *Exclusive use* appears to mean: "Use of a specific portion of a dwelling unit *solely* for the purpose of carrying on a trade or business."

Any personal use whatsoever would seem to disqualify the space as a home office.

Nothing in the Code or Committee Reports refers to a separate room per se. Section 280A refers to "a portion of a dwelling unit"; the Committee report refers to "a specific part of a dwelling unit." Yet the IRS says that there must be a physical separation, except for qualified storage. This would seem to mean that it considers a "portion" to be a separate room entirely.

NOTE, HOWEVER:

In Weightman (TCM 1981-301) the court denied the taxpayer home office deductions, but ruled that a portion of his bedroom could be used exclusively for business even though it was not physically separated.

Regular basis. Proposed regulations state that a decision as to the qualfication of this factor will be made based on all "facts and circumstances." Presumably expenses attributable to the exclusive but incidental or occasional use will not be deductible.

Profit-seeking activities, such a those entered into by investors, do not qualify for the office-at-home deductions. The activity must be a trade or business.

Where to deduct home office expenses. All employees, including outside salespersons who have deductions for related business expenses such as office supplies and depreciation for business furniture and equipment, should add these costs to their deduction for a home office on Form 2106 (Employee Business Expenses).

In general, if the taxpayer is an employee, he or she may deduct expenses for an office at home only if deductions are itemized.

An outside salesman may deduct expenses for business use of home even if deductions are not itemized. Form 2106 should be utilized.

Self-employed persons should include the home office expenses on Schedule C.

8.5 HANDLING THE AUDIT

Items listed in Section 8.3 of this chapter should be reviewed for assurance that these questions can all be handled properly.

A worksheet for figuring the deduction for business use of a home is contained in IRS Publication 587 and is included here as Figure 8-2.

If not already done, this worksheet should be prepared and made ready for presentation to the IRS examiner. Data contained therein should satisfy most government queries.

Basis of residence. This should be documented wherever possible, as mentioned in Chapter 7. The revenue person will not be difficult to satisfy in this respect, particularly if the basis has been used for a substantial length of time and is reasonable.

In the case of an employee, a statement should be secured from the employer to the effect that the employee is required to maintain an office at home. To make it easy for the employer (who is probably a busy person), prepare a checklist of reasons why an office away from the taxpayer's place of employment is necessary. This will generate a quicker and more helpful reply.

Worksheet for Figuring the Deduction for Business Use of a Home

Step 1—Percentage your home is used for business[1]

1) Area of home used for business (in square feet) _____
2) Total area of home _____
3) Divide (1) by (2) to get the percentage your home is used for business _____

Step 2—Time the business part is used to provide services (For day-care facilities)

1) Total hours used for facility(_____ days ×
_____ hrs.) _____
2) Total hours available (24 hrs. × 366 days) ____8784____
3) Divide (1) by (2) to get the percentage of time used _____

Step 3—Figuring depreciation for your home

1) Adjusted basis of your home[2] _____
2) Estimated useful life _____
3) Divide (1) by (2) to get the depreciation for your home _____

Step 4—Expenses for business use[3]

1) Direct expenses (100% deductible)
   a) Repairs to business part of home _____
   b) Painting of business part of home _____
   c) Other direct expenses _____
   d) Total _____
2) Indirect business expenses (multiply total expense by percentage in Step 1 or, for day-care facilities, multiply by percentage in Step 1 then by percentage in Step 2)

Expense	Total Expense	Business Part
Real estate taxes[4]	_____	_____
Mortgage interest[4]	_____	_____
Lights	_____	_____

Heating

Insurance, 1 yr.

Exterior painting

Roof repair

Depreciation for home (Step 3)

Miscellaneous

3) Add (1) and (2) to get the total expenses for business use

Step 5—Deduction Limitation

1) Gross income from business[5]

2) Less business part of the following items (multiply total expense by percentage in Step 1 or, for day-care facilities, multiply by percentage in Step 1 then by percentage in Step 2):

a) Real estate taxes

b) Mortgage interest

c) Casualty losses

3) Total deduction limitation

Step 6—Deduction for business use of your home

1) Step 4, total expenses for business use, or Step 5, total deduction limitation, whichever is less. (Expenses that are more than the deduction limitation are not deductible.)

[1]To allocate on room basis, see *Business Part*.

[2]The adjusted basis generally is acquisition cost plus capital improvements, see *Depreciation*.

[3]For information on the forms to use to record these expenses, see *Where to Deduct*.

[4]Remaining part of real estate taxes and mortgage interest after the percentage business deduction is the personal part deductible on Schedule A (Form 1040).

[5]If you get gross income from the use of your home and from the use of other facilities, you must divide this income to determine the part you got from the business use of your home.

Figure 8-2

8.6 PERTINENT COURT DECISIONS—PRO AND CON

Pro
Edwin R. Curphey, 73 TC 766

Findings of Fact

Taxpayer, a dermatologist, also managed six rental properties as a second business.

Opinion

The Tax Court ruled that he could deduct expenses of his home office in connection with his rental business—and also cost of travel between that office and his rental properties.

Con
Joel A. Sharon, 66 TC 515, aff'd, (9Cir; 1978)
43 AFTR 2d 79-335, 591 F2d 1273

Findings of Fact

The taxpayer, an IRS attorney, set aside one room of his three-bedroom apartment for use as an office, claiming business necessity. The room was used in performing work in connection with his employment and with investments in property held for the production of income. Occasionally, the room was also used for handling personal correspondence and for house guests.

Opinion

Appeals Court agreed with the Commissioner and the Tax Court. Taxpayer's home office expenses were personal in nature under Section 262 and not deductible.

His employer did not require him to work at home. On the contrary, the IRS provided him with an office—and with a key so that he could work after hours if he so desired. Taxpayer's use of a home office was adopted to make his evening work more pleasant and convenient.

8.7 RELEVANT CODE AND REGULATION SECTIONS AND IRS PUBLICATIONS

Code

Section 280A	Disallowance of Certain Expenses in Connection with Business Use of Home, Rental of Vacation Homes, etc.
280A(a)	General Rule
280A(c)	Exceptions for Certain Business or Rental Use; Limitations on Deductions for Such Use
280A(c)(2)	Certain Storage Use
280A(c)(5)	Limitation on Deductions
1034	Rollover of Gain on Sale of Principal Residence
280A(c)(1)	Certain Business Use

IRS Publications

523	Tax Information on Selling Your Home
587	Business Use of Your Home

8.8 APPLICABLE IRS MANUAL REFERENCES (INVESTIGATIVE TECHNIQUES)

The IRS *Standard Explanations Handbook* (MT 428-11-15), under "Office in the Home," pays particular attention to the following computation methods or expenses which were more frequently disallowed in past investigations:

- Method of arriving at allocation percentage.
- All office expenses because of failure to prove necessity for business use.
- Personal expenses included in the deduction.
- Indirect costs such as lawn care.
- Repairs to personal portion of residence.
- Some home office expenses for lack of proof.
- Certain expenses which are deductible only as itemized deductions. (Standard deduction was used.)
- All expenses for lack of proof that an employer-required office was necessary.
- All deductions because office portion of residence was not used regularly and exclusively for business.

Charitable Contributions
(Section 170)

9

9.1 IDENTIFYING THE PROBLEM

Search almost any area of the charitable contribution deduction issue and a problem will appear. There is a plethora of them.

At first look, a gift of $100 to the Red Cross would appear to be a simple enough transaction—and it is. The taxpayer donates the money, retains his or her cancelled check, and takes the deduction, but after this straightforward cash donation to a public charity, things become involved.

Prior to 1974 there was no limitation on charitable deductions. Now they abound. Gifts of different types of property bring on different computation requirements. Donations, of whatever type, necessitate separate handling, depending on the classification of the donee organization. Regulations differ as between individuals and corporations. Code Section 170, (Charitable, etc., Contributions and Gifts) which is lengthy and involved, governs.

Some of the basic questions that must be answered are these:

- Which donee organizations qualify for the charitable contribution deduction and to what extent?
- Which is a public charity and which is private?
- Who can deduct contributions?
- When may donations be deducted?
- Exactly what type of gift is deductible?
- How are gifts of "appreciated property" handled?
- What are the 50 percent, 30 percent and 20 percent limitations and how are they applied?
- What is a charitable "bail-out"; is it legal; how does it work?
- What are charitable remainder trusts and how can they be established so that maximum gift deductions can be obtained?

■ How are deductions for "bargain sales" computed?

■ How can "valuation" difficulties be overcome?

■ When do capital gain and ordinary income problems enter the picture—and how are they handled?

■ How is "donative intent" measured?

■ What is the "as if" rule—and how does the IRS use it to its advantage?

■ What about carryovers of unused contributions?

Read on for solutions to these and dozens of other smaller stumbling blocks.

9.2 HOW THE IRS SEES THE ISSUE

For the ordinary taxpayer the IRS approach is direct and simple. The matter will probably be handled by an office auditor. This individual will simply want to see a listing of the qualified organizations to which contributions were made, and proof of each gift.

Unsubstantiated cash contributions for individual employees will not be disallowed out of hand, but only if such gifts do not measure up as a logical possibility after the "available cash" test has been applied—and after a determination has been made regarding the general condition of the return. (Was it prepared carelessly and was documentation of other deductions generally lacking?)

If the latter situation exists and if it does not appear that the taxpayer could have retained sufficient funds to cover the unsubstantiated cash contributions, the deductions will be disallowed for lack of proof.

How the "Available Cash" Test Works

The "available cash" test is made through use of the following formula:

GROSS INCOME, LESS PAYROLL DEDUCTIONS—LESS OTHER ITEMIZED DEDUCTIONS AS CLAIMED—LESS ESTIMATION OF PERSONAL LIVING EXPENSES—LESS ESTIMATED INCOME TAXES PAID—PLUS NONTAXABLE INCOME SUCH AS SOCIAL SECURITY OR THE TAX-FREE PORTION OF CAPITAL GAINS.

After consideration of these factors, the IRS arrives at what it considers to be "cash available for use in making the unsubstantiated cash contributions."

EXAMPLE:

Computed available funds amount to $1,000—the questionable contributions were listed at $3,000. The difference, unless otherwise proven, would be disallowed— particularly if the condition of the balance of the return appears to have been carelessly prepared as previously mentioned. Depending upon the examiner, *all* of such contributions might be disallowed.

When the Audit Will Go Deeper

In situations *where the taxpayer derived substantial tax benefits from contributions of appreciated property, or where bargain sales exist,* the audit will go deeper. An Internal

Revenue Agent will usually conduct the examination as a field audit. Valuations, limitations, types of donees, basis of properties—all become important.

In instances where *exceptionally large amounts are involved*—no matter who the donee—the taxpayer can expect a visit from the IRS. This situation includes deductions for gifts of partial interests, gifts in trust, gifts of homes or farms, and the like. Documentation will always be required.

Internal Revenue Agents, from collective experiences, have learned that *people in business sometimes switch expenditure categories* to suit their own aims. For example, if a taxpayer does not intend to itemize deductions, he or she might record a gift to a college building fund as "advertising," thereby salvaging an otherwise lost expenditure. The agents do not consider this cricket and look for such situations.

9.3 FACTORS WHICH THE IRS CONSIDERS WHEN MAKING ITS AUDIT DECISION

Initially, as previously indicated, the Service looks for proof of payment, then qualification of donees. When in doubt as to the latter, the examining officer uses Publication 78 (Cumulative List of Organizations). This is the government's listing of qualified contribution donees. Should the charity in question not appear in this publication, the IRS person will probably contact the Exempt Organization Master File Clerk in his or her EO key district (Employee Plans and Exempt Organization Division) to verify the status of the doubtful payee.

When the deduction may still be salvaged. Even if a favorable reply is not received from this last source, the deduction may yet be salvaged. Under the following circumstances (presuming existence of proof of payment) the agent still may allow the contribution deduction:

1. If the contribution was made to an organization whose exempt status was revoked on or before the date on which the Service had announced the revocation in an IRS Bulletin.
2. If the payment was made to a bona fide church, even though the church had never applied for exempt status.
3. If made to an organization whose application for exempt status was being held up due to a lack of sufficient information from which a determination could be made.
4. If made to an organization which had secured qualification status but whose name had erroneously been omitted from Publication 78

Audit Checklist

After the first casual inspection, the IRS person, whenever the situation warrants, will get down to some serious auditing. The following checklist will be used:

■ Was the deduction taken by the actual donor? (It must have been.)
■ Was the deduction taken for the purchase of something of value—maybe a ticket for a benefit dinner? (Only the amount which exceeds the fair market value of the meal is deductible.)
■ Was the value of donated services deducted as a contribution? (It should not have been.)

■ If the contribution was made to a school or college, was any portion applicable to attendance costs for a dependent?

■ If property was contributed, was it correctly valued and did the taxpayer relinquish the proper amount of control over ownership of the asset? (Explanation in Section 9-4)

■ Were the donee organizations 50 percent or 20 percent charities and were contribution limitations correctly applied?

■ Was the contribution of appreciated property subjected to the 30 percent limitation?

■ If the taxpayer was an accrual basis corporation, were accrued contributuions paid within the required 2½ months? Were they authorized by the Board of Directors? Were they deducted in only one year?

■ Did the contributuion consist of the transfer of a future interest in tangible personal property such as a painting? (If so, the value is not deductible.)

■ For closely held corporations or partnerships, were contributions deducted twice—once on the business return and once on the individual returns?

■ Were gifts of stock in trade valued at Fair Market Value? (They should not have been. Generally the amount of the contribution is reduced by the amount of gain that would not have been long-term capital gain if the property contributed had been sold by the taxpayer at its FMV.)

■ Were gifts of stock in trade deducted twice—once as cost of goods sold and again as a contribution?

■ Were carryover contributions correctly computed originally and properly carried forward?

■ Was an alleged contribution, represented by a cancelled check, actually remitted as payment for a purchase, such as for a television set from a church rummage sale?

■ Were items, as recorded in the advertising account, actually contributions?

■ Were gifts of property, valued in excess of $200, fully documented as required by law? (For details, see Section 9-5, "Handling the Audit.")

This list is not by any means complete, but it does touch at least the main bases. It will be enlarged upon before the chapter is finished.

9.4 CONSIDERATIONS WHEN PREPARING THE RETURN

IMPORTANT:

A well-planned program of charitable giving can produce substantial savings in tax dollars—but not before all the ins and outs are traced and regulation wrinkles ironed out. The following paragraphs will take you through this labyrinth!

Who Qualifies as Donor and Donee?

Fortunately, most charitable contributuions are made in cash to public institutions such as schools, churches, hospitals, and combined community campaigns. The only problem to be considered under these circumstances is the 50 percent limitation (governing this type of giving) under Section 170(b)(1)(A). This is the simplest way to make a gift. No complex rules enter the picture. At the same time, *the cash method does not usually generate maximum tax benefits*. (See reference to contributions of appreciated property as it follows in this book section.)

Who may deduct contributions? Only the donor. Those eligible are individuals, corporations, partners, trusts, and estates.

Who are qualified donees? Those charities which are commonly called Section 170(b)(1)(A) organizatioins—churches, schools, hospitals, etc. (See Figure 9-1).

When the qualifications of a charity are in doubt, use Publication 78. This booklet and its quarterly supplements can be obtained from the Superintendent of Documents, U. S. Government Printing Office, Washington, D. C. 20402, on a subscription basis.

(b) Percentage Limitations—

(1) **Individuals.**—In the case of an individual, the deduction provided in subsection (a) shall be limited as provided in the succeeding subparagraphs.

(A) General rule.—Any charitable contribution to—

(i) a church or a convention or association of churches,

(ii) an educational organization which normally maintains a regular faculty and curriculum and normally has a regularly enrolled body of pupils or students in attendance at the place where its educational activities are regularly carried on,

(iii) an organization the principal purpose or functions of which are the providing of medical or hospital care or medical education or research, if the organization is a hospital, or if the organization is a medical research organization directly engaged in the continuous active conduct of medical research in conjunction with a hospital, and during the calendar year in which the contribution is made such organization is committed to spend such contributions for such research before January 1 of the fifth calendar year which begins after the date such contribution is made,

(iv) an organization which normally receives a substantial part of its support (exclusive of income received in the exercise of performance by such organization of its charitable, educational, or other purpose or function constituting the basis for its exemption under section 501(a)) from the United States or any State or political subdivision thereof or from direct or indirect contributions from the general public, and which is organized and operated exclusively to receive, hold, invest, and administer property and to make expenditures to or for the benefit of a college or university which is an organization referred to in clause (ii) of this subparagraph and which is an agency or instrumentality of a State or political subdivision thereof, or which is owned or operated by a State or political subdivision thereof or by an agency or instrumentality of one or more States or political subdivisions.

(v) a governmental unit referred to in subsection (c)(1),

(vi) an organization referred to in subsection (c)(2) which normally receives a substantial part of its support (exclusive of income received in the exercise or performance by such organization of its charitable, educational, or other purpose or function constituting the basis for its exemption under section 501(a)) from a governmental unit referred to in subsection (c)(1) or from direct or indirect contributions from the general public.

(vii) a private foundation described in subparagraph (D), or

(viii) an organization described in section 509(a)(2) or (3),

shall be allowed to the extent that the aggregate of such contributions does not exceed 50 percent of the taxpayer's contribution base for the taxable year.

Figure 9-1

Donative intent. This causes a great deal of difficulty with the IRS, because the taxpayer may have received something of value in exchange for the so-called gift.

Illustration: A church owns a large parcel of land, part of which the taxpayer needs to extend his or her parking lot.

If the businessperson buys the property, there would be no tax advantage, only an increase in the basis of the land. If he or she contributes, say $5,000, to the church and the church reduces the selling price by that amount, the taxpayer receives a charitable deduction.

WARNING:

In this situation the IRS cries "Foul." No charitable intent existed, nor was any true contribution made.

Contribution Limitations

In the case of individuals, contributions made to public charities (mainly churches, schools, hospitals, government units, and other publicly supported charities such as the Red Cross) and to certain private foundations can be deducted in an amount that does not exceed 50 percent of the taxpayer's adjusted gross (without inclusion of any net operating loss carryback). (Section 170(b)(1)(A))

NOTE:

Unused contributions may be carried over for five years.

Under Code Section 170(b)(1)(B) contributioins made *for the use of* (rather than *to)* 50 percent public charities and certain private foundations—and *to or for the use of* other qualified charities—carry a 20 percent limitation. These donations may be deducted only in the year made and only if the 50 percent limit has not been exhausted—but only to the extent of the lesser:

1. 20 percent of the contribution base (generally adjusted gross income) *or*
2. 50 percent of your contribution base, minus the 50 percent limit contributions deductible for the year.

Now comes the Economic Recovery Tax Act of 1981. Beginning in 1982 this new law allows "above the line deductions" (No itemization) as follows:

In 1982 and 1983 the deduction is limited to 25 percent of contributions up to maximum giving of $100—a $25 deduction.

In 1984 the limit is still 25 percent; but the maximum goes to $300—a $75 deduction.

In 1985 the deduction climbs to 50 percent of all contributions—and in 1986 to 100 percent.

In 1987 the law expires, and we go back to nothing for nonitemizers.

Married taxpayers filing separately are limited to $50 in 1982 and 1983 and $150 in 1984.

Corporations. For tax years beginning after 1981, the corporate charitable deduction increases from 5 percent of taxable income, as adjusted, to 10 percent.

In addition, corporations will receive a much larger charitable deduction for gifts of ordinary income scientific property to a college or university for research purposes. See ERTA Section 222 for formula.

Gifts of appreciated capital assets or Section 1231 property used in a trade or business are subject to a 30 percent limitation. The value of such appreciated gifts is added to either 50 percent limit or 20 percent limit contributions for computing amounts deductible under these classes.

AN ALERT:

To maximize the 30 percent-limit deduction, an individual can elect to reduce the amount of such contribution by 40 percent of the amount of long-term capital gain that would have resulted from its sale and disregard the 30 percent-limit rule. (Section 170 (b)(1)(C))

Order of Deductibility

Contributions are computed and deducted in the following sequence:

1. Where there are no gifts of 30 percent appreciated property, deduct
   a. Current gifts of 50 percent limitation charities.
   b. Carryovers of gifts to 50 percent charities.
   c. Current 20 percent limitation gifts.

2. Where there are 30 percent property limitation gifts of appreciated property, deduct
   a. Current gifts to 50 percent limitation charities.
   b. Carryovers of gifts to 50 percent organizations.
   c. Current gifts of 30 percent property applicable to 50 percent charities.
   d. Carryovers of 30 percent property applicable to 50 percent charities.
   e. Current gifts of 20 percent property.
   f. Current gifts of 30 percent property applicable to 20 percent charities.

WARNING:

Unused 20 percent-limitation gifts may not be carried forward.

What Constitutes a Contribution?

Personal services do not generate a deduction, but the following expenses which are incident to such services do:

- Transportation costs—actual oil and gas, *or* the charitable mileage allowance, plus parking fees and tolls.
- Cost of meals and lodging—but only while away from home overnight.
- Cost of uniforms and other accessories if not suitable for general wear.

In Rev. Rul. 73-597, 1973-2 CB 69, the IRS declared that baby-sitting expenses, to allow the taxpayers to perform volunteer charitable work, were not deductible. The Tax Court, however, in Alfred D. Kingsley, TC Summary Opinion 1978-74, held that such expenses should be treated the same as any other out-of-pocket expenses for charitable purposes—and were deductible.

In addition, the following are also considered allowable charitable contributions:

- Gifts of property
- Gifts of partial interests
- Gifts in trust

■ Gifts of partial interests not in trust

■ Gifts of undivided property interests

Gifts of property (Regulation 1.170-1(c)). If *depreciable property* is contributed, the deduction is the FMV, less depreciation recapture. A recapture of investment credit may also be necessary.

If the contribution is in the form of a *capital asset,* such as land or stock which was held for investment for 12 months or less, the deduction is the FMV or cost, whichever is less. This rule applies, no matter the classification of the donee. If held for more than 12 months, the FMV may be deducted, even though it includes substantial appreciation since date of purchase.

IMPORTANT:

Obviously, the benefits of giving long-term, capital-gain assets are excellent. The appreciation is not taxed. The 30 percent limitation causes no great problem, since the unused portion may be carried forward for five years. Careful timing of the gift may even eliminate this limitation.

BUT NOTE:

If the gift is to a private foundation (one not qualifying for the 50 percent limitation), the deduction would be limited to 60 percent of the appreciation.

If the gift is *stock in trade (inventory) or other ordinary income property,* such as short term capital gain assets or works of art created by the donor, the deduction is limited to basis (usually cost). This rule applies for all classes of donees.

Special rules apply, however, in the case of *corporations that donate inventory or other ordinary-income property* to public charities or private foundations whose purpose is the care of the sick, or the needy, or children. In these instances, the deduction is cost plus 50 percent of the property's appreciation—but in no event can the deduction exceed twice the basis of the donated property.

If the gift is *tangible personal property* which would have yielded long-term capital gain when sold, and if the donation would be used in a fashion which would not further the donee's tax-exempt status, the deduction would have to be reduced by 40 percent of the appreciation. *Example:* A painting which had grown in value but which would be sold by the donee after receipt.

SUGGESTION:

Contributions of this sort should be made (if tax benefits are paramount) only upon receipt of a letter of intent—in this instance that the painting would be used as an educational prop in the art department.

Valuation of property. Real estate generally does not pose a problem. Good appraisals can nearly always be obtained and will generally be accepted by the IRS if otherwise substantiated as follows:

1. Insurance coverage was sufficient to cover the gift valuation.

2. The appraisal was performed by at least two professional appraisers of good repute.

3. The value, as set, was realistic and reasonable (comparable to the recent selling price of like properties).

4. No unsuccessful attempt had been made to sell the property. If such had occurred, this would undoubtedly lower an otherwise reasonable valuation, since FMV turns on the amount a willing buyer would pay to a willing seller.

WARNING:

In situations where the deduction is substantial, and in dispute, the IRS may call in its own engineers to do an appraisal. It then becomes a matter of compromise.

Used household goods have a value that is generally minimal, depending upon condition and age. Appraisals should be obtained. Pictures should be taken. Original costs and dates of purchase should be secured.

Used clothing can be valued by rule of thumb as previously mentioned. The easiest and best valuation can be established by securing an itemized receipt from the donee organization.

Jewelry, gems, paintings, antiques, and other art objects should all be evaluated by expert appraisers or certified gemologists.

Stocks and bonds. If marketable on an exchange, the mean of the highest and lowest quoted selling prices on the contribution date is considered to be the valuation per share or bond.

For securities of closely held corporations, valuations can be controversial. For bonds, the IRS considers

1. The soundness of the security
2. The yield
3. The date of maturity
4. Other relevant factors

For stocks, the company's net worth, prospective earning power, dividend-paying capacity, and other relevant factors are all considered.

Gifts of partial interests. In general, a taxpayer can secure a deduction for a remainder or income interest in property only if it is placed in a trust or other specified form as described by Regulation 1.170A-6.

Gifts of partial interests not in trust. There are, however, five situations in which deductions can be obtained for donated property not transferred in trust:

1. Gift of a personal residence
2. Gift of a donor's farm
3. Gift of an *undivided* interest
4. Gift of a lease, option to purchase, or easement concerning real property given in perpetuity to a charity exclusively for conservation purposes
5. Gift of a remainder interest in real property that is given to a charity exclusively for conservation purposes

Gifts of undivided property interests. In addition, under Regulation 1.170A-7, a contribution will be allowed for *partial interests* if they represent the donee's entire interest in the property.

Gifts in trust (Section 170(f)(2)(A)) of remainder interests can be deducted if one of the following three classifications can be established:

1. *Annuity Trust.* This instrument will specify in dollars the amount of the annuity that will be paid to the income beneficiary. The payments must be made at least yearly.

2. *Unitrust.* Under this trust the payout is specified as a percentage of the FMV of the trust's assets as computed on a yearly basis.

3. *Pooled Income Funds.* Trusts maintained by public charities which have an irrevocable remainder interest in the contributed assets. The trust is generally comprised of funds donated by donors who keep an income interest for life.

The tax deduction, under these instruments, is arrived at by computing the present value of the remainder interest, as measured by the FMV of the property at time of gift—less any estimated future drop in value as the result of depreciation or depletion—multiplied by the remainder factor for the donee's life expectancy (as taken from Treasury tables)—discounted at 6 percent or other rate as determined by the IRS.

Establishment of these charitable remainder trusts as described respectively in Sections 664(d)(1), 664(d)(2), and 642(c)(5) are involved matters and should be undertaken by only the thoroughly informed.

Watch Out for the "As If" Rule

The "As If" rule is designed to plug a loophole in charitable contribution statutes.

In instances where charitable gifts include property that would have resulted in ordinary income if sold (instead of being contributed) the amount of the donation must be reduced by the appreciation that would have been ordinary income.

The IRS goes even further with this "As-If-Sold" theory and claims that it also applies in establishing the appreciation as a capital gain or ordinary income. Frequent gifts, for example, can be classed as frequent sales—and as such can place a taxpayer "in the business of selling the items in question in the course of an ordinary trade or business." This forced classification removes the opportunity for a charitable deduction.

EXAMPLE:

Taxpayer, an investor, purchased 100 books, held them in a warehouse for more than one year and then donated them to qualified charities at their retail list price.

The IRS claimed that, under the "As If" rule, the investor was actually a book dealer and disallowed his charitable deductions (Rev. Rul. 79-419, 1979-52 IRB 9). This is a wrinkle to watch when planning a giving program.

Corporate "Bail Out" Through Contributions

The IRS allows owners of closely held corporatioins to donate portions of their stock to qualified charities with the understanding that such charities will sell the stock back to the corporation. These maneuvers produce two favorable results:

1. The taxpayer personally receives a charitable deduction which was made with cash from his corporation at no tax consequence to the latter. (Such a gift deduction is usually made even more attractive because the stock has, more than likely, substantially appreciated in value.)

2. The corporation benefits to some degree in that its "accumulated earnings" risk has been reduced.

CAUTION:

> While the IRS does not seem to object to a prearranged transaction of this type, it will treat the arrangement as a stock redemption, leading to a shareholder dividend, "if the donee is legally bound, or can be compelled by the corporation, to surrender the shares for redemption." (Rev. Rul. 78-197, CB 1978-1, 83)

"Above-the-Line Deductions" Under The Economic Recovery Tax Act of 1981. Beginning in 1982 this law allows "above-the-line deductions" (no itemization) as follows:

In 1982 and 1983 the deduction is limited to 25 percent of contributions up to maximum giving of $100—a $25 deduction.

In 1984 the limit is still 25 percent but the maximum goes to $300—a $75 deduction.

In 1985 the deduction climbs to 50 percent of all contributions—and in 1986 to 100 percent.

In 1987 the law expires, and we go back to nothing for nonitemizers.

Married taxpayers filing separately are limited to $50 in 1982 and 1983 and $150 in 1984.

Corporations. For tax years beginning after 1981, the corporate charitable deduction increases from 5 percent of taxable income, as adjusted, to 10 percent.

In addition, corporations will receive a much larger charitable deduction for gifts of ordinary income scientific property to a college or university for research purposes. See Act Section 222 for formula.

9.5 HANDLING THE AUDIT

Be sure that the "available-cash" test can be met for cash gifts that do not have documentation. See Section 9.2 of this chapter.

For businesses, review the advertising account to reassure yourself that no contributions are hidden therein.

If the deduction is large enough to warrant the effort—and if the qualification of the donee organization is in doubt and cannot be determined in any other fashion—secure a copy of its Exempt Status Certificate.

Review the previously mentioned *Audit Checklist* and attempt to legally arrange evidence so as to satisfy the items of inquiry as listed.

Cancelled checks to donee charities are not always acceptable proof of deductible contributions, especially when made out to churches, schools, hopspitals, and the like. They might represent personal gifts to a clergyman, payment of school tuition, or medical bills, etc. Secure donee statements or receipts which list dates of gift, purpose, and amounts contributed.

Personal notes or pledges are not deductible contributions. Use of credit cards to make gifts, however, is acceptable to the IRS. Date of charge is governing—not date debt was paid. Secure credit card invoices.

For gifts of property valued at more than $200 the following information should have been attached to the return (Regulation 1.170A-1(2)(ii)). If this was not done, secure the data now:

■ Name and address of the charity

■ Date of gift

■ A description of the property in enough detail to identify it—if tangible property, state its physical condition.

■ For securities, the name of the issuer, type of security, and how it is traded.

■ How and when donated property was acquired; i.e., gift, inheritance, purchase.

■ FMV of the property at time of gift, giving method used in determining value. (Attach appraisal if one was acquired.)

■ For appreciated property, the cost or adjusted basis.

■ For certain appreciated property, the amount by which the contribution is reduced by the amount that would have represented ordinary income if sold at its FMV.

■ Any agreement relating to the use, sale, or other disposition of the donated property, such as "Rare book—will be used for research in library."

■ The amount claimed as a deduction. If less than the entire interest is given, state the amount claimed as a deduction in any earlier years for gifts of other interests in the property. Give also the name and address of each donee, the location where the property (if tangible) is located, and the name of the individual having possession if other than the organization to which originally given.

Charity travel away from home overnight. Details of the necessity for such travel should be secured from the organization involved. Documentation should be obtained along with a written statement to the effect that none of the expenses were reimbursed.

Know this: Expenses incurred while attending a church convention solely as a member of the church, rather than as a duly chosen representative, are not deductible.

In general, review this chapter and meet all recommendations as they apply. This contribution issue has ramifications never envisioned before being encountered.

Most Revenue persons will not question small contributions to unfamiliar donee organizations unless the return contains an unusually large number of such charities.

9.6 PERTINENT COURT DECISIONS—PRO AND CON

Pro
Jerome and Myrtle Scheffres et al (TC Memo 1969-41)

Findings of Fact

Petitioners entered into a joint venture with others (called Greenbelt Associates) to purchase a 390-acre tract of land for investment purposes. On the same date, members of Greenbelt Associates also entered into an agreement whereby the land would be developed through the construction of apartment houses and other income-producing improvements.

The sellers of the 390-acre tract, the Perkins and Kramer families, were also 20 percent owners of Greenbelt Associates. The contract under which these sellers originally agreed to purchase the tract provided that consummation of the purchase was contingent upon their obtaining a change in zoning from industrial to residential so as to permit the construction of garden-type apartments on approximately 300 acres of the land.

Subsequently, the Perkins and Kramer families made application for the zoning change. They were granted the change after assuring the county that they would contribute ten acres of their tract for use as a school site. (If the promised gratuitous conveyance had not been made, the Board of Education could have acquired the 10-acre parcel upon the payment of a price, by negotiative purchase, or condemnation.)

The sellers, in their contract of sale to Greenbelt Associates, required an acknowledgment from the buyers that the gift of the 10 acres would be made for the purpose stipulated. It subsequently was, with each of the Associate's partners taking a "charitable contribution" for his fair share of the FMV of the property. The IRS objected.

Opinion

The court agreed that the Board of Education is an organization referred to in Section 170(c)(1) and that the 10-acre tract was to be used exclusively for public purposes.

No one acting on behalf of Greenbelt Associates or petitioners ever made any gift commitment to the Board of Education. No special economic benefit inured to Greenbelt Associates, since the board testified that it would have acquired the school land anyway—either by purchase or by condemnation—and would have located it upon the 390-acre tract.

Held for the petitioners.

Con
Sol Minzer, et ux, v U.S. (DC Tex; 1975)
35 AFTR 2d 75-1416

Findings of Fact

The plaintiffs, Sol and Margaret Minzer, transferred approximately 2½ acres of land to the County of Dallas for use as a road right of way and deducted the FMV of $107,767 as a contribution.

The government claimed that

A transfer of property does not qualify as a charitable contribution merely because the person making the transfer was not paid for his property. In order to be deductible the benefits received or expected to be received by the transferror must not be greater than those received by the general public. If the benefits received or expected to be received by the transferror are substantial, and meaning by that, benefits received or expected to be received are greater than those that inure to the general public from transfer for charitable purposes, then in such case the transferror has received or expects to receive benefits sufficient to remove the transfer from the realm of deductibility.

Opinion

The jury decided that the benefits which inured to the plaintiffs were greater than those received by the general public and

That the FMV of the conveyed property was 50¢ per square foot. Judgment for the government.

9.7 RELEVANT CODE AND REGULATION SECTIONS, PLUS PUBLICATIONS

Code

Section 170	Charitable, etc., Contributions and Gifts
170(a)	Allowance of Deduction
170(b)	Percentage Limitations
170(b)(1)(B)	Other Contributions
170(b)(1)(C)	Special Limitation with Respect to Contributions of Certain Capital Gain Property
170(c)	Charitable Contributions Defined
170(d)	Carryovers of Excess Contributions
170(e)	Certain Contributions of Ordinary Income and Capital Gain Property
170(e)(3)	Special Rule for Certain Contributions of Inventory and Other Property
170(f)	Disallowance of Deduction in Certain Cases and Special Rules
170(f)(2)(A)	Remainder Interests

Regulations

Section 1.170A-1(2)(ii)	Contribution by Individual of Property Other Than Money
1.170A-6	Charitable Contributions in Trust
1.170A-7	Contributions Not in Trust of Partial Interests in Property
1.170A-1(c)	Contribution in Property

Publications

78	Cumulative List of Organizations
526	Charitable Contributions
561	Determining the Value of Donated Property

9.8 APPLICABLE IRS MANUAL REFERENCES (INVESTIGATIVE TECHNIQUES)

Data from the following manual or handbook sections have been included in the body of this chapter:

MT 4231-36	Part IV - Audit	Section 741
MT 4231-42	Audit Technique Handbook	Section 679
MT 4233-1	Part IV - Audit	Section 520.1(16)
MT 4234-12	Part IV - Audit	Section 778

Moving Expenses
(Section 217)

10

10.1 IDENTIFYING THE PROBLEM

With some 30 percent of our U.S. population yearly changing locations, the moving-expense deduction has become an increasingly important tax consideration—particularly since it is allowed in arriving at adjusted gross without the necessity for itemizing deductions.

From a practitioner's viewpoint, there are two completely segregated groups of problems. Employees, retirees, survivors, and self-employed persons require one set of rules—employers, another.

For the individual, the following moves require identification and different handling:

■ Moves to or within the U.S.

■ Moves to or within a foreign country or from one foreign country to another

■ Moves by the military

■ Moves by retirees or survivors returning to the U.S.

Within these movement categories are other important considerations:

■ Distance and Time requirements

■ Deduction limitations

■ Direct or indirect expenses

■ Reasonableness of moving expenses

■ Handling of reimbursements

■ Sale of a residence (Should costs be deducted as moving expenses or added to basis?)

For the employer, payroll taxes come into play. Since moving expenses are personal in nature, any reimbursement is taxable income under Section 82 (Reimbursements for Expense of Moving). Employers, therefore, must subject such payments to payroll scrutiny and must furnish each transferred employee with Form 4782 (Employee Moving Expense Information). Details later.

Problems are not insurmountable; they are more tricky than difficult. These suggestions should help.

10.2 HOW THE IRS SEES THE ISSUE

For the most part, the IRS sees moving expenses as a rather straightforward problem. The law is relatively clear. Facts document legal requirements—or they don't. Most court cases seem to have turned on factual matters.

10.3 FACTORS WHICH THE IRS CONSIDERS WHEN MAKING ITS AUDIT DECISION

An IRS examiner will first categorize the move. Normally, it will be that of an employee-taxpayer transferring from one point in the U.S. to another. After this, the auditor will want to determine whether it was a legitimate move under the law.

■ Was the purpose of the move to begin a new principal place of employment?

■ Did the move traverse a sufficient number of miles?

■ Did the employee work full time for a qualifying number of weeks at the new location?

■ Were direct and indirect dollar limitations adhered to?

■ Were expenses, as deducted, proper?

Instructions for the handling of each category and each legal requirement will be detailed in the next section.

10.4 CONSIDERATIONS WHEN PREPARING THE RETURN

Code Section 217, MOVING EXPENSES, governs the deduction. Paragraphs (a) and (b) are reproduced below:

(a) *Deduction Allowed.*—There shall be allowed as a deduction moving expenses paid or incurred during the taxable year in connection with the commencement of work by the taxpayer as an employee or as a self-employed individual at a new principal place of work.

(b) *Definition of Moving Expenses.*—
   (1) *In general.*—For purposes of this section, the term "moving expenses" means only the reasonable expenses—
   (A) of moving household goods and personal effects from the former residence to the new residence,
   (B) of traveling (including meals and lodging) from the former residence to the new place of residence,
   (C) of traveling (including meals and lodging), after obtaining employment, from the former residence to the general location of the new principal place of work and return, for the principal purpose of searching for a new residence,
   (D) of meals and lodging while occupying temporary quarters in the general

location of the new principal place of work during any period of 30 consecutive days after obtaining employment, or

(E) constituting qualified residence sale, purchase, or lease expenses.

Two Tests That Must Be Satisfied

From this basic position, the Code requires that two tests be satisfied before consideration of the deduction can continue

The distance test requires that the new principal job location be at least 35 miles farther from the taxpayer's former residence than the old one was. No reference is made as to the location of the new home. (Regulation 1.217-2(c)(2))

What it means is this: If the old job was 5 miles from the former residence, then the new job location must be at least 40 miles from the original home. If a person, such as a student, did not have an old job location, then the new job spot must be at least 35 miles from his or her former home.

NOTE:

This distance test does not apply to the military where the move was due to a permanent change of station.

The time test. Employees must work full time for at least 39 weeks during the 12-month period following arrival in the general area of the new job location. Such a work schedule need not be continuous. (Regulation 1.217(c)(4))

COMMENT:

If the taxpayer is married, either spouse may satisfy this 39-week, full-time test. They may not, however, combine their work periods.

In the case of self-employed individuals, they must work full time for at least 39 weeks during the first 12 months and a total of 78 weeks during the 24 months after arrival in the new job area.

Either an employee or a self-employed person can meet these 39/78-week time tests, even if they have not met them by date for filing.

Taxpayer expects to meet time test. If such expectation does not materialize, the taxpayer would then be required to report the amount of the deduction as income in the year the requirement could not be met or file an amended return for the year of the deduction.

The time test does not have to be met by:

1. Members of the Armed Forces who are permanently transferred
2. Movers to the U.S. who are retirees or survivors of a person who died while living and working outside the U.S.
3. Movers, whose job has ended due to disability, transfer for the employer's benefit, or layoff other than for willful misconduct.

Deduction limitations. Having passed these tests, now come the deduction limitations ($3,000 for persons moving to or within the U.S.—$6,000 for movers to or within a foreign country or from one foreign country to another). However, before the limitation formula can be illustrated, "direct" and "indirect" moving expenses should be defined.

Direct moving expenses. These include *reasonable costs of transporting household goods and personal effects*—for the taxpayer and the members of his or her household who were classified as such before and after the move. Such members do not include tenants, employees, or personal attendants or friends. Direct expenses also extend to costs of *travel, meals, and lodging* while moving from old to new residence.

NOTE:

There is no limitation on the amount of allowable deductions to cover these two types of moving expenses, but travel expenses are limited to one trip per family member.

Indirect moving expenses. These items, too, must be *reasonable* in amount. They include house-hunting expenses, temporary living costs, qualified residence sale, purchase, or lease expenses. Their deduction is limited to $3,000, only $1,500 of which can be attributable to house-hunting and temporary living expenses.

Reasonableness is defined in Regulation 1.217-2(b)(2) as movement:

1. By the shortest and most direct route.

2. By the conventional means of transportation actually used.

3. In the shortest period of time commonly required to travel the distance.

WARNING:

Circuitous sightseeing trips will not be allowed. The cost of lavish or extravagant temporary quarters or meals will not be deductible.

One-year rule. According to Regulation 1.217-2(a)(3), moving expenses, in order to be deductible, must have been incurred within one year of date of commencement of work at the new location—or a reasonable approximation thereto. It defines the latter in the following terms:

> Moving expenses incurred after the 1-year period may be considered reasonably proximate in time if it can be shown that circumstances existed which prevented the taxpayer from incurring the expenses of moving within the 1-year period allowed.

Making the computation. A good illustration of the computation required for a domestic move is included in Publication 521 (Moving Expenses).

Foreign moves are computed through use of Form 3903F (Foreign Moving Expense Adjustment). The computation is much the same as for Form 3903 with the following exceptions:

1. Costs of moving possessions to and from storage—and for storing them for all or part of the time the new job location outside of the U.S. remains a principal job location—are deductible.

2. Costs of temporary living are allowed for 90 days instead of the 30 days for movers to or within the U.S.

3. House-hunting and temporary living expenses are limited to $4,500 instead of the domestic $1,500.

4. The overall limitation is $6,000 instead of the domestic $3,000.

Business expenses. While we are primarily concerned here with the cost of moving a family, let us not forget that the cost of moving an office is still deductible as an ordinary business expense.

Costs of exchanging residences. These include:

Sale-related expenses such as real estate commissions, cost of advertising house for sale, cost of deed preparation, and other legal expenses, escrow fees, "points" paid to obtain an FHA mortgage for the buyer and state transfer taxes. They do not include "fix-up" expenses or any loss on sale of the residence.

Purchase-related expenses such as legal, escrow, and appraisal fees—title costs, "points," or loan placement charges which do not represent interest and other reasonable expenses necessary to the purchase.

NOTE:

These sale-and-purchase-related expenses may be used either as moving expenses or to reduce the gain on sale of old residence or to increase the basis of the new. It is generally (but not always) better to use such expenses as moving deductions. Any unused portions can be used to reduce gain or increase basis as mentioned.

Lease expenses such as cost of settling an unexpired lease such as payments to lessor for discontinuance of contract, legal fees, real estate commissions, advertising for a sub-lessee, etc. Expenses incident to obtaining a new lease at the new locationn are also deductible, but not prepayments on the lease contract or security or other such deposits.

House-hunting expenses, covered in Regulation 1.217-2(b)(5). They include the cost of transportation, meals, and lodging for the taxpayer and members of his or her household while traveling to and from the area of the new job, and while there. Such costs may be deducted only if incurred after the new job has been obtained, and only if such expenditures were made primarily for the purpose of securing a new place to live.

NOTE:

There is no limit to the number of house-hunting trips that may be made, but the monetary costs are subject to limitations as previously explained.

Car expenses incurred in the moving process, or in shipping the automobile itself (if not driven) can be deducted as follows:

1. Actual out-of-pocket expenses such as for gas, oil, and repairs (but not depreciation) and for tolls and parking fees, or
2. The standard mileage rate may be used.
3. The cost of shipping a car is entirely deductible.

All *reimbursements* are includible in income in the year received, no matter whether received or accrued, directly or indirectly, in cash or in kind—and no matter whether such reimbursements were deductible moving expenses or not (Section 82).

They include, but are not limited to

■ All moving and transportation costs
■ Allowances for loss on sale of former residence

- Allowances for costs of new drapes, carpeting, and the like
- Storage charges for items not in transit
- Movement of persons not members of taxpayer's household
- Transportation of furniture, whether paid by employer or performed by employer
- Moving costs in excess of limitations

How Moving or Travel Allowances Should Be Handled by an Employer

The following book section will detail the manner in which such reimbursments or allowances should be handled by an employer.

NOTE:

An obvious saving to the employee can be realized if his or her employer purchases the taxpayer's residence and sells it at a loss—rather than reimburse the employee for the loss. It makes no difference to the employer in taxes.

Withholding, Social Security, and FUTA. No withholding of income tax or social security is required for allowances or reimbursements of moving expenses, nor are these amounts subject to the Federal Unemployment Tax Act (FUTA) if the employer reasonably believes that the employee will:

1. Realize deductible moving expenses, and
2. Meet the 35-mile distance test, and
3. Meet the 39-week time test.

CAUTION:

If the employee is not expected to meet these requirements, then the reimbursement becomes subject to all three types of taxes.

If the reimbursement will cover both deductible and nondeductible moving expenses, with no specific allocation to either, the employer must allocate the allowance first to the deductible portion which is not subject to withholding—and the remainder to the non-deductible classification which makes it subject to the three payroll taxes.

For withholding purposes, if the reimbursement is included with regular wages, the total amount is treated as though it were wages. If the reimbursement is paid separately, the employer can either withhold a flat 20 percent or include the payment with the current or last preceding payroll period within the calendar year.

Social security is withheld, where required, until both salaries and the moving reimbursement reach the maximum wage limit.

Movers Checklist of Moving—Deduction Requirements

A Movers Check List is included as Figure 10-1. This will provide for quick location of most moving-deduction requirements.

10.5 HANDLING THE AUDIT

The IRS approaches the moving-expense issue from various qualfication and limitation angles, most of which have already been mentioned. In addition, the Service will be interested as to—

MOVERS CHECK LIST

	(1) Moves Within or to the U.S. Employees	(2) Self-Employeds	(3) Retired Persons and Survivors Moving to the U.S.	(4) Moves to or Within a Foreign Country
Distance Test	New job location must be at least 35 miles farther from former home than old job location was	Same as for (1)	Same as for (1). (Move must be made within six months of death of survivor's spouse or other decedent)	Same as for (1)
Time Test	Must work full time for at least 39 wks during the 12 month after the move—or expect to	Must work full time for at least 39 wks during the first 12 months and 78 wks during the first 24 months after the move —or expect to.	None required	Same as for (1)
Time Allotment for Temporary Quarters	30 Days	30 Days	30 Days	90 Days
Dollar Deduction Limits:				
Cost of Moving Household Goods	None. (Includes in-transit storage)	None. (Includes in-transit storage)	None. (Includes in-transit storage)	None. (Includes storage and transportation to and from storage.)
Cost of Travel to New Location	None	None	None	None
All Other Allowable Expenses	$3,000	$3,000	$3,000	$6,000
Reimbursements	Must be incl. in gross inc. except if rec'd under Uniform Relocation Assistance and Real Property Acquisition Policies Act of 1970	Same as for (1)	Same a for (1)	Same as for (1)

Figure 10-1

■ Whether reimbursements have been reported.

■ Whether the taxpayer, after the move, was a full-time employee. (In the case of seasonal employment, off-season weeks in which there is no work are counted as full-time employment only if the employment contract covers the off-season period which must be less than six months—as in the case of school teachers, for example.)

CAUTION:

For a self-employed person, the full-time requirement is decided by the customary practices of the occupation or trade or business in the geographical area. A surgeon, for example, qualifies as full time if he or she works four days a week and all others in the same profession, in the same area, do the same.

■ Whether the move took place within one year. If it didn't, the examiner may disallow the expenses out of hand.

RED FLAG:

Remember the rule under Regulation 1.217-2(a)(3)—the one-year period may be waived where circumstances existed that prevented the timely move. For example, the family may not have moved because they wanted a child to graduate from high school with his or her class. Don't allow the examiner to win this issue by default.

■ Whether any lease-breaking or mortgage penalties were included in the moving-expense deduction.

■ Whether living expenses, before or after the move, were deducted. (They should not have been, not even if they were temporary.)

■ Whether moving-expense deductions included such nondeductible costs as new curtains or carpeting, or wallpapering, or the like.

■ Whether deductions such as allocated real estate taxes were taken as itemized deductions or as moving expenses. (They should have been deducted in the former manner.)

■ Whether all of the earned income during the year of the move—and the year following—was taxable. (Moving expenses are considered business expenses attributable to the employment for which the move was made. If a husband and wife, for example, were both over 65 and did not earn enough to produce earned taxable income, their moving expenses could not be deducted against dividend and interest income.)

■ Whether moving-expense deductions were taken in a situation where the earned income was not subject to U.S. income taxes. (They should not have been.)

Additional Steps That Will Aid in Handling the Audit

1. Prepare a Form 3903 or 3903F if one has not been completed. Secure or prepare the required Forms 4782, as the case may be.

2. If an employee situation is in question, make sure that the 4782 has been properly computed. Secure a statement from the employer as to the necessity for the move.

3. Question the taxpayer concerning the following additional moving expense deduction possibilities:
   a. Cost of connecting or disconnecting appliances such as stoves, washers, etc.
   b. Cost of meals on day of arrival.
   c. Lodging en route, including day of arrival.

WARNING:

Under the Cohan Rule, the IRS will generally allow an estimated amount for unsubstantiated expenses, such as for the reasonable cost of meals, tolls, parking fees, and the like. But the taxpayer probably will not receive the entire deduction as requested unless he or she possesses at least a record of such expenses, including dates, amounts, and purpose of expenditures. If a record does not exist, one should be reconstructed before the audit begins. Taxpayers think much more clearly and calmly while not under the direct scrutiny of an IRS auditor.

10.6 PERTINENT COURT DECISIONS—PRO AND CON

Pro
(Rev. Rul. 72-195, 1972-1 CB 95)

Findings of Fact

Advice was requested as to whether moving expenses, under circumstances described below, are attributable to a taxpayer's trade or business in determining the net operating loss deduction allowable under Section 172 of the Code.

The taxpayer, a manufacturer's representative, worked for a corporation which assigned him to its New York City office. In December of 1970 his territory was changed to San Francisco.

He relocated but was not reimbursed for his moving expenses so he claimed them as a deduction on his 1970 return. In the same year his manufacturer's representative business suffered a net operating loss which he could carry back to prior years.

Question: Can the moving expenses be classified as business expenses for the purpose of arriving at the NOL?

Opinion

The legislative history of Section 217 gives evidence that Congress considered such expenses attributable to a taxpayer's trade or business. House Report No. 749 of the 88th Congress states:

> The deductions allowed by your committee's bill with respect to moving expenses are to be deductible in computing "adjusted gross income." This means that these expenses are *treated essentially the same as business expenses;* these expenses, therefore, are deductible whether the individual involved itemizes his personal deductions or takes the standard deduction. This treatment is provided not only because *these expenses are substantially similar to business expenses,* but also because when they are incurred, they are likely to be relatively large.

Held that the moving expenses in question are allowable as a deduction in full in determining taxpayer's NOL.

Con
(Rev. Rul. 78-174 1978-1 CB 77)

Findings of Fact

A was employed on a full-time basis by X Corporation. This employment was terminated after 12 years and A remained without work for a period of 2 months. Upon securing a new job, A sold his old residence, bought a new one, and moved.

The distance between A's former residence and former principal place of work was 25 miles. The distance between A's former residence and new principal place of work is 55 miles, thus exceeding by 30 miles the distance from A's former residence to A's former principal place of work.

Section 217(c)(1) provides in part that, if a person has *no former principal place of work* (my emphasis) the qualifying distance need be only 35 miles between former residence and the new principal place of work.

If A, indeed, had no former principal place of work because of his layoff, he would qualify under 217(c)(1) for a moving-expense deduction.

Advice was sought as to whether A could be allowed the moving deduction.

Opinion

A was not seeking full-time employment for the first time, nor could he be considered as re-entering the labor force after a substantial period of unemployment, in view of the fact that he was unemployed for a period of only 2 months. Deduction denied.

10.7 RELEVANT CODE AND REGULATION SECTIONS, PLUS PUBLICATION

Code

Section 1.217-2	Deduction for Moving Expenses Paid or Incurred in Taxable Years Beginning After December 31, 1969
1.217-2(a)(3)	Commencement of Work
1.217-2(b)(2)	Reasonable Expenses
1.217-2(b)(5)	Expenses of Traveling for the Principal Purpose of Looking for a New Residence.
1.217-2(b)(9)	Dollar Limitations
1.217-2(c)(2)	Minimum Distance
1.217-2(c)(4)	Minimum Period of Employment

Publication

5.2	Moving Expenses

10.8 APPLICABLE IRS MANUAL REFERENCES (INVESTIGATIVE TECHNIQUES)

Audit Technique Handbook For Internal Revenue Agents

MT 4231-36	Section 749	Moving Expenses

Standard Explanations Handbook

MT 428(11)-15	Section 47	Moving Expenses

Child and Disabled Dependent Care

(Section 44A)

11

11.1 IDENTIFYING THE PROBLEM

Many of the difficulties that have arisen in taking this deduction have occurred because

1. The child and dependent care expenses were not properly work related.
2. The "Qualifying Persons" test was not met.
3. "Dollar" and "Earned Income" limitations were not correctly applied.
4. A determination could not be made as to which divorced parent provided more than one-half the cost of keeping up a home.
5. Of the necessity for keeping records and subjecting wages to employment tax procedures.
6. Of the difficulty in employing household workers who are willing to participate in the employment tax requirements.

CAUTION:

Referring to (6), and being realistic, good housekeepers or sitters who are available for this purpose, are frequently persons who are retired or who receive welfare payments. They are not worried about income taxes because their taxable income is generally insufficient for them to qualify, but they do object to paying Social Security and certainly do abhor the thought of having to report income for welfare purposes.

Accordingly, many refuse to work unless they receive their wages in cash without withholding considerations.

Suggestion: Wherever possible, employ a day care center of some sort. The IRS defines such a facility as one that provides care for more than six individuals and complies with all applicable laws and regulations of a state or unit of local government.

WARNING:

The other alternative—that of ignoring the payroll tax requirement—is not practical since Form 2441 (Figure 11-1) must accompany a return before this credit will be

Form **2441** Department of the Treasury Internal Revenue Service (0)	**Credit for Child and Dependent Care Expenses** ▶ Attach to Form 1040. ▶ See Instructions below.	OMB No. 1545-0068 **198__** 26

Name(s) as shown on Form 1040 | Your social security number

1 See the definition for "qualifying person" in the instructions. Then read the instructions for line 1.

(a) Name of qualifying person	(b) Date of birth	(c) Relationship	(d) During 1981, the person lived with you for:	
			Months	Days

2 Persons or organizations who cared for those listed on line 1. See the instructions for line 2.

(a) Name and address (If more space is needed, attach schedule)	(b) Social security number, if applicable	(c) Relationship, if any	(d) Period of care		(e) Amount of 1981 expenses (include those not paid during the year)
			From Month—Day	To Month—Day	

To Figure Your Credit, You MUST Complete ALL Lines That Apply

3 Add the amounts in column 2(e) **3**

4 Enter $2,000 ($4,000 if you listed two or more names in line 1) or amount on line 3, whichever is less **4**

5 Earned income (wages, salaries, tips, etc.). See the instructions for line 5. An entry MUST be made on this line.

  (a) If unmarried at end of 1981, enter your earned income . . . .

  (b) If married at end of 1981, enter:

    (1) Your earned income . . . $ _____ Enter the lesser

    (2) Your spouse's earned income $ _____ of b(1) or b(2) . . . ▶ **5**

6 Enter the amount on line 4 or line 5, whichever is less **6**

7 Amount on line 6 paid during 1981. An entry MUST be made on this line . . . . ▶ **7**

8 Child and dependent child care expenses for 1980 paid in 1981. See instructions for line 8 . . . **8**

9 Add amounts on lines 7 and 8 . . . . **9**

10 Multiply line 9 by 20 percent **10**

11 Limitation:

  a Enter tax from Form 1040, line 37 . . . . **11a**

  b Enter total of lines 38, 39, and 41 through 43 of Form 1040 . . **11b**

  c Subtract line 11b from line 11a (if line 11b is more than line 11a, enter zero) **11c**

12 Credit for child and dependent care expenses. Enter the smaller of line 10 or line 11c here and on Form 1040, line 40 . **12**

13 If payments listed on line 2 were made to an individual, complete the following: | Yes | No

  (a) If you paid $50 or more in a calendar quarter to an individual, were the services performed in your home? . . . .

  (b) If "Yes," have you filed appropriate wage tax returns on wages for services in your home (see instructions for line 13)? . . . . .

  (c) If answer to (b) is "Yes," enter your employer identification number . . . . . . ▶

Paperwork Reduction Act Notice.—The Paperwork Reduction Act of 1980 says we must tell you why we are collecting this information, how we will use it, and whether you have to give it to us. We ask for the information to carry out the Internal Revenue laws of the United States. We need it to ensure that you are complying with these laws and to allow us to figure and collect the right amount of tax. You are required to give us this information.

General Instructions

If you or your spouse worked or looked for work, and you spent money to care for a qualifying person, this form might save you tax.

What Is the Child and Dependent Care Expenses Credit?—This is a credit you can take against your tax if you paid someone to care for your child or dependent so that you could work or look for work. You can also take the credit if you paid someone to care for your spouse. The instructions that follow list tests that must be met to take the credit. If you need more information,

please get **Publication 503**, Child and Disabled Dependent Care.

For purposes of this credit, we have defined some of the terms used here. Refer to these when you read the instructions.

Definitions

A qualifying person can be:

● Any person under age 15 whom you list as a dependent. (If you are divorced, legally separated, or separated under a written agreement, please see the Child Custody Test in the instructions.)

● Your spouse who is mentally or physically not able to care for himself or herself.

● Any person not able to care for himself or herself whom you can list as a dependent, or could list as a dependent except that he or she had income of $1,000 or more.

A **relative** is your child, stepchild, mother, father, grandparent, brother, sister, grandchild, uncle, aunt, nephew, niece, stepmother, stepfather, stepbrother, stepsister, mother-in-law, father-in-law, brother-in-law, sister-in-law, son-in-law, and daugh-

ter-in-law. A cousin is not a relative for purpose of this credit.

A full-time student is one who was enrolled in a school for the number of hours or classes that is considered full time. The student must have been enrolled at least 5 months during 1981.

What Are Child and Dependent Care Expenses?

These expenses are the amounts you paid for household services and care of the qualifying person.

Household Services.—These are services performed by a cook, housekeeper, governess, maid, cleaning person, babysitter, etc. The services must have been needed to care for the qualifying person as well as run the home. For example, if you paid for the services of a maid or a cook, the services must have also been for the benefit of the qualifying person.

Care of the Qualifying Person.—Care includes cost of services for the well-being and protection of the qualifying person.

(Continued on back)

Care does not include expenses for food and clothes. If you paid for care that included these items and you cannot separate their cost, take the total payment.

Example: You paid a nursery school to care for your child and the school gave the child lunch. Since you cannot separate the cost of the lunch from the cost of the care, you can take all of the amount that you paid to the school.

This example would not apply if you had school costs for a child in the first grade or above because these costs cannot be counted in figuring the credit.

You can count care provided outside your home if the care was for your dependent under age 15.

You can claim medical expenses you paid for the qualifying person if you paid them so you could work or look for work. If you itemized deductions, you may want to take all or part of these expenses on Schedule A. For example, if you can't take all of the medical expenses on Form 2441 because your costs for care have reached the limit ($2,000 or $4,000), you can take the rest of the medical expenses on Schedule A. If you show all of the medical expenses on Schedule A, you cannot take on Form 2441 that part you could not deduct on Schedule A because of the 3-percent limit.

To Take This Credit.—You must file Form 1040, not Form 1040A, and you must meet all of the tests listed below.

(1) You paid for child and dependent care so you (and your spouse if you were married) could work or look for work.

(2) One or more qualifying persons lived in your home.

(3) You (and your spouse if you were married) paid more than half the cost of keeping up your home. This cost includes rent; mortgage interest; utility charges; maintenance and repairs; property taxes and property insurance; and food costs (but not dining out).

(4) You must file a joint return if you were married. There are two exceptions to this rule. You can file a separate return if:

(a) You were legally separated; or

(b) You were living apart and:

• The qualifying person lived in your home for more than 6 months; and

• You paid more than half the cost of keeping up your home; and

• Your spouse did not live in your home during the last 6 months of your tax year.

(5) You paid someone, other than your spouse or a person for whom you could claim a dependency exemption, to care for the qualifying person.

You are allowed to pay a relative, including a grandparent, who was not your dependent. If the relative is your child, he or she must also have been 19 or over by the end of the year.

Child Custody Test.—If you were divorced, legally separated, or separated under a written agreement, your child is a qualifying person if you had custody for the longer period during 1981. The child must also have:

• Received over half of his or her support from the parents, and

• Been in the custody of one or both parents for more than half of 1981, and

• Been under 15, or physically or mentally unable to care for himself or herself.

Credit Limit.—The credit is generally 20% of the amount you paid someone to care for the qualifying person. The most

you can figure the credit on is $2,000 a year for one qualifying person ($4,000 for two or more).

Line-by-Line Instructions

Line 1.—*In column (a)* list the name of each qualifying person who was cared for during 1981 so you could work or look for work. In column (b) show the date of birth of each person. In column (c) show that person's relationship to you (for example: son or daughter). In column (d) show the number of months and days each person lived in your home during 1981. Count only the times when the person was qualified.

Line 2.—*In column (a)* show the name and address of the person or organization who cared for each qualifying person. If you listed a person who was your employee and who provided the care in your home, then in column (b) enter that person's social security number. Leave column (b) blank if the person: was not your employee; was self-employed; was an employee of an organization or a partnership; or did not provide the care in your home.

In column (c) write none if the person who provided the care was not related to you. If the care was provided by a relative, show the relationship to you. See definition of relative on the front of the form.

In column (d) show the period of time each person or organization provided care.

In column (e) list the amount of your 1981 expenses including those not paid during the year.

Line 3.—Add the amounts in column 2(e) and enter the total.

Line 4.—Enter $2,000 ($4,000 if more than one person is listed on line 1) or the amount on line 3, whichever is less.

Line 5.—This line is used to figure your *earned income.* Generally, you can figure earned income using steps (a) through (c). If you are unmarried, enter your amounts from Form 1040 when they are needed for the steps below. If you are married, each spouse's earned income will have to be figured separately and without regard to community property laws.

(a) Enter one spouse's amount from Form 1040, line 7 . . . _____

(b) Enter the same spouse's net profit or (loss) from Schedule C or Schedule F (Form 1040) if applicable _____

(c) Combine amounts on lines (a) and (b). (If the result is zero or less, enter zero.) . . . _____

If you are unmarried, enter the amount from line 5. If you are married, enter the amount from (c) on line 5(b)(1) and go back and figure your spouse's earned income using steps (a) through (c). Enter your spouse's earned income from (c) on line 5(b)(2). Enter the lesser of line 5(b)(1) or line 5(b)(2) on line 5.

If your spouse was a full-time student or not able to care for himself or herself, use the greater of your spouse's monthly earned income or $166 ($333 if you listed two qualifying persons on line 1(a)) to determine his or her total income for the year.

If, in the same month, both you and your spouse were full-time students and did not work, you cannot use any amount paid that month to figure the credit. The same ap-

plies to a couple who did not work because neither was capable of self-care.

Line 6.—Enter the amount from line 4 or line 5, whichever is smaller.

Line 7.—How much of the amount on line 6 did you pay in 1981? Enter this amount on line 7. Do not list any amounts for 1981 that you did not pay until 1982.

Line 8.—If you had child and dependent care expenses for 1980 that you did not pay until 1981, add them and enter the total on this line. Be sure the total is not over your 1980 limit. Attach a sheet similar to the example below, showing how you figured the amount you are carrying over to 1981.

Example: In 1980 you had child care expenses of $2,100 for your 12-year-old son. For one child, you were limited to $2,000. Of the $2,100, you paid $1,800 in 1980 and $300 in 1981. Your spouse's earned income of $5,000 was less than your earned income. You would be allowed to figure a credit on $200 in 1981, as follows:

(1) 1980 child care expenses paid in 1980 . $1,800

(2) 1980 child care expenses paid in 1981 . 300

(3) Total 2,100

(4) Limit for one qualifying person . . . 2,000

(5) Earned income reported in 1980 . . . 5,000

(6) Smaller of line 3, 4, or 5 2,000

(7) Subtract child care expenses on which credit was figured in 1980 1,800

(8) 1980 child care expenses carried over for credit this year (1981) . . . . . $ 200

Line 9.—Add lines 7 and 8 and enter the total on line 9.

Line 10.—Multiply the amount on line 9 by 20% and enter the result on line 10.

Line 11.—Your credit for child and dependent care expenses cannot be more than your tax after subtracting certain credits. To figure the allowable credit, enter your tax from Form 1040, line 37, on line 11a. Add the amounts, if any, you entered on Form 1040, lines 38, 39, and 41 through 43. Enter the total of these lines on line 11b. Subtract line 11b from 11a and enter the difference on line 11c. If line 11b is more than line 11a, enter zero on line 11c.

Line 12.—Enter the smaller of line 10 or 11c on this line and Form 1040, line 40. This is your credit for child and dependent care expenses.

Line 13.—On line 13(a), check the yes box if you paid cash wages to an employee for household services. Check the no box if you did not. In general, if you paid cash wages of $50 or more in a calendar quarter for household services to a person such as a cook, housekeeper, governess, maid, cleaning person, babysitter, etc., you must file an employment tax return. If you are not sure whether you should file an employment tax return, ask the Internal Revenue Service or get Form 942, Employer's Quarterly Tax Return for Household Employees. **Note:** You should file a Form 940, *Employer's Annual Federal Unemployment Tax Return,* for 1981 by February 1, 1982, if you paid cash wages of $1,000 or more for household services in any calendar quarter in 1980 or 1981.

On line 13(b), check the yes box if you have filed appropriate wage tax returns. Check the no box if you have not.

On line 13(c), enter your employer identification number if you checked the yes box on line 13(b).

☆ U.S. GOVERNMENT PRINTING OFFICE: -1981-343-452 E.I. 61-088-2708

Figure 11-1

allowed. Notice that the name, address, and Social Security number of the employee must be entered on the form. Then realize the possibility that this data might be dropped into an IRS computer for the purpose of determining whether the required payroll Forms 940, 942, W-2, and W-3 had been filed. If not, the employer will be in trouble.

11.2 HOW THE IRS SEES THE ISSUE

The Service feels strongly that there is a great deal of noncompliance in this Child and Dependent Care area—so strongly, in fact, that they recently instituted a study of 6,000 returns at the Atlanta, Brookhaven, and Fresno Service Centers. The purposes of the study are to

1. determine the compliance level of the payer and payee.
2. evaluate the feasibility of a compliance program in this area.
3. determine the most effective and efficient way to conduct such a program.
4. determine whether changes should be made to Form 2441 (Credit for Child and Dependent Care Expense).

RED FLAG:

Prominent in the instructions for this study (Audit Manual Supplement 40 RDD-75) is the following paragraph:

In previous studies by Internal Audit, TX and Examination, the sample selection was limited to individuals incurring the Child Care Expense (Payer). These studies indicated a potential low level of payer compliance. This study will provide information on the 1976 Tax Reform Act's effect on payer's compliance, *as well as determine if the payments for these expenses were picked up as income by the recipient (payee) and self-employment tax paid or whether the payee is an employee and is liable for his/her share of FICA on wages received* (my emphasis).

Under Section 10 (Examination Procedures) this Manual supplement states that: "there are no surveys before or after assignment except to payer returns erroneously selected during screening." This means that *no* taxpayer will be allowed to escape the study unless wrongfully chosen; i.e., maybe the deduction was too small.

NOTE:

Under Section 11 (Examination of Payer Return) (4) instruction reads:

If the payer taxpayer responds with substantiation of child and dependent care expenditures, take appropriate action to requisition payee(s) return and continue examination simultaneously as one case.

WARNING:

This last instruction, if for no other reason, makes it strongly advisable that a taxpayer follow Child and Dependent Care regulations to the letter. Becoming involved in any manner with unreported income or failure-to-file allegations is never pleasant—and can in fact be downright costly. One last manual instruction bears this out.

If the payee taxpayer responds and indicates on Form 6451 (Questionnaire Income Received for Child and Dependent Care Services and Payments by Employers of Social Security Tax) that the child and dependent care services were performed in the employer's home, and the employer did not pay social security taxes on such wages, the payee's returns along with the payer's related case file should be transferred to district offices for completion.

RED FLAG:

"For completion" means for audit—and for preparation of all missing employment tax returns for a period (in most cases) of at least three yearrs.

11.3 FACTORS WHICH THE IRS CONSIDERS WHEN MAKING ITS AUDIT DECISION

The government will particularly search for qualification and statutory requirements. But they will not limit their audit to these. Going deeper, the IRS person will request the following additional information:

If taxpayer is a divorced or separated parent

• What was date of divorce or separation?
• What were dates of custody of qualifying individual?
• What were dates during which the other parent had custody of qualifying individual?

If the qualifying dependent was disabled

• Proof of disability will be requested.
• Location of care will be questioned.

If care was provided at a residence by an individual

• Were withholding requirements property met?
• Were all required employment tax returns correctly filed?
• Was the person providing the care a dependent or the taxpayer's child under age 19? (Neither qualifies.)

If portions of Form 2441 were left blank, expect that a request will be made to rectify this omission

• Were deductions taken for travel to the care location? (They should not have been.)
• Was the employee who provided the care a gardener or a chauffeur? (They do not qualify.)
• Was the taxpayer legally married and living with spouse on the last day of the taxable year? (If so, then a joint return must have been filed before the credit could be taken.)
• Was qualifying work unpaid or for a nominal salary? (If so, no deduction will be allowed.)
• Did the taxpayer receive any aid to families with dependent children (AFDC)? (If so, such amounts will not be considered part of the expenses of "keeping up a home.")
• Did more than one family live in the qualified residence? (If so, each is treated as a separate household.)

- Were job-related expenses paid for other than care and household services? (If so, they are unrelated and not deductible, unless minimal in nature.)

- Was cost of schooling for first grade or higher included in care credit? (It should not have been.)

- Was taxpayer ill and away from work during any of the time for which care expenses were paid? (If so, such costs are not deductible.)

- Were care expenses paid in the year the credit was taken? (They should have been.)

- Was a credit taken for prepaid expenses in the year the services were performed? (Only then would the credit apply.)

- Were any expenses deducted both as medical expenses and in computing the care credit? (They should not have been.)

- If the employer qualified under the Work Incentive Program (WIN), was his or her salary taken as such, or as a child or dependent care credit? (The former applies.)

- If the taxpayer was married to more than one person during the taxable year, was the earned income of the couple computed by using the person's salary to whom the taxpayer was married on the last day of the year? (It should have been.)

11.4 CONSIDERATIONS WHEN PREPARING THE RETURN

In order to secure the credit for child and dependent care expenses, certain rules, tests, and qualifications must be met. The basic requirements are listed in Regulation 1.44A-1 (Expenses for Household and Dependent Care Services Necessary for Gainful Employment) and are outlined below:

In general, Code Section 44A allows a credit against tax for the cost of caring for a child or disabled dependent (including a spouse)—in a qualified household—whenever such expense is necessary to enable the taxpayer to be gainfully employed or to seek employment.

Maintaining a qualified household. (Regulation 1.44A-1(d)) This requirement is satisfied if the home is the principal residence of the taxpayer and the qualifying child or dependent—and if the taxpayer (and spouse, if married) provided more than one-half of the cost incurred for its upkeep.

Expenses of maintaining a household include property taxes, mortgage interest, rent, utility charges, home repairs, and food consumed on the premises. They do not include payments for clothing, education, medical treatment, vacations, life insurance, transportation, mortgage principal, or for the purchase, improvement, or replacement of property.

Who may claim the credit? (Regulation 1.44A-1(a)(2)) Any person who maintains the above qualified household may claim the credit. Such individuals include taxpayers who are

1. Single.
2. Married and filing jointly, even though one or both spouses work only part time, or even if one works and one is a full-time student.
3. Divorced or separated parents where one (the claimant) has custody of a child under 15 years of age for a longer period of time than the other.
4. Abandoned spouses who maintain a qualifying household alone for the last six months of the year.

Who are Qualifying Individuals?

Qualifying individuals, under Regulation 1.44A-1(b), are:

1. A dependent under age 15 who is a person for whom the taxpayer is entitled to a personal-exemption deduction under Section 151(e) (Additional Exemption for Dependents).

PLEASE NOTE:

This dependent need not be a child of the taxpayer. It can be a brother, or sister, or anyone classed as a dependent under Section 152 (Dependent Defined). See Figure 11-2.

2. A dependent (not described in 1) who is mentally or physically incapable of self-care.

3. The taxpayer's spouse who is physically or mentally incapable of self-care.

4. A child (of divorced or separated parents) whose age is under 15, or who is physically or mentally handicapped—who received more than one-half of his/her support from such parents—and who was in the custody of one or the other, or both such parents, for more than one-half of the year.

NOTE:

The parent who held the longest custody may take the credit.

Qualification of an individual is determined on a daily basis. Thus, if a dependent or spouse ceases to be a qualifying person on September 16, he or she is considered to have been a qualifying individual through September 15 only.

SEC. 152. DEPENDENT DEFINED

(a) **General Definition.**—For purposes of this subtitle, the term "dependent" means any of the following individuals over half of whose support, for the calendar year in which the taxable year of the taxpayer begins, was received from the taxpayer (or is treated under subsection (c) or (e) as received from the taxpayer):

(1) A son or daughter of the taxpayer, or a descendant of either,

(2) A stepson or stepdaugther of the taxpayer,

(3) A brother, sister, stepbrother, or stepsister of the taxpayer,

(4) The father or mother of the taxpayer, or an ancestor of either,

(5) A stepfather or stepmother of the taxpayer,

(6) A son or daughter of a brother or sister of the taxpayer,

(7) A brother or sister of the father or mother of the taxpayer,

(8) A son-in-law, daughter-in-law, father-in-law, mother-in-law, brother-in-law, or sister-in-law of the taxpayer, or

(9) An individual (other than an individual who at any time during the taxable year was the spouse, determined without regard to section 143, of the taxpayer) who, for the taxable year of the taxpayer, has as his principal place of abode the home of the taxpayer and is a member of the taxpayer's houschold.

Prior amendments.—Sec. 152(a) was previously amended by the following:

Sec. [1[(b) of Public Law 90-78, Aug. 31, 1967, effective (Sec. 2 of P.L. 90-78) with respect to taxable years beginning after Dec. 31, 1966.*

Sec. 4(a) of Public Law 85-866, Sept. 2, 1958 (qualified effective date rule in Sec. 1(c)(1) of P.L. 85-866).*

(b) Rules Relating to General Definition.—For purposes of this section—

(1) The terms "brother" and "sister" include a brother or sister by the halfblood.

(2) In determining whether any of the relationships specified in subsection (a) or paragraph (1) of this subsection exists, a legally adopted child of an individual (and a child who is a member of an individual's household, if placed with such individual by an authorized placement agency for legal adoption by such individual), or a foster child of an individual (if such child satisfies the requirements of subsection (a)(9) with respect to such individual), shall be treated as a child of such individual by blood.

Last amendment.—Sec. 152(b)(2) appears above as amended by Sec. 912(a) of Public Law 91-172, Dec. 30, 1969, effective (Sec. 912(b) of P.L. 91-172) with respect to taxable years beginning after Dec. 31, 1969.

Prior amendment.—Sec. 152(b)(2) was previously amended by Sec. [1](a) of Public Law 86-376, Sept. 23, 1959, effective (Sec. [1](b) of P.L. 86-376) for taxable years beginning after Dec. 31, 1958, Sec. 152(b)(2) as so amended is in P-H Cumulative Changes.

(3) The term "dependent" does not include any individual who is not a citizen or national of the United States unless such individual is a resident of the United States or of a country contiguous to the United States. The preceding seentence shall not exclude from the definition of "dependent" any child of the taxpayer legally adopted by him, if, for the taxable year of the taxpayer, the child has as his principal place of abode the home of the taxpayer and is a member of the taxpayer's household, and if the taxpayer is a citizen or national of the United States.

Prior amendments.—Sec. 152(b)(3) was previously amended by the following:

Sec. [1](a) of Public Law 92-580, Oct. 27, 1972, effective (Sec. [1](c) of P.L. 92-580) with respect to taxable years beginning after Dec. 31, 1971.*

Sec. 4(b) of Public Law 85-866, Sept. 2, 1958, effective (Sec. 4(d) of P.L. 85-866) for taxable years beginning after Dec. 31, 1957.*

Sec. 2 of Public Law 333, Aug. 9, 1955 (qualified effective date rule in Sec. 3(b) of P.L. 333).*

*Sec. 152(a) as so amended is in P-H Cumulative Changes.

Reproduced from the *Prentice-Hall Federal Taxes* Service (1983 edition) with the permission of the publisher.

Figure 11-2

Employment-Related Expenses

Employment related expenses under Regulation 1.44A(c), are considered as such only if they are incurred to allow the taxpayer (and spouse) to be gainfully employed or to actively search for gainful employment. They are not work related merely because they were incurred while the taxpayer was working.

NOTE:

A spouse is considered to have worked if he or she was a full-time student during each of five months during the year, or was physically or mentally incapacitated.

Work-related expenses include those which were expended to provide for the well-being and protection of a qualifying individual—and are generally considered to include care and household services. The latter cannot be included without the former.

Such care can qualify for the credit only if provided:

1. For a child under 15 years of age and/or a disabled dependent *within* a qualifying household, or

2. For a child under 15 years of age *outside* of the home—not for a disabled dependent.

CAUTION:

> Beginning in 1982, expenses incurred for the care of both types of individual *outside the home* qualify for the credit provided that such individuals spend at least eight hours a day in the taxpayer's household.

Household care expenses include salaries of baby sitters, maids, cooks, housekeepers, and nurses who provide care in the home. Gardeners and chauffeurs do not qualify. A relative may be employed provided he or she is neither a dependent nor a taxpayer's child who is under 19 years of age.

Salaries include related employment taxes, cost of meals, lodging, and medical services as given to the employee.

IMPORTANT:

> Child care expenses may also include the cost of nursery schools and such, outside the home, even if some portion of the expense has to do with educational purposes. Once a child reaches first grade, however, this type of expense no longer qualifies for the credit.

Limitations on Amount of Credit (Regulation 1.44A(2)(a))

There are two types of limitations: (1) those applicable to a *dollar* amount and (2) those applicable to an *earned income* amount.

Annual dollar limit. Work related expenses may be taken into account in computing the credit only to the extent that they do not exceed:

1. $2,000 for the care of one qualifying individual ($2,400 beginning in 1982).
2. $4,000 for the care of two or more ($4,800 beginning in 1982).

The earned income limitation. Work-related expenses may be considered only to the extent they do not exceed:

1. An individual taxpayer's earned income for the year, or
2. A married taxpayer's earned income of that of his or her spouse, whichever is the lower.

NOTE:

> In considering the earned income limitation, a spouse who is a full-time student or disabled is considered to have earned $166 a month, if there is one qualifying dependent in the home—or $333 a month if there are two or more ($200 and $400 beginning in 1982).

The credit is computed by using Form 2441. It will be the lesser of 20 percent of the Annual Dollar Limit (for a maximum of $800)—or 20 percent of the Respective Earned Income Limitation. For example, if the earned income of a disabled spouse was considered to be $3,996 (12 × $333) the final allowable credit would amount to $799.

Beginning in 1982 the credit increases. If the adjusted gross income is $10,000 or less, an individual's credit is 30 percent of his or her employment-related expenses. This phases downward, however, by 1 percent for each $2,000 of adjusted gross income, or fraction thereof, in excess of $10,000, but never lower than 20 percent.

CAUTION:

The child and dependent care credit cannot be used to produce a refund. It is allowable only to the extent that it does not exceed the tax due after such tax has been reduced by the following:

Foreign Tax Credits

Credit for the Elderly

Investment Credit

WIN Credit

Political Contribution Credit

Employment Taxes

If a taxpayer employs a household employee—and if such a worker earns $50 or more during a calendar quarter—this individual's earnings are subject to social security taxes. Both the employer and the employee must contribute 50 percent of the required percentage.

As mentioned in the first section of this chapter, such wages are also subject to federal unemployment taxes and other employment tax considerations.

Exclusion for Dependent Care Assistance to Employees

Under the Economic Recovery Tax Act of 1981, employees may exclude from income amounts paid or incurred by their employers for furnishing dependent care assistance to them under a dependent care assistance program.

IMPORTANT:

For purposes of this new assistance exclusion, "employees" include self-employed individuals (sole proprietors and partners). A sole proprietor is treated as his own employer. A partnership is treated as the partners' employer.

11.5 HANDLING THE AUDIT

If it appears that the child and dependent care credit will be at issue, carefully review Sections 11.2 and 11.3 of this chapter.

Locate every possible answer which might satisfy questions raised in these book sections—and which might become the subject of an examiner's inquiries.

Recompute all limitation and qualfication tests. Substantiate

- Ages of dependent children.
- Custodial dates involved.
- Disability status of dependents or spouse.
- Student status of spouse, etc.
- Divorce or legal separation dates.
- Qualifying household expenses. (If there is a controversy between divorced persons as to which one paid more than 50 percent, be sure that this problem is solved before date of audit.)
- Wages and other costs attendant on care services.

Prepare a proper Form 2441 if one was not filed.

CAUTION:

> Review the status of in-home employees for employment tax considerations. If proper forms were not filed, prepare them—but for one year only. The IRS examiner might not request those for other years, particularly if the amount due is inconsequential.

11.6 PERTINENT COURT DECISIONS—PRO AND CON

Pro
Carol Janice and John Charles Freeman
(TC Memo 1979 - 288)

Findings of Fact

In 1975 petitioners were legally married and maintained a household for the entire year. Carol was gainfully employed. John spent the year in jail where he worked 56 hours a week to reduce his sentence.

The Freemans have a son who in 1975 was of preschool age. They paid $1,034 to The Cliff Temple Baptist Church for child care.

The IRS, using Code Section 214(e), claimed that both spouses were not gainfully employed—and therefore were not entitled to a child-care deduction. The Service relied on the fact that John did not receive compensation for his work to support its position that he was not gainfully employed.

Opinion

The court held that compensation need not be in the form of cash—that the petitioner was not required to work while incarcerated—and that nothing can be more valuable than working for one's freedom. Held for the petitioner! He was gainfully employed.

Con
Rodney A. and Dorothy M. Buras
(TC Memo 1977 - 325)

Findings of Fact

Petitioners were both gainfully employed. During the years in question Dorothy's mother (Josephine Landry) resided in their household but did not contribute toward household expenses, even though she had income of some $2,000 a year.

Since she was in ill health, the taxpayers employed a person one day a week to clean Mrs. Landry's room and to do odd jobs around the house.

The taxpayers claimed her as an exemption and deducted $240 for dependent care in one of the years at issue.

Opinion

The court noted that the petitioners did not call Mrs. Landry as a witness—because of her bad health and the possibility that she would be a hostile witness. No evidence was introduced as to who paid her medical bills. The taxpayers did not make a diligent effort to prove that they contributed more than one-half of Mrs. Landry's support and, consequently, did not reach first base in establishing her as a qualifying individual under Section 214(b)(1). Nor was any evidence produced to the effect that the alleged dependent was physically or mentally incapable of caring for herself.

Dependent care deduction denied.

11.7 RELEVANT CODE AND REGULATION SECTIONS, PLUS PUBLICATION AND FORM

Code

Section	44A	Expenses for Household and Dependent Care Services Necessary for Gainful Employment
	151(e)	Additional Exemptions for Dependents
	152	Dependent Defined

Regulations

Section	1.44A-1	Expenses for Household and Dependent Care Services Necessary for Gainful Employment
	1.44A-1(a)(2)	In General
	1.44A-1(b)	Qualifying Individual
	1.44A-1(c)	Employment Related Expenses
	1.44A-1(d)	Maintenance of Household
	1.44A-2(a)	Annual Dollar Limit on Amount Creditable

Publication

503	Child and Disabled Dependent Care

Form Required

2441	Credit for Child and Dependent Care Expenses

11.8 APPLICABLE IRS MANUAL REFERENCES (INVESTIGATIVE TECHNIQUES)

Audit Manual Supplement

40 RDD-75	Child and Dependent Care Study

Standard Explanations Handbook

MT 428(11)-14	Child and Dependent Care

Mail Questionnaire

Form 4746	Expenses for Household and Dependent Care Services

Form 6451   Income Received for Child and Dependent Care Services and Payments by
                   Employers of Social Security Tax

Material from the Manual has been incorporated into this chapter. The Form 4746 Questionnaire will probably arrive from the IRS in instances where Form 2441 was not filed with a return.

Sale of a Residence
(Sections 1034 and 121)

12

12.1 IDENTIFYING THE PROBLEM

Ownership of a home is commonly known as the All-American Tax Shelter—and it is just that. Over the years, most dwellings appreciate substantially in value, while their owners are not paying rent but are realizing good tax advantages through use of such itemized deductions as mortgage interest and real estate taxes. Additionally, gain on sale of a home or homes can be deferred indefinitely.

Under the following two Code sections, Congress has supplied the means whereby a home owner can—with careful planning—provide himself or herself with a retirement annuity, the cost of which can have been realized from completely tax-free dollar accumulations.

Section 1034 -Rollover of Gain on Sale of Principal Residence
Section 121 -One-time Exclusion of Gain from Sale of Principal Residence by Individual Who Has Attained Age 55

The taxpayer simply pays a higher price for each succeeding residence (not difficult these days)—deferring the gain each time—until he or she reaches 55 years of age. At this point the residence can be sold with no taxes being paid on the gain, because of the $125,000 ($62,500 in the case of married filing separately) one-time exclusion.

NOTE:

If any profit still remains, it can be invested in a more modest principal residence such as a condominium, with the excess gain still being deferred (Regulation 1.121-5(g)).

The large, tax-free residual from the sale can then, of course, be used to invest in any desired fashion to produce retirement income.

Basic rules: In summary, Sections 1034 and 121 allow a taxpayer to defer gain on sale of a principal residence or (in the case of those 55 or older) to exclude all or part of the gain from taxation. Requirements are these:

Deferral of Gain

1. New principal residence must be purchased within 24 months before or 24 months after sale of the old.
2. Construction of new principal residence must begin before or within 24 months of the sale of the old *and* the new home must be occupied not later than 2 years from date old residence was sold.

$125,000 Exclusion of Gain

1. Old principal residence must have been utilized as a principal residence for at least 3 years during the 5-year period ending on date of sale.
2. *Neither* spouse may have previously elected the $125,000 exclusion.

WARNING:

Deferral of gain on sale of principal residence is mandatory. Such a deferral is merely the reduction of the basis of a new property by the untaxed gain on the sale of the old. Form 2119 (Sale or Exchange of Principal Residence) should be completed and filed with the appropriate tax return.

Solving Two Sets of Problems

In utilizing the advantages of Sections 1034 and 121, there are two sets of completely different problems:

1. Satisfying the Internal Revenue Service
2. Satisfying the taxpayer's personal goals

From the IRS viewpoint the data contained on Form 2119 (Sale or Exchange of Principal Residence) will not be considered proof of anything. The government will treat this document as merely a worksheet and will require substantiation for all information contained thereon. In addition, its agents will want to delve into such issues as home-office use and casualty-loss reduction of basis

Personal considerations. To a greater degree than for probably any other tax matter, this "Sale of a Principal Residence" can be traumatic. It normally required deep, life-affecting personal decisions. To most taxpayers, the buying or selling of a home is usually the largest, most important transaction of their lives—not only in a total value sense, but from a net, after-taxes overlook. *Example:*

Aldea and Bill are 55 years of age. They are widowed and are considering marriage to each other. Each owns a principal residence that has substantially increased in value. They are in a quandary.

1. Before marriage, should they sell hers—or his?
2. Before marriage, should they sell both homes, then buy another after marriage?
3. Should they get married—live in one—rent one—and then decide?

CRITICAL:

Sentimental considerations aside, (2) is by far the most attractive option. Following this idea (deceased spouses qualifying), *each* could elect the $125,000 once-in-a-lifetime exclusion. After marriage, the extra $125,000 would not have to be recaptured by either, jointly or otherwise.

Following (1) (sale before marriage), the spouse who sold would become "tainted" for life. The exclusion would not only be unavailable to this individual thereafter, but to anyone whom he or she marries in the future.

Following (3) (sale of both homes) would result in loss of one property as a principal residence.

Out-of-pocket loss under (1) or (3) would be the tax on $125,000 of capital gains.

Personal considerations such as these continue for all sorts of human possibilities—divorce, gifts, choice of neighborhood, etc. Section 12.4 of this chapter will discuss the matter further.

12.2 HOW THE IRS SEES THE ISSUE

Unlike many bristly areas of taxation, "Sale of Residence" at a gain does not usually cause anyone in the Service to become overly aggressive. As concerns the most difficult phase—establishing the original basis for older, longer-held homes—examiners appear to be reasonable indeed. They will, however, require all of the formal substantiation that is available.

After this beginning, the Service sees the issue as one of factual realities and will proceed in a normal investigative manner to examine all facets of the case. the IRS examiner, therefore, will want to discuss the ramifications of

- Adherence to legal time requirements for:
  Years of ownership
  Years of principal residency
  Repurchase period
  Period for building a new home
- Qualification of home as a "principal residence"
- Capital additions which might have altered the original basis
- Prior sales of residential property which would affect the basis of the home in question
- Correct handling of casualty-loss deductions (if existent) when arriving at adjusted basis
- Proper division of values and expense of sale in situations where the residence was partially rented or used as a home office, including:

  Section 1231 considerations (Property Used in the Trade or Business and Involuntary Conversions)
  Sale of Section 1245 property (Gain from Disposition of Certain Depreciable Property)
  Sale of Section 1250 property (Gain from Dispositions of Certain Depreciable Realty) as concerns recovery of accelerated depreciation excess over straight-line method.

12.3 FACTORS WHICH THE IRS CONSIDERS WHEN MAKING ITS AUDIT DECISION

In an examination where the once-in-a-lifetime, $125,000 exclusion of gain has been elected, the IRS will bring into play a generally unpublicized tool.

RED FLAG:

Special Examination Feature: known as **LTEX**, this investigative tool allows an auditor to determine whether a taxpayer, or spouse, has *ever* made the $125,000 exclusion election. Such information is maintained from the date of election by the taxpayer to his or her date of death, no matter the number of divorces or deceased spouses involved. Once "tainted" by this $125,000 election, neither the taxpayer nor his or her spouse may ever use its generosity again (Section 121(c)).

After having made this exclusion determination, the examining officer will want to be satisfied that the requirements of Section 1034 (Rollover of Gain on Sale of Principal Residence) have been met. In so doing, the IRS person will generally cover the points as previously set forth in 12.2, plus such offshoot questions as

1. Since Schedule D lists the profitable sale of a residence, why is Form 2119 missing? (Deferral of gain is mandatory if the sale qualifies under Section 1034 rollover rules.

2. Question 1(c) on Form 2119 has not been answered: "Have you ever claimed credit for purchase or construction of a new principal residence?" (If the answer is "Yes," the taxpayer may be required to file Form 5405 (Recapture of Credit for Purchase or Construction of New Principal Residence) for the purpose of recapturing such a credit.)

3. Are capital expenditures included in the "basis of property"? If so, of what do they consist? (Here, the IRS is searching for repair items which should have been classed as personal expenses—and not added to value of dwelling. Receipted bills will be requested, or invoices and cancelled remittances. Checks alone will usually not suffice.)

4. Was the value of personal labor included in capital improvement costs? (If so, it should not have been.)

5. Particularly if residence is in a resort area, was it rented at any time? (Auditor may be looking for unreported income—application of Section 1231 concerning sale of property used in a trade or business—or violations of Section 280A (Vacation Homes and Other Dwelling Units). For a discussion of the latter, see Chapter 7 of this book.

In general, an examiner will request proof of all items on Form 2119 and/or Form 5405 as the case may be. If the period-of-residency limitation was not met because of a job-related move (Section 1034(d)), the auditor will request proof that the move was necessary. See Chapter 10 for further details concerning moving expenses.

KNOW THIS ALSO:

The Service has begun selecting returns which indicate a change of address in situations where real estate taxes were deducted and where no Form 2119 was filed. They are looking, of course, for unreported gains on sales of residences.

In placing the matter on its "Prime-Issue" list (no. 0167.02-04) the IRS shows its special interest in the following situation.

Whether a taxpayer who ceases to use a property as residential property and immediately offers it for sale, without attempting to rent the property, is entitled to deductions for depreciation and maintenance during the period prior to sale.

The Service says that such expenses are not deductible. Obviously, then, the ex-residence should be put up for sale *and/or* rent, It can, after all, be rented for a period of up to two years if it had been a principal residence for the previous five without loss of deferral rights.

BUT BE CAREFUL:

> **Rev. Ruling 82-26 (IRB 1982-6) quotes Rev. Rul. 59-72 as holding that "where all the facts and circumstances indicate that property sold by a taxpayer was used by the taxpayer as the taxpayer's principal residence, the taxpayer will be entitled to relief provided for by Section 1034 of the Code, notwithstanding the fact that the taxpayer temporarily rented out the residence prior to its sale.** *Thus the Service looks to the use of the property at the time of sale."*

12.4 CONSIDERATIONS WHEN PREPARING THE RETURN

Here are some manipulative thoughts which might help in making advantageous personal decisions—

When utilizing Section 121 to exclude gain, the maximum benefit is $125,000. This does not mean, however, that unused portions can be carried forward.

WARNING:

> **The exclusion can be used only once in a lifetime—either to cover $1,000 or $100,000 or $125,000, i.e., if gain is $40,000 and the exclusion is elected, the balance of $85,000 is lost forever.**

This is not to say that the exclusion should not be taken. Personal situations should govern. If the taxpayer is moving into an inexpensive vacation home where he or she intends to remain—and this person's health is good—so that eventually the principal residence will lose its status as such if not sold, then the election should be made to take the exclusion.

If an individual is undecided as to whether he or she should elect the $125,000 exclusion, the decision can be postponed for up to 24 months by attaching a statement to the tax return for the year of sale. Gain should be noted, along with the notation to the effect that a replacement residence has not yet been purchased.

When persons over 54 are contemplating marriage, a determination should be made as to whether one spouse is "tainted" in the exclusion sense. If the situation exists, the other potential spouse should consider whether to sell *before* the nuptial ceremony. Marriage to a person who has already used the exclusion eliminates the election for both individuals thereafter—so long as they remain married to each other. Apparently, the stigma disappears from the untainted person, however, if a divorce occurs.

To defer gain, the proceeds of a sale must be reinvested, but the funds need not necessarily be identical. For example, a taxpayer may use $10,000 of the gain to purchase a trip around the world—then increase the mortgage on the new residence by this amount. The only requirement is that the total purchase price of the replacement property include the untaxed gain.

A principal residence may be a boat. Therefore, should a taxpayer wish to reside in a southern climate aboard a yacht (as his or her principal residence), Section 1034 or 121 may be utilized.

Divorce considerations can be tricky. Since both spouses must elect to take the exclusion, a nonowner spouse, obviously, should not agree since this would cause such a person to become "tainted," to no tax advantage.

Revocation of election. Should personal problems or situations change a married couple's lifestyle—and should they wish to revoke their election—they may do so by filing a statement with the District Director where the election was filed. However, see Regulation 1.121-4(c) for "Manner of Revoking Election."

Purchase of more than one residence within two years. If during the replacement period an individual acquires more than one residence, only the last one qualifies for deferral of the gain. Gain on sale of the other temporary homes is taxed—and possibly at "short-term" rates.

IMPORTANT EXCEPTION:

Job-related moves are an exception to this rule. If the taxpayer can meet the requirements of Section 217 (Moving Expenses) then both houses qualify for the deferral of gain.

If a taxpayer rents an apartment and at the same time owns an appreciated home—and if such a person contemplates selling the property at some future date—he or she should move into the home so as to cause it to qualify as principal residence before selling. As it stands, the rented property is the principal residence.

Technical Advisories for Deferring or Eliminating Gain on Sale of a Principal Residence

There are, of course, a number of rules to follow in deferring or eliminating the gain on sale of a principal residence. Some of the most important will be discussed here.

Definition of principal residence. According to Regulation 1.1034-1, a principal residence is the home in which a person lives. If an individual owns more than one home, then the principal residence is the one in which he or she lived during the majority of the time. Such a residence presumably includes all contiguous acreage that is utilized for living purposes such as for recreation, personal gardening, or for the purpose of grazing personally-utilized livestock or riding horses—or, for that matter, for just plain walking and enjoying.

What about ownership of a nonworking ranch with a principal residence in the middle of 5,000 acres??? The purpose for which it was bought and actual use of the land would probably govern. If the property was purchased for investment *and residency,* profit on most of the land would not be likely to qualify for deferment or exclusion.

Definition of "Sale" includes (1) an exchange of a residence for other property, (2) a trade-in of an old home for another, and (3) seizure of a home through requisition or condemnation or threat or imminence thereof (Section 1034(i)).

Definition of "Purchase" includes an acquisition of a residence through exchange, construction, or partial construction.

The building time limit, as previously stated, must be strictly adhered to. The new residence must be completed—and the taxpayer moved in—before the expiration of two years following sale of old principal residence. This rule applies, even if the delay lies with the contractor.

SUGGESTION:

Place a paragraph in the building contract to the effect that the taxpayer will be indemnified against loss should the building not be completed on time.

Upon death of a taxpayer the surviving spouse will still be entitled to deferment or exclusion of gain, provided that:

1. The deceased spouse met the occupancy requirements, and
2. The surviving spouse (in using Section 121 for the exclusion) is at least 55 years of age and has not remarried.

Gain on sale of a residence as a tax preference item. At one time such a sale was considered a tax-preference item. It no longer is.

How to make the Section 212 (Rollover of Gain) election. The election under Section 121(a) is made by attaching a statement to the tax return for the year in which the sale was made. Required data is set forth in Regulation 1.121-4(b) which is reproduced below as Figure 12-1.

(b) *Manner of making election.* The election under section 121 (a) shall be made in a statement signed by the taxpayer and (where required) by his spouse and attached to the taxpayer's income tax return, when filed, for the taxable year during which the sale or exchange of his residence occurs (see Form 2119 and the accompanying instructions). The statement shall indicate that the taxpayer elects to exclude from his gross income for such year so much of the gain realized on such sale or exchange as may be excluded under section 121. The statement shall also show—

(1) The adjusted basis of the residence as of the date of disposition;

(2) The date of its acquisition;

(3) The date of its disposition;

(4) The names and social security numbers of the owners of the residence as of the date of sale, the form of such ownership, and the age and marital status (as determinued under paragraph (f) of §1.121-5) of such owner or owners at the time of the sale:

(5) The duration of any absences (other than vacation or other seasonal absence) by such owner or owners during the 5 years (8 years under the transitional rule) preceding the sale; and

(6) Whether any such owner or owners have previously made an election under section 121 (a), the date of such election, the taxable year with respect to which such election was made, the district director with whom such election was filed, and, if such election has been revoked, the date of such revocation.

Figure 12-1

Installment sale reporting of gain in excess of the $125,000 exclusion is proper, if the requirements of the Installment Sales Revision Act of 1980 and Section 453 (Installment Method) of the Code can be met.

Don't overlook this excellent tax-saving possibility. A married couple is retiring. Both are over 65. Their taxable income will be sharply reduced. They sell their principal residence at a profit of $140,000 and retain a five-year first mortgage in the amount of $15,000.

Under Section 1202 (Deduction for Capital Gains) 60 percent of the profit (after exclusion) or $9,000 is nontaxable. The remaining $6,000 of taxable gain, when paid over five years, would probably generate little, if any, additional taxes.

Residence used partially for business. Only gain on the portion of the building which qualifies as a principal residence can realize the benefits of Sections 1034 or 121. The sale must be treated as two sales—one governed by either of the above sections—one by Section 1231 (Property Used in the Trade or Business and Involuntary Conversion).

NOTE, HOWEVER:

Chapter 8 (Home Office) contains a method for relief from this regulation.

Statute of Limitations, as pertains to sale of a residence, does not begin to run until the IRS receives a written notification as required by Regulation 1.1034-1(i). (See Figure 12-2.)

(i) *Statute of limitations.*(1) Whenever a taxpayer sells property used as his principal residence at a gain, the statute period prescribed in section 6501(a) for the assessment of a deficiency attributable to any part of such gain shall not expire prior to the expiration three years from the date of receipt, by the district director with whom the return was filed for the taxable year or years in which the gain from the sale of the old residence was realized (section 1034(j)), of a written notice from the taxpayer of—

(i) The taxpayer's cost of purchasing the new residence which the taxpayer claims results in nonrecognition of any part of such gain.

(ii) The taxpayer's intention not to purchase a new residence within the period when such a purchase will result in nonrecognition of any part of such gain, or

(iii) The taxpayer's failure to make such a purchase within such period. Any gain from the sale of the old residence which is required to be recognized shall be included in gross income for the taxable year or years in which such gain was realized. Any deficinecy attributable to any portion of such gain may be assessed before the expiration of the 3-year period described in this paragraph, notwithstanding the provisions of any law or rule of law which might otherwise bar such assessment.

(2) The notification required by the preceding subparagraph shall contain all pertinent details in connection with the sale of the old residence and, where applicable, the purchase price of the new residence. The notification shall be in the form of a written statement and shall be accompanied, where appropriate, by an amended return for the year in which the gain from the sale of the old residence was realized, in order to reflect the inclusion in gross income for that year of gain required to be recognized in connection with such sale.

Figure 12-2

For computation of gain on sale of residence, see the following section, 12.5.

12.5 HANDLING THE AUDIT

An Internal Revenue auditor will begin with Form 2119 and look for verification of its amounts. It is, therefore, important that a practitioner or taxpayer recompute the form, collecting all available substantiation as the job progresses.

Worksheets for Substantiating Form 2119. Review Lines 1 and 2 for accuracy, then proceed to Lines 3, 4, 6, and 10 where the meat of the matter lies. Use worksheets and check lists of the type illustrated in Figure 12-3.

Line 3. Selling price of residence is generally the amount realized, less selling expenses. See suggested Worksheet A (Figure 12-3).

Line 4. Expense of sale. See checklist on Worksheet A.

Line 6. Basis of residence sold. The adjusted basis is usually cost plus, or minus, items as indicated on Worksheet B (Figure 12-4). Not all principal residences are purchased. The following chart will help in determining bases for those which are not:

Property Acquired	Basis
For services rendered	Agreed-upon price or fair market value (FMV)
Through gift	Generally, donor's adjusted basis—but see Publication 551 (Basis of Assets)

Property Acquired	Basis
Through inheritance	FMV at date of decedent's death, or the later alternative valuation date, if chosen for federal estate tax purposes.

Worksheet A
Form 2119—Sale or Exchange of Principal Residence
Line 3—Selling Price of Residence

Total Received:

Money
Notes Receivable
Mortgage Held by Seller
Mortgage Assumed by Buyer
Condemnation Election
Other Property (FMV)
Other Consideration (FMV)   _____   _____
   Total Selling Price

Line 4—Expenses of Sale

Allowable Expenses:

Commissions
Legal Fees
Advertising
Appraisal Fees
Escrow Fees
Maps
Surveys
Mortgage Satisfaction Fees
"Points" or Loan Processing Fees
Recording Fees
Title Abstract Fees
*State Transfer Taxes
Other   _____   _____

   Total Expenses
Amount Realized (Line 4)   _____

*Utilize only where not applied to better advantage in itemized deductions.

Figure 12-3

Line 10, cost of new residence, includes capital amounts expended within the 36-month (or 42-month for new construction) replacement period—or within 48 months after July 20, 1981.

The basis also includes debts to which the property is subject and the face amount of the taxpayer's notes or other liabilities such as purchase money mortgages or deeds of trust—plus buying expenses, much the same type as for "Sale of a Residence" (Figure 12-3).

Worksheet B
Form 2119—Sale or Exchange of Principal Residence
Line 6—Basis of Residence Sold

Cost   _____

Plus: Expenses of purchase, such as brokerage commissions, legal fees, etc.
      Cost of capital improvements
      Restoration expenditures after casualty loss
      Capital expenditures for installation of energy conservation or
      renewal sources   _____

Less: Any allowable depreciation
      Any deductible casualty loss, plus insurance recovery
      Energy credits, if previously allowed
      Nontaxable gain on sale of a previous residence   _____

Basis of residence sold (Line 6)   _____

Figure 12-4

CAUTION:

The once-in-a-lifetime $125,000 exclusion, **because of its tremendous possibilities, will be closely examined by the IRS. Make sure that all previously mentioned requirements, in this regard, have been met—then check to determine whether the taxpayer could have utilized Section 1034 along with 121 to defer any residual gain, but did not. He or she still may have time to make this election and collect a refund.**

How to Establish Original Basis for Older Homes

Frequently, original homes are sold for the first time. Purchase records have long been lost. Memories fade. Possibly the property was inherited.

The IRS, nevertheless, will want to know how this beginning valuation was arrived at. If the taxpayer just guessed, when filing his or her return some digging is in order. In my experience, the Service has been reasonable in this respect—but not careless.

Checklist for locating documentation: Do everything possible to locate some documentation. Take these steps in order:

- Begin with appropriate public real estate records (whether state, county, or municipal). Secure a copy of the legal instrument through which the taxpayer acquired title to his residence. Goverment Excise Tax regulations, at one time, required that Documentary Stamps be purchased and affixed to all Deeds of Conveyance. Since the amount of such stamps was determined by the value of the transaction, old property costs can easily be ascertained wherever the stamp law applied.

- Contact the law firm which prepared the deed and handled the title transfer. Possibly their files will contain a settlement sheet, or other helpful data.

- Search old real estate Grand Lists or other such tax records which will produce at least assessed valuations.

- Contact zoning control offices for information as to valuations of newly constructed buildings, or improvements.

- Bank records usually contain property valuations along with mortgage data—also information as to capital improvements, old insurance coverage, etc.

- Attempts should be made to locate appropriate gift or estate tax returns, divorce papers, appraisals, and old insurance policies.

- A practitioner should sit down with the taxpayer and spouse. Do some brainstorming. List dates and amounts, names of contractors, improvements made, and the like.

IMPORTANT:

A Revenue person will be much more likely to accept an estimate if it was clearly arrived at through obvious effort rather than through a simple guess.

12.6 PERTINENT COURT DECISIONS—PRO AND CON

Pro

(Rev. Rul. 75-238, 1975-1 CB 257)

Findings of Fact

Prior to their marriage in January of 1975, A and B each owned a principal residence.

In March of 1975 the couple purchased and occupied a new home. Each contributed one-half of the purchase price, taking joint title to the property.

A and B thereafter both sold their old residences at a gain. Can these gains be deferred?

Opinion

Reference is made to Rev. Rul. 74-250 1974-1 CB 202 which holds that the nonrecognition provisions of Section 1034(a) apply separately to the gains realized by a husband and wife from the sale of their single principal residence under circumstances in which they agreed to live apart and separately purchased and occupied replacement principal residences.

Held that no recognition of gain for either A or B was required.

Con
Harry and Martha Lokan (TC Memo 1979-380)

Findings of Fact

In April 1973, while residing in a principal residence that they owned in Clearwater, Florida, the petitioners took out a first mortgage on this property and with the proceeds purchased 7½ acres of land in New Port Richey, Florida, for $20,500 (approx. $2,733 per acre).

In May of 1973 they began construction of a new home on their new acreage. In November of 1973 they sold their old residence at a gain of $19,688.

In December of 1973 they purchased a trailer for $2,109 and moved it to their New Port Richey property where they entered residence. Cost of moving and establishing trailer home—$2,636. This made their total new home cost $4,745, exclusive of land.

The petitioners, at that time, were the parents of four children. Although Harry had been working on the new home, it was far from finished. They quickly completed one bedroom and a bath so that three of the children could sleep in the new residence while the balance of the family slept in the trailer, which was located nearby.

Within 6 months, two of the older children moved back to Clearwater. The other child remained in the house until it was substantially completed in September of 1976.

In 1974 and 1975 petitioners used six acres of their New Port Richey land in the business of farming.

The taxpayers did not report any realized gain from the sale of their old principal residence.

The IRS claimed that the petitioners did not meet the requirements of Section 1034 and assessed additional taxes.

Petitioners claimed that the use of both trailer and new home should be considered one residence under the circumstances.

Opinion

Neither petitioner lived in the building that was to be their new residence within the required 18 months. As was clearly noted in Bayley v. Comm. 35 TC 288,295 (1960) "Used as a principal residence" means physical occupancy. The trailer was their real, new, principal residence until September of 1976.

In determining its cost, only 1½ acre of land should be considered, since 6 acres were utilized in the business of farming. Regulation 1.1034-1(c)(3)(ii) provides in part that if a new residence is used only partially for residential purposes, only so much of its cost as is allocable to the home portion may be counted as cost of purchasing the new residence.

Held for the government.

12.7 RELEVANT CODE AND REGULATION SECTIONS, PLUS PUBLICATIONS

Code

Section	121	One-time Exclusion of Gain from Sale of Principal Residency by Individual Who Has Attained Age 55
	121(a)	General Rule
	121(c)	Election
	217	Moving Expenses
	280A	Disallowance of Certain Expenses in Connection with Business Use of Home, Rental of Vacation Homes, etc.
	453	Installment Method
	1034	Rollover of Gain on Sale of Principal Residence
	1034(d)	Limitation
	1231	Property Used in the Trade or Business and Involuntary Conversions
	1202	Deduction for Capital Gains

Regulations

Section	1.121-1	Gain from Sale or Exchange of Residence of Individual Who Has Attained Age 55

1.121-1(c)	Ownership and Use
1.121-4(b)	Manner of Making Election
1.121-4(c)	Manner of Revoking Election
1.1034-1	Sale or Exchange of Residence
1.1034-1(a)	Nonrecognition of Gain; General Statement
1.1034-1(i)	Statute of Limitations

Publications

| 523 | Tax Information on Selling Your Home |
| 551 | Basis of Assets |

12.8 APPLICABLE IRS MANUAL REFERENCES (INVESTIGATIVE TECHNIQUES)

Audit Technique Handbook

| MT 4231-24 | Gains and Losses from Sale or Exchange of Property |

Tax Audit Guidelines

| MT 4233-1 | Capital Gains and Losses |

Audit

| MT 4234-5 | Gains and Losses from Sale or Exchange of Property |

Material from the above Manual Sections has been incorporated into this chapter.

Income Tax

| MT 4200-412 426(32) | Lifetime Gain on Sale of Personal Residence (LTEX) |

Bribes, Illegal Payments, and Kickbacks

13

(Section 162(c))

13.1 IDENTIFYING THE PROBLEM

Today's marketplace is cluttered with bribes, illegal payments, kickbacks, rebates, volume discounts, and incentive grants. Call them what you will, they all constitute some sort of a payout to drum up business. The difficulty is in determining which of these are deductible and which are not.

Individuals operating outside the law have no difficulty with this question. A payment to a local police official so that a floating crap game can circulate unmolested is clearly illegal and nondeductible, but who cares? The operator reports little of his true income, if any; the police official reports none of his, since to do so would jeopardize his job.

In the so-called straight world, however, things are not so clear cut. Here's a quick list of questions that will set forth most of the problems facing legitimate business people:

1. What constitutes nondeductible illegal payments? (Some are illegal but nevertheless deductible, if the governing state laws are not generally enforced.)

2. What does "generally enforced" mean?

3. Which kickbacks enter the category of "common practice in the trade" and thus become immune to the nondeductible stigma?

4. Do rebates go beyond the pale because they are given in merchandise, which circumvents price-control laws?

5. Are payments to employees, to influence employers' actions, deductible commissions, or referral fees, or what?

6. When is commercial bribery not considered a crime?

7. If payments are made to foreign officials to further the business ends of a taxpayer, are such deductible if they violate only the laws of the purchasing country?

8. What's the kickback or rebate situation under Medicare and Medicaid?

9. Must Forms 1099 NEC (Non-Employee Compensation) be filed with the IRS to cover kickbacks and other such payments?

10. Who has the burden of proving that payments are legal or illegal?

Answers are fairly well provided in Code Section 162(c), included here as Figure 13-1. Further details will follow in Section 13.4 of this chapter.

(c) Illegal Bribes, Kickbacks, and Other Payments.—

Last amendment.—Heading of Sec. 162(c) appears above as amended by Sec. 310(a)(2) of Public Law 92-178, Dec. 10, 1971, effective (Sec. 310(b) of P.L. 92-178) with respect to payments after Dec. 30, 1969. Heading of Sec. 162(c) as it read before this amendment is in P-H Cumulative Changes.

(1) Illegal payments to government officials or employees.—No deduction shall be allowed under subsection (a) for any payment made, directly or indirectly, to an official or employee of any government, or of any agency or instrumentality of any government, if the payment constitutes an illegal bribe or kickback or, if the payment is to an official or employee of a foreign government, the payment is unlawful under the Foreign Corrupt Practices Act of 1977. The burden of proof in respect of the issue, for the purposes of this paragraph, as to whether a payment constitutes an illegal bribe or kickback (or is unlawful under the Foreign Corrupt Practices Act of 1977) shall be upon the Secretary to the same extent as he bears the burden of proof under section 7454 (concerning the burden of proof when the issue relates to fraud).

Last amendment.—Sec. 162(c)(1) (Formerly (c)) appears above as amended by Sec. 288(a) of Public Law 97-248, Sept. 3, 1982, effective (Sec. 288 (c) of P.L. 97-248) for payments made after Sept. 3, 1982.

Prior amendment.—Sec. 162(c)(1) (formerly (c)) was previously redesignated and amended by Sec. 902(b) of Public Law 91-172, Dec. 30, 1969 (qualified effective date rule in Sec. 902(c) of P.L. 91-172). Sec. 162(c)(1) (formerly (c)) as so amended is in P-H Cumulative Changes.

Addition.—Sec. 162(c)(1) (formerly (c)) was added by Sec. 5(a) of Public Law 85-866, Sept. 2, 1958 (qualified effective date rule in Sec. 5(b) of P.L. 85-866).

(2) Other illegal payments.—No deduction shall be allowed under subsection (a) for any payment (other than a payment described in paragraph (1)) made, directly or indirectly, to any person, if the payment constitutes an illegal bribe, illegal kickback, or other illegal payment under any law of the United States, or under any law of a State (but only if such State law is generally enforced), which subject the payor to a criminal penalty or the loss of license or privilege to engage in a trade or business. For purposes of this paragraph, a kickback includes a payment in consideration of the referral of a client, patient, or customer. The burden of proof in respect of the issue, for purposes of this paragraph, as to whether a payment constitutes an illegal bribe, illegal kickback, or other illegal payment shall be upon the Secretary to the same extent as he bears the burden of proof under section 7454 (concerning the burden of proof when the issue relates to fraud).

Last amendment.—Sec. 162(c)(2) appears above as amended by Sec. 310(a)(1) of Public Law 92-178, Dec. 10, 1971, effective (Sec. 310(b) of P.L. 92-178) with respect to payments after Dec. 30, 1969. Sec. 162(c)(2) as it read before this amendment is in P-H Cumulative Changes.

Addition.—Sec. 162(c)(2) was added by Sec. 902(b) of Public Law 91-172, Dec. 30, 1969 (qualified effective date rule in Sec. 902(c) of P.L. 91-172).

Income Taxes *(I.R.C.)* **25,175**

(3) Kickbacks, rebates, and bribes under medicare and medicaid.—No deduction shall be allowed under subsection (a) for any kickback, rebate or bribe made by any provider of services, supplier, physician, or other person who furnishes items or services for which payment is or may be made under the Social Security Act, or in whole or in part out of Federal funds under a State plan approved under such Act, if such kickback, rebate, or bribe is made in connection with the furnishing of such items or services or the making or receipt of such payments. For purposes of this paragraph, a kickback includes a payment in consideration of the referral of a client, patient, or customer.

Last amendment.—Sec. 162(c)(3) appears above as amended by Sec. 310(a)(1) of Public Law 92-178, Dec. 10, 1971 (qualified effective date rule in Sec. 310(b) of P.L. 92-178). Sec. 162(c)(3) as it read before this amendment is in P-H Cumulative Changes.

Addition.—Sec. 162(c)(3) was added by Sec. 902(b) of Public Law 91-172, Dec. 30, 1969 (qualified effective date rule in Sec. 902(c) of P.L. 91-172).

Reproduced from the *Prentice-Hall Federal Taxes* Service (1983 edition) with the permission of the publisher.

Figure 13-1

13.2 HOW THE IRS SEES THE ISSUE

In the matter of bribes, illegal payments, or kickbacks, the IRS works both sides of the street. It considers that all such payments, whether in the form of cash, goods, or services, are payable to the recipient and possibly not deductible by the payer.

Because of the latter possibility, it expects that payments of this nature will be hidden somewhere in the payer's records—and eventually not reported for tax purposes by the receiver.

To stifle this possibility, it requires that all payers file information returns, Forms 1099 NEC, in each instance where payments of $600 or more are made to any individual—whether or not such expenses were deductible. This regulation causes double trouble for a business person in the form of

1. Additional taxes where kickbacks were not allowed on audit.

2. Penalties for failure to file the Forms 1099.

In its *Techniques Handbook for In-Depth Examinations* (NIT 4235-5) the IRS begins with three clear statements that epitomize the government's feelings in this matter:

(1) The receipt of income from kickbacks can occur in nearly every segment of business, large or small.

(2) The payment of kickbacks can take the form of cash, goods, or services to or for others for some kind of preferential treatment or to influence another party for such treatment.

(3) Because of the difficulty involved in tracing the receipt or payment of kickbacks, it has become a favorite source of revenue to organized crime. Kickbacks can be difficult to trace through records as they could be hidden in a maze of bookkeeping entries and buried in any number of accounts such as cost of sales, sales returns, advertising, repairs, travel and entertainment, loans and exchanges, promotional

expenses, miscellaneous expenses, or practically any other account. Additional difficulty occurs where the kickbacks do not appear on the books and records of the business at all, e.g., an individual will pay a kickback from his/her personal account or from personal cash on hand. Further, if such a payment is uncovered, there is the additional problem of determining who actually received the payment as the payor will often refuse to identify the payee.

The Service then sets its basic philosophy.

In dealing with kickbacks that are discovered, it is generally agreed that:

(a) kickbacks are always taxable to the recipient;

(b) if the name of the recipient is not disclosed, no deduction will be allowed to the payor;

(c) kickbacks are not deductible unless they are both ordinary and necessary business expenses.

RED ALERT:

After a succession of defeats in the Tax Court and the Ninth Circuit Court of Appeals, the IRS has finally surrendered, and now agrees that illegal payments that are part of the cost of goods sold, or an exclusion from gross sales (and not a deduction), are now deductible (Rev. Rul. 82-149).

Example: **A wholesale liquor dealer gives his customers one free bottle for each case purchased. This amounts to a price rebate which violates state law. Nevertheless, such a practice is now allowable under the Code.**

In Section 773 of this same manual the IRS sets forth its kickback samples. (See Figure 13-2.)

---

773 *(4-11-80)*   4235
Examples of Kickback Areas

(1) The following are illustrative of the types of kickback payments, made or received, and schemes that are used in this area of tax abuse.

(a) Loans are arranged for individuals or corporate entities that would otherwise be difficult for them to obtain. These loans are arranged through financial institutions or other third parties. For this "service" a substantial fee would be paid to the individual(s) arranging the loan, e.g. an individual needing a loan for one million would be given a loan for one million one hundred thousand dollars. The additional one hundred thousand dollars would then be paid to the individual, or representative of the individual, who arranged the loan that could not otherwise have been obtained.

(b) Members of organized crime involved with labor unions will receive extorted funds or payoffs for preventing, or not initiating strike action by the members of the union.

(c) Customers or clients are "steered" to business concerns who in turn will pay kickbacks based on the income received from these customers (popularly called "finders fees").

(d) Business entities owned or operated by members of organized crime will make large purchases which are paid for by check and covered by a bill for the full amount. The supplier would then be required to kickback, in cash, a certain percentage of the payment.

(e) The contract price for the acquisition of property could be overstated in a scheme whereby part of the purchase price is kicked back to the purchaser and the money used to set up a slush fund. The contractor/seller will refund the money as a reduction of sales price and the funds are diverted into a slush fund account or to the personal benefit of the purchaser. The examining agent should consider employing the following techniques to detect these transactions.

1. Examine contracts for changes in acquisition price without corresponding changes in contract plans, i.e., excessive purchase price.

2. Examine correspondence between the parties to the contract for indications of diversion of funds.

3. Examine add on costs, such as legal fees, consultant

fees, settlement fees, and finders fees to determine the reasonableness of expenditures.

4. When examining contractors, test refunds or reduction of contract price for correctness. Examine refund cancelled checks for areas of deposit by the purchaser.

Prepare information reports on the purchaser for unusual or large refunds by the contractor.

(2) These examples are illustrative only and investigation should not be restricted to these areas of business activities.

Figure 13-2

13.3 FACTORS WHICH THE IRS CONSIDERS WHEN MAKING ITS AUDIT DECISION

In its attempt to locate kickbacks and illegal payments, the IRS goes far afield, both as to payers and payees. Some of its recommended investigative techniques follow:

Kickbacks by Payers

■ Determine whether employers remit all applicable union dues and welfare payments. If not, this may be an indication that monies are being paid in cash to union officers to insure labor peace.

■ Carefully examine corporate loans where they are unsecured and interest free. Who received them? Was there a business purpose? Was the recipient only a middleman with the proceeds passing through to another? Were the loans possibly repaid in cash and the funds then paid off to someone else?

■ Watch for payments made to individuals or concerns allegedly for consulting fees or commissions. Trace them to their destination. They could be kickbacks or payoffs.

■ Examine all other accounts which could be conduits for illegal payments.

Kickbacks to Payees

■ Checking and saving accounts of payees and immediate relatives should be closely scrutinized for unexplained deposits—as should investment accounts.

■ Loans received by a corporation from an outside party should be carefully examined to establish source and disposition.

■ Sales should be analyzed to determine unexplained income for which there is no documentation or there are no shipping records.

MT 4235-5 further admonishes its examiners to "think kickbacks" and to use imaginative investigation techniques. Only a few have been portrayed above.

Sections 780 and 814.3 of the Handbook devote several additional pages to PAYMENTS TO OR FOR PUBLIC OFFICIALS. Subheadings include:

Types of Payments   Kickbacks in the Construction Industry
Examples of Payments   Investigative Techniques
Methods of Payment

Corporate Slush Funds and Improper Payments

Investigations of some major corporations by the Service and other enforcement agencies have disclosed intricate schemes designed to generate large amounts of cash for illegal or improper use. The end result of these schemes was to illegally reduce taxes. Most were perpetrated by high-ranking corporate officials.

As a result of these findings, the Service instituted a policy whereby examining officers are required to secure—in suspect circumstances—from selected corporate officials and key employees, answers to the following questionnaire UNDER PENALTIES OF PERJURY. Presumably, this quiz can be used also for individual proprietorships.

Questionnaire

The following questions are submitted in connection with an examination by the Internal Revenue Service of the corporation's Federal tax liabilities. You may state your position with the corporation and your particular area of responsibility. However, the questions are not limited to knowledge acquired in the course of your official responsibility, but should be answered on the basis of your knowledge, belief, and recollection from whatever source.

You should state under the penalties of perjury that you believe your answers to be true and correct as to every material matter. You may provide explanatory details with your answers. If you are unsure whether a particular transaction comes within the scope of the question, you may discuss the matter with the examining agent. If, after the discussion, you believe that any answer requires qualification, you should state clearly the nature of the qualification. If the examining agent concludes that any qualification is ambiguous or unreasonable, or if the response to any question requires further information, the agent may submit additional questions to you for response.

All references to corporation herein shall include not only the particular corporation referred to, but any subsidiary, parent, or affiliated corporation, and any joint venture, partnership, trust, or association in which such corporation has an interest.

1. During the period from _____ to _____ , did the corporation, any corporate officer or employee, or any other person acting on behalf of the corporation, make, directly or indirectly, any bribe, kickback, or other payment of a similar or comparable nature, whether lawful or not, to any person or entity, private or public, regardless of form, whether in money, property, or services, to obtain favorable treatment in securing business or to obtain special concessions, or to pay for favorable treatment for business secured or for special concessions already obtained?

2. During the period _____ to _____ , were corporate funds, or corporate property of any kind, donated, loaned, or made available, directly or indirectly, for the benefit of, or for the purpose of opposing, any government or subdivision thereof, political party, political candidate, or political committee, whether domestic or foreign?

3. During the period from _____ to _____ , was any corporate officer, employee, contractor, or agent compensated, directly or indirectly, by the corporation, for time spent or expenses incurred in performing services, for the benefit of, or for the purpose of opposing, any government or subdivision thereof, political party, political candidate, or political committee, whether domestic or foreign?

4. During the period from _____ to _____ , did the corporation make any loan, donation, or other disbursement, directly or indirectly, to any corporate officer or employee, or any other person, for contributions made or to be made, directly or indirectly, for the benefit of, or for the purpose of oppposing, any government or subdivision thereof, political party, political candidate, or political committee, whether domestic or foreign?

5. During the period from _____ to _____ , did the corporation, or any other person or entity acting on its behalf, maintain a bank account, or any other account of any kind, whether

domestic or foreign, which account was not reflected in the corporate books and records, or which account was not listed, titled, or identified in the name of the corporation?

IMPORTANT:

Obviously, the government is taking this matter of bribes, illegal payments, and kickbacks very seriously. You should, too. Make sure that any clients who might come within the purview of this Questionnaire can completely and honestly reply to its queries.

13.4 CONSIDERATIONS WHEN PREPARING THE RETURN

Before all else, we should recognize the definition of a legal, Section 162, ordinary and necessary kickback. Let's begin with the most common kind.

Kickbacks to Persons Other Than Public Officials.

This type of payment (direct or indirect) is illegal and nondeductible if it violates any law of the U. S. or any state law (but only if such state law is "generally enforced") that subjects the taxpayer to a criminal penalty or the loss (including a suspension) of a license or privilege to engage in a trade or business.

NOTE:

The penalty or loss of license need not actually be imposed upon the taxpayer.

A kickback also includes those payments which are made as a reward for referral of a client, patient, or customer. Regulation 1.162-18(b)(1).

Laws of the U. S. shall be deemed to include only federal statutes, including state laws which are assimilated into federal law by federal statute and legislative and interpretative regulations thereunder. The term shall also be limited to statutes which prohibit some act or acts for the violation of which there is civil or criminal penalty.

WARNING:

The deduction will denied whether or not the payer is convicted. Regulation 1.162-18(a)(4).

Generally enforced. A state law shall be considered to be "generally enforced" unless it is never enforced or the only persons normally charged with violations thereof are infamous or those whose violations are extraordinarily flagrant. Thus, it would appear that in a state where a commercial bribery statute exists—if, in practice, it is never enforced—the deduction would apparently be allowed even if the payer was convicted as an exception to the nonenforcement practice. Regulation 1.162-18(b)(3).

Commercial bribery. To my knowledge the federal government does not have on its books a general commercial bribery statute. Some states do, however. The New York State law (N.Y. Penal Law 180.00, 180.03(McKinney 1979)) reads in part:

A person is guilty of commercial bribery when he confers, or offers or agrees to confer, any benefit upon any employee, agent, or fiduciary, without the consent of the latter's employer or principal, with intent to influence his conduct in relation to this employer's or principal's affairs.

If this law is "generally enforced," then the paramount issue would be whether the employer had knowledge of the act and consented to it.

In Fiambolis v. U. S. (57-2 USTC 9805, 152 F. Sup. 19 (DC S.C.)) the case revolved about one point—whether amounts paid by the taxpayers, in their business of ship chandlery, to officers of foreign flagships were deductible as ordinary and necessary business expenses.

The taxpayers proved that the practice of rebating five percent of the invoice price of the ship's stores, as billed out by the ship chandler, had existed "from time immemorial," and was common to the industry. The court found that the ship owners not only knew of this practice but approved of it—and held for the taxpayers.

Illegal Payments to Government Officials or Employees

No deduction shall be allowed for any amount, paid or incurred directly or indirectly to any official or employee of any government, or agency thereof, which violates any state or federal law. This statute does not apply to representatives of foreign governments. Regulation 1.162-18(a).

Payments to Foreign Officials

In this respect the payment, to be disallowed, need be in violation of federal laws only. The place where the bribe was paid is immaterial. It also matters not whether the payment violated any of the laws of the foreign country. Section 162(c)(1).

Upon the enactment of TEFRA (Sept. 3, 1982) however, Section 162 was altered to read that kickbacks to foreign officials would not be allowed, *only* if the payment was in violation of the 1977 Foreign Corrupt Practices Act.

Kickbacks, Rebates, and Bribes Under Medicare and Medicaid

See Regulation 1.162-18(c) (Figure 13-3).

(c) Kickbacks, rebates, and bribes under medicare and medicaid. No deduction shall be allowed under section 162(a) for any kickback, rebate, or bribe (whether or not illegal) made on or after December 10, 1971, by any provider of services, supplier, physician, or other person who furnishes items or services for which payment is or may be made under the Social Security Act, as amended, or in whole or in part out of Federal funds under a State plan approved under such Act, if such kickback, rebate, or bribe is made in connection with the furnishing of such items or services or the making or receipt of such payments. For purposes of this paragraph, a kickback includes a payment in consideration of the referral of a client, patient, or customer.

Figure 13-3

NOTICE:

Under this regulation the bribe or kickback *need not be illegal*.

13.5 HANDLING THE AUDIT

Unlike most tax issues, the burden of proof here is *not* on the taxpayer, but upon the Commissioner. See Regulation 1.162-18(b)(4) below:

Burden of Proof. In any proceeding involving the issue of whether, for purposes of Section 162(c)(2), a payment constitutes an illegal bribe, illegal kickback, or other illegal payment, the burden of proof in respect of such, such issue shall be upon the Commissioner to the same extent as he bears the burden of proof in civil fraud cases under Section 7454 (i.e., he must prove the illegality of the payment by clear and convincing evidence....

COMMENT:

Such proof is not easily obtainable. Section 6653(b) (Fraud) says simply that: "If any part of any underpayment (as defined in subsection (c)) of tax required to be shown on a return is due to fraud, there shall be added to the tax an amount equal to 50 percent of the underpayment."

Neither the Code nor the judiciary have chosen to specifically define "fraud." Courts have traditionally interpreted the weight of evidence needed to support both civil and criminal fraud along the same vein. It is apparent, therefore, that the burden of proof in this instance is burdensome indeed. For this reason, I would insist that the Service produce very strong evidence of an illegality in respect to this issue before agreeing to any disallowance.

How to Handle the IRS Bribery Questionnaire

Consider first whether your client operates the type of business in which kickbacks are commonplace:

Construction   Foreign Oil

Beer and Wine Sales   Ship Chandlery

If he or she, or their corporation is involved in such an operation, review the questionnaire with them.

RED FLAG:

Impress upon such taxpayers, in strong terms, that they should not give any false answers to an IRS person. Neither the taxpayer nor you can possibly be sure of the knowledge which the examiner possesses.

Code Section 7206(1) (FRAUD AND FALSE STATEMENTS) says that any person who:

Willfully makes and subscribes any return, statement, or other document, which contains or is verified by a written declaration that it is made under the penalties of perjury, and which he does not believe to be true and correct as to every material matter ... shall be guilty of a felony and, upon conviction thereof, shall be fined not more than $5,000, or imprisoned not more than 3 years, or both...

Under a somewhat overlapping statute (Section 1001 of Title 18 of the U. S. Code), a proven false statement can result in a fine of not more than $10,000 or imprisonment for not more than five years or both.

EXTREMELY IMPORTANT:

NEVER DEAL IN FALSEHOODS (WRITTEN OR ORAL) WHEN DEALING WITH THE IRS. Rely on the Fifth Amendment to the Constitution if you must, and refuse to answer on the grounds that your answer might tend to incriminate you, but do not lie.

IRS Audit Techniques

In searching for illegal payments or kickbacks, the IRS may take all or some of the following audit steps—or more, in addition to those mentioned in book Sections 13.2 and 13.3:

To locate false invoices agent will

1. Inquire into who prepared the document and from what source data.
2. Look for business checks that have been cashed and attempt to identify the ultimate recipient.
3. Compare checks listed on business back statements with deposits in personal accounts of the taxpayer.
4. Look for unusual payers or endorsements.
5. Look for unusual patterns.
6. Reconcile debit balances in accounts payable for particular vendors.
7. Match selected check register payments with vendor invoices.
8. Trace suspicious invoices to points of origin to locate outright fakes.
9. Where appropriate, consider third-party contacts to determine if the taxpayer's suppliers are making large payments to other parties at the same time they receive monies from the taxpayer. Possibly, portions of the payments are being returned to the taxpayer, either directly or indirectly.

The *IRS In-Depth Handbook* makes no specific mention of the following two moves but they have been used to hide kickbacks:

1. The taxpayer writes frequent checks to a local department store. They are charged to various expense accounts, although actually used for the purchase of gift certificates for buyers or others. Generally, they can be traced, because they must be endorsed before cashing.
2. The taxpayer writes checks to a bank. Purpose: purchase of government bonds to be used as kickbacks. These, also, are traceable through their applications and endorsements.

To locate payments to public officials agents will look for bargain sales, fictitious rents, purchase of corporate stock of an organization set up to funnel kickbacks, bad debts written off in favor of a politician or a politician-controlled corporation, large campaign contributions, indirect payments through attorneys' trust accounts, public relations, advertising, or accounting firms.

NOTE:

Large bonuses to corporate officials will be perused with interest. Where they authorized in the minutes? Were they warranted? Were they reported for tax purposes? Did they actually accrue to the benefit of the individuals involved? What path did the check take? If it was deposited in the officer's personal account, was a similar withdrawal made—and to whom? And so on.

Generation of kickback cash. The IRS may look to customers' checks for leads. Were they cashed and not run through sales? Were the checks sent to a bank for collection? If so, the bank would issue a receipt to the taxpayer and process the check as though it were deposited. Upon collection, the bank would pay the depositor with cash or a bank check. Such funds would not have been reported as income, and would be available for bribes or kickbacks.

SUGGESTION:

> **The list of schemes is endless. Practitioners, therefore, should be cautious. They should closely question all suspect clients regarding this issue. The questions and answers should be written down in their workpapers and dated.**

WARNING:

> **Where kickbacks are located, they should be investigated thoroughly with the contents of this chapter in mind—and legitimized to the highest degree possible. Practitioners should never aid or cover up in any fashion any clearly illegal scheme.**

13.6 PERTINENT COURT DECISIONS—PRO AND CON

Pro
Conway Import Company Inc. v. U.S.
(D C NY; 1969 - 25 AFTR2d 70-352,
311 F Supp 5)

Findings of Fact

The plaintiff, a food-processing company, made gifts and gratuities to employees of its customers over a period of many years. Such payments were alllowed by IRS examiners at all times until 1957 when a Regional Analyst reversed the decision of the original auditor. The taxpayer paid additional taxes of $98,262, then sued to recover.

The government claimed that public policy required disallowance of the payments as commercial bribes. The gratuities (about 10 percent of sales) were paid to Conway salesmen who in turn distributed the cash to employees of customers. Records were kept to show the payments to salesmen.

An Internal Revenue survey (in which the Intelligence Division cooperated) determined that the practice of gratuity payments to chefs, stewards, maitre d's, receiving clerks, etc., was common in the wholesale food industry.

Opinion

The court found that the gifts were made as ordinary and necessary business expenses to influence the continuing purchase of the taxpayer's products, that they were not made without knowledge of the customer-employers, and that they were common in the industry.

The court noted particularly the case of Lilly v Com. 343 U.S. 90 (41 AFTR 591) 72 S.Ct. 497-1952, in which kickbacks paid by a manufacturer of eyeglasses to optometrists were allowed because they reflected a nationwide practice and were regarded as essential to the taxpayer's business operation.

Held for the plaintiff.

Con
James C. Tooke (TC Memo 1977-91)

Findings of Fact

Taxpayer operated, under various names, as a property tax consultant. As such, he represented businesses by preparing property tax returns for local assessors and by negotiating with such assessors or their delegates concerning the assessed valuation of properties.

While supplying such services, the taxpayer made illegal payments to individuals employed in the offices of property tax assessors. These payments were claimed as deductible business expenses.

Opinion

The court found that one significant aspect of the taxpayer's business was to secure favorable property tax treatment through the use of bribes—that such bribes were not ordinary and necessary business expenses and not common in the trade. They were illegal in the state and consequently not allowable under Section 162(c)(1) which has to do with illegal payments to employees of any government or agency thereof.

13.7 RELEVANT CODE AND REGULATION SECTIONS

Code

Section	162	Trade or Business Expenses
	162(c)	Illegal Bribes, Kickbacks, and Other Payments
	162(c)(1)	Illegal Payments to Government Officials or Employees
	162(c)(2)	Other Illegal Payments
	162(c)(3)	Kickbacks, Rebates, and Bribes Under Medicare and Medicaid
	6653	Failure to Pay Tax
	6653(b)	Fraud
	7206	Fraud and False Statements
	7206(1)	Declarations Under Penalties of Perjury
	7454	Burden of Proof in Fraud, Foundation Manager and Transferee Cases

Regulations

Regulation	1.162-18	Illegal Bribes and Kickbacks
	1.162-18(a)	Illegal Payments to Government Officials or Employees
	1.162-18(a)(4)	Laws of the United States
	1.162-18(a)(5)	Burden of Proof
	1.162-18(b)(1)	Other Illegal Payments—in General
	1.162-18(b)(3)	Generally Enforced
	1.162-18(b)(4)	Burden of Proof
	1.162-18(c)	Kickbacks, Rebates, and Bribes Under Medicare and Medicaid

13.8 APPLICABLE IRS MANUAL REFERENCES (INVESTIGATIVE TECHNIQUES)

Techniques Handbook for In-Depth Examination

MT 4235-5

Sec.	770	Kickbacks and Payoffs
	771	Introduction
	772	Income and Deduction Features
	773	Examples of Kickback Areas
	774	Investigative Techniques
	780	Payments to or for Public Officials
	781	Introduction
	782	Types of Payments
	783	Examples of Payments
	784	Methods of Payment
	814.3	Kickbacks and Payoffs to Public Officials
	814.4	Investigative Techniques

Manual
Supplement 42G-378   Corporate Slush Funds and Improper Payments

42G-380   Guidelines for the Use of the Corporate Slush Fund Questionnaire

NOTE:

The subject, Corporate Slush Funds, is dealt with in the IRS *National Office List of Prime Issues* or the *Appeals Coordinated Issues List as it is now called.*

Educational Expenses
(Section 162-Regulation 1.162-5)

14

14.1 IDENTIFYING THE PROBLEM

The Code makes no direct reference to "educational expenses." Instead, governing Section 162 states that:

> There shall be allowed as a deduction all the ordinary and necessary expenses paid or incurred during the taxable year in carrying on any trade or business...

Regulations, in 1.162-5(a), backs into the matter by stating that educational costs are deductible as ordinary and necessary business expenses if they are not of the type described in paragraph (b). See below for summation.

Defining educational expenses:

■ Qualifying educational expenses are those which aid a taxpayer in maintaining or improving skills which will be used in an already established profession or business, or

■ Which will help in meeting the express requirements of an employer or of applicable law imposed as a condition of such employment or salary status.

■ Such expenses *will not* be considered ordinary and necessary if they are expended to meet minimum educational requirements for qualification in employment or other trade or business, or

■ For qualification in a new trade or business.

These seem to constitute a relatively simple set of rules, except that a little stretching here and there causes problems.

• A CPA studies law as an aid to increased efficiency in the conduct of his accounting practice.

• A college professor spends the summer traveling in Europe as a means of improving his teaching skills.

- A tax practitioner attends a two-day tax seminar 2,000 miles from home, while in the middle of a thirty-day vacation.
- A Michigan architect attends an art festival in Miami, Florida, in February so as to broaden his creativity.

All want to deduct costs as qualifying educational expenses. Court decisions jump all over the spectrum, allowing full deductions for some, such as for the architect—for pieces, as in the case of the tax practitioner—and nothing for the CPA.

Above or Below the Line Deductions

More problems arise when it comes time to enter the deductions on a return. Are they adjustments to income in arriving at adjusted gross (above the line) or are they itemized deductions which are allowable only in arriving at taxable income (below the line)? The correct choice here is important, not only from a legal sense but because it can mean a substantial difference in tax results.

Deciding the primary objective of a dual-purpose trip (study and pleasure) can be troublesome—and costly—if not planned correctly.

Where local transportation is involved, computing the mileage allowance can be tricky. Going from work to home, then to night school can bring about different results than going directly from work to school.

KEY POINT:

IRS people do their best to sort things out and give each taxpayer his or her just deserts. Don't let the likelihood of their scrutiny deter you. There are many more benefits in the educational area than are quickly apparent. Know the rules and use them.

14.2 HOW THE IRS SEES THE ISSUE

The Service sees affluent taxpayers as taking vacations at the government's expense—or educating themselves with the same type of tax-deductible dollars. It also looks closely at Educational Assistance Programs which provide free education for employees who may, at the same time, be the paying employers.

In Private Letter Ruling No. 7746068, the IRS indicated that it will rule adversely on questions of deductible educational expenses unless the taxpayer shows

...a direct and proximate relationship between the education and the skills required in your particular field. Therefore, you must provide information as to the subject matter or the scope of the courses which you intend to take or as to any relationship that the study of such courses may have to the maintaining or improving of particular skills required in your employment.

The teaching profession comes into particular focus, mainly because travel can be uniquely necessary for the maintenance of instructing skills—and yet, at the same time, can be a pleasing, recreational activity.

14.3 FACTORS WHICH THE IRS CONSIDERS WHEN MAKING ITS AUDIT DECISION

The IRS manuals and handbooks instruct their auditors and examiners to look for answers to the questions enumerated below:

1. Does the education deduction meet the requirements of Section 162 insofar as it applies to ordinary and necessary business expenses?
2. Does it adhere to the principles of Regulation 1.162-5(a) as they apply to the improving of skills or were such expenses incurred to meet minimum educational requirements or to qualify in a new trade or business?
3. In the case of school teachers, are they studying to meet minimum requirements of a local or state Board of Education—even while employed? (Not deductible.)
4. For deductions which represent substantial travel expenses, what portion of time was actually expended on direct, educational-improvement activities? (Fishing, hiking, sightseeing, soccer games, don't count.)
5. Has the deduction been claimed in the proper year?
6. Was any reimbursement received?
7. Did the studies bear a direct relationship to the taxpayer's duties? (If not, they probably won't be allowed—for example, a chemist studying law.)
8. Is substantiation available for expenses incurred and/or mileage traveled? (If not, difficulties arise.)
9. Were the deducted educational costs incurred before reentry into a trade or profession? (If so, they would not be deductible.)
10. Were the training expenses incurred while the taxpayer was not actively engaged in a trade or business or not employed? (Not deductible.)
11. Were individually paid expenses incurred for a dependent? (Not deductible.)
12. Were unreimbursed educational expenses such as tuition, books, and supplies deducted in arriving at adjusted gross? (They should not have been—only travel and transportation expenses are allowed in this respect.)

14.4 CONSIDERATIONS WHEN PREPARING THE RETURN

Prior to the Revenue Act of 1978, employees were required to cope with a bundle of problems in determining whether their employer-furnished educational benefits were taxable.

Educational assistance programs, as established under Act Section 164 and Code Section 127 (Educational Assistance Programs) removed most of these difficulties.

IMPORTANT:

For the years 1979 through 1983, employer-paid educational assistance is to be considered a nontaxable fringe benefit, whether job related or not.

This assistance, however, must be provided under a qualified employer program which is established under the following conditions. The plan

- Must be in writing and must operate for the exclusive benefit of employees.
- Need not be funded or approved in advance by the IRS.
- Must be publicized sufficiently so that eligible employees will have reasonable notice of its availability.
- Must benefit a broad class of employees.
- May not permit employees to choose taxable benefits instead of educational benefits.
- May not discriminate in favor of employees who are officers, shareholders, self-employed, or highly compensated—or in favor of dependents of such employees. (A plan is considered discriminatory if more than five percent of the amounts paid or incurred by the employer in any year go to shareholders or owners—or their spouses or dependents—who own more than five percent of the employer.)
- Must exclude from consideration those employees who are covered by a collective bargaining agreement where there is evidence that educational assistance benefits were the subject of good-faith bargaining between the employer and employee representatives.
- May not include education or training involving sports, games, or hobbies unless they are directly related to the employer's business.

Program benefits include, but are not limited to, payments for tuition, fees, and similar expenses—and for books, supplies, and equipment—but not for tools and supplies that may be retained by the employee after completion of the course of instruction. Nor may they include cost of meals, lodging, or transportation.

IMPORTANT:

The Committee Report ('78 Revenue Act) states, "There is no restriction as to who may furnish the educational assistance. It may be furnished by an educational institution *or any other party."* (Emphasis mine.)

Who may qualify. Code Section 127(b)(1) says that the program shall exist "for the exclusive benefit of employees to provide such employees with educational assistance."

This statement is clear enough, but Section 127(b)(2) seems to go further to include dependents. It reads in part:

The program shall benefit employees who qualify under a classification set up by the employer and found by the Secretary not to be discriminatory in favor of employees who are officers, owners, or highly compensated, *or their dependents*. (Emphasis mine.)

There are no regulations as yet on this subject and neither the Code nor the Committee Report come out flatly to say that beneficiaries under the plan can include "dependents."

CAUTION:

Dependents are *not* to be included. The Code really means, in this case "Dependents Who Are Employees."

Employees and employers are defined in Section 127(c)(2) and (3) as including in the first instances an individual who is an employee within the meaning of Section 401(c)(1)—relating to self-employed individuals.

Employers include individuals who own the entire interest in an unincorporated trade or business and individual members of a partnership.

LOOK!

An owner of a solely operated proprietorship, since he or she is also an employee for purposes of Section 127, can set up a plan and educate himself or herself with funds deducted as a business expense under Section 162.

Two Types of Expenditures That Cannot Be Deducted

Two categories of expenditures are definitely not deductible:

Minimal educational requirements (Regulation 1.163-5) are decided by considering an employer's demands, applicable law and regulations, and the standards of the profession, trade, or business. The fact that an employee is performing a particular job does not mean that such an individual has met the minimum requirements for the position.

A teacher without a degree, for example, may be functioning as an instructor in a post that requires at least a bachelor's degree. The expense of acquiring such a degree would not be deductible.

New trade or business (Regulation 1.162-5). Educational expenses that are part of a program to qualify a person in a new trade or business are considered capital expenditures and not deductible.

SPECIAL NOTE FOR TEACHERS:

Teachers, however, are given much latitude in this respect. Once they have met the minimum requirements for the position, the cost of most studies is deductible, i.e., to change from elementary to secondary teaching—from teaching to becoming a principal—from being an English instructor to teaching history.

Educational Travel: Taxpayers Should Exercise Caution

Normally, the cost of qualified transportation expenses, including meals and lodging, are deductible. But, if personal pleasure is involved, the taxpayer should be cautious.

The deduction, under these conditions, swings on the amount of time utilized for each purpose—study or fun.

BEWARE:

If the primary purpose for the trip is pleasure, *no* deduction can be taken for travel. The cost of meals and lodging will be deductible only for the time actually expended on educational activities.

EXAMPLE:

Attorney Zelse travels to Miami, Florida, to attend a two-day law seminar. While there he vacations for two weeks. He may not deduct transportation costs but he may deduct 1/7 of his meals and lodging expense, plus the attendance cost.

Whether a trip is primarily personal or educational depends upon the time spent for each purpose. Studying eight days out of ten would allow the travel to be categorized as mainly for educational purposes—and would allow transportation expenses to be deductible in their entirety.

How to Deduct

Expenses such as the cost of tuition, books, lab fees, and similar items may be taken as itemized deductions. An explanatory statement should be attached to the return.

The cost of the following qualifying educational expenses may be deducted in arriving at adjusted gross whether or not deductions are itemized:

- Travel and transportation
- Educational expenses of outside sales persons
- Reimbursed expenses up to the amount included in income (Form 2106—Employee Business Expenses—should be used in reporting these three items.)

Self-employeds may deduct qualifying educational expenses by entry directly onto their Schedule C's.

14.5 HANDLING THE AUDIT

The IRS examiner will, of course, wish to satisfy himself or herself that the educational expenses meet the basic rules as summarized in Section 14.4 of this chapter.

If a Form 2106 is applicable but was not filed, prepare one.

For out-of-town travel in particular collect all possible data or substantiation which will prove educational-participation time. As previously mentioned, much depends upon the primary purpose of the trip. The auditor will expect to see a tour folio, registration receipt, and other evidence, such as a studies transcript.

Where education was voluntarily undertaken—if not under an employer-assistance plan (Secton 127)—make sure that evidence exists to prove "improvement of skills" or "employer or legal requirements." A statement from the employer might be necessary.

Where reimbursement was received, be prepared to show that it was included in income, or if not, that it did not exceed costs and that an accounting of such expenses was made to the employer.

NOTE:

If the educational deductions were taken by a teacher on sabbatical, taking graduate studies, expect to document that such leave of absence was for one year or less (Rev. Rul. 68-591).

Be prepared to prove distances where mileage allowances were taken.

CAUTION:

If the taxpayer goes home before going to school, he or she may deduct the cost of traveling from *home to school*, but only to the extent that it does not exceed the cost of going from *work to school*.

WARNING:

Local travel costs on a nonworking day are considered personal commuting expenses and are not deductible.

Be careful of situations where the taxpayer, while attending a university, accepts employment leading to a degree (such as that of an instructor or research assistant). The government says that

> If such employment was secured at or near the time of attendance and studies—and for the purpose of providing funds to pursue studies—it can hardly be said that the educational expenses were primarily incurred to increase proficiency in the taxpayer's present employment.

14.6 PERTINENT COURT DECISIONS—PRO AND CON

Pro
Toner v Com. (3 Cir 1980) 46 AFTR 2d
80-5156, F2d-Rev'g 71 TC 772

Findings of Fact

The taxpayer accepted a teaching position at a parochial school where the minimum employment requirements were a high school diploma. At the time she commenced work, she had completed two years of a four-year college degree program.

As a condition to her employment the school required that she sign an agreement to the effect that she would take a minimum of six college credits each year until she obtained a degree. This she did, taking 15 credit hours in one year and deducting the resultant expenses on her tax return.

The IRS and Tax Court both denied the deduction. The latter came forth with a split decision in that some of the judges ruled that the taxpayer's education was for the purpose of meeting minimal requirements—and others ruled that it was to prepare her for a new profession because she then became qualified to teach in a public school.

Opinion

The Appeals Court reversed the decision, ruling that the taxpayer had met the minimum standards for employment and that she furthermore was required by her employer to undertake additional studies. She did not study to qualify for a new profession, since she was already a teacher—whether in a parochial or public school notwithstanding.

Con
Danielson v. Quinn (D C VI; 1980)
45 AFTR 2d 80-1555 F Supp

Findings of Fact

Danielson, a CPA, became specialized in the fields of taxation and business planning. In 1971 he attended law school and eventually obtained his degree and passed the bar examination.

Upon returning to public practice, he continued in his areas of specialization, refusing to represent clients in any other fields of law. He deducted his educational costs, including travel expenses.

The taxpayer claims, and the IRS denies, deductions for maintaining and improving his skills.

Opinion

The court ruled for the government, holding that Danielson's studies had qualified him for a new profession. It mattered not that he remained in his same general areas of practice.

14.7 RELEVANT CODE AND REGULATION SECTIONS, PLUS PUBLICATIONS

Code

Section 127	Educational Assistance Programs
127(b)(1)	In General
127(b)(2)	Eligibility
127(c)(2)	Definition: Employee
127(c)(3)	Definition: Employer
162	Trade or Business Expense
401(c)(1)	Definitions and Rules Relating to Self-Employed Individuals and Owner-Employees

Regulations

Section 1.162-5	Expenses for Education
1.162-5(a)	General Rule

Publications

508	Educational Expenses
529	Miscellaneous Deductions
535	Business Expenses and Operating Losses

14.8 APPLICABLE IRS MANUAL REFERENCES (INVESTIGATIVE TECHNIQUES)

Audit Guidelines for Examiners

MT 4231-46	Section 576	Educational Expenses

Tax Audit Guidelines for Tax Auditors

MT 4234-5	Section 77(12)	Educational Expense

Handbook of Standard Explanations

MT 428(11)-14	Sec. 39	Educational Expense

EXEMPTIONS AND DEPENDENTS

15

(Sections 151 and 152)

15.1 IDENTIFYING THE PROBLEM

Many and varied rules govern this ofttimes controversial subject. In reviewing prominent court cases, legal confrontations seem to appear most frequently in areas involving

- Gross income of dependents
- Status of dependents—cousins, for example, adopted children, nonrelated residents of taxpayers' homes.
- Classification of support—and its valuation.
- Proof of more than 50% suppport.
- Conflicting claims between taxpayers, i.e., husband and wife, brothers and sisters.
- Noncustodial parents claiming child dependents.
- Marital status at end of tax year.

In addition, the IRS "Related Cases" program causes difficulties in that information obtained from the examination of one return leads to the audit of another.

15.2 HOW THE IRS SEES THE ISSUE

Probably because of the millions of exemptions and dependents in this country—and the fact that each is worth at least $1,000 off the top of someone's tax return—the IRS does not see this as a minor issue. It may become even more serious in 1985 when indexing begins.

Look to the Service's voluminous Questionnaire (Form 2038), Figure 15.1. This document goes out to taxpayers wherever there is doubt as to the validity of an exemption.

Form **2038** (Rev. Jan. 1978)	Department of the Treasury—Internal Revenue Service **QUESTIONNAIRE—EXEMPTION CLAIMED FOR DEPENDENT**	In reply refer to
Names of taxpayers	Name of dependent as shown on the return	Taxable year ended

The information requested on this questionnaire is needed to support the exemption for a dependent claimed on your Federal income tax return. Please complete this form by giving information about the dependent named above. The attached information guide contains tests for claiming dependents and other helpful instructions.

PART I

1. Full name of dependent

2. Was dependent a citizen, resident, or national of the United States, or a resident of Canada or Mexico during the year? ☐ Yes ☐ No

3. Relationship of dependent to you

4. Dependent's age at end of taxable year

5. Number of months dependent lived with you during year ➡

If the dependent lived with you less than 12 months, please complete item 6. below.

6. Names and addresses of others with whom dependent lived *(If dependent entered or left the Armed Forces during the year, show "AF" and date of entry or discharge.)*

	Relationship to dependent	Number of months

7. Was dependent married during any part of the year? ☐ Yes ☐ No *(If Yes, complete items 8 and 9.)*

8. Name and address of dependent's spouse

9. Did dependent file a joint income tax return with spouse? ☐ Yes ☐ No

PART II — Complete this part only if the exemption claimed is not for your child.

10. If dependent was a minor, give names and addresses of dependent's parents *(If dependent's parents are not living, write "Deceased" and show dates of death in the spaces provided below.)*

a. Mother's name and address

b. Father's name and address

PART III — Complete this part only if the exemption claimed is for your child.

11. If the dependent was 19 or older, was dependent a full-time student? ☐ Yes ☐ No *(If Yes, complete items a, b, and c.)* ▶

a. Name and address of school

b. Dates of school attendance: From / To

c. Dependent attended ☐ Day school ☐ Night school

12. Did you and the other parent of the dependent file a joint return for the year shown above? ☐ Yes ☐ No

If Yes, skip questions 13 and 14 and complete the parts on the back of this form.
If No, complete the remaining questions on both front and back of this form.

13. Name and address of other parent of dependent

a. Amount you contributed to the support of dependent *(Do not include arrearage payments for earlier years.)* $ ....

14. Were you and the dependent's other parent divorced, legally separated, or separated under a written separation agreement for any part of the year shown above? ☐ Yes ☐ No

If Yes to either question, complete items a, b, and c below, and attach a copy of any decree or agreement under which support payments were made or that states which parent can claim an exemption for the dependent.

If Yes, does the decree of divorce or separate maintenance, or written agreement, state which parent can claim an exemption for the dependent? ☐ Yes ☐ No

If No to both questions, do not complete items a, b, and c below. Show amount other parent contributed to the dependent's support: $_____

(Do not include arrearage payments for earlier years' support.)

a. Date of separation

b. Date of divorce

c. Was the child in your custody during the taxable year? If Yes, complete item d. ☐ Yes ☐ No

d. Show period of custody: From _____, 19____, to _____, 19____.

Return This Part to IRS   Form **2038** (Rev. 1-78)

PART IV.— Include in this part only the income and expenses for the part of the year the dependent lived with you.

15. Did dependent receive any income, such as wages, interest, dividends, pensions, rents, social security, welfare? ☐ Yes ☐ No
(If Yes, please complete items a, b, c, and d, below.)

	Gross Amount	Source
a. Income	$	
	$	
	$	
	$	
	$	

b. Amount of the dependent's income used for his or her support		$
c. Amount of the dependent's income used for other purposes		$
d. Amount of dependent's income saved		$

Expenses for entire household *(Where dependent lived)*		Expenses for dependent only	
16. Lodging *(Complete items a or b, and item c if applicable)*	a. Rent paid. $	24. Dependent's portion of household expenses *(Item 23)*	$
	b. If not rented, show fair rental value of home *(if dependent owns home, include this amount in item 31)* $	25. Clothing	$
	c. If you completed item b, show below the name and address of the owner of the home	26. Education	$
		27. Medical-Dental	$
	Homeowner's name and address	28. Travel-Recreation	$
		29. Other *(Specify)*	
17. Food	$		
18. Utilities *(heat, light, water, etc.)*	$		
19. Repairs *(not included in item 16a or item 16b)*	$		$
20. Other *(Do not include expenses of maintaining residence, such as mortgage interest, real estate taxes, and insurance.)*	$	30. Total cost of dependent's support for the year *(Add items 24 through 29.)*	$
21. Total household expenses *(Add items 16 through 20.)*	$	31. Amount dependent contributed for own support *(item 15b, plus amount from item 16b if dependent owns home)*	$
22. Number of persons *(including dependent)* living in household	*(Number)*	32. Amount others contributed for dependent's support *(include amounts by State, local, and other welfare societies or agencies.)*	$
23. Dependent's portion of household expenses *(item 21 divided by item 22)*	$	33. Amount you contributed for dependent's support	$

34. If you are claiming the dependent under a multiple support agreement, please show the amount spent for dependent's support by each member of the multiple support group who contributed.

PART V

If the dependent did not live with you the entire year and you are unable to furnish complete information for Part IV, it will help support your claim to the exemption if the person with whom the dependent lived will either (a) complete the following Certificate, or (b) submit a signed statement that you furnished more than half the dependent's total support and the dependent was not claimed on that person's Federal income tax return.

Certificate

I certify that during the taxable year 19____, _____

(Name of person claiming dependent)

provided more than half the total cost of support for _____

(Name of dependent)

and I did not and will not claim the dependent's exemption on my Federal income tax return for the above year.

Signature	Address	Date

PART VI

Declaration (If a joint return, both you and your spouse must sign)

I declare I have examined the information entered on this form, and to the best of my knowledge and belief it is true, correct, and complete.

Your signature	Date	Spouse's signature	Date

If you decide you are not entitled to claim an exemption for the dependent, please complete the withdrawal statement below.

Withdrawal Statement (If a joint return, both you and your spouse must sign)

I no longer believe I am entitled to claim an exemption for _____

(Name of dependent)

and I withdraw my claim to this exemption. Please make the necessary adjustments to my income tax return for the year shown on the other side of this form.

Your signature	Date	Spouse's signature	Date

Form **2038** (Rev. 1-78)

Figure 15-1

The IRS manuals and handbooks additionally devote what would seem at first glance to be a disproportionate amount of space to "Exemptions and Dependents." Nay. The potential volume spells millions in additional government income.

Not even the Criminal Investigation Division writes this one off. Many individuals have been convicted of criminal fraud after willfully taking deductions for totally unqualified dependents. Dogs, cats, and unborn children don't count. A stillborn child doesn't count either.

15.3 FACTORS WHICH THE IRS CONSIDERS WHEN MAKING ITS AUDIT DECISION

In its drive to eliminate false exemptions, the Service has instituted additional requirements for processing Forms W-4 (Employee's Withholding Allowance Certificate). Under this enforcement program, employers are required to submit to the IRS all copies of all Forms W-4 which meet the following two tests:

1. Claim more than nine exemptions, or
2. Claim exemption from withholding and the employer reasonably expects the employee's wages usually to be more than $200 a week.

Copies of the certificates must be forwarded together with Forms 941, 941-E, or 941-M, as the case may be, along with a statement showing the employer's name, address, I.D. number, and number of certificates submitted.

Following this action, the employer will continue to withhold on the basis of the W-4 for which copies were submitted. If the IRS claims that a material misstatement exists—or that it lacks information to verify whether or not the certificate is correct—the employer will treat the W-4 as defective.

The employer will then provide the employee with the government notice and request a new certificate. Until one is provided, withholding will be on the basis of a single person with no exemptions. (Regulation 31.3402(g))

Five Major Exemption Tests

IRS audit procedures call for a variety of tests—and tests within tests. Tax Audit Guidelines make this point to its examiners:

> If any of the five major (exemption) tests cannot be met, then there is no reason to pursue the others—so check the easiest first.

Here are the five tests in stated order with a summary of interesting government comments. Parenthesized material is mine:

Gross Income Test: (with two exceptions which concern children, gross income of a qualified dependent must be less than $1,000 (Section 151(e)(1))

1. Gross income does not include tax-exempt income.
2. **Gross receipts from rents are includible in gross income (no matter the ultimate taxable loss).**

3. Net partnership income is included. (This instruction is probably incorrect. Code Section 151(e)(1) mentions "gross income." Pub. 501, *Exemptions,* says: "Partnership income of a dependent is a partner's share of the gross—not a share of the net partnership income.")

4. For persons who sell products, gross income is sales minus cost of goods sold.

5. A capital gain deduction is excluded. (Watch for the taxable portion, however. It counts.)

In community property states, one-half of the income of one spouse may be gross income to the other. In instances where a taxpayer cannot substantiate the gross income of a dependent, the former should request a written statement from the dependent setting forth the sources of such income.

Member of Household or Relationship Test: (Qualifying relationships, generally lineal descendants, are described in Code Section 152(a) and also in book section 15.4.)

1. Temporary absences of a dependent for reasons such as illness, school, or vacation do not preclude claiming the exemption.

2. An individual may not be considered a household member if the relationship with the taxpayer is in violation of local law.

3. Relationships once established by marriage are not terminated by death or divorce. (For purposes of this section, for example, a mother-in-law is always a mother-in-law and may qualify as a dependent.)

4. If a child, prior to adoption, is placed in a taxpayer's home by an authorized adoption agency, the child meets the relationship test if he or she is a member of the household. (Otherwise, the child can be a bona fide dependent under this section, if he or she was a member of the taxpayer's household for the entire year.)

Citizenship Test: (A dependent must be a citizen or national of the U.S., or a resident of the U. S., Canada, or Mexico at some time during the calendar year in which the taxpayer's year begins (Section 152(b)(3).)

1. The physical presence of a person in a particular country does not mean that he or she is a resident.

2. Where such presence is questionable, the taxpayer should be requested to explain the dependent's purpose and length of stay, as well as the type of visa which permitted entry. (Wherever citizenship or residency is questionable, a practitioner should ask the taxpayer to provide copies of birth certificates, visas, adoption papers, or other proof which might aid in meeting this test.)

Joint Return Test: (Generally, a dependent may not file a joint return with another (Section 151(c)(2).)

1. Should a married daughter file a joint return with her husband—even though she is supported by her father—this eliminates her exemption from the father's return

NOTE HOWEVER:
If such a dependent had income of less than the amount required before a return must be filed—and if such filing was for the purpose of acquiring a refund—the parent would not lose the exemption. See Rev. Rul. 54-567 and 65-34.

Support Test: (A taxpayer generally must furnish more than one-half of a dependent's support for the calendar year in which the taxpayer's taxable year begins (Section 152(a).) Some exceptions are described in book section 15.4.

The "Support" *Audit Guidelines* are voluminous. They present seven sections on approximately three pages. Should you have any particular difficulty with the IRS concerning this corner of the subject, it might prove helpful to secure the respective manual section:

MT 4234-5   Tax Audit Guidelines for Tax Auditors

As mentioned in Chapter 10, such guidelines are available through the IRS Freedom of Information Reading Room for a very small fee.

Here is a summary of the seven sections as the IRS presents them to their auditors:

• In situations where the dependent resides in the taxpayer's home, difficulty arises in determining support, because documentation undoubtedly does not exist for such expenses as food, clothing, and lodging. Here, the auditor should consider the income of the taxpayer and the number of persons in the family.

• Where total support is claimed, a statement should be secured to the effect that the dependent had no income or other funds, received no aid, and was not the owner of the dwelling which he or she occupied.

• Particularly in the case of dependents who entered the Armed Forces—as to who furnished more than one-half of the total support—consideration must be given to basic support items, such as clothing, food, quarters, etc., as furnished by the military.

• It is the taxpayer's responsibility to furnish the support amount. Therefore, in cases where the dependent resided elsewhere, it is incumbent upon the taxpayer to secure support data from the other household.

• Watch for inclusion of value of services in support total. (Not allowed.)

• (Here's one for the taxpayer.) Expenses may be accepted without verification, if reasonable. To establish reasonableness, consider:

Number of persons in family

Available funds

Area of country in which dependent resided

Standard of living, etc.

• Make the cash-availability test. If household expenses and the direct expenses of the dependent, together with itemized deductions—and a reasonable estimate of unrelated expenses—exceed reported income and other funds, it is evident that the expenses have been overstated or available funds understated.

• In the absence of any other acceptable means of allocation, the dependent's total support will include a pro rata portion of general household expenses based on the number of members in the household. Variables include special foods which the dependent may require, medical care, and unusual clothing.

• Auditors are cautioned to be alert to the fact that the disallowance of a dependency may also lead to disallowance of medical expenses for such an individual.

• *Amounts furnished by dependent:*

1. Look for social security payments. In the absence of records, one-half of the amount expended from a single joint social security check is considered to have been furnished by each spouse, regardless of the fact that benefits in the check may differ.

2. Determine if other income exists—welfare or relief payments or incidental earnings. The source and tax status of funds is immaterial.

3. If a claim is made that dependent's funds were placed in savings, examine the passbook or bank statement.

4. The following benefits, received by or for the dependent for his or her support, must be considered as having been so used regardless of how expended:
   a. Public benefit payments based solely on need.
   b. Support received under a court order or divorce decree. (Arrearage payments received for child support are not considered support payments.)

5. Unless the taxpayer can establish otherwise, the dependent's available funds are to be considered as having been used for his or her own support.

15.4 CONSIDERATIONS WHEN PREPARING THE RETURN

All parties to tax matters know that—as concerns this simple issue—every taxpayer will resolve the question in his or her own favor.

All should expect, however, that at some time they may receive the IRS mind-busting Form 2038 (Questionnaire-Exemption Claimed for Dependent). This form is included in book section 15.2 as Figure 15-1. Practitioners, before completing a tax return, should review this form with the client—and be positive that the situation at least approximates its requirements. If it doesn't, by a wide margin, the preparer may be tagged with a negligence penalty.

Personal Exemptions for Marrieds

Personal exemptions for marrieds are actually deductions that come "off the top" in computing income tax. Statutorily, at this writing, the deduction is $1,000 for each of the following but may go higher with indexing in 1985:

• The taxpayer (even though in some instances he or she may be the dependent of another as in the case of a student).

• A spouse (if legally married on the last day of the year even though not residing in taxpayer's household).

• Additional exemptions for taxpayer and spouse who are 65 or over.

WATCH THIS ONE:
A person born on January 1 is legally considered to have been born on December 31.
The extra exemption can initially be taken in the prior year.

• Additional exemptions for taxpayer and spouse for blindness. (The Regulations in 1.151-1(d) define blindness as existing in cases where

1. The person's central visual acuity does not exceed 20/200 in the better eye with correcting lenses, or

2. The fields of vision are so limited that the widest diameter of the visual field subtends an angle no greater than 20 degrees. In cases where vision can be corrected beyond these limits only by contact lenses that can be worn only briefly because of pain, infection, or ulcers, the extra blind exemption may be taken. Certification of eye condition must be attached to returns as indicated in Publication 501 (Exemptions).

These personal exemptions are always deductible in full in cases where individuals were legally married on the last day of the year or at date of death. No proration is necessary except in cases where there was a change in accounting period.

Personal Exemptions for Single Taxpayers

Personal exemptions for single taxpayers include all of those as described for individual partners to a marriage—and under the same citizenship requirements.

Dependent Exemptions

Dependent exemptions may be taken if such individuals meet the five dependency tests as enumerated in book section 15.3 and in Regulation 1.151-2.

Related Dependents

Related dependents are those as defined in Code Section 152(a) and are generally considered to be those as summarized in Publication 501, Figure 15-2.

A dependent related to you in any of the following ways need not live with you or be a member of your household for you to claim the exemption:

Your child, grandchild, or great grandchild, etc., (a legally adopted child is considered your child).

Your stepchild,

Your brother, sister, half brother, half sister, stepbrother, or stepsister,

Your parent, grandparent, or other direct ancestor, but not foster parent,

Your stepfather or stepmother,

A brother or sister of your father or mother,

A son or daughter of your brother or sister,

Your father-in-law, mother-in-law, son-in-law, daughter-in-law, brother-in-law, or sister-in-law.

Any relationships that have been established by marriage are not ended by death or divorce.

Before legal adoption, a child is considered to be your child if he or she was placed with you for adoption by an authorized agency and was a member of your household. If the child was not placed with you by such an agency, you may take the child as a dependent only if the child was a member of your household for your entire tax year.

A foster child is considered to be your child if your home is the child's principal home and the child is a member of your household for the entire year. See *Foster Child,* later.

If your foster child was born or died during the year, you may take the dependency exemption if the child lived in your household for the part of the year the child lived. This does not include any required hospital stay following birth or other temporary absences.

An exemption for your cousin ordinarily is not allowed unless the cousin lives with you as a member of your household for the entire year. A cousin is a descendant of a brother or sister of your father or mother.

If you file a joint return, you need not show that the dependent is related to both of you. You may, for example, claim an exemption for your spouse's uncle who receives more than half his support from you, even though the uncle does not live with you.

If you and your spouse file **separate returns,** you may not claim an exemption for your spouse's uncle, unless he is a member of your household and lives with you for the entire tax year.

Figure 15-2

CAUTION:

> The relationship classification, as you may have noticed, is important since such relatives need not have resided in the taxpayer's home for the exemption to be taken—whereas a nonrelated individual must have resided in the household for the entire year.

Where a joint return is filed, dependents may be related to either spouse.

IMPORTANT:

> There is no support requirement for a spouse. He or she may be supported by a father, for instance, and yet can still file jointly with the opposite married partner. Daddy gets no exemption.

Children of Divorced Parents

Unfortunately, when divorce becomes imminent, individuals generally do not think rationally or clearly. If they would, the tax audit could be made less harmful to both sides.

Divorced Parents Are Defined as:

"Parents who are legally separated under a decree of divorce or separate maintenance, or separated under a written separation agreement."

NOTE:

> When a person is divorced, he or she may not claim the other as a dependent even though the taxpayer contributes more than 50% of the ex-mate's support.

The custodial parent gets the dependency where he or she has custody of the child for the greater part of the year. It does not matter whether the parent actually provided more than one-half the support—unless *one* of thhe following exceptions applies:

1. The noncustodial parent provides at least $600 toward each child's support during the calendar year *and* the decree of divorce or separate maintenance, or other agreement between the parents, states that the noncustodial parent will be allowed the dependency exemption.

NOTE:

> Under this exception the parent must attach a copy of such an agreement to each tax return upon which the exemption is entered.

2. The parent without custody provides $1,200 or more of support for each child *and* the former spouse cannot prove that he or she provided more.

NOTE:

> This rule applies even though the decree or written agreement gives the exemption to the parent with custody.

Government becomes a referee. Under the above second exception, either parent may request that the other advise if that parent intends to claim, or has claimed, the child as a dependent. An itemized statement of support may also be requested. Both the requests and answers must be in writing.

For complete details, and the IRS judgment of the matter, see a copy of "Itemized Statement" from Publication 501.

Multiple support agreement. It happens on occasion that no one individual provides more than 50 percent of a dependent's support. The IRS becomes understanding in this respect and allows somebody to take the exemption—provided that this person has supplied more than 10 percent of the dependent's support—and provided that the other contributors agree to let such a person take the dependency.

WARNING:

If they do not agree, then no one who has not donated more than 50 percent gets the deduction.

If an agreement is arrived at (And why not? Each can take the benefit in alternating years, if necessary), then the taxpayer receiving the dependency exemption must file with his or her tax return Form 2120 (Multiple Support Declaration) as signed by each of the other contributors.

Items Excluded from Total Support

Certain benefits received by or on behalf of a dependent need not be included in a total-support determination. They are:

1. Scholarships received by a taxpayer's child, stepchild, or legally adopted child who is a student.
2. The value of room and board furnished by an accredited school of nursing for the benefit of a student nurse.
3. The value of education, room, and board provided for a handicapped child by a state.

Certain expenses are also excluded from the total-support determination:

1. Income and social security taxes
2. Life insurance premiums
3. Capital expenditures such as the cost of furniture or automobiles
4. Funeral expenses

15.5 HANDLING THE AUDIT

The key to a good presentation is Form 2038 (Figure 15-1). With good substantiation this document should wash away any applicable IRS doubts.

Also available are "Itemized Statements" as described in section 15.4. If such material has not been secured, you might as well bite the bullet and get the two parents together. Such a meeting can only help. No matter how exemptions were deducted, the IRS Related Cases Program will lay bare the whole matter. Better to discuss the situation and get things squared away *before* IRS time—not *during*.

In instances where applicable, Multiple Support Declarations (Form 2120) should be secured.

A practitioner should review sections 15.2 and 15.3 of this chapter for identification of IRS questions that are likely to appear. Preparation—preparation—can't be beaten!

The IRS Information Guide—Exemptions for Dependents—is reproduced here as Figure 15-3. It presents a good summation of the subject and contains much concise information that will be helpful in preparing for an audit.

The IRS support computation will probably materialize in somewhat the following manner:

Assume that a father and two sons (John and Harry) reside in the same household. A third son, Peter (the taxpayer), sends money home to his father requesting that it be used for the support of Harry. In the absence of records which identify Harry's support payments, the taxpayer's contributions would be applied as follows:

	Total	Father	John	Harry
Total Cost of Support	3500	1700	900	900
Furnished by:				
Father	2900	1700	600	600
Peter	600		300	300

Because the taxpayer did not provide more than $450 of his brother Harry's support, he is not entitled to his exemption. The father is. However, let us suppose that the latter had no need for the deduction. A Multiple Support Declaration could then be made to work nicely, since Peter paid more than 10 percent of the cost of his brother's support.

15.6 PERTINENT COURT DECISIONS—PRO AND CON

Pro
(Rev. Rul. 66-28 1966-1 CB 31)

Findings of Fact

An elderly woman—unrelated to the taxpayer but a permanent member of his household and a legal dependent prior to becoming ill—had to be placed in a nursing home where she remained for several years. The taxpayer paid all of her confinement expenses.

Could she be considered as having been temporarily absent from her principal place of abode for the purposes of determining whether she qualifies as the taxpayer's dependent under Section 152(a)(9)?

Opinion

In view of the decision in the case of Walter J. Hein v. Comm. 28 TC 826 (1957) Acquiescence, CB 1958-2,6, a period of time during which a dependent is confined to a nursing home because of illness will be considered a temporary absence due to special circumstances even though such absence is for an extended period of time.

Accordingly, in this instance, the elderly woman remains a dependent under Section 152(a)(9) of the Code.

Con
Jaque H. Soskis (TC Memo 1978-499)

Findings of Fact

A noncustodial father supplied more than $1,200 a year to his ex-wife for support of their daughter Anna—and claimed her as a dependent for each of the years in question. The custodial family also claimed the child as a dependent in the same years. The IRS disallowed

Department of the Treasury
Internal Revenue Service
Information Guide-Exemptions for Dependents

This guide will help you determine the dependents you are entitled to claim on your Federal income tax return.

Qualifications for Dependents

Each dependent claimed must meet all of the following tests:

1. Gross Income Test—Received less gross income than the deductible amount allowable for a dependency exemption. If the dependent is your child who was under 19 or was a full-time student, this test does not apply.

2. Joint Return Test—Did not file a joint return with spouse.

3. Citizenship or Residence—Was either a citizen, resident, or national of the United States, or a resident of Canada or Mexico; or was an alien child adopted by and living with a United States citizen abroad.

4. Relationship—(a) Was related to you (or to your spouse if you file a joint return) in one of the following ways:

Child (see note below)	Mother-in-law
Stepchild	Father-in-law
Mother	Brother-in-law
Father	Sister-in-law
Grandparent	Son-in-law
Brother	Daughter-in-law
Sister	The following if related by
Grandchild	blood:
Stepbrother	Uncle
Stepsister	Aunt
Stepmother	Nephew
Stepfather	Niece

or (b) was a member of your household and had your home as principal residence for the entire tax year.

Note: Includes your son, daughter, stepson, stepdaughter, or a child who is a member of your household if placed with you by an authorized placement agency for legal adoption, or a foster child who is a member of your household for the entire year.

5. Support—Received more than half of support from you (or from your spouse if you file a joint return). This requirement does not apply if:

1. Form 2120, Multiple Support Declaration, statements are filed with your tax return.

2. You are a divorced or separated parent entitled to use the special rules discussed later in this information guide.

Before you can determine whether you furnished over half the support for a dependent, you must determine the total support furnished by you, by the dependent, and by others. Total support for a dependent is the sum of:

1. The fair rental value of lodging furnished.

2. Items of expenses paid or incurred directly by or for the dependent.

3. A proportionate share of expenses that cannot be attributed directly to a particular individual, such as cost of food for the entire household. The total cost, not the period of time over which you furnish the support, is the deciding factor.

The following are some typical items that are includible or not includible in the determination of total support:

Items Includible in Total Support

Food
Shelter
Clothing
Medical and dental care
Medical insurance premiums
Basic Medicare benefits
School tuition, lunches, and milk
Tuition payments and allowances under G.I. Bill
Child care expenses
Armed Forces dependency allotments
Board
Haircuts
Personal hygiene expenses
Movies and other entertainment
Gifts to dependent
Recreation
Travel
Transportation costs
Church contributions
Baby-sitting expenses
Tax-exempt military quarters allowances
Armed Services academy appointment

Support received for or by the dependent under a court order or divorce decree. (This must be considered as having been so used, regardless of how spent. Arrearage payments received for child support are not considered as support payments.)

Items Not Includible in Total Support

Federal, State, local, or FICA taxes paid by a dependent on own income

Life insurance premiums

Funeral expenses

Arrearage payments of child support

Medical insurance benefits

Supplementary Medicare benefits

Scholarships received by taxpayer's child, stepchild, foster child, or legally adopted child who is a student

Payment received under the War Orphan's Educational Assistance Act of 1956 and used for the recipient's support. (This is considered a scholarship.)

Student nurse's room and board furnished by an accredited school of nursing

Value of education, room, and board provided by educational institution for a handicapped child. (This is considered a scholarship.)

Student

A student is an individual studying full time at a recognized educational institution during any 5 months of the year, or taking a full-time on-farm training course under the supervision of an accredited agent of an educational institution or of a State, county, or local government agency. For income tax purposes, a student must be your child, stepchild, foster child, or legally adopted child.

In figuring whether you provided more than half the support of a student, do not include amounts received as scholarships.

Multiple Support

If two or more persons contributed toward the support of an individual but no one of them alone contributed more than 50 percent and any one of them could claim the person as a dependent except for the support test, then any one of them who contributed more than 10 percent of the support may claim the exemption for the dependent. Each of the others must file a Form 2120, Multiple Support Declaration. These declarations must be filed with the income tax return of the person who claims the exemption.

Divorced and Separated Parents

Special rules apply to determine which of separated parents will be considered to have furnished over half the support for their children (including stepchildren). These rules apply only to parents who are divorced, legally separated, or separated under a written agreement and not filing a joint return. And the rules are further limited to the children (including stepchildren) of such parents: (a) who were in the custody of one or both of the parents over half of the year; and (b) who received over half their support for the year from one or both of the parents, and (c) who were not included in a Multiple Support Declaration filed for the year.

If all the above conditions are present, the general rule provides that the parent who had custody of the child for the greater amount of time during the year (more time than the other parent) is considered to have contributed over half the child's support.

There are two exceptions to the general rule. The parent who did not have custody of the child (or had custody for the lesser time) will be considered to have furnished over half the child's support for the year if that parent:

1. Provided at least $600 for the child's support for the year, and the decree of divorce or of separate maintenance (or a written agreement between the parents) states that that parent is entitled to the exemption, or

2. Provided $1,200 or more for the child's support (or for the support of each child, if more than one) for the year and the parent who had custody (or had custody for the longer time) cannot prove that he or she furnished more for the child's support than the other parent furnished.

Any amounts spent for the support of a child or children are to be treated as received from the parent who did not have custody to the extent that the parent provided amounts for child support.

Custody is normally determined by the terms of the most recent decree of divorce or separate maintenance, or subsequent custody decree, or, if there is no decree, by written separation agreement.

Figure 15-3

Jaque's dependency claim on the grounds that he did not supply more than one-half of Anna's support.

Opinion

The court's opening remarks appear to be of sufficient importance to warrant full quotation:

> In dealing with the special dependency situation of a child of divorced parents, we must turn to section 152(e), which provides a special test to determine which parent is entitled to

the personal exemption for the dependent child. Generally, the custodial parent is allowed the exemption. For the instant case, however, we look to section 152(e)(2)(B) for an exception which allows the non-custodial parent, petitioner here, to claim the child as dependent if that parent has provided $1,200 or more for the child's support and the custodial parent can not clearly establish that she provided more support for the child during the taxable year than did the other parent. Clearly, petitioner jumps the first hurdle since it is agreed that he provided $1,500 in support payments in both 1973 and 1974. Thus, the burden of proof is shifted to the custodial parent under section 152(e)(2)(B)(ii) to show a greater support contribution. However, the mother, custodial parent, is not before the Court; therefore, the burden is placed upon the Commissioner, as respondent. Labay v. Commissioner, 55 TC 6, 11 (1970), affirmed per curiam 450 F.2d 280 (28 AFTR 2d 71-5895) (5th Cir., 1971). It is the respondent's burden, then, to show "by a *clear preponderance* of the evidence" that the mother contributed more than half of the support for Anna in 1973 and again in 1974. Labay v. Commissioner, supra, at 13. Certain contributions to Anna's support by her mother have already been noted in the findings of fact as sufficiently proven.

In addition to the contributions noted in the findings of fact as being made by the mother for Anna's support, contributions by the step-father are also to be treated as from the mother. Colton v. Commissioner, 56 T.C. 471 (1971); Rev.Rul. 73-175, 1973-1 C.B. 59; Rev.Rul. 78-91, 1978-11 I.R.B. 6.

The custodial parent was able to prove that she and her second husband provided more than one-half of the child's support. Held for the government.

15.7 RELEVANT CODE AND REGULATION SECTIONS, PLUS PUBLICATIONS

Code

Section 151	Allowance of Deductions for Personal Exemptions
151(e)(1)	Additional Exemption for Dependents-In General
151(e)(2)	Exemption Denied in Case of Certain Married Dependents
152	Dependent Defined
152(a)	General Definition
152(b)(3)	Rules Relating to General Definition (Citizenship)

Regulations

Section 1.151-1	Deductions for Personal Exemptions
1.151-1(c)	So-called Old Age Exemptions
1.151-1(d)	Exemptions for the Blind
1.151-2	Additional Exemptions for Dependents
31.402(g)	Supplemental Wage Payments

Publications

501	Exemptions
519	U.S. Tax Guide for Aliens

15.8 APPLICABLE IRS MANUAL REFERENCES (INVESTIGATIVE TECHNIQUES)

Tax Audit Guidelines for Tax Auditors

MT 4234-5   Section 776   Exemptions and Dependents

Income Tax

MT 4200-377   Section 4224.2   Dependency Exemption Cases
MT 4200-268   Section 4224.3   Related Cases

Standard Explanations Handbook

MT 428 (11-13) Section 41   Exemption

This handbook section contains some 50 useful clues which will help you to penetrate the IRS exemption audit screen. Again—if pertinent to your type of practice—secure a copy of this training guide.

BAD DEBTS
(Section 166)

16

16.1 IDENTIFYING THE PROBLEM

With the credit crunch plaguing today's marketplace, bad debts assume a greater role than ever. Liberalized bankruptcy laws do not help. And to add to taxpayers' woes, the IRS scrutiny of this deduction continues to become ever more acute.

For purposes of clarity and brevity, no attempt will be made here to include special and exceptional rules such as for banks and financial institutions. Listed below are some of the more obvious problems in the consideration of uncollectibles:

- When is a debt business-oriented, and when it is not? (The answer is important, since the latter is treated as a short-term capital loss subject to limitations.)

- How and when does a debt become worthless? (Both questions must be answered—and proved—before the deduction will be allowed.

- What is the adjusted basis of the debt? (Only this is deductible.)

- Does the deduction cover a *loss* or a *bad debt?* (If the former, the statute of limitations for filing a claim for refund is three years. For the latter, seven years under Section 6511(d).)

- Is the recovery taxable or not? (Sometimes—under the "recovery-exclusion" rule—it is not.)

- Is the debt completely worthless or partially so? (The former is deductible only in the year it becomes totally uncollectible. The latter can be deducted in later years.)

- How should bad debts be deducted—through specific write-off or through a reserve method? ("Specific" might be easier but "reserve" can be more advantageous.)

- Under the reserve method for computing the bad debt deduction, what is a "reasonable addition" to the reserve?

Read on to learn additional details concerning these questions, and to find out what the IRS thinks and does about them.

16.2 HOW THE IRS SEES THE ISSUE

Internal revenue auditors are taught to approach certain types of bad-debt deductions with a jaundiced eye—those, for example, where transactions appear to have been disguised as bad debts and used to avoid or evade taxes.

Assume, if you will, that an alleged loan was made to an individual with no tangible wealth or visible regular income—a person who is judgment-proof against forced legal collection—and therefore not open to suit. A ficititious loan to such a person could easily be converted into a bad-debt deduction.

The IRS, in its *Handbook for In-Depth Examinations* (MT 4235-5), has this to say to its examiners:

> Before it can become "bad" a debt has to exist. In order for a debt to exist, a transaction, either in the form of a loan or sale, had to occur. The occurrence had to happen with the expectation of receiving payment without any attached contingency and with the expectation of collecting, based on the borrower's financial condition when loan or sale is made.

The handbook suggests, under these conditions that:

1. The instrument which created the loan be examined to determine if the loan calls for the payment of interest at the then going rate.
2. A determination be made as to whether the interest payments were timely honored—as to whether they were ever honored—and, if honored temporarily, how soon after the transaction did they cease to be honored?

WARNING:

Under these tests and in accordance with the handbook's cautionary remarks—all tests being negative—the deduction would undoubtedly be disallowed.

Other IRS bad-debt suspicions include:

- Hasty write-offs, as evidenced by a large volume of recoveries.
- Debt deductions not becoming worthless within the applicable year.
- "Business" bad debts that are actually "nonbusiness" in nature.
- Additions to reserves, probably inflated.
- Loans to officers and related taxpayers, possibly hidden in the charged-off accounts.
- Repossessions not considered.
- Recoveries never recorded, but pocketed. (*Be careful of this one:* It happens far too frequently, and is traceable.)
- In the case of a nonbusiness bad debt, it may have been a gift to a relative.
- Illegal payments and/or kickbacks frequently go the bad-debt route.

In general, expect that the above thoughts are near the surface in the minds of IRS examiners. Specifically, they will check out the deduction as indicated below.

16.3 FACTORS WHICH THE IRS CONSIDERS WHEN MAKING ITS AUDIT DECISION

One recommended audit technique calls for use of the taxpayer's computer to verify accounts receivable and the bad-debt deduction. This was done at a gambling casino. The computer did the mathematics and cross checking, reporting the discrepancies per patron and in totals. The results were evidently satisfactory since the IRS calls attention to this audit method in one of its handbooks.

Additional Recommendations Which the IRS Makes to Its Agents

1. Examine prior RAR's (Revenue Agent's Reports) to insure that an unauthorized change has not been made from one write-off method to another. (Presumably, this prior year examination would include tax returns.)

2. Examine write-offs. If they include corporate officers, shareholders, relatives, police, politicians, etc., consider *not only* their removal from the business return *but also* their addition to the respective individual return.

3. In determining worthlessness—and the correct year of deduction—consider the financial condition of the debtor.

NOTE:

Don't be deterred by bankruptcy. In itself it does not establish worthlessness unless it is obvious that there will be no recovery.

4. Be alert to worthlessness of securities. Except in the case of banks, losses in such cases may not be treated as bad debts. They are subject to capital gain and loss treatment.

DEFINITION:

Securities, in this instance, are those as described in Section 165(g)(c): "a bond, debenture, note, or certificate, or other evidence of indebtedness, issued by a corporation or by a government or political subdivision thereof, with interest coupons or in registered forms."

5. Look for charged-off items that arose out of transactions never reported as income. This situation arises at times in the case of small business people, professionals, and others on the cash basis.

6. The loss charge-off for installment receivables should be limited to cost. The remainder should properly be charged to the unrealized gross profit account.

7. In the case of sizable write-offs, it might be advisable to confirm the bad debt through the debtor. This could disclose an unreported recovery.

8. In the year of payment, the noncorporate guarantor, endorser, or indemnitor of a noncorporate obligation may deduct the sustained loss as a business bad debt—but only if he or she can establish that the proceeds of the loan were used in the trade or business of the borrower.

9. Watch for forgiven loans that may actually be gifts.

10. In closely held corporations, be alert to the possibility that loans from stockholders may actually be additions to capital.

11. Make sure that additions to a bad-debt reserve are "reasonable." (Reasonableness is discussed at length in book section 16.5)

12. If a business which used a reserve write-off method has been discontinued, ascertain whether the reserve was restored to income.

13. Test check charged-off accounts with subsidiary ledgers. Sales activity, subsequent to write-off, may indicate that a premature deduction was taken.

14. Absence of bad-debt recoveries on books may indicate diversion of funds.

15. When installment notes, held by a finance company, become worthless, they are charged off on their books—either against the dealer's reserve or directly to the taxpayer.

    In either case, the loss represents a bad debt to the dealer. Note, however: Dealers must prove such accounts are worthless to them. The action of the finance company does not constitute a final determination.

16. If a dealer maintains a reserve for guaranteed debt obligations, it must be kept separate from his or her Section 166(c) bad-debt reserve.

    Examiners will then find it easier to determine whether repossessed property was taken in at less than FMV. If it was, the effect of such undervaluation is to inflate bad debts and produce a fictitious bad-debt loss experience on which additions to the reserve are based.

17. Be watchful. The amount of the charge-off should be the basis of the receivable *plus* cost and expense of reducing it to the taxpayer's possession *less* the value of the repossessed article.

18. Make sure that repossessions of real estate follow Section 1038 (Certain Reacquisitions of Real Property).

16.4 CONSIDERATIONS WHEN PREPARING THE RETURN

Probably the best place to begin is with the classification of a bad debt. Is it business or nonbusiness?

Business Bad Debt

A business bad debt is defined in Section 166(d)(2) as

1. a debt created or acquired (as the case may be) in connection with a trade or business of the taxpayer or

2. a debt the loss from the worthlessness of which is incurred in the taxpayer's trade or business.

The Supreme Court, in U.S. v. Generes 405 U.S. 93 AFTR2d 72-609, ruled that there must be a very close relationship between the debt and the business—"proximate with a dominant business motivation."

With the exception of loans to officers and stockholders, all legitimate bad debts of a corporation are considered to be business bad debts and are deductible in full in the year in which they become worthless. Partial losses are also deductible but can be used in later years if desired. Debts that are evidenced by securities are excluded from partial write-off provisions.

Nonbusiness Bad Debt

Nonbusiness bad debts, according to Section 166(d)(2), are all those not covered by (1) and (2) above. Some examples:

- Loans to a taxpayer's closely held corporation, if he or she is not in the business of lending money. The company's business is not the taxpayer's.
- Loss of deposit on purchase of a personal auto because dealer opted for bankruptcy.
- Loans to a friend or relative for the purpose of starting a new business. The business does not belong to the taxpayer.
- Loss from a venture into the stock market. Investing is not the loser's business.

Nonbusiness bad debts must be taken as short-term capital losses on Schedule D's of Form 1040.

BE CAREFUL:

They are deductible only if totally worthless.

RED ALERT:

If fraud is involved, a theft loss (limited only to the $100 floor) will be allowed.

Example: Suppose the taxpayer makes a $1,000 deposit toward the construction of a home. The contractor was proved to be an embezzler who never intended to build the home. The $1,000 loss can be treated as a theft loss.

"Bad Debt" Defined

Defining a bad debt, in accordance with Regulation 1.166-1(c): "A bona fide debt, is a debt which arises from a debtor-creditor relationship based upon a valid and enforceable obligation to pay a fixed or determinable sum of money."

IMPORTANT:

The three main points as set forth above are extremely significant. All must exist:
DEBTOR-CREDITOR RELATIONSHIP
VALID AND ENFORCEABLE OBLIGATION
FIXED OR DETERMINABLE SUM OF MONEY

In proving worthlessness, the following situations are helpful, but not necessarily sufficient unto themselves, to substantiate the deduction:

Bankruptcy of debtor	Ill health or death of debtor
Debtor in receivership	Seizure by foreign government
Debtor insolvent	Collateral becomes worthless
Debtor out of business	Disappearance of debtor

Creditors' actions are important. Continued dealing with the debtor, for example, can be damaging. Lack of collection effort—or a weak effort—can cause the IRS to allege that the deduction is inconsistent with the taxpayer's claim of worthlessness.

TAX TIP:

If you are in doubt as to the date of worthlessness, the deduction should be taken at the earliest practicable time. Since the completely worthless bad debt can be taken only in the year it became bad, the deduction will be lost if that year is missed and the statute of limitations has tolled.

On the other hand, if the IRS claims that the year utilized was not the year of worthlessness, the deduction still has a chance in following years.

IMPORTANT:

If disallowed, keep taking the deduction as long as you believe that it is proper.

How to Deduct Business Bad Debts

There are two methods: (1) specific write-off and (2) reserve method.

Under (1), Specific Write-Off, an unlimited deduction may be taken for each bona fide bad debt that becomes worthless, or partially worthless, during the tax year. Burden of proof is upon the taxpayer as to each debtor.

Partial worthlessness can be applied to specific debts only, not to groups of two or more, and can be deducted in a year of choice.

Under (2), Reserve Method, a deduction may be taken for a reasonable addition to a reserve for bad debts. The reserve is an estimate of the uncollectible portion of accounts receivable on hand at any particular time.

The taxpayer decides what constitutes a "reasonable addition," and the IRS agrees or not through its use of a six-year moving average formula which is based on prior years' experience. In years prior to March 12, 1979, a taxpayer could add to its reserve or not, as he or she pleased. Since that date, however, a businessperson must add to the reserve and deduct an amount not less than that called for under his or her normal and proper method of computing yearly reserve additions.

When a business is first established, an election may be made to adopt the bad-debt reserve method. For an established business, however, permission must be obtained from the IRS before a change can be made from the specific write-off to the reserve method.

If the reserve method is used, a statement must be attached to the tax return showing

1. The total amount of all charge sales and other credit transactions for the tax year and the percentage the reserve is of that toal.

2. The total amount of all notes and accounts receivable at the beginning and at the end of the tax year.

3. The total amount of all bad debts that have been charged against the reserve account during the year.

4. The manner in which the addition to the reserve was computed.

Defining "reasonable addition" has always caused a great deal of controversy. Technically, a taxpayer can use any computation formula he or she wishes—past experience, current evaluation, unusual circumstances, such as one large credit customer going bankrupt, but the IRS has no obligation to accept the addition. Generally, its agents will follow the *Technique Handbook for Internal Revenue Agents* (MT 4231-35, Section 676(4)) and/or its six-year moving average or Black Motor Formula in making its reasonableness determination. The *Handbook* section seems sufficiently enlightening to warrant reproduction here. See Figure 16-1.

Audit Technique Handbook for Internal Revenue Agents   page 4231-75
(5-7-79)

(4) *Reserve method*—Under the reserve method reasonableness is the criterion for deduction. The test for reasonableness is based on the status of the reserve account after the year's provision has been made. If the examiner determines that the reserve per return is too high at that point, he/she is justified in reducing the year's provision to effect a more correct amount. This may involve allowing the taxpayer no provision in a given year.

(a) There are four methods of checking reasonableness. Two of these are statistical, based on the past experience of the taxpayer over a term of years. A third is based on the condition of the receivables as good, bad, and doubtful at the end of the year. The fourth is known as "aging" and involves classifying the year-end receivables by current, and number of days past due status. Special methods are established for determining the reserve additions of banks and other financial institutions, which methods are not covered herein.

(b) All four methods are described in the Individual Income Tax Law course and the various tax services. If the agent is not familiar with them he/she should assemble the information described below while at the taxpayer's place of business. He/she should then familiarize himself/herself with the principles of the four methods after he/she returns to his/her own office.

(c) *Statistical method*—Assemble for at least each of the five preceding years, the charge sales (or total sales if charge sales were not segregated), the charge-offs, the recoveries, and the total receivable balances at the beginning and end of each of the years. Determine if all years are comparable, that is, were credit terms the same each year, and was the same type of merchandise sold.

(d) *"Condition of receivable" and "aging" methods*— These are factual and to some extent the discussion under the specific charge-off method above is pertinent. Both involve using a percentage factor. For instance, under the "aging" method a taxpayer might be using 5% on the over 30-day-old receivables, 20% on the 60-90-day ones and 50% on those over 90 days old. This can only be checked by reference to the accuracy of his earlier years' estimates as applied to each category.

(e) It might be wise in some cases to check the reserve by more than one method. If they coincide, determination is simplified. In general the receivables against which the reserve is applied should exclude employee's stockholder's, and intercompany loans. Likewise the reserve against installment receivables should be based on the cost element as discussed earlier. When a taxpayer sells both on charge and installment terms separate reserves should be maintained.

(f) Whether a dealer who discounts his/her installment accounts with recourse is entitled to a reserve against them has been extensively litigated in the courts. Two courts of appeal have ruled that the taxpayer is entitled to such a reserve but the Commissioner does not agree.

(g) The extent to which hindsight may be used in determining the propriety of a write-off or the adequacy of the reserve is a debatable question. The collection of the bulk of the receivables between the year end and the filing date may at times indicate the taxpayer himself/herself knew the receivables were good at the same time he/she was claiming they were bad in filing his/her tax returns. Likewise, the determination as to how many of the receivables which existed at the end of the year under examination, actually became bad in subsequent years, may aid in establishing the reserve as being excessive.

Figure 16-1

Regulation 1.166-4(b)(1) defines reasonableness as:

Relevant factors—What constitutes a reasonable addition to a reserve for bad debts shall be determined in the light of the facts existing at the close of the taxable year of the proposed addition. The reasonableness of the addition will vary as between classes of business and with conditions of business property. It will depend primarily upon the total amount of debts outstanding as of the close of the taxable year, including those arising currently as well as those arising in prior taxable years, and the total amount of the existing reserve

The end of this definition seems to describe the Black Motor Co. Formula fairly well. An illustration of how the formula works is included here as Figure 16-2.

BLACK MOTOR CO. FORMULA

This is a percentage method of computing a reasonable addition to a reserve for bad debts. It consists of four steps:

1. Find the ratio of the total of the net bad debts for the taxable year and the five preceding years to the total of accounts and notes receivable for the same 6-year period.

2. Apply this ratio to the receivables as of the last day of the taxable year.

3. Add to the figure arrived at in 2) the total amount of bad debts charged to the reserve during the taxable year and then subtract the amount of recoveries in the taxable year; this is the "total reserve requirement" for the year.

3. Subtract from the total reserve requirement the balance in the reserve at the end of the immediately preceding taxable year. The result is the amount deductible as a "reasonable addition" to the reserve for the taxable year.

Example: Taxpayer, in the 6-year period 19xx-19x9, had a ratio of 22.36% of bad debts to accounts and notes receivable, arrived at as follows:

Year	Receivables	Bad Debts (Net)	Ratio of Losses
19xx	$50,000	12,500	25%
19xx	60,000	15,600	26%
19xx	80,000	19,200	24%
19xx	100,000	23,000	23%
19x8	120,000	24,000	20%
19x9	110,000	22,000	20%
Total	$520,000	$116,300	22.36%

Accounts and notes receivable December 31, 19x9 . . . . $110,000

Reserve at December 31, 19x9 as adjusted (22.36% of $110,000) . . . . $ 24,596

Add: Losses charged to reserve in the taxable year (19x9) $22,500
      Less recoveries. . . . .   500 $ 22,000

Total reserve requirement . . . . $ 46,596

Deduct: Reserve as adjusted December 31, 19x8 . . . . $ 21,800

Allowable addition to reserve for taxable year . . . . $ 24,796

Figure 16-2

Bad Debt Recoveries

Bad debt recoveries are generally taxable when received. This occurs under the specific write-off method when such receipts are simply added to income. See below under "Recovery exclusion" for exception.

Under the reserve method, recoveries are credited to the bad debt reserve. This has the effect of reducing the amount of the bad debt deduction which will be added to the reserve at the end of the year—thereby accomplishing the purpose of increasing taxable income.

Recovery exclusion. Under the specific charge-off method, the recovery is excluded from income consideration to the extent that the bad debt was not included in the deduction and did not result in a reduction of tax.

Loan Guarantees—Bad Debt or Nonbusiness Loss

Since the beginning of 1976, nonbusiness guarantees have been treated as direct loans. This means that a loss on a guaranty, connected with a trade or business, is an ordinary bad-debt loss.

On the other hand, a loss on a guaranty entered into for profit—but not connected with a business—is treated as a nonbusiness bad debt, or a short-term capital loss.

16.5 HANDLING THE AUDIT

If audited, four issues will be paramount:

1. Is the debt bona fide or some sort of a sham?
2. Is it "business" in nature or "nonbusiness"?
3. Is it truly worthless—and when did it become so?
4. If a reserve method is used, was the addition to the reserve "reasonable"?

A review of previous book sections 16.2 and 16.3 will explain in detail how the IRS will approach these issues. From a practitioner's viewpoint, he or she should expect to show in addition that

- Serious efforts were made to collect the debt.
- The taxpayer is no longer doing business with the debtor.
- The debtor is no longer solvent or continuing in business.

If the reserve method was used and the additions seem excessive—the IRS person will, in most cases, apply the Black Motor Formula. Know too that, in addition to applying this formula, the examiner will probably probe into the write-offs against the reserve. They must also pass the test of worthlessness as for the specific write-off method. See Figure 16-1 for details.

If your case is weak in any of the above respects, do your best to prove extenuating circumstances which might warrant an excess bad debt deduction:

- Several large customers are leaning toward bankruptcy.
- Your particular industry—construction, for example—is being particularly hard hit because of high interest problems.

16.6 PERTINENT COURT DECISIONS —PRO AND CON

Pro
Jamil and Mahason Diab (TC Memo 1979-475)

Findings of Fact

Jamil, a real estate developer, lent $300 to an acquaintance. The money was never repaid so the taxpayer claimed that the debt became worthless in 1966—and took a bad-debt deduction in that amount.

The government contended that the petitioner had made no effort to collect the debt but instead gratuitously discharged the obligation.

Mr. Diab did not deny lack of collection effort but instead claimed that, because of the debtor's extremely poor financial condition, his age, and ill health, attempts to collect would have been useless.

Opinion

Referring to Regulation 1.166-2(b) and Sherman v. Comm. 18 TC 746,752 (1952), the court ruled that nothing in the law requires a creditor to engage in futile acts.

Under the circumstances, the taxpayer was justified in refraining from instituting legal proceedings and acted properly in determining the debt to be worthless.

Con
Appalachian Trail Company (TC Memo 1973-119)

Findings of Fact

Petitioner is in the wholesale business of manufacturing and selling oak flooring. Its normal procedure is to take orders and ship directly to its wholesalers' customers. During the years 1963 through 1965 and for most of 1966, it followed this sales procedure with the Northerlin Company, Inc.

Normally, Northerlin paid promptly, but by the end of the taxpayer's fiscal year on February 28, 1967, it owed Appalachian $39,154. Petitioner's president did not learn of this fact until April of 1967. Upon receipt of this knowledge, he traveled to the Northerlin office to collect. Here, he found that this customer was "terribly insolvent."

Before Appalachian filed its tax return on May 15, 1967, Northerlin had made payments so that the account was reduced to $25,553. An additional sale was also made to this company in the amount of $2,769 on March 17, 1967. Still, the petitioner took a bad-debt deduction in the amount of $25,553 for the FY ending 2-28-67.

The IRS claimed that the debt did not become worthless in that year.

Opinion

Held for the government. Petitioner did not prove worthlessness. The record did not contain any precise information as to Northerlin's financial condition on the crucial date. Furthermore, petitioner collected a total of $16,370 in March and April of 1967 and made a credit sale to Northerlin in the amount of $2,769 after the close of its taxable year.

16.7 RELEVANT CODE AND REGULATION SECTIONS, PLUS PUBLICATION

Code

Section 111	Recovery of Bad Debts, Prior Taxes, and Delinquency Amounts
165(g)(c)	Security Defined
166	Bad Debts
166(c)	Reserve for Bad Debts
166(d)(2)	Nonbusiness Debt Defined
1038	Certain Reacquisitions of Real Property
6511(d)	Limitations on Credit or Refund (Special Rules Applicable to Income Taxes)

Regulations

Section 1.166-1(c)	Bona Fide Debt Required
1.166-4(b)(1)	Reasonableness of Addition to Reserve—Relevant Factors

Publication

548	Deduction for Bad Debts

16.8 APPLICABLE IRS MANUAL REFERENCES (INVESTIGATIVE TECHNIQUES)

Audit Technique Handbook for Internal Revenue Agents

MT 4231-24	Section 445	Exceptions to the General Rule—Claims, Bad Debts, or Worthless Securities
MT 4231-30	Section 676	Bad Debts

Specialized Industries Audit Guidelines

MT 4232.2-4	Section 263.1	Specific Charge-Off Method
	Section 263.2	Reserve Method

Tax Audit Guidelines, Individuals, Partnerships, Estates, and Trusts and Corporations

MT4233-1	Section 321.1(21)	Nonbusiness Bad Debts
	322.1(14)	Bad Debts
	520.1(12)	Bad Debts

Techniques Handbook for In-Depth Examinations

MT 4235-5	Section 6(12)0	Bad Debt and Interest Expenses
	7(21)4	Methods of Computer Application—(6) Verify Accounts Receivable and Bad-Debt Deduction

Inadequate Books and Records 17
(Section 6001)

17.1 IDENTIFYING THE PROBLEM

In the tax world of small and moderate-sized clients, lack of proper records is frequently seen as an inconsequential matter. This is dangerous and faulty thinking. Inadequate books and records can trigger all sorts of difficulties—all the way up to, and including, criminal fraud allegations.

IMPORTANT:

> **Inadequate books and records do not mean a "total lack." An entire bookkeeping program can be perfect except in one area—and still be classed as inadequate.**

One taxpayer wrote checks to "cash" and charged them to "purchases." The court held that such records were inadequate because of a lack of endorsements or other evidence showing the ultimate recipients of the payments. (Est. of Sperling, TC Memo. 1963-260, aff'd 341 F. (2d) 201, cert. den. 382 U.S. 827, 15L ed 2d 72)

WARNING:

> **Identifying inadequate records can many times be a problem in itself. How bad can they be before the IRS takes offense? If you take a chance and they turn out to be improper, you can be assured of a follow-up examination in the next year.**

Where records do not correctly reflect income, the government may resort to their own means of securing information—even to the service of summonses. These are served on a taxpayer's customers, banks, and others, demanding their records concerning dealings with your client. Very bad for business!

Inadequate records cause the IRS to look deeper. Failing to obtain proper records, the IRS can use any method it desires in arriving at correct taxable income—net worth, bank deposit, source and application of funds, etc. (Regulation 1.446-1(b)(1).

RED FLAG:

> In using these indirect methods, agents delve into all sorts of areas which they normally ignore—cash hoards, cost of living, vacation trips, safe deposit boxes. In so doing, they may discover manipulations that can be embarrassing.

In a fraud case, the absence or inadequacy of books and records is considered to be one of the "badges of fraud" which are used to determine whether or not a taxpayer is guilty of evasion.

Remember this as a problem: Once an IRS examiner embarks on an indirect, time-consuming trip such as one called "net worth," he or she has no intention of wasting these efforts. The auditor must realize some production (additional taxes) from the efforts or be criticized by superiors.

Civil and criminal penalties lurk in the background. Failure to keep proper books and records exposes the taxpayer to a 5 percent negligence penalty (Section 6653). Willful failure can result in a fine of not more than $10,000 or one year's imprisonment or both (Section 7203).

Poor records as they damage professional practices. If left unimproved, poor records leave the door open not only to taxpayer penalties but to practitioner fines as well. For example, should a professional allow the use of checks to "cash" as previously mentioned, he or she on audit would undoubtedly be assessed at least the $100 preparer-negligence penalty.

TAKE NOTE:

> The stigma of inadequate records will carry over to a practitioner—if frequent enough—labeling him or her a shiftless, careless professional and may even get such a practitioner into the "Problem Preparer's Program," where the government gives special attention to his or her clients' returns.

17.2 HOW THE IRS SEES THE ISSUE

The Service believes—and with some justification—that a lack of records or maintenance of inadequate books and records is often deliberately arranged to avoid—or even evade—taxes.

It believes that Section 6001 (below) is clear and should be obeyed:

> SEC. 6001. NOTICE OR REGULATIONS REQUIRING RECORDS, STATEMENTS, AND SPECIAL RETURNS.
>
> Every person liable for any tax imposed by this title, or for the collection thereof, shall keep such records, render such statements, make such returns and comply with such rules and regulations as the Secretary may from time to time prescribe. Whenever in the judgment of the Secretary it is necessary, he may require any person, by notice served upon such person or by regulations, to make such returns, render such statements, or keep such records, as the Secretary deems sufficient to show whether or not such person is liable for tax under this title. The only records which an employer shall be required to keep under this section in connection with charged tips shall be charge receipts and copies of statements furnished by employees under Section 6053(a).

17.3 FACTORS WHICH THE IRS CONSIDERS WHEN MAKING ITS AUDIT DECISION

The IRS defines inadequate records as a "lack of records, or records so incomplete that correctness of taxable income cannot be determined.

Its agents approach the problem by establishing a preexamination plan—one in which they anticipate that the records will not lend themselves to proper examination. They expect, in other words, that they will have to utilize some indirect method of constructing income. So they proceed accordingly, securing all information that they possibly can during the first interview.

Section 350 of IRS Manual MT 4235-5 (In-Depth Examinations) gives a good insight into examiners' modus operandi:

350

Inadequate Records

(1) Inadequate records is defined as the lack of records, or records so incomplete that correctness of taxable income cannot be determined.

(2) Chapter 900 of IRM 4231, Audit Technique Handbook for Internal Revenue Agents, covers the subject of inadequate records in detail.

(3) The approach to this problem must start with the preexamination plan in which the agent recognizes the probability that any records presented will not lend themselves to proper examination. Furthermore, since illegal income is generally not fully recorded, the indirect method of construction of income will probably have to be employed.

(4) In addition, the preparation of a net worth statement will probably be required in all cases; therefore, planning must be directed accordingly.

(5) Emphasis is placed on preexamination planning since it is highly possible that the most important phase of the investigation will revolve around the initial interview. This is the time the agent is afforded the opportunity to obtain information that may not be forthcoming at a later date.

(6) Since the interview should be developed to its utmost, it is advisable when an inadequate record situation is anticipated to have a witness to help document all answers and to attest to their accuracy. The interrogation must be preplanned and well conceived. Details for developing the initial interview are covered under heading of Initial Contract.

Note the emphasis on collection of information "which might not later be available"—and on the "presence of a witness."

WARNING:

Investigations of this type are dangerous. Taxpayer divulgence of the amount of a cash hoard, for example, can be fatal. See book section 17.5 (Handling the Audit) for suggestions as to how to proceed under these circumstances.

How the IRS Makes the Inadequate Records Decision

The initial decision as to whether records are improper rests with the examiner. If this individual believes that they are, he or she will discuss the matter with his or her superior. They jointly use the following criteria in making the ultimate decision—and decide whether an inadequate records notice (Letter 978(DO)) and Form 2807 (Agreement to Maintain Adequate Books of Account and Records) will be issued:

1. Prior history and present degree of noncompliance.
2. Indications of willful intent.
3. Evidence of refusal to keep records.
4. Other evidence of harm to the government.
5. Probability that the bookkeeping inadequacies will result in significant under-reporting of tax.
6. Likelihood that compliance can be enforced if the taxpayer fails or refuses to correct inadequacies.
7. Anticipated revenue in relation to the time and effort required to obtain compliance.

If Agreement (Form 2807) is utilized and signed by the taxpayer, it is attached to the inadequate records notice, Letter 978(DO) (Figure 17-1). The letter is then served upon the taxpayer.

It is the responsibility of the Service Center to associate Letter 978 (DO) and attachment with the income tax return of the taxpayer for the first taxable year beginning after the notice was delivered. Subsequently, a follow-up examination will occur. If the records are later found to be inadequate still, penalties may be meted out under circumstances as previously explained.

INTERNAL REVENUE SERVICE   **DEPARTMENT OF THE TREASURY**
District Director

    Date: **Social Security or**
                                      Employer Identification Number:

                                      Person to Contact:

                                      Contact Telephone Number:

    Our review shows that you are not keeping adequate records to determine your correct Federal tax liability. The reasons why your records are not adequate are explained below.

    You are required by law to keep permanent records and supporting documents. Penalties may be charged for your not doing so. The applicable provisions of the Internal Revenue Code and Regulations are printed on the back of this letter.

    This letter is your official notice to keep complete records so your correct tax liability may be determined. The records you keep must show all of the following information.

(1) The date and a description of each transaction you engaged in.
(2) The date and amount of each item of gross income received.
(3) A description of the nature of income received.
(4) The date and amount of each payment you made.
(5) The name and address of the payee.
(6) A description of the nature of each payment.

    If you have any questions, please contact the person whose name and telephone number are shown above.

                                        Sincerely yours,

                                      District Director

Your records are not adequate in the following ways:

APPLICABLE PROVISIONS OF THE INTERNAL REVENUE CODE AND REGULATIONS

Section 6001 of the Internal Revenue Code provides as follows:

"Every person liable for any tax imposed by this title, or for the collection thereof, shall keep such records, render such statements, make such returns, and comply with such rules and regulations as the Secretary may from time to time prescribe. Whenever in the judgment of the Secretary it is necessary, he may require any person, by notice served upon such person or by regulations, to make such returns, render such statements, or keep such records, as the Secretary deems sufficient to show whether or not such person is liable for tax under this title."

Section 1.6001-1(e) of the Regulations under the Internal Revenue Code provides as follows:

"(e) Retention of Records.—The books or records required by this section shall be kept at all times available for inspection by authorized internal revenue officers or employees, and shall be retained so long as the contents thereof may become material in the administration of any internal revenue law."

Section 7203 of the Internal Revenue Code provides as follows:

"Any person required under this title to pay any estimated tax or tax, or required by this title or by regulations made under authority thereof to make a return (other than a return required under authority of section 6015), keep any records, or supply any information, who willfully fails to pay such estimated tax or tax, make such return, keep such records, or supply such information, at the time or times required by law or regulations, shall, in addition to other penalties provided by law, be guilty of a misdemeanor and, upon conviction thereof, shall be fined not more than $10,000, or imprisoned not more than 1 year, or both, together with the costs of prosecution."

ORIGINAL OF THIS NOTICE SERVED AS INDICATED

Taxpayer's name	Social security or employer identification number

Date (day, month, year) taxpayer was verbally told records were not adequate

Agreement Form 2807 solicited ☐ Secured ☐ Not secured	Date solicited (day, month, year)
Original of this notice personally served on (name)	Date (day, month, year)

Address where notice was served

Signature of person serving notice	Title

Figure 17-1

WARNING:

If section 7203 seems to have been violated, and if the practitioner is not an attorney, one should be retained so that arrangements can be made for the practitioner to work under the attorney's umbrella of privilege.

Indirect Methods of Constructing Income

The Service generally uses one of two indirect methods to arrive at correct income—Net Worth or Bank Deposit. In criminal cases, it may use both or tie them in with specific items of unreported income.

The Net Worth method of determining income is based on the theory that increases or decreases in the taxpayer's net worth during a taxable period—adjusted for nontaxable income and nondeductible expenditures—must be the result of taxable income. It is generally used where more than one year is involved and where a likely source of taxable income can be proved.

The Bank Deposit method is well illustrated in U.S. v Parks 74-1 U.S.T.C. 9312 (5th Cir. 1974). In this case the court required the government to demonstrate that the taxpayer had a business of lucrative nature (a source of taxable income) and that during the years in question Parks made regular periodic deposits in bank accounts in his own name or in accounts over which he exercised control. Where the annual deposits exceeded exemptions and deductions, the balance represented taxable income.

This basic formula is generally refined by adding cash expenditures and deducting nontaxable income.

NOTE:

The courts have many times rejected the IRS use of indirect methods of reconstructing income in instances where proper records existed.

17.4 CONSIDERATIONS WHEN PREPARING THE RETURN

Certainly, if a new client has been previously served with an inadequate records notice—and still maintains substantially poor records—your first job should be to put them in order. Check below to determine what types of books and records are considered "adequate."

Primary and secondary records and their use in adhering to regulations is described in *IRS Audit Guidelines for Examiners.* MT 4231-46, Chapter 700. Paragraphs (2), (3), and (4) of 710 (Accounting Records) are reproduced below:

> (2) The primary (informal) records common to all types of businesses and their accounting systems are those documents upon which are recorded the individual transactions of buying and selling merchandise, supplies, services, assets used in the business, and capital assets. These documents include invoices, vouchers, bills, receipts, and tapes. When inventories are an income-determining factor, the primary records include detailed inventory lists. Also to be included are such evidences of financial transactions as canceled checks, duplicate deposit slips, bank statements and notes.

(3) The secondary (formal) records, which are utilized regardless of the accounting method employed by the taxpayer, are the permanent books, worksheets, tallies, etc. These records list or summarize the primary records in proper classifications of income or expense and reflect adjustment when necessary. They are designed to aid taxpayers in determining their financial status and profit or loss at the end of any given period. These secondary records may consist of a single book or record, a simple set of books, or a complicated set of records in which numerous analyses, consolidations, or summarizations are made before the final result is obtained.

(4) The only taxpayers not required to keep these so-called secondary records are those whose sole source of gross income is from salaries, wages, or similar compensation for personal services rendered, or from farming. All taxpayers are required to keep the primary records and are required to be prepared to show how each item of income and expenses on the return was computed. All records shall be retained so long as the contents thereof may become material in the administration of any internal revenue law.

Books and records. These two nouns are synonymous in meeting government regulations in that they *both* must be maintained in a proper manner. Otherwise, the inadequacy claim may pop up. As previously mentioned, checks to "Cash" charged to "Purchases" brought on the IRS charge of inadequate records.

Checks to an establishment, such as a large general mail-order house, can be meaningless as to proof of purpose. (Personal items may have been purchased.) Paid invoices are needed. If a sufficient number of the latter are missing for this type of expenditure, records can be classed as unsatisfactory.

In one instance, IRS audit agents found that all cancelled checks were missing. Records were otherwise perfect. The taxpayer's bookkeeper posted from check stubs, but none of the paid bills for merchandise purchased matched the stubs. The invoices called for larger amounts.

What sort of a scheme was this? In the end—after much reproduction of checks from bank Recordak films—it was determined that the taxpayer intentionally understated his purchases because he was also understating his sales and wanted the markup percentage to present a correct ratio. An IRS inadequate-records allegation and fraud charge resulted.

17.5 HANDLING THE AUDIT

In book section 17.3 a brief explanation of the Service's preexamination plan was given. The gist of government's technique: "Prepare carefully for the initial interview where inadequate records are suspected; then secure all the information possible at this first meeting because it might not be available later."

The government, in its *Audit Technique Handbook for Internal Revenue Agents,* suggests the following means of developing inadequate records suspicions. Its agents should

1. Read prior examination reports and discuss the condition of the taxpayer's records with the prior Revenue Agent.
2. Obtain existing accountant's audit reports in a search for any mention of inadequate records.
3. Inspect trial balances and balance sheets as of the beginning and ending of the year.

4. Where necessary, reconcile income per books with income per return and observe whether earned surplus and capital accounts in the books agree with these same accounts on the balance sheets.

NOTE:

Presumably (3) and (4) are accomplished through use of practitioner workpapers. It isn't likely that books could be obtained *before* the initial interview.

You and the Revenue Agent Put Your House in Order at the Outset.

The examining officer, therefore, may be visiting the practitioner first. If this happens to you, do not allow such a person to walk in unexpectedly—ask for your workpapers—and immediately receive them. Learn all you can regarding the purpose of his or her visit; then make an appointment for a future time.

In the interim, carefully review your workpapers and your client's books and records. Do not alter either in any way. Secure backup material. Make sure that the books and your material mesh properly. Inquire of your client as to the prior existence of any inadequate records notices. Put your house in order. Then consider the intensity of the Initial Interview Technique.

Should Your Client Be Present at Audit Time?

This is an old and troublesome question. It can probably be answered in this situation by reference to paragraph (3) of Figure 17-2. Note the all-important necessity for the proving of "starting cash." Without this figure solidly established, the government is actually not in a good position to use indirect methods of establishing income, such as net worth and bank deposit.

Cash on hand may consist of undivulged bank accounts or cash hoards developed over the years from tax paid or nontaxable sources. Both can be available to legitimately increase a taxpayer's net worth or to fatten bank deposits without the existence of tax evasion or avoidance.

VERY IMPORTANT:

It is imperative, therefore, that the government solidify the amount of this asset before proceeding further with indirect methods. Why then should your client, in a fit of cooperation, testify against his or her own interests?

For this reason and because of all the dangers inherent in this inadequate records dilemma, I'd think twice before allowing a client to be present at this initial interview.

This is not to deny the government its answers, but to insure that all replies are correct and carefully weighed for the possible existence of indications of fraud—violation of inadequate records statutes or existence of falsehoods.

Should any of these appear, you would want to be in a position to recommend that your client take advantage of the Fifth Amendment to the Constitution which allows a person not to answer government questions on the grounds that such replies might be incriminating.

Certainly no harm can come from your sifting through questions and answers before their delivery, and employing an attorney if the situation requires such a move.

INSIDE TIP:

> Rarely will agents become upset because your client is not present. They won't work harder and they won't be vindictive, but they will be jubilant if your client appears, goes the whole route, and
>
> > Admits to a complete lack of "starting cash."
> > Provides cost-of-living statements for each year in question.
> > Identifies all assets and liabilities.
> > Admits to never having received any type of nontaxable income.
> > Opens the safe-deposit box for inspection.

In other words, your client provides a nice beginning for a net-worth attack.

Recommendation: Secure a power of attorney from your client (Form 2848). Attend the initial interview at the location requested. It will probably be at your client's office, because the agent will want to look things over—your client included. After this first interview, suggest that any subsequent sessions be held in your office.

After your client meets the agent, he or she should leave. You take over. Answer all questions concerning the books and records for which you confidently know the answers. Write all others down for later replies. Write down also all personal questions concerning your client. Later, after matching queries with correct answers, you will be in a position to judge which route is most advantageous for your client to follow—with or without client's cooperation.

WARNING:

> If you do not feel comfortable with your knowledge of rules of evidence, tax fraud, etc., *do* recommend to your client that he or she employ a knowledgeable tax attorney.

---

60 5-81   Audit Guidelines for Examiners   7245-27

Chapter 800

INDIRECT METHODS

810 (4-23-81)
Introduction

(1) There are two basic methods of determining or proving income; the direct or specific item method and the indirect method. The specific item method involves the verification or determination of each questionable item of income and expense which affects the taxpayer's liability. The indirect method involves the development of circumstantial proof of income by the use of net worth, bank deposits, source and application of funds, etc. The indirect methods of determining income will be discussed here.

(2) The indirect methods of proving income described in this Chapter will be used primarily in the examination of business returns. However, they can be successfully employed to determine additional income and verify deductions on nonbusiness returns. Further, these methods are not limited to situations where records appear inadequate. To the contrary, these methods can be used to show inaccuracies, intentional or otherwise, in what may at first appear to be well kept and accurate books and records.

820 (4-23-81)
Initial Interview Techniques

(1) One of the most important phases of any examination is the initial interview with the taxpayer. This is especially true when the records are inadequate, nonexistent, or there is reason to believe that they are false.

(2) During the initial interview, in addition to securing all business information, it is advisable to secure as much

information as possible about the taxpayer's personal living habits, expenses, and financial history.

(3) Determine the extent of the taxpayer's cash on hand and cash hoards. In many instances, the entire case may hinge upon the correct determination of these items. It is important that the examiner structure any questions in such a manner as to leave little doubt as to what is asked. If it appears that this may be a significant area, it may be necessary to secure an affidavit from the taxpayer or have a witness to corroborate the answer given. In some cases, the taxpayer will later claim that a large amount of cash was on hand at the beginning of the period in an attempt to counteract understatements determined by these methods. In other words, the taxpayer may allege that the cash utilized to acquire assets, pay expenses, etc., in the years under examination, was accumulated in prior years. The examiner is then faced with the problem of verifying the taxpayer's contentions.

(a) A prime consideration in the determination and allowance of cash on hand at the beginnning of a period, is the taxpayer's filing history. An analysis of net income reported in prior years may indicate that cash accumulations claimed would be an impossibility when compared to the income previously reported. The only defense the taxpayer could offer is that the income was from a nontaxable source or income was understated in prior years.

(b) In many instances the taxpayer may have filed balance sheets with financial or credit organizations. This may assist the examiner in the determination of the opening cash accumulations.

(c) Loans and chattel mortgages on automobiles, personal furniture and other equipment, especially if at a high interest rate, may be evidence that the taxpayer would not have any sizeable cash accumulations during that period.

(4) Other items which should be covered during the initial interview include:

(a) Loans receivable and payable.

(b) Assets owned, bought, and sold including: real estate, equipment, auto, household, securities, government bonds, notes, etc.

(c) Bank accounts and location—checking and savings accounts, personal and business, certificates of deposit.

(d) Safe deposit box location.

(e) Employee reimbursements received.

(f) Nontaxable income such as gifts, inheritances, social security payments, unemployment compensation, and insurance proceeds.

(g) Operation of business—internal control, personal use of merchandise, years involved in business, bartering activities, etc.

(h) Information on inventories, method used in determination, and any workpapers used in the computations.

(i) Listing of the taxpayer's equipment, showing dates of acquisition and disposition, costs, selling prices, suppliers, trade-ins, whether financed or paid for without borrowed funds.

MT 42 31-46   **820**

Figure 17-2

Defensing Net Worth and Bank Deposit Methods

Books can be written on this subject; so I'll touch upon only a few highlights.

WARNING:

It is the government's responsibility to prove both harmful and helpful evidence in the development of their indirect methods. Agents, however, are not as diligent in producing the latter as the former.

In a bank deposit case, for example, all unexplained deposits are considered taxable income. The agents total the deposits—remove any obviously nontaxable income—then claim all else to be taxable. It is up to you and your client to prove otherwise. Here are some possibilities:

1. If your client has not talked and talked and talked, possibly unknown bank accounts exist from which funds were transferred to known accounts.

2. Maybe there were transfers from brokerage accounts of which the agents did not have knowledge.

3. Deposits (with check or otherwise) may represent sale of capital assets which were reported on the tax return—proceeds only partially taxable.

4. All sorts of nontaxable deposits may have been made. Down payment on purchase of taxpayer's home, for instance—returned when deal fell through.

5. Deposits may have been made with cash from accumulated savings held at home.

How do you prove the existence of this cash hoard? Sometimes easily.

Proving a Cash Hoard

■ Possibly the taxpayer has a record of accumulated cash—with dates of additions, deletions, or sources.

■ Possibly a relative or friend has assisted in counting the money and can so testify.

■ Occasionally, cash withdrawals from bank accounts can be utilized to indicate additions to cash hoard where no record of a corresponding expenditure can be found.

■ Maybe a personal asset was sold at no gain, the cancelled check for which gives indication that it was cashed.

■ Sale of a capital asset for cash—only the gain subject to tax.

■ Cash receipts of an individual proprietorship, received and reported in the prior year but not deposited in any bank. Added to hoard.

■ Gifts of cash as attested to by the donor.

■ Cashed checks representing federal income tax refunds.

■ Occasionally the IRS will accept corresponding visitation dates to a safe-deposit box and a savings account as evidence that the amount of the deposit may have come from a cash hoard.

The list is long. Be sure to search all nooks and crannies.

NOTE:

One taxpayer saved his salary checks from his closely held corporation for three years then cashed them all on the same day. The IRS got excited, but to no avail. The taxpayer produced the cancelled check and proved the legitimacy of the surfaced currency.

Defensing the bank deposit method requires careful and complete analysis of all deposits and withdrawals. Proving errors in the government's position goes a long way toward casting doubt on its claims that unexplained deposits are taxable income.

The net worth method of reconstructing income is strongly dependent upon a taxpayer's cooperation. Without it, the government will have considerable difficulty in proving the opening net worth position.

This position, if shown to be erroneous, can cause a court to reject the government's case. It is easily understood why. The higher the opening net worth, the lower the increase that the IRS considers additional taxable income.

Omitted assets such as "cash on hand"—understated liabilities and asset costs—all cause trouble for the IRS. Proof of a taxpayer's cash hoard can be obtained as indicated above under the bank deposit method. Most defenses applicable to this latter method also apply to net worth.

If not furnished by the taxpayer, such items as cost of living, cash on hand, gifts, nontaxable income, and inheritances will have to be either estimated by the government or hunted down, if possible. Without cancelled checks, the job of putting together a net worth method becomes infinitely more difficult.

RED FLAG:

> **Again I say, "Don't allow your clients to unnecessarily cooperate themselves into tax or fraud trouble."**

The practitioner should do the analyzing, comparing, answering, and cooperating—not the taxpayer. This applies even in office audit cases where the questions and requests for documentation are clear-cut and easily complied with. Normally, the examiner will inquire only into matters listed in his letter to the taxpayer. Should the practitioner however, become garrulous and open up new areas of possible noncompliance, a whole new ball game could result.

17.6 PERTINENT COURT DECISIONS—PRO AND CON

Pro
(TC Memo 1963 - 145)

Findings of Fact

The taxpayer, John N. Gounaris, a Greek National, entered this country by jumping ship in the port of New York. At that time he possessed $500 in cash and had a fifth-grade education.

For many years thereafter he held various menial positions in restaurants until he finally became a kitchen manager. He lived frugally, worked double shifts whenever possible, and frequently worked as a waiter at special parties. He did not gamble or drink intoxicants. Mistakenly, he did not report tips, which he believed were gifts.

Eventually he became a partner in the operation of two restaurants. His associate handled the cash and recorded the sales. Unfortunately, at the time of audit, the sales journal for one of the restaurants, or "black book" as it was called, was missing. The IRS claimed inadequate records and utilized a net worth method to establish civil fraud and a large deficiency. No "opening cash" was allowed.

Petitioner Gounaris claimed, through his representative, that the opening net worth was grossly in error—that the government's computations were incorrect, that no fraudulent intent existed, and that the statute of limitations had, in fact, expired on all years except one.

Opinion

The court found an abundance of evidence which proved the existence of $15,000 in opening cash, a government error of some $14,000 to $16,000 in opening bank balances, and other indications of faulty considerations and excess cost-of-living additions.

The main point here is the court's approach to the importance of the opening net worth position. It relied on a landmark case, Holland v. U.S., 348 U.S. 121 (46 AFTR 943), in which the Supreme Court said:

We agree with petitioners that an essential condition in cases of this type is the establishment, with reasonable certainty, of an opening net worth, to serve as a starting point from which to calculate future increases in the taxpayer's assets. The importance of accuracy in this figure is immediately apparent, as the correctness of the result depends entirely upon the inclusion in this sum of all assets on hand at the outset....

Since the court had received evidence of outright IRS errors and testimony that Gounaris had used large denomination currency (smelling of moth balls) to purchase assets, it ruled in favor of the taxpayer.

(Please let me say again—no taxpayer, when requested to do so by the IRS, should voluntarily provide opening net worth figures.)

Con
(Rev. Rul. 68-420, 1968-2 CB 257)

Findings of Fact

The taxpayer, a domestic building and loan association, to which Section 593 applies, deducted additions to its bad-debt reserve for the tax years in question and recorded such in its general ledger. The various subsidiary reserve accounts as maintained by the association did not, however, contain any entries for the years at issue.

Details of these reserve accounts (four in number) were maintained in a public accountant's work papers and not associated with the books and records of the taxpayer.

Opinion

Quoting from Rev. Rul. 58-601, the IRS noted that "accountants' work papers may not be considered as meeting the requirements of permanent auxiliary records unless they are sufficiently complete and accurate to provide a reliable and reasily accessible basis for reconciling the regularly maintained books of account and the tax returns—and if the originals of such work papers are turned over to the taxpayer and associated with the taxpayer's regular books of account."

Held that record-keeping requirements were not met. Thus no deduction could be allowed for additions to the bad-debt reserve.

17.7 RELEVANT CODE AND REGULATION SECTION, PLUS PUBLICATION

Code

Section 446	General Rule for Methods of Accounting
446(b)	Exceptions
6001	Notice or Regulations Requiring Records, Statements, and Special Returns
6653	Failure to Pay Tax
6361(a)	Collection of State Individual Income Taxes—General Rules—Collection and Administration
7203	Willful Failure to File Return, Supply Information, or Pay Tax

Regulations

Section 1.446-1(b)(1)		Statutory Provisions: General Rule for Methods of Accounting—Exceptions
1.6001-1(a)		Records—in General
	(b)	Farmers and Wage Earners
	(c)	Exempt Organizations
	(d)	Notice by District Director Requiring Returns, Statements, or the Keeping of Records
	(e)	Retention of Records

Publication

583	Record Keeping for a Small Business

17.8 APPLICABLE IRS MANUAL REFERENCES (INVESTIGATIVE TECHNIQUES)

Audit Guidelines for Examiners

MT 4231-24	Section 510	Accounting Records and Methods
	520	General Adequacy of Records
	710	Accounting Records
	820	Initial Interview Techniques
	·940	Badges of Fraud
	962	Attitude and Conduct of the Taxpayer

General

MT 4000-159 Section 4022.3	Factors to Consider Before Issuing Summons

Income Tax Examinations

MT 4200-399 Section 4297	Procedure Where Taxpayers Have Failed to Maintain Proper Records

Specialized Industries Audit Guidelines

MT 4232-7 Section 322	Inadequate Records

In-Depth Examinations

MT 4235-5 Section 350	Inadequate Records

Travel and Entertainment Expenses

18

(Sections 162, 212, 274)

18.1 IDENTIFYING THE PROBLEM

The problem is nearly as old as taxes themselves. Because of the opportunity for tax-free living and enjoying, traveling or selling persons have always been subjected to more than their share of IRS auditing, and there doesn't seem to be any relief in sight. In fact, the Service yearly becomes more demanding in its proof requirements and restrictions.

The writers of Section 274 (Disallowance of Certain Entertainment, etc., Expenses) totally disbelieved the ancient saying that "casting bread upon the waters will cause it to return a hundredfold."

Instead, this section sternly lays out a large grouping of "can'ts and don'ts"—but even before these restrictions apply, deductions for travel, entertainment, or gifts must otherwise qualify under Chapter I (Income Tax) of the Code. They must be ordinary and necessary business expenses under Section 162 (Trade or Business) or Section 212 (Expenses for Production of Income).

Section 274 Restrictions

In planning a travel and giving budget, a salesperson has the problem of steering a qualifying path through a maze of limitations. Section 274 says that

- An expenditure for entertainment cannot be lavish or extravagant, and it must meet one of two tests:
  1. Directly related to, or
  2. Associated with, the active conduct of a trade or buisness.
- Entertainment deductions cannot include the cost of visitations to night clubs, floor shows, or sporting events, except before or after a legitimate business meeting. More details later.

■ Expenses relating to entertainment facilities, such as the purchase and upkeep of yachts and hunting lodges, are generally not deductible. This rule also covers losses on sale of such facilities.

■ The cost of customer gifts may not exceed $25 if they are to be deductible.

■ Club dues and fees are deductible only if the taxpayer proves that the facility was used primarily to further the trade or business—and that the cost was "directly related."

■ To deduct the cost of meals and drinks, a taxpayer's meeting with a customer must adhere to the "quiet business meal" rule. The atmosphere at the rendezvous point must be conducive to a business discussion—at home, for example, or in a quiet restaurant.

■ Rules for taking deductions for foreign conventions changed drastically beginning in 1981. No deductions will be allowed unless it is "reasonable" for the convention to be held outside North America. Seminars or conventions on cruise ships are out.

■ Amounts paid to employees or independent contractors for travel and entertainment (T&E) carry their own particular set of rules.

■ Travel requires the "away from home" status to be deductible and generally includes meals and lodging. It also must meet all other requirements of Sections 274, 162, or 212.

■ Per diem and mileage allowances—or actual expense deductions—enter the picture. Which are best?

■ Substantiation rules are tough and demanding.

Additional problems, including such items as temporary employment, outside salespersons, traveling with a spouse, and trips that are split between business and pleasure—all add to T&E difficulties. Frequent changes in T&E rules over the years haven't helped matters either.

18.2 HOW THE IRS SEES THE ISSUE

When T&E enters the picture, visions of all sorts of tax-free goodies float into the minds of IRS auditors—sumptuous meals, very dry martinis, lively yacht parties, fancy country clubs, elaborate vacation trips—all at Uncle's expense, and much of which is not technically deductible.

Examiners also feel that four unsavory situations are likely to exist:

1. T&E expenses will be hidden in various record corners, such as automotive expenses, advertising, selling and/or miscellaneous expenses—anywhere but in "travel and entertainment" where they belong.

2. Luncheons, dinners, sporting events will be contrived to somehow remotely dodge the requirements of Section 274. For instance—and the IRS says this—not I:

> The entertainment of other doctors and patients which is of a reciprocal nature should not be allowed. An example of this would be a group of doctors who customarily refer patients to one another and who also attend social events together for which they take turns purchasing the tickets. Another example would be the reciprocal cost of meals by doctors who are associated with the same hospital or who share a medical suite and lunch together.

3. In the case of employees, T&E expenses could have been deducted in situations where such expenditures were not required by the employer, or were actually commuting expenses, or were incurred while traveling away from a residence instead of away from a "tax home," or were not incurred while "away from home overnight."

4. Correct allocation of business and pleasure—or spouse and taxpayer—expenses may not have been made in computing the deduction.

18.3 FACTORS WHICH THE IRS CONSIDERS WHEN MAKING ITS AUDIT DECISION

According to Internal Revenue Audit Manuals, the Service asks its examiners to be especially alert to the following T&E facts or circumstances which might yield additional revenue:

- Deductions which do not meet the "ordinary and necessary" business expense requirements.
- Substantiation which does not establish
  1. The relationship of the expenditure to business.
  2. The payee and place of expenditure.
  3. The identity of the persons involved, including parties enertained, if any.
  4. The amount of the expenditure.
- Employer expense allowances not properly accounted for on employee returns.
- Personal expenses possibly buried in T&E accounts.
- Company owned or rented automobiles, hunting lodges, resort property, yachts, airplanes, apartments, or hotel suites.
- Families at conventions or business meetings.
- Expense-paid vacations of owners and employees, or members of their families, not reported on Form W-2.
- Cash expenditures or checks payable to owners—or to employees closely related by blood or marriage to them.
- Lack of records so that an "insufficient records notice" should be prepared and served.
- Employer-paid vacations or trips issued as prizes to individuals other than employees. (Were Forms 1099 filed?)
- Lack of T&E schedules or Forms 2106 (Employee Business Expenses) for returns where they would normally appear; e.g., employees who are sales or public relations persons.

18.4 CONSIDERATIONS WHEN PREPARING THE RETURN

A practitioner, when preparing a return with T&E issues, should be particularly concerned with the requirements of Section 274. Before moving along to specifics, let's get one (to be deductible) essential out of the way. This will eliminate frequent repetition of this single point:

ALL EXPENDITURES, OF WHATEVER CLASSIFICATION, MUST FIRST OF ALL MEET THE "ORDINARY AND NECESSARY BUSINESS-EXPENSE" TEST AS COVERED BY EITHER SECTION 162 OR SECTION 212.

Travel and Transportation Expenses

These are somewhat related but different in application. "Travel" generally includes the cost of movement from one place to another *plus* expenses applicable to meals and lodging while "away from home overnight."

"Transportation" means the cost of travel by air, bus, rail, taxi, etc., and the cost of maintaining and driving a car, but *not* the cost of meals and lodging.

Away from home overnight does not always mean what it says in a literal sense. If a trip is of sufficient duration to allow for sleep or rest, then it qualifies.

Example: An airline pilot leaves home at 6:00 A.M. and returns at 11:00 P.M. At his layover point he rents a motel room and gets a few hours' sleep. The trip is considered to have been "away from home overnight." (Rev. Rul. 75-170, 1975-1 Cum. Bul. 60)

Where is home? In an old precedent-setting case (Comm. v. Flowers (1946) 326 U.S. 465, 34 AFTR 301) the court ruled that the taxpayer's tax home was where his business was, not where he resided. In other words, your residence can be in Philadelphia while your principal place of employment or business is in New York.

IMPORTANT:

The IRS insists that your tax home is in the latter location. The cost of traveling to and from New York is "commuting" and not deductible.

Temporary employment is defined by the IRS as being that which is "of a definite, limited duration up to one year." Presumably, an indefinite employment period will not qualify, although in Harvey v. Comm. (CA-9, 1960) 283 F. 2d 491, 6 AFTR 2d 5780, the court ruled that an indefinite period which extended a little beyond one year did qualify. The IRS objected—and still does. Here's what transpired:

Harvey was transferred by his employer to a locality beyond commuting range for an indefinite period. He received a per diem allowance which the IRS claimed was additional compensation because his stay did not meet "temporary" rules. The court ruled that it did.

INSIDE TIP:

The government's position in this instance seems strange, since scores of its own representatives in all branches of civil service are constantly being assigned to temporary duties which frequently extend far beyond one year. These agents receive per diem allowances. Not one, to my knowledge, ever classified such reimbursement as addditional compensation. Nor do I believe that they should, since few, if any, volunteered for their assignment.

Traveling with a spouse. The question to be answered here is whether or not you can prove that the presence of a spouse was *essential* to a business purpose. Mere convenience will not qualify nor will performance of incidental services. Court decisions have gone every which way.

Observation: For this reason, my suggestion would be to take the deduction for spouses in all instances where it appears that the taxpayer qualifies. After all, the full cost of travel for the principal can always be deducted as though he or she made the trip alone. (Rev. Rul. 56-168, 1956-1 CB 93)

Foreign travel carries generally the same rules as those for domestic movements. Allocations between business and nonbusiness activities, however, do differ.

- For domestic travel no allocation of expenses is necessary—not even for transportation costs. All that's required is that direct, nonbusiness expenses not be deducted and that the purpose of the trip be primarily for business.

- For foreign travel, an allocation is required unless the trip is no more than seven consecutive days in duration, or unless the time spent on nonbusiness matters is less than 25 percent of the total time spent away from home.

Conventions—Foreign and Domestic

Prior to 1981 no more than two foreign meetings could be attended in any one year, and the cost deducted. Beginning in 1981, however, any number may be enjoyed, but the qualification rules are tougher. Now, no deduction will be allowed for expenses attributable to conventions that are held outside North America unless it is "reasonable" for such a gathering to be held in the foreign location.

Reasonableness is decided by application of three factors:

1. The purpose of the meeting and the activities indulged in,
2. The purpose and activities of the sponsoring organization, and
3. The residences of the active members of the sponsoring organizations and places where other meetings of the sponsors have been or will be held. (Sections 274(h)(1)(A)-(D))

Other relevant factors will, of course, be considered.

NOTE:

Pacific Island Trust Territory is exempt from the North American rule—and Jamaica has recently been added by the signing of a new tax treaty.

Other regional countries such as the U.S. Virgin Islands, Puerto Rico, the Bahamas, and Bermuda may also eventually be exempt, since they are presently complaining bitterly, "Why Jamaica and not us?"

The cost of attending conventions, both foreign and domestic, will be allowed only if such expenditures meet the following criteria:

1. The primary purpose of the trip is to maintain or improve skills required in business or employment.
2. The cost is an ordinary and necessary business expense (Section 162).
3. The meeting is attended to aid in the management, conservation, or maintenance of property held for the production of income (Section 212).
4. The expense is incurred in connection with the determination, collection, or refund of any tax.

Transportation Expenses

All business-purpose costs of public transportation, plus automobile expenses, within the United States are deductible—tips, toll charges, parking fees as well—but not the cost of meals unless the taxpayer is in travel status. Such expenses are generally applicable to local itineraries and are deductible in arriving at adjusted gross.

In taking the deductions, care must be exercised that they do not stray into the "commuting" classification. Transportation expenses are nondeductible.

Example: If the taxpayer is a plumber with a office and warehouse ten miles from home, transportation to his or her place of business is not deductible—only the traveling from there to customer locations qualifies. Going home directly after the last stop is part of commuting and not deductible.

Car expenses and mileage allowances. Either employees or independent business people may use one of two methods in deducting automobile expenses (portion applicable to business):

1. Actual costs include *depreciation, insurance, investment credit, property taxes, finance charges, etc. Good records are a necessity.
2. Standard mileage rate is allowed by the IRS under the following stipulations. Taxpayer must
   a. Own the car.
   b. Not use it for hire, such as for a taxi.
   c. Not operate a fleet of cars, using two or more at the same time.
   d. Not have claimed depreciation using any method other than straight-line.
   e. Not have claimed additional first year depreciation on the car.

*A vehicle is considered fully depreciated at the end of 60,000 miles of business use. At this time the mileage allowance will be reduced *but not eliminated*. See Publication 463 (Travel, Entertainment and Gift Expenses).

RECOMMENDATION:

Since the auto mileage rate traditionally lags far behind actual costs, it is strongly suggested that taxpayers at least test each method. Usually the actual-cost method will be most advantageous. If the car is used 50 percent for business and 50 percent for personal purposes, it is a simple matter to apply the business percentage.

For additional details concerning this subject, see Chapter 27 (The Business Automobile).

Reimbursed Expenses

In general four situations exist:

1. Excess of reimbursement over actual expenses must be included as income.
2. Excess of expenses over reimbursement may be deducted but only where *all* expenses are proven and information is furnished as for (4) below.
3. If employees are required to account to their employer for costs of travel, transportation, etc., then they need not report such reimbursement on their tax returns, but may be required to prove that they did not realize any gain from these receipts (Regulation 1.274-5(e)(2)).
4. If employees *do not* account to their employers for such expenditures, they are required to report total amounts received as advances or reimbursements, their occupation, number of days away from home, the amount of business expenses paid or incurred, and the specific identity of each. In addition, they must maintain records and documentation for such expenditures (Regulation 1.274-5(e)(3)).

Form 2106 (Employee Business Expenses) can be used for reporting purposes in this instance and for all other like purposes.

Accounting to an employer. This is accomplished by furnishing the employer with a record of all data as listed in (4) above, along with substantiation of applicable expenditures. Normally, under these circumstances, the IRS will not require further proof. It might, however, where the employee is a majority stockholder or is a close relative of the employer.

Per diem allowances. If an employer pays per diem allowances, excluding transportation costs, of a flat amount instead of actual travel and living expenses, the employee need not report such income unless the amount expended

1. Exceeded the per diem received, or
2. Exceeded the maximum per diem rate authorized by the federal government to its employees in the locality traveled.

This government rate moves up and down like a yo-yo. For Great Falls, Montana, the allowance can be $41 a day, while in Barbados it can be $140. Most tax services list the approved rates. See Prentice-Hall #16,961 or the official government listing in Federal Property Management Regulations, Temp. Reg. A-11, Supp. 11, GSA.

Entertainment

This segment of T&E took a particularly bad beating from Section 274 and allowed the IRS to become really hard-nosed about the entire subject of entertainment. There are two key tests which must be passed before the deduction can be taken. Expenses must be

1. Directly related to, or
2. Associated with the active conduct of a trade or business (Regulation 1.274-2(a)(1)).

Directly related. To meet this requirement an entertainment expense must show that the taxpayer

1. Had more than a general expectation of securing income or some other specific benefit at some future time. (This test presumably would include development of good will.)
2. Did engage in business with the person being entertained.
3. Intended that the entertainment meeting be held primarily for business purposes.
4. Did not allocate such expenses to individuals other than the customer, or persons closely connected with the customer. (According to Regulation 1.274-2(d)(4) this reference includes a customer's spouse—and under these circumstances, the taxpayer's spouse as well.)

SEE THIS:

There is no requirement to show that business income actually resulted from the entertainment meeting.

Associated entertainment must meet two tests: that such amusement

1. Was associated with the active conduct of a trade or business as defined in "Directly related," and
2. Directly preceded or followed a substantial and bona fide business discussion.

"Directly" means on the same day—or in the case of out-of-town visitors—the preceding day or the day after the business dealings.

Quiet meals rule. For deductibility, a meal must be held in a locality which is conducive to a business discussion. Entertainment at a sporting event, busy cocktail lounge, or night club doesn't qualify unless the visit directly preceded or followed a bona fide business discussion as in "Associated entertainment" above.

Entertainment facilities such as hunting lodges and yachts, or the rental thereof, do not qualify as direct or associated entertainment aids. Consequently, applicable depreciation, repairs, maintenance, etc., are not deductible.

The actual and direct costs of entertaining *at* such facilities, however, are deductible if they otherwise meet the requirements of the Code (a dinner party, for example, aboard the Sea Gull following a recognized business meeting).

Club dues are an exception to this "facilities" rule. They may be deducted if the club in question is utilized more than 50 percent of the time for business purposes, but there's a hitch here. Only the portion of use "directly" related to commerce may be deducted. The percentage applicable to development of good will, for instance, won't count. Suppose you meet the "over 50 percent" requirement but use the club only 20 percent for directly related visits; you will be able to deduct only 20 percent of the dues paid.

Gifts are generally not deductible if they exceed $25 to any one individual. There are some exceptions, however:

- Contributions in the form of scholarships, prizes, and awards do not carry limitations.
- Gifts of advertising displays are not treated as gifts.
- Gifts of novelty advertising items which do not cost more than $4 each need not be considered in the $25 limitation.
- The $25 ceiling also does not apply to gifts costing up to $100 to an employee for length of service or safety achievement. ($400 after The Economic Recovery tax Act of 1981)

Exceptions to entertainment rules. Subject to the ordinary and necessary test, the following costs may be deducted:

- Food and beverages, if otherwise deductible, furnished to any person under the "quiet meals" rule
- Expenses for food and beverages and related facilities furnished on the employer's business premises primarily for employee use
- Items treated as compensation to employees
- Reimbursements to an employee or independent contractor to cover outlays by them.
- Expenses for recreational or social activities (including facilities) for employees—holiday parties, for example
- Expenses of business meetings of employees, agents, stockholders, and directors
- Expenses directly related to business meetings and conventions of exempt trade associations, chambers of commerce, etc.
- Expenses for goods, facilities, and services made generally available to the public
- Expenses in producing entertainment sold to the public

Guidelines for Substantiation of T&E Deductions

Substantiation of T&E deductions is covered by Regulation 1.274-5 and is summarized below:

■ A complete and accurate diary must be maintained—entries to be made at the time of occurrence or as soon thereafter as practical. "Complete" means who, what, when, where, and why, plus the amount.

■ Documentation must be obtained for:

   • All lodging costs, no matter how small.

   • Any T&E expense of $25 or more, except, for transportation charges, documentary evidence will not be required if they are not readily available or are impractical to secure.

18.5 HANDLING THE AUDIT

Having knowledge of IRS requirements, and thinking, will allow you to focus on preparation to present facts in their most favorable light.

The diary, as required by Regulation 1.274-5(c)(2), will be of prime importance. If one is not available, however, you or the taxpayer should not rush out, buy one, and immediately load it with estimated data—that is, unless you fully intend to admit to the examining agent that you did so.

A spanking new diary with identical writing, ink coloring and shadings is a dead giveaway. Should you or your client lie—and say that the entries were made at the time of expenditure, the government can easily prove, through its handwriting experts, that all were made at one sitting—so admit the truth.

IMPORTANT:

Show that the entries, as they appear in the newly prepared diary, were made after substantial research—and with the use of mind refreshers such as paid bills, cancelled checks, credit cards, and penciled notes made at the time of the expenditures. Some credence is better than none—and an IRS person can accept this sort of proof under Regulation 1.274-5(c)(3) (Substantiation by other sufficient evidence) if he or she so desires.

Schedule of expenses. If the return does not include such a schedule, the tax auditor will request a Form 2106. One should, therefore, be prepared and documented to the highest degree possible. This form, along with evidentiary material and an inclusive diary will go a long way toward satisfying the IRS.

The taxpayer's occupation should give a good indication of whether T&E expenses were business oriented or not. If such a question does exist, then the taxpayer should secure a statement from his employer to the effect that he or she was obligated to travel and entertain, etc.—and that reimbursement was or was not made, and in what amounts.

If the taxpayer is the principal stockholder in a corporation, a letter would obviously be useless. In this instance the examiner would probably look to the minutes for an answer.

Travel away from home. The IRS Manual, MT 4234-5 *(Tax Audit Guidelines for Tax Auditors)* in Section 774.2 suggests that the following questions be asked at examination time:

1. Name and location of employer.

2. City where hired and date.

3. Location of job and inclusive dates of employment.

4. Length of time the taxpayer expected to be there at the outset. Why?

5. Any change in expectation thereafter? Why?

6. Where was taxpayer's family living?

7. Where was the taxpayer living?

8. Company facilities or transportation provided and if not used, why?

9. Name and address of local union to which the taxpayer belonged and length of membership.

10. Permanent residence address, if any. Why? How long? Is it owned?

11. Where did the taxpayer live between jobs and why?

12. Work history. Where is the taxpayer usually employed? When was he or she last employed there? For how long?

13. Expenses incurred.

14. Reimbursement or allowance received.

Similar question lists are recommended by the IRS for all categories of T&E deductions

Local Travel	Travel Outside the U.S.
Automobile Expenses	Entertainment
Use of Entertainment Facilities	Gifts, etc.

Each of these queries ties in with regulation requirements. Answers—unless well thought out—will trap taxpayers into damaging admissions. For this reason, I suggest—in instances where T&E is of major importance—that manual sections MT 4234-5 and MT 4231 be purchased from the IRS Freedom of Information Reading Room, 1111 Constitution Avenue, Washington, DC 20224, and used to identify each question and its relevance to the Code.

For example, when the auditor asks how long the taxpayer "expected" to work at the location in question, he or she is attempting to determine whether or not the job was temporary (one year or less) or permanent.

ATTENTION:

Remember a previous section: An "indefinite" employment period will not qualify for travel deductions.

After the purpose for each question has been determined, the practitioner can then assist in the preparation of proper answers *without prevarication*.

The T&E issue is one of the most difficult for a practitioner. Preparation for the audit interview is nowhere more important than in this instance. Lack of it—along with poor records and documentation—will most certainly cost the taxpayer money.

VERY IMPORTANT:

The Cohan Rule, **which allows for an approximation of deductible expenses in most federal tax matters, will be allowable here *only* as its doctrine affects local travel—and then only if they meet three requisites:**

1. **That the expense claimed is so directly related to the business of the taxpayer that it qualifies as an ordinary and necessary expense;**

2. **That some expense was actually incurred; and**

3. That a basis for approximation has been constructed from available evidence both as to amount and business purpose of the expenditure claimed.

Should all other substantiation be inadequate, a practitioner should at least do everything possible to meet the above three requisites—and attempt to salvage something through the Cohan Rule.

18.6 PERTINENT COURT DECISIONS—PRO AND CON

Pro
Raymond C. Burke (TC Memo 1979 - 195)

Findings of Fact

Petitioner was employed as a flight engineer by Braniff Airways and also served as an officer in the U.S. Naval Reserve. In these capacities he frequently traveled in an away-from-home capacity. Some of his travel expenses were disallowed as commuting costs. The main point to be made here, however, concerns the taxpayer's diary, which was maintained during the year in question.

Opinion

The court found that travel outside the taxpayer's home base of Dallas, Texas, was ordinary and necessary and that the deductions for transportation, food, lodging, and tips were reasonable in amount. It paused when considering the diary, because Burke had added entries at a time subsequent to the expenditures.

In the end, however, it did accept as credible the petitioner's statement that such additional entries had been made only for the purpose of recording the source of funds which had been used to pay the travel expenses.

Then the court turned to the substantiation issue. In this respect the taxpayer had been lax, but in the end was able to fill in some of the gaps by alternate methods of proof through use of flight logs, active duty orders, etc.

Finally, the court did allow some $900 in nonreimbursed expenses but not until it was satisfied that all requirements of Section 274 had been at least reasonably met.

Con
(Rev. Rul. 78-373 1978 - 2 CB 108)

Findings of Fact

Advice was sought concerning the deductibility of entertainment expenses by members of Congress for items such as lunch with a constituent, a party for staff members, a cocktail party and buffet for constituents, etc.

Opinion

As to lunch with a constituent, the cost would be considered an ordinary and necessary business expense, but only if the meeting was not for the purpose of socializing or for discussing campaign matters.

In substance, parties for staff members would not be deductible, because the required employee-employer relationship under Section 274(e)(5) would not exist. Secretaries and aides are not employees of a member of Congress—but of the federal government which pays the salaries. Not directly related and not deductible.

As for the cocktail party and buffet, the surroundings would not be conducive to the discussion of business and would not, therefore, be deductible under Regulation 1.274-2(c)(7).

18.7 RELEVANT CODE AND REGULATION SECTIONS, PLUS PUBLICATION

Code

Section 162	Trade or Business
212	Expenses for Production of Income
274	Disallowance of Certain Entertainment, etc., Expenses
274(h)(1)(A)-(D)	Attendance at Conventions, etc.

Regulations

Section 1.274-1	Disallowance of Certain Entertainment, Gift and Travel Expenses
1.274-2	Disallowance of Deductions for Certain Expenses for Entertainment, Amusement, or Recreation
1.274-2(a)(1)	Entertainment Activity
1.274-2(b)	Entertainment Defined
1.274-2(c)	Directly Related Entertainment
1.274-2(d)	Associated Entertainment
1.274-2(d)(4)	Expenses Closely Connected with Directly Related Entertainment
1.274-2(e)	Expenditures with Respect to Entertainment Facilities
1.274-3	Disallowance of Deduction for Gifts
1.274-4	Disallowance of Certain Foreign Travel
1.274-5	Substantiation Requirements
1.274-5(c)(2)	Substantiation by Adequate Records
1.274-5(c)(3)	Substantiation by Other Sufficient Evidence
1.274-5(e)(2)	Reporting of Expenses for Which the Employee Is Required to Make an Adequate Accounting to His Employer
1.274-5(e)(3)	Reporting of Expenses for Which the Employee Is Not Required to Make an Adequate Accounting to His Employer
1.274-5(e)(4)	Definition of an Adequate Accounting to the Employer

Publication

463	Travel, Entertainment and Gift Expenses

18.8 APPLICABLE IRS MANUAL REFERENCES (INVESTIGATIVE TECHNIQUES)

Standard Explanation Handbook

MT 428(11)-15	Section 54	Travel and Entertainment
4231-46	6(14)2.49	Travel and Entertainment
4231-46	547	Employee Business Expenses
4231-46	547.1	General

Audit Technique Handbook for Internal Revenue Agents

MT 4231-27	Section 67(13)	Travel and Entertainment
4231-24	733	Travel and Entertainment

Tax Audit Guidelines, Individuals, Partnerships, Estates, Trusts and Corporations

MT 4233-1	Section 321.14	Travel and Entertainment
	322.1(22)	Travel and Entertainment
	520.1(26)	Travel and Entertainment

NOTE:

This subject of T&E is undoubtedly listed on the government's National Office List of Prime Issues.

Abandonment and Demolition Losses
(Sections 165, 167, 280B)

19

19.1 IDENTIFYING THE PROBLEM

Abandonment losses must be considered in light of two Regulations
1. Regulation 1.165-2. Obsolescence of Nondepreciable Property
2. Regulation 1.167(9)-8. Gains and Losses on Retirement (Permanent Withdrawal of Depreciable Property)

Losses under (1) (Section 165) can be deducted by individuals and noncorporate taxpayers as ordinary deductions against gross income, if such losses were incurred in business or in transactions entered into for profit. Corporations may generally take the deduction for any qualifying abandonment.

Losses under (2) are subject to a different set of rules set forth in regulations which cover Depreciation (Section 167).

Demolition of buildings is covered by Regulation 1.165-3.

Difficulties occur when attempts are made to define qualifying abandonment, retirement, obsolescence, demolition, intent, etc. Are they true losses or dispositions of capital assets which bring into play Section 1231 (Property Used in a Trade or Business or Involuntary Conversions)?

In abandonment situations the most common IRS controversies arise

- When determining whether or not the property was actually abandoned. Did the taxpayer own it? Did he or she intend to abandon it? Was control over the asset truly relinquished?

- Was the abandonment actually the *sale* of a capital asset—or "deemed" to have been such? (If so, an ordinary loss will not be allowed.)

- Was the retirement normal or abnormal? (Loss may or may not be recognized depending upon this classification.)

- If the asset was retired from a multiple-asset account, a single-item account, or a vintage account, different rules will apply.

In a demolition situation the primary problem seems to evolve into one of "intent." Regulation 1.165-3(a) (Demolition of Buildings) defines the word:

Intent to demolish formed at time of purchase.

(1) Except as provided in subparagraph (2) of this paragraph, the following rule shall apply when, in the course of a trade or business or in a transaction entered into for profit, real property is purchased with the intention of demolishing either immediately or subsequently the buildings situated thereon:

No deduction shall be allowed under section 165(a) on account of the old buildings even though any demolition originally planned is subsequently deferred or abandoned. The entire basis of the property so purchased shall, notwithstanding the provisions of 1.167(a)-5, be allocated to the land only. Such basis shall be increased by the net cost of demolition or decreased by the net proceeds from demolition.

NOTE:

There is an exception to this denial rule. It occurs in instances where buildings are not immediately demolished but rented or used in the taxpayer's trade or business or for the production of income.

When this happens, a portion of the property's basis may be allocated to the buildings and depreciated over the rental or use period. Such allocation, however, cannot exceed the present discounted value of the right to receive income from the buildings over the period of their intended use, based on interest rates recognizable in the money market.

The formula for determining this limitation is somewhat involved and will be detailed later under book section 19.4.

19.2 HOW THE IRS SEES THE ISSUE

Since abandonment and demolition losses are deductible from gross income without regard to Section 1231, IRS agents believe that close scrutiny of such deductions very well may produce more favorable government options. Usually IRS audit changes in this area are substantial in amount and well worth an examiner's time.

Possibly, abandonment or demolition did not even occur—maybe the property was completely depreciated, or transferred to the owner, or held for resale. Details concerning how the IRS will search these issues follow.

19.3 FACTORS WHICH THE IRS CONSIDERS WHEN MAKING ITS AUDIT DECISION

IRS audit guidelines call for varied approaches. *In searching the abandonment issue*

1. Did the taxpayer actually own the property as opposed to having only the right of purchase?

2. Did the property actually become worthless?

3. Was it truly abandoned—and when?

4. Did a foreclosure occur before abandonment? (If so, the transaction may be considered an

involuntary transfer and treated as a sale (Hamel v. U.S. 311 U.S. 504, 41-1 USTC #9169, 24 AFTR 1082 S. Ct. 1941)).)

5. How does the adjusted basis compare with the related depreciation reserve?

6. Is the loss applicable to the correct tax year?

7. If the property was used in, or relates to, the operation of a mineral property where percentage depletion was claimed, was the loss included as an operating cost?

8. Was the asset only taken out of service and stored? (No abandonment.)

9. Did the abandonment loss occur as the result of disappearance or theft? (In such cases, the taxpayer must prove the year of loss.)

10. If the loss occurred due to threat of seizure by a foreign govrernment, where is proof?

11. Is an abandonment loss specifically allowed under the taxpayer's method of accounting for depreciable property?

Audits concerning demolition center to an important degree around intent at time of acquisition. If the intent was to demolish, then the cost is not deductible but must be added to the cost of the land.

RED FLAG:

You and/or the taxpayer may believe that *a state of mind*—at any given time—cannot be proven, but it can. Here are some of the ways in which the IRS goes about it:

1. A short holding period would seem to indicate demolition intent.
2. Examination of corporate-minutes books produces clues.
3. Cross-examination of the taxpayer occasionally bears fruit in the form of a careless, not well-thought-out answer.
4. Dates on construction contracts for replacement buildings tell a convincing story.
5. Questioning of bookkeepers and other knowledgeable employees usually produces clues.
6. If a land lease was involved, its contents may indicate that demolition was required as one of its stipulations. (In this instance dismantling costs would have to be amortized over the life of the lease.)
7. Where a building was demolished prior to a sale of land, the sales contract may indicate that such demolition was a condition of sale. (If so, the loss may not be allowed.)
8. Questioning of involved real estate people can be informative.

19.4 CONSIDERATIONS WHEN PREPARING THE RETURN

Practitioner thinking at filing time should be guided by the 19 IRS approaches as presented in section 19.3 above.

IMPORTANT:

Both abandonment and demolition losses require prior planning for successful implementation. Particularly in these two instances, but actually in any financial transaction, taxpayers should never enter into business dealings without first fully discussing the matter with their tax consultants. It is infinitely more difficult to reconstruct a deal from the top down than to structure it from the bottom up.

Here are some major points which should be considered:

Abandonment

What is abandonment? It results under Regulation 1.165-2 when, for nondepreciable property, three conditions are met:

1. There is an intention to permanently abandon.
2. Some act takes place which evidences such intention.
3. It can be proved that the loss occurred in the tax year when claimed.

NOTE:

The taxable year in which the loss is sustained is not always the year in which (1) and (2) and loss of title occurred. Be careful of this point.

The deduction is the difference between adjusted basis and the salvage value, if any.

Under Regulation 1.167(a)-8, a tax-effective transaction results when depreciable property is placed in a supplies or scrap account, or is abandoned. Gain or loss is determined by considering whether the retirement was normal or abnormal—and whether the asset withdrawal was from a single-asset account.

Retirement assets from vintage accounts under the CLADR system carry still different rules. See Publication 534 (Depreciation) for details.

Normal retirement is accomplished in instances where a permanent withdrawal of depreciable property is made within the useful life originally established and at a time when the asset had reached a condition at which it would customarily have been retired.

Abnormal retirement occurs when an asset is withdrawn for reasons not contemplated at the time that the depreciation rate was set—retirement earlier than expected, or damage by casualty, or sudden and extraordinary obsolescence.

For an asset not disposed of or abandoned no gain is recognized, but a loss may be allowed if the retirement is

1. Abnornal.
2. Normal from a single-asset account in which the life of eash asset is determined separately.
3. A normal retirement from a multiple-asset account in which the depreciation rate is based on the maximum expected life of the longest-lived asset and the loss occurs before expiration of the full useful life. (No loss is allowed, however, if the depreciate rate is based on the average useful life of the assets in the account.)

Loss is computed by subtracting the asset's estimated salvage or fair market value at the time of retirement, whichever is greater, from its adjusted basis.

Assets retired from a single-asset account. If abandoned, the amount of the recognized loss is the asset's adjusted basis as computed for a sale or exchange. If the retired property was added to a supplies or scrap account, any gain would not be recognized. Loss would be measured as in the first paragraph above.

Assets retired from a multiple-asset account. For a normal withdrawal, if depreciation was computed by using the *average* expected useful life, the adjusted basis is the estimated salvage value which was anticipated at the time the asset was originally acquired.

BE CAREFUL:

If depreciation was figured using the maximum expected useful life of the *longest-lived* asset in the account, the taxpayer must use the method of depreciation used for the multiple-asset account and a rate based upon the maximum expected useful life of the asset retired (not the remaining useful life).

For an abnormal retirement from a multiple-asset account, the adjustment for depreciation is made at the rate which would have been proper had the asset been depreciated in a single-asset account. The method of depreciation used for the multiple-asset account should be used. The rate is based upon either the average expected useful life or the maximum expected useful life of the retired asset, depending upon the method used to determine the rate of depreciation for the multiple-asset account.

Dry Hole Losses

When such a deduction appears on a tax return the IRS suspects a doubling-up situation … and usually begins a search for the following elements:

1. *Intangible drilling costs under an election to deduct such expenses.* Section 162. (These are deductible whether the well is productive or not, as long as the taxpayer has not elected otherwise in an earlier year. Even after an election to capitalize has been made, a second option is given to either write off these capitalized expenses when a dry hole has been dug, or to capitalize them as depletable cost of the overall property on which the dry well was drilled.)

IMPORTANT:

This second election once made, is binding thereafter.

2. *Intangible drilling expense capitalized under an election but now written off because of the dry hole.* (Like (1) above, previously made elections should not be contrary to the dry hole deduction.)

3. *Lease costs under any of the various forms previously discussed written off as an abandonment loss.* (Abandonment will be verified. Complete relinquishment of title is considered the best verification but not the only evidence of abandonment. The taxpayer will probably be asked to furnish Form 927 (Proof of Worthlessness of Mineral Rights).)

NOTE:

Besides being of value to the IRS in consideration of the loss deduction, this form also provides for an affidavit whereby the taxpayer agrees that if he or she subsequently receives income from the abandoned property, no depletion will be claimed on such income until the worthlessness loss is recouped.

Sale vs Abandonment

It is critical in this instance to retain the abandonment classification. If a taxpayer is "deemed to have sold" an asset, the transaction will be treated as if it were a regular sale of a capital asset—unless of course Section 1231 intervenes. Where it does, if losses from the sale or exchange of property used in a trade or business (including losses from certain conversions) exceed the gains from such sales, exchanges, and conversions, such gains and losses will be treated as ordinary gains and losses, rather than as capital gains and losses.

CAUTION:

> In general, the government considers that if a taxpayer receives any consideration, however small, for the conveyance of property, "sale," not an abandonment, will have resulted, e.g., under the following circumstances:
>
> • Taxpayer transfers property on which he or she is personally liable for delinquent real estate taxes and the transferee assumes the liability, or
>
> • Taxpayer transfers property on which he or she is personally liable for a nonrecourse mortgage and the new owner assumes the debt.

If foreclosure is imminent, a taxpayer should abandon the property prior to the occurrence. In Hamel v. U.S. (311 U.S. 504, 41-1 USTC 9169, 24 AFTR 1082 (S. CT 1941)), the Supreme Court ruled that a foreclosure was a "sale."

Demolition

Costs of demolition are allowable deductions in instances where the following tests are met:

1. The expense was incurred in business or in a transaction entered into for profit.
2. The demolition occurred as the result of a plan formed *after* acquisition of the property.
3. The demolition was not pursuant to the terms of a lease or not a condition of a sales contract.

In most controversies with the IRS, (2) causes the most difficulties ... Intent!

According to regulations, *Evidence of Intention* depends upon an examination of all the surrounding facts and circumstances, and not solely upon statements of the taxpayer. Regulation 1.165-3(c) sets forth clear suggestions for measuring before and after acquisition intentions and is reproduced here as Figure 19-1.

(c) *Evidence of intention*. (1) Whether real property has been purchased with the intention of demolishing the buildings thereon or whether the demolition of the buildings occurs as a result of a plan formed subsequent to their acquisition is a question of fact, and the answer depends upon an examination of all the surrounding facts and circumstances. The answer to the question does not depend solely upon the statements of the taxpayer at the time he acquired the property or demolished the buildings, but such statements, if made, are relevant and will be considered. Certain other relevant facts and circumstances that exist in some cases and the inferences that might reasonably be drawn from them are described in subparagraphs (2) and (3) of this paragraph. The question as to the taxpayer's intention is not answered by any inference that is drawn from any one fact or circumstance but can be answered only by a consideration of all relevant facts and circumstances and the reasonable inferences to be drawn therefrom.

(2) An intention at the time of acqusition to demolish may be suggested by:

(i) A short delay between the date of acquisition and the date of demolition;

(ii) Evidence of prohibitive remodeling costs determined at the time of acquisition;

(iii) Existence of municipal regulations at the time of acquisition which would prohibit the continued use of the buildings for profit purposes;

(iv) Unsuitability of the buildings for the taxpayer's trade or business at the time of acquisition; or

(v) Inability at the time of acquisition to realize a reasonable income from the buildings.

(3) The fact that the demolition occurred pursuant to a plan formed subsequent to the acquisition of the property

may be suggested by:

(i) Substantial improvement of the buildings immediately after their acquisition;

(ii) Prolonged use of the buildings for business purposes after their acquisition;

(iii) Suitability of the buildings for investment purposes at the time of acquisition;

(iv) Substantial change in economic or business conditions after the date of acquisition;

(v) Loss of useful value occurring after the date of acquisition;

(vi) Substantial damage to the buildings occurring after their acquisition;

(vii) Discovery of latent structural defects in the buildings after their acquisition;

(viii) Decline in the taxpayer's business after the date of acquisition;

(ix) Condemnation of the property by municipal authorities after the date of acquisition; or

(x) Inability after acquisition to obtain building material necessary for the improvement of the property.

Figure 19-1

Buildings rented before demolishment. As indicated in book section 19.1, some portion of an otherwise totally lost demolition deduction can be salvaged by using or renting the structure before tearing it down. The IRS however considers the purpose for which the property was acquired and allows only an allocated portion of the basis for depreciation purpose. See Regulation 1.165-3(a)(2)(iii) which sets forth an example of the allocation computation as required (Figure 19-2).

(iii) The application of this subparagraph may be illustrated by the following example:

Example. In January 1958, A purchased land and a building for $60,000 with the intention of demolishing the building. In the following April, A concluded that he would be unable to commence the construction of a proposed new building for a period of more than 3 years. Accordingly, on June 1, 1958, he leased the building for a period of 3 years at an annual rental of $1,200. A intends to demolish the building upon expiration of the lease. A may allocate a portion of the $60,000 basis of the property to the building to be depreciated over the 3-year period. That portion is equal to the present value of the right to receive $3,600 (3 times $1,200). Assuming that the present value of that right determined as of June 1, 1958, is $2,850, A may allocate that amount to the building and, if A files his return on the basis of a taxable year ending May 31, 1959, A may take a depreciation deduction with respect to such building of $950 for such taxable year. The basis of the land to A as determined under subparagraph (1) of this paragraph is reduced by $2,850. If on June 1, 1960, A ceases to rent the building and demolishes it, the balance of the undepreciated portion allocated to the buildings, $950, may be deducted from gross income under section 165.

Figure 19-2

Demolition of certain historic structures. Under Code Section 180B, no demolition deduction shall be allowed for destruction of a certified historic structure unless the Secretary of the Interior shall rule that it is not such an edifice. This section shall apply with respect to demolitions commencing after June 30, 1976, and before January 1, 1984.

19.5 HANDLING THE AUDIT

If the person being audited is your client—and you followed closely the pages of this chapter—you should have no difficulty with an audit.

If the taxpayer is a new client—and you are totally unfamiliar with his or her abandonment or demolition situation—you should obtain all documentation possible to place his or her deduction in a creditable position. Use these pages as a checklist to accomplish this purpose.

You may find that what's done is done, but it's possible that putting data into a correct perspective will salvage the deduction.

TAX TIP:

Being knowledgeable before the IRS auditor will certainly help.

Be sure, for example, that the examiner correctly applies Section 1231 in a situation where he or she changes an abandonment loss to a sale. Under such circumstances, if this were the only qualifying transaction, the audit change would have no effect. The loss would still emerge as ordinary.

Where a building was rented or used in business before demolition, make sure that the Revenue person utilizes the taxpayer benefits of Regulation 1.165-3(a)(2). Continue the procedure item by item.

IMPORTANT:

Remember, too, that the taxpayer's words are strongly considered in all abandonment and demolition decisions. Do not hesitate to provide the IRS with a sworn affidavit from the taxpayer to substantiate his or her contentions—of course, only in a situation where you are convinced that such testimony is true and correct and cannot be disproved. Always remain alert to the possibilities of the Red Flag warning at the end of book section 19.3.

19.6 PERTINENT COURT DECISIONS—PRO AND CON

Pro
Montgomery National Bank (DC Ky. 1971)
27 AFTR 2d 71-1443 330 F. Supp. 1246

Findings of Fact

On March 4, 1963, the bank's board of directors authorized the purchase of the Trimble Theatre building in Mt. Sterling, Kentucky. The purchase was accomplished on June 17, 1963, the purpose being to give the bank an additional facility that would include a drive-in window.

On June 16, 1963, the bank's executive vice-president wrote a letter to the Bank Building and Equipment Corporation of America stating that the bank had just purchased a building which it intended to raze—and asked for suggestions, presumably for demolition and reconstruction.

Testimony and affidavits from board members stated that the vice-president had no authority to make such an inquiry. To substantiate their testimony, they produced the board minutes of September 9, 1963, which showed that it was the unanimous decision of its members to remodel the newly purchased structure. They even voted at that time to attempt to negotiate a contract toward this end.

After several unsuccessful attempts at formulating a satisfactory remodeling contract, it became apparent that such construction would be impractical; all this proven by copies of board minutes.

On January 13, 1964, the board voted to demolish the structure—and eventually did so. The IRS disallowed the loss.

Opinion

Judgment was entered in favor of the plaintiff. The minutes and actions of the bank and its board of directors clearly established that it was their intention, at time of acquisition, to remodel—and not to demolish—the structure.

NOTE THE EXTREME IMPORTANCE OF GOOD MINUTES.

Con
Elvin K. & Jacqueline H. Wheeler (TC Memo 1979, 333)

Findings of Fact

Petitioners acquired four buildings in November 1970 and subsequently leased them to others. In 1971 the structures were damaged in an earthquake and not repaired.

On May 10, 1973, the Department of Building and Safety ordered the owners to make certain repairs. The order was ignored. On August 29, 1973, the department ordered that the properties be vacated until the required repairs were made. Petitioners were able to extend this last order into 1974. By the end of 1973 they still had not decided whether to repair or demolish. The latter was accomplished in December 1974, after an estimate of reconstruction costs had been obtained.

The petitioners claimed that the vacate order was sufficient cause for them to be able to claim, in 1973, an abandonment loss or one due to extraordinary obsolescence. The IRS disagreed.

Opinion

The court relied in part on Regulation 1.165-1(d)(1) which states that

A loss shall be treated as sustained during the taxable year in which the loss occurs as evidenced by closed and completed transactions and as fixed by identifiable events occurring in such taxable year.

The plaintiffs continued dealings with the Department of Building and Safety, and their indecision as to repair or demolition until the end of 1974 was strong evidence to the court that no "closed transaction" for the purpose of Section 165(a) occurred in 1973.

Held for the government.

19.7 RELEVANT CODE AND REGULATION SECTIONS, PLUS APPLICABLE PUBLICATION

Code

Section 162	Intangible Drilling and Development Costs—Option to Expense or Capitalize
165	Losses
167	Depreciation

280B	Demolition of Certain Historic Structures
1011	Adjusted Basis for Determining Gain or Loss
1012	Basis of Property—Cost
1231	Property Used in a Trade or Business or Involuntary Conversions

Regulations

Section 1.165-1(d)(1)	Year of Deduction
1.165-2	Obsolesence of Nondepreciable Property
1.165-3	Demolition of Buildings
1.165-3(a)(2)(iii)	Example
1.165-3(c)	Evidence of Intention
1.167(a)-8	Gains and Losses on Retirement (Permanent Withdrawal of Depreciable Property)

Publication

534	Depreciation

19.8 APPLICABLE IRS MANUAL REFERENCES (INVESTIGATIVE TECHNIQUES)

Audit Technique Handbook for Internal Revenue Agents

MT 4231-24 Section 657.4		Dry Hole Losses
4231-42	67(10)	Losses—Abandonment and Demolition

Audit Guidelines for Examiners

MT 4231-46 Section 5(10)3	Abandonment and Demolition Losses

Tax Audit Guidelines, Individuals, Partnerships, Estate and Trusts, and Corporations

MT 4233-10 Section 322.1(12)		Abandonment and Demolition Losses
4233-10	520.1(18)	Abandonment and Demolition Losses

Tax Audit Guidelines for Tax Auditors

MT 4234-13 Section 878	Losses—Abandonment and Demolition

Divorce and Alimony
(Sections 71 and 215)

20

20.1 IDENTIFYING THE PROBLEM

The Code's definition of "husband and wife" (Section 7701(a)(17)) will give you some idea of the difficulties you are about to encounter when approaching this subject.

As used in sections 71, 152(b)(4), 215 and 682, if the husband and wife therein referred to are divorced, wherever appropriate to the meaning of such sections, the term "wife" shall be read "former wife" and the term "husband" shall be read "former husband,"— and if the payments described in such sections are made by or on behalf of the wife or former wife to the husband or former husband instead of vice versa, wherever appropriate to the meaning of such sections, the term "husband" shall be read "wife" and the term "wife" shall be read "husband."

Having neatly and clearly topped that hurdle, the Code faces many others:

- When does divorce or legal separation occur?
- What is an interlocutory decree and how does it affect the marital status?
- Does alimony differ from child care in taxes? How is each handled under the Code?
- How are property settlements taxed?
- Who may claim the children as dependents—and under what circumstances?
- What about the legal fees? Are they deductible?
- Is it possible to structure a divorce to minimize the tax consequences for each party?
- Can former spouses live apart from each other in the same home and be considered legally divorced or separated for tax purposes?

Entwined with these problems are numerous traps for the unwary, such as alimony payments that do not qualify as "periodic" and thus become nondeductible to the payor and nontaxable to the payee; periodic payments tied to a contingency which may alter tax treatment; or application of state laws which may upset tax planning for divorce.

For purposes of this chapter the taxpayer will be considered an ex-husband who will be making payments to an ex-wife. Gift or estate tax applications will not be approached.

TAKE NOTE:

Simply speaking, qualifying alimony is taxable to the wife and deductible by the husband to the extent that it is included in the former wife's income. The deduction is made from gross income (Sections 71 and 215).

Child support is not deductible or taxable but may be considered in arriving at the exemption deduction.

20.2 HOW THE IRS SEES THE ISSUE

Frequently, divorce decrees or separation agreements are not clear as to which portion is applicable to alimony and which to child support. In such instances where combination payments are made, the Service considers that child support is paid first. It looks, therefore, to the controlling documents for guidance as to this point and several others.

1. Dates are important since each periodic payment and obligation must be considered on a periodic, rather than on a calendar year, basis. If the total payments for the year exceed the obligations for that year, the excess will be considered payment for child support arrearages, unless the taxpayer can establish that the excess exceeded such arrearages.

2. Back payments made for alimony are deductible only in the year paid.

3. Even separated individuals are considered married until the date of the final decree of divorce or separate maintenance.

4. Insurance premiums are considered alimony paid to a wife, if the policy has been irrevocably assigned to her.

5. Payments on a home mortgage, as well as interest and real estate taxes, are not considered alimony to the extent the husband retains ownership rights in the property.

6. Use of a home by an ex-spouse does not constitute a "periodic payment" (definition later) and is therefore not an allowable deduction.

7. Legal fees in connection with a divorce are not deductible.

NOTE:

The IRS in its operational manual doesn't tell all concerning this point—attorney fees, in connection with tax planning for divorce, are deductible (Rev. Rul. 72-545, 1972-2 CB 179).

8. If the opposing spouse lives in a jurisdiction other than the audit location, an Information Report (Form 4298) will be filed with the other jurisdiction so that the government can be assured the payee is reporting alimony income correctly. If the recipient resides in the same jurisdiction, the return will be secured for analysis.

9. Verbal agreements will not be considered.

10. Occasionally, a spouse will pay alimony in an amount which exceeds that specified in a decree or agreement. The excess is not deductible.

20.3 FACTORS WHICH THE IRS CONSIDERS WHEN MAKING ITS AUDIT DECISION

Where payments as a result of divorce appear on either spouse's tax return, and become an audit issue, expect that both returns may be examined as in (8) above.

The IRS will want to see the divorce decree or separation agreement, plus cancelled checks with evidence payments. They will ask for the name and address of the former spouse. If payments are not made directly but are paid from endowment or annuity contracts, the Service will ask to see the governing documents.

Possibly a domestic relations court collects and transmits support payments. Under these conditions, court reports will be requested.

Children of divorced or separated parents. Examining agents will delve deeply into such dependency deductions. So that we may escape redundancy, please refer to Chapter 15 (Exemptions and Dependents) for complete coverage of this issue.

Foreign divorces are considered null and void if the parties remarry in the following year. The couple must file as married for both years. Since the advent of the Economic Recovery Tax Act of 1981 this issue is not likely to be as troublesome as in the past.

The transfer or sale of property in satisfaction of marital rights will be examined carefully by the IRS. Did the property appreciate in value? If so, the husband may have realized a taxable gain from the transaction.

Whether the asset is depreciable property or not is important, since Section 1239 (Gain from Sale of Depreciable Property Between Certain Related Taxpayers) may come into play, making the gain ordinary in nature (more later).

IMPORTANT:

If the taxpayer took a loss—and the transfer preceded the divorce decree—Section 267 (Losses, Expenses, and Interest with Respect to Transactions Between Related Taxpayers) would eliminate the deduction.

The payment of residential expenses carries all sorts of traps for the careless. The manner of ownership becomes important. Joint tenants or tenants by the entirety produce one rule; tenants in common, another rule; residence owned by husband, still another. (More later on this subject.)

Miscellaneous payments will be carefully analyzed by examining auditors and will be disallowed as alimony if they fit into categories as listed below:

1. Any payment not required by the decree or agreement
2. Any payment that does not arise out of the marital relationship, such as repayment of a loan to a spouse
3. Any payment made before the decree or agreement
4. Any payment agreed upon before the decree but paid later
5. Any payment made after death of the divorced spouse, even if required by the decree or agreement

6. Any lump-sum cash or property settlement required by a decree or agreement

Periodic or lump-sum? One is deductible under the correct situations; the other is not. The IRS will certainly want to be satisfied as to which is which. These terms will be fully discussed in section 20.4.

20.4 CONSIDERATIONS WHEN PREPARING THE RETURN

Tax planning, in this complex area of taxation, is an absolute necessity. Choosing legal and tax representatives should be high on the priority list. If both cannot be found in one person, then two should be employed—a divorce lawyer and a knowledgeable tax professional. Frequently, what's good for one spouse may be harmful to the other. When correctly handled, there can be a numbing of the tax blow for each.

Tax Planning for Divorce

A juggling of payments between alimony and child support can frequently produce good after-tax results for both parties. Structuring installments on lump-sum settlements to cover more than ten years can help the husband and possibly not harm the tax position of the wife. Maybe her income will come only from the divorce settlement. Increasing her divorce payments to cover her additional taxes might save a large amount for the husband.

Providing for a dependency agreement in the court decree can many times save taxes. When transferring property in satisfaction of marital rights, use of high basis (and not heavily appreciated) property can save payment of tax on the gain.

The list is long. Circumstances should dictate the way to go. Generally involved in the arbitration process are

Alimony	Child Support
Alimony vs.Child Support	Property Settlements
Dependency Exemptions	Legal Fees

Some of the basic considerations will be discussed below.

What Constitutes Divorce?

The state law governs. But generally, for tax purposes, a divorce or legal separation occurs at the time of execution of a

1. Court decree of divorce or separation.
2. Written separation agreement executed after August 16, 1954, or materially altered or modified thereafter.
3. Decree for support.
4. Interlocutory decree (not final).
5. Decree of Alimony "pendente lite" (while awaiting action on the final decree or agreement) entered into after March 1, 1954.
6. Decree of annulment:
   (Andrew M. Newburger, 61 TC 457, Acq.)
   (George F. Reisman, 49 TC 570, Acq.)

NOTE:

> In the latter situation (Reisman) no valid marriage ever legally existed, so the parties to the decree must file amended returns for all open years.

Payments for Alimony, Separate Maintenance, etc.

Payments for alimony, separate maintenance, or the like are deductible to the husband and taxable to the wife under varying circumstances.

Under A Decree of Divorce or Separate Maintenance the payments must

1. Qualify as periodic;
2. Be paid *after* decree;
3. Be paid to discharge a legal obligation based on the marital or family relationship or be attributable to property transferred in discharge of those obligations; and
4. Be unopposed pursuant to a decree or a *written* instrument incident to a divorce or separation.

Under A Written Separation Agreement the payments must

1. Qualify as periodic;
2. Be paid after execution of the agreement;
3. Result from the marital or family relationship;
4. Be made under, or be attributable to, property transferred under the agreement;
5. Be paid after parties are separated;
6. Have been paid pursuant to an agreement which was executed after August 16, 1954 (or as materially modified after that date); and
7. Have been paid while the parties were not filing joint returns.

Under A Decree for Support the payments must

1. Have been required under a decree or court order;
2. Qualify as periodic;
3. Be paid after parties are separated; and
4. Be paid when joint returns are not filed.

Periodic payments are required in each of the above three situations if they are to be treated as alimony or separate maintenance (deductible to the husband and taxable to the wife). Payments are considered "periodic" when they are

- In fixed amounts for an indefinite period.
- In indefinite amounts for either a fixed or an indefinite period.
- Principal sum payments payable over a period which exceeds 10 years.

A *lump-sum settlement* to be paid to a wife, as stated in a decree, cannot be considered "periodic" even if paid in installments—and consequently is not taxable to the wife or deductible by the husband.

Ten-year exception: Under this omission, payments may be considered "periodic" if they are to be paid out over a period of more than ten years—or even over a period of less than ten years if the following specific contingencies exist:

They are to end or change in amount on

- The death of either spouse, or
- The remarriage of the receiving spouse, or
- A change in the economic status (amount of money or property owned) of either spouse.

Such contingencies may be set forth in the terms of the decree or agreement *or may be imposed by local law.*

Transfer of Property in Satisfaction of Marital Rights

Where this move occurs, gain or loss is computed on the difference between the adjusted basis and the fair market value at time of transfer.

VERY IMPORTANT:

The FMV of the asset is considered equal to the FMV of the inchoate marital rights (the discharged obligation). The wife, therefore, has no gain or loss. Her basis becomes the FMV of the property received.

Depreciation and investment credit recapture apply wherever applicable. Here are some of the other problems which exist:

If depreciable property is transferred, caution is advised. Section 1239 (Gain from Sale of Depreciable Property Between Certain Related Taxpayers) may apply. If it does, any gain will be classed as ordinary.

TAX TIP:

To avoid this trap, the transfer should be planned so as not to occur prior to the date of the final or interlocutory decree. The parties are man and wife until then.

Having escaped Section 1239, planning considerations should then look to the best use of Section 1231 (Property Used in the Trade or Business and Involuntary Conversions) where different combinations of gains and losses can produce good results.

If appreciated Section 1221 (Capital Asset Defined) property is transferred such as a vacation home, the transfer can generate a capital gain. Use of a high-basis property should, therefore, be considered when making divorce settlements in a lump sum.

If property is transferred at a loss, several points of law should be considered. Under Section 165 (Losses) deductions are allowed to individuals only for losses sutained in a trade or business, in a transaction entered into for profit, or for casualty losses. This eliminates any possible deduction because of the unfavorable transfer of a residence.

Under Section 267 (Losses, Expenses, and Interest with Respect to Transactions Between Related Parties) the transfer of property at a loss would not carry with it a deduction—unless the asset was transferred *after* the final decree of divorce was granted.

NOTE:

Section 267 does not include an "interlocutory decree" as does Section 1239 (Gain From Sale of Depreciable Property Between Certain Related Taxpayers).

Of course, the husband can always sell the Section 267 property to a third party, take the loss, and transfer the cash to his wife.

Residential Expenses

These are also tricky. They are guided by the various types of ownership:

Joint Tenants or Tenants by Entirety

Under this ownership, a home is held jointly. Both parties are responsible for the mortgage. If the divorce decree states that (from money paid by the husband) the wife must pay mortgage and interest, the payor may deduct only one-half of such principal and interest payments; the wife must take one-half into income.

Tenants in Common

Each party owns one-half of the property. The husband pays all principal, interest, insurance, and taxes. The payor may deduct one-half of his amount; the spouse must include one-half in income.

If Wife Owns the Home

Qualifying payments for principal, interest, etc., may all be deducted by the paying spouse. The total of such is taxable to the owner spouse.

If Husband Owns the Home

If the wife lives there rent free, the husband may not deduct the mortgage payments or the fair rental value of the home—but may deduct interest and taxes as itemized deductions. If covered by the final decree, he may deduct the cost of any utilities that he paid. The wife must report this amount as income.

Divorced persons residing in the same home. With rents sky high, divorced individuals frequently find it impossible to maintain two residences. So they live in the same structure—apart in all respects. For purposes of the alimony deduction under Section 215, can this be called being "separated"? The IRS says no, but the Eighth Circuit Court in a unanimous decision says yes.

In Sydnes v Comm. (8 Cir; 1978) 42 AFTR 2d 78-5143, the court held that determining whether parties are living separately in the same residence for tax purposes presented a factual issue which should be decided on the evidence—and overturned the decision of the Tax Court.

Handling Legal Fees in a Divorce Proceeding

Legal fees are usually substantial and certainly an important consideration in any divorce proceeding. Under Regulation 1.262-1(b)(7)

> Generally, attorneys' fees and other costs paid in connection with a divorce, separation, or decree for support are not deductible by either the husband or the wife. However, the part of an attorney's fee and the part of other costs paid in connection with a divorce, legal separation, written separation agreement, or a decree for support, which are properly attributable to the production or collection of amounts includible in gross income under Sec. 71 are deductible by the wife under Sec. 212.

TAKE CARE:

This means therefore that deductions may be taken for legal fees which are directly attributable to the obtaining of tax advice for divorce. But substantiation is crucial. Rev. Rul. 1972-2 CB 179 suggests that a statement be obtained from the tax person involved setting forth the following information:

An itemized statement from the attorney or accountant setting forth time expended, degree of difficulty of the tax question, amount of taxes involved, fee regularly charged for similar services, and results obtained.

SUGGESTION:

Ideally, the taxpayers should retain a separate tax person not connected with the divorce attorney. Substantiation would then be no problem. Note also that the wife can deduct legal fees for the production or collection of taxable alimony under Section 212 (Expenses for the Production of Income.)

BE CAREFUL:

Even though the husband is forced by the court decree to pay his wife's legal fees, he may not deduct them since he is not the appropriate person who incurred the expense.

20.5 HANDLING THE AUDIT

If the IRS concern is mainly with the divorce situation, probably an office auditor will be the government's prime mover. This person will notify the taxpayer of a date for appearance, and will ask for a list of specific documentation, i.e., divorce decree, cancelled checks, etc. All such data should be collected and reviewed for adequacy. The existence of an unusual situation should be fully explored.

Example of the latter: A divorced taxpayer paid his ex-wife's alimony by writing checks to a bank for deposit to her account. If such a happening occurs, secure backup proof such as a letter from the ex-wife and copies of the bank statements involved. Prove that the account was carried in the name of the ex-wife and that the subject checks were indeed deposited therein.

Look forward to producing clear evidence. Where it doesn't exist, secure it. Save yourself a second trip and your client some worry time. In involved situations where there is a transfer of property, expect a requirement to prove basis and fair market value. Where good tax planning for divorce has occurred, this should be no problem; but serioius difficulties will pop up where no planning was attempted.

Child support and the dependency problems usually become part of the audit where apropos. Use Chapter 15 (Exemptions and Dependents) as a preparation guide to meet this difficulty.

The divorce and alimony issues actually carry with them such a wide range of Code applications that it would be impossible to cover every possibility here. My best suggestion would be to fragment and separate each issue involved, then move forward to study these various points—documenting and strengthening each fragment to make it usable to an audit aid.

Review this chaper, the regulations, Publication 504 (Tax Information for Divorced or Separated Individuals) and, of course, your tax service. Include also the pertinent sections of the IRS audit manuals. They tell a story in themselves.

20.6 PERTINENT COURT DECISIONS—PRO AND CON

Pro
Liberty Nat'l Bank & Trust Co., Exec., v U.S.
(DC Ga. 1969) 24 AFTR 2d 69-5824

Findings of Fact

Plaintiffs were Pearle R. Nabors, widow of the deceased taxpayer, and his estate. They claimed that $5400 paid by Mr. Nabors to his former wife was in satisfaction of his past and present alimony obligations and was therefore deductible.

The IRS, on the other hand, claimed that part of this payment represented a lump-sum amount paid to obtain a release from future support payments and was not deductible.

Opinion

The judge charged the jury in part:

Back alimony is deductible in the year paid. A lump-sum payment of back payments is deductible even though the agreement fixing the amount to be paid also relieves the taxpayer of liability for part of back payments or for all or part of future payments.

To make this clearer, if the payment that Mr. Nabors made to his former wife was simply a lump-sum back payment of alimony and the agreement fixing the amount of back payment contained a provision stating that Mr. Nabors would not be required to make future payments, then you could allow a deduction for all he paid.

However, if you find that only part of the sum Mr. Nabors paid to his former wife was back payments of alimony and part of the sum he paid was paid for the purpose of obtaining a release of all future payments, then only the part he paid representing back payment of alimony would be deductible.

The jury held for the plaintiffs. All of the $5400 payment was deductible.

Con
Evelyn Barrett v U.S. (5 Cir. 1961)
8 AFTR 2d 5816, 296 F 2d 309

Findings of Fact

Appellant was convicted on four counts of failing to file income tax returns for the years 1954 through 1959. The government based its case on the taxability of Evelyn's alimony payments, her only source of income.

She contended that such amounts were not "periodic" and therefore not taxable to her. They consisted of $750 a month for five years and $500 a month thereafter, until the death or remarriage of the appellant.

Opinion

The judge remarked that it has many times been held that payments are periodic within the meaning of the statute where the monthly payments, pursuant to a decree, are contingent and uncertain and may be reduced or terminated upon the happening of certain events, such as death or remarriage—and a principal sum payable in money or property is not specified.

After quoting from numerous previous court decisions to this effect, he stated that the payments were clearly "periodic" and ruled that the evidence did not warrant submission of this question to the jury.

20.7 RELEVANT CODE AND REGULATION SECTIONS, PLUS PUBLICATION

Code

Section 62(13)	Adjusted Gross Defined—Alimony Excepted
71	Alimony and Separate Maintenance Payments
152	Dependent Defined
165	Losses
212	Expenses for the Production of Income
215	Alimony, etc., Payments
267	Losses, Expenses and Interest with Respect to Transactions Between Related Taxpayers
682	Income of an Estate or Trust in Case of Divorce, etc.
1221	Capital Asset Defined
1231	Property Used in the Trade or Business and Involuntary Conversions
1239	Gain from Sale of Depreciable Property Between Certain Related Taxpayers
7701(a)(17)	Definitions—Husband and Wife

Regulations

Section 1.71-1	Alimony and Separate Maintenance Payments; Income to Wife or Former Wife
1.215-1	Periodic Alimony, etc., Payments
1.262-2(b)(7)	Personal, Living, and Family Expenses
1.1239-1	Gain from Sale of Depreciable Property Between Certain Related Taxpayers After October 4, 1976

Publication

504	Tax Information for Divorced or Separated Individuals

20.8 APPLICABLE IRS MANUAL REFERENCES (INVESTIGATIVE TECHNIQUES)

Audit Technique Handbook for Internal Revenue Agents

MT 4231-36	Section 747	Alimony and Separate Maintenance Payments
MT 4231-46	513.2	Children of Divorced or Separated Parents
	543	Alimony

Standard Explanation Handbook

MT 428(11)-15	Section 30	Alimony

Bartering
(Section 61)

21

21.1 IDENTIFYING THE PROBLEM

The problem, very simply, has its roots in excessively burdensome taxes and inflation. These cause the public to search continuously for a way out. Barter exchanges, although operationally legal, offer a tempting means of tax evasion.

The exchanges work as a clearing house for members, as reciprocal trade agencies. Both services and inventory may be exchanged for "credits" which can later be used to obtain other services or goods.

All bartering transactions do not by any means pass through these formal exchanges. Many occur directly between friends and neighbors or between professionals and clients, e.g., a roof repair for a tooth filling. These friendly trades are nearly impossible to locate, so the government intends to concentrate on organized barter exchanges of which there are more than 200 in the U.S.

From what I can determine, "bartering income" has been placed on the *National Office List of Prime Issues* and is destined for concentrated enforcement effort as part of the UIP (Unreported Income Program). Prime targets will be "barter clubs" and their members, but professional persons and ordinary taxpayers will not be ignored.

Internal Revenue shows its concern by establishing a Barter Exchange Project. In Section 2 (Background) of its Manual Supplement 45G-324, the Service has this to say:

> The growth of the number of organized barter exchanges, their franchise activity, and the number of members have resulted in widespread publicity concerning the advantages of noncash transactions. Such transactions represent a potentially significant area of noncompliance.

21.2 HOW THE IRS SEES THE ISSUE

Under the "great gobbler," Section 61 (Gross Income Defined)

> Gross income means all income from whatever source derived, unless excluded by law. Gross income includes income realized in any form, whether in money, property, or services.

The IRS interprets this to mean that the earning of barter credits constitutes taxable income (Rev. Rul. 80-52, IRB 1980-8,12)—and the courts so far have agreed. Subsequent to Rev. Rul. 80-52 a district court ruled that the IRS can compel a barter club to identify its members (Constantinides, DC, Md., 11-16-80).

Later, the IRS issued a summons to a barter exchange demanding

- Records that listed each member.
- Every bartering transaction.
- Dates, participants, and amounts.

When the exchange refused to comply, the IRS asked for a court order. On appeal, the Third Circuit held that the Service had reasonable cause to believe that unknown taxpayers may have failed to comply with requirements of the Code, and ordered that the summons be complied with. (Pittsburgh Trade Exchange, Inc., CA-3, 3-27-81. To the same effect in Maxwell, DC Nev. 3-3-81.)

In its *Audit Guidelines for Examiners,* MT 4231-46, Section 520 (Income) the Service makes these statements:

Examiners must be alert to detect the possibility of omitted income. Two sources are moonlighting income and income from bartering.

TAX TIP:

Being "alert" means: If reported income appears insufficient to meet the taxpayer's cost of living plus other disbursements, including those claimed on the return and substantiated during the examination, examiners will want to know where the obviously missing funds came from—bartering, moonlighting, inheritance, gifts, or where.

21.3 FACTORS WHICH THE IRS CONSIDERS WHEN MAKING ITS AUDIT DECISION

From the viewpoint of enforcement, the IRS feels that the best place to begin is with identification and location of barter exchanges. To this end their Barter Exchange Project, as outlined in Manual Supplement 45G-324, calls for the following identification methods:

- Review of barter trade journals, business periodicals, telephone books and newspapers. (Presumably IRS people, who are assigned to the project, would be responsible for this review in each of their respective locales.)
- Inquiries at the Chamber of Commerce or Better Business Bureau.
- Information obtained from the examination of any return that would identify the existence of a barter exchange.
- All such collected data will be coordinated with a District Examination UIP Coordinator and moved along from there.

Selection and examination of barter exchange returns (Manual Supplement 45G-324, Section 4) will include specific steps:

1. After identification, barter exchange returns will be pulled for classification along with those of owners and operators. Those with potential for tax change will be selected for examination.

2. During the examination, members of the exchange will be identified along with the amount of barter transactions for each.

3. The list of members with their respective transactions will be sent to the District Examination UIP Coordinator. He or she will determine a sample of returns (from this list) which should be pulled.

4. After these returns are obtained, they will be classified by experienced Revenue Agents. All such taxpayers will have been involved in bartering either through a business, moonlighting activities, "hobby" or nonbusiness operations. Where the barter transactions do not appear, the returns will be assigned for audit.

DIF (Discriminate Function System). This is a system for classifying returns which will insure a high degree of "audit potential." Through a secret formula DIF assigns a numerical value to certain specific factors—ten for a home office, for instance. When the total reaches a selected number, the computer calls for an examination of the return.

According to the Manual Supplement, the DIF score is not specifically constructed to identify barter transactions. Therefore, the sample returns may be scored high or low. Current list-year returns with high DIF scores will be classified for all DIF issues in addition to bartering. In a situation such as this, the unreported bartering income obviously would trigger an audit not otherwise likely.

NOTE:

DIF can assign scores only to those items or situations which appear on a return. Most barterers, of course, do not report or identify swapping income.

WARNING:

In instances where returns have already been audited, the examination will be reopened to include unreported bartering income.

21.4 CONSIDERATIONS WHEN PREPARING THE RETURN

Probably the best approach is to understand the workings of a barter exchange. Typically, it is a corporation which receives its income in the form of initiation fees, commissions, or override fees on purchases, annual dues, advertising, and—in some instances—from the sale of franchises.

In return the exchange publishes directories of goods and services as provided by members, and maintains an accounting for members' transactions.

When goods or services are received, no cash payment is made. Instead, the barterer is issued trade credits which are then available to purchase goods or services from other members of the exchange. Members usually receive a monthly summary of transactions and a billing notice for commissions or various charges such as for membership fees or advertising in the exchange magazine. These charges are generally payable in cash.

BE CAREFUL:

> **Organized clubs carefully steer clear of the tax issue, referring members to their own tax advisors.**

Since employees of some exchanges are frequently paid with trade credits, the IRS has a special interest in assuring itself that employment tax regulations are satisfied.

KNOW THIS:

> **After July, 1, 1983, as a result of TEFRA and TD 7873, 3-3-83, barter exchanges will be required to file information returns on exchanges of property or services whenever there are 100 or more such exchanges within a calendar year.**
>
> **Reporting is to be on a transactional basis. Form 1099 will in the reporting vehicle. Beginning in 1984 exchanges must use magnetic media unless they can show undue hardship. (Reg. 1.6045-1)**

Types of Clients Who Barter

Clients who barter can be placed in four categories:

1. Members of organized exchanges
2. Business people who swap services for goods or other services
3. Nonbusiness individuals who exchange their expertise
4. Friends and relatives who swap personal assets or personal services

The degree of tax risk, if such bartering is unreported, decreases from one to four in the order shown.

One. In situations where the member is appreciably active in earning the trading "credits," the risk of detection is great. The UIP search is thorough. If your client escapes, it will be only because the classifier did not feel that his or her return was worthy of good production.

BEWARE:

> **If apprehended, your client will be required to take into income all "credits" earned regardless of whether they were used.**

Two. Business persons. These taxpayers can possibly secure some relief from normal taxation by the manner in which they set fair market values. IRS Publication 525 (Taxable and Nontaxable Income) reads:

> *Property or services (bartering).* An exchange of property or services for your property or services is sometimes called bartering. Income that you receive in the form of property or services must be included in income at its FMV on the date received. If you receive the services of another in return for your services and you both have definitely agreed ahead of time as to the value of the services, that value will be accepted as FMV unless the value can be shown to be otherwise.

TAX TIP:

> **From this paragraph, it appears that, if low values are set, the burden of proving the correct FMV shifts to the IRS. In a practical sense, unless the bartering values are**

substantial (and obviously set very low), the examining officer will usually accept them as recorded. The tax advantages here are obvious—the lower the FMV the lower the taxable income.

Three. Ordinary individuals. A taxpayer whose hobby is gardening swaps services with another who is adept at tying trout flies—maybe twice a year. Who knows, and who cares? Probably de minimus in the eyes of the IRS.

IMPORTANT:

The key here seems to lie in the answer to the question: Was the swap entered into for profit? If it was, it will probably be classed as taxable.

Four. Friends and relatives who swap personal items such as a no-longer-needed baby crib for a bed—or a day's work for a reciprocal amount of time. Certainly no Revenue Agent would waste time on this sort of thing. He or she probably engages in the same type of neighborliness.

Legitimate swaps can be made under the law. They include

• Like-for-like exchanges of property held for business purposes or investment.

• Property for stock in a closely held corporation.

• Legitimate gifts between friends and relatives where there is no business connection.

• Other nontaxable exchanges under Regulation 1.61-6(b).

BE CAREFUL:

Practitioners have the most to fear from *One* (clients who are members of an organized barter exchange). If there is any suspicion of such membership, particularly in the case of professional persons, the taxpayer should be asked point-blank whether he or she is a member. If the answer is in the affirmative, request all exchange statements and report the value of all "earned credits" on the tax return.

NOTE:

There doesn't seem to be any requirement that barter income be so identified on a tax return—only that its FMV be reported. For a business person, therefore, it might be a good idea to simply include the value in sales.

21.5 HANDLING THE AUDIT

Section 6 of the IRS Manual Supplement 45G-324 presents a clear picture of what to expect at the time of a barter audit. See Figure 21-1.

Note particularly paragraph .02(1)

During the initial interview, the member taxpayer should be asked the specific, direct question,

ARE YOU A MEMBER OF A BARTER ORGANIZATION OR HAVE YOU PARTICIPATED IN ANY BARTER TRANSACTIONS? (Emphasis mine)

VERY IMPORTANT:

If your client is a member of an organized exchange, you should presume that the government auditor already knows the answer to this question. Prep your client not to

reply falsely. Trouble—nothing but trouble—can come from fabrication. The truth might bring on a 5 percent negligence penalty; a lie a much greater penalty.

Section 6. Audit Techniques—Members

.01 The barter organization should be asked for copies of the records of member transactions. These should be checked against members' returns (those which have been selected for examination under this project) for verification of the reporting income. Each member's account with the barter exchange receives credits when goods are sold or when services are rendered. Credits are reduced when purchases are made. Generally, one credit received will equal one dollar received.

.02 The following audit techniques should be useful in examining members' returns in the absence of the organizations' records.

1. During the initial interview, the member taxpayer should be asked the specific, direct question, "Are you a member of a barter organization or have you participated in any barter transactions?" The purpose of this question is to determine whether the taxpayer is a member of more than one barter organization or has participated in a direct (outside of an organization) type of barter transaction. If the response to this question is in the affirmative, copies of the monthly statements of transaction received from the barter exchange should be requested from the taxpayer. If the taxpayer refuses, consider issuing a summons to the barter exchange under the provisions of Section 7 of this Supplement.

2. In a double entry system of accounting, certain accounts in the general ledger should be analyzed in detail:

a. exchange account or suspense account.

This account should normally contain debits when goods or services are provided (sold) by the member and credits when the right to receive benefits from the previous barter transaction is exercised (bought).

b. proprietor's drawing or capital account.

The analysis of these accounts should disclose credits representing personal benefits obtained from the barter of business goods and services.

c. accounts Receivable/Receivable from or payable to Officers.

Credits to this account (other than cash payments or write-offs) may include payment (of the account) by means of bartered goods or services received.

3. In both double entry and single entry systems of accounting, to determine whether there is unreported income from bartering transactions, the following accounts should be analyzed to detect possible payments of initiation fees, annual dues, and commissions/overrides to the barter organization:

a. dues and subscription accounts: These accounts may reflect cash payments for the initiation fee and annual dues.

b. interest, business promotion, sales expense, miscellaneous accounts, etc.:

4. These accounts may reflect cash payments of the (commission/override) percentage charged by the barter organization on each bartered transaction. In addition, this commission or override fee, as a percentage of the barter transaction, should permit the examiner to compute the gross amount of the barter transactions if not reported in gross income. Payments may also be charged to the advertising account for advertisements in the exchange directory. Interest expense may reflect payments to a barter organization for purchases made in excess of credits earned or for a line of credit extended to the member by the exchange.

5. Payments of fees may also be made by means of credit cards. Payments made in this manner should alert the examiner to check for unreported income from bartering.

.03 After indications of bartering are discovered, request that the taxpayer furnish copies of all transactions with the exchange. If these are not available, the taxpayer should request duplicates from the exchange. Consideration should be given to the issuance of a summons if the information is not provided.

.04 Trade credit values for goods or services rendered may not reflect their fair market value. Therefore, you should test check these values with arms-length standards. Once established, any lower values (example, a distress sale) would have to be justified based upon factual considerations.

45G-324, 41G-133,   42G-405,   9G-114

Figure 21-1

Should your client be in the category *Two* on an infrequent basis, no great problems should arise when the truth is told. Most agents will probably shrug off affirmative answers to *Three* and *Four*.

WATCH OUT:

> **There should be no devious plan or clearly outright attempt to evade taxes. If you, as a practitioner, uncover such a scheme while preparing a tax return, you should scotch it in its infancy. If your client insists on the evasion attempt, do not prepare the return. It can mean your hide—and do him no service.**

21.6 PERTINENT COURT DECISIONS—PRO AND CON

Pro

No favorable court cases could be located at this early date—and none are expected which will aid formal barter exchange members.

Con
(Rev. Rul. 80-52 IRB 1980-8 p. 12)

Opinion

Members of a barter club that used credit units to obtain goods and services from other members had to include the dollar value of such in income.

See also section 21.2 (How the IRS Sees the Issue).

21.7 RELEVANT CODE AND REGULATION SECTIONS, PLUS PUBLICATION

Code

Section 61	Gross Income Defined

Regulations

Section 1.61-1	Gross Income
1.61-2	Compensation for Services, Including Fees, Commissions, and Similar Items.
1.61-2(d)(1)	Compensation Paid Other Than in Cash
1.61-6(b)	Nontaxable Exchanges

Publication

Pub. 525	Taxable and Nontaxable Income

21.8 APPLICABLE IRS MANUAL REFERENCES (INVESTIGATIVE TECHNIQUES)

Audit Guidelines for Examiners

MT 4231-46 Section 521	Income—Introduction
523	Income from Bartering

Collateral Procedures

Manual Supplement 45G-324	Barter Exchange Project Unreported Income Program (UIP)

Compensation, Excessive or Not 22
(Section 162)

22.1 IDENTIFYING THE PROBLEM

The issue of unreasonable (and therefore nondeductible) compensation generally arises in situations where there is a close relationship between the taxpayer and the employee:

- The majority stockholder or stockholders of a closely held corporation
- The parent or children of an individual proprietor

We will be concerned here primarily with the closely held corporation. Presumably, where the compensated employee does not control the amount of his or her salary, no issue exists. The president of General Motors, for example, is limited only by what he can get. For the vulnerable taxpayer, however, three major problems exist:

1. There are no precise rules that can be used to determine what is reasonable and what is not. (Regulation 1.162-7 defines *reasonable* as "only such amount as would ordinarily be paid for like services by like enterprises under like circumstances.")
2. Burden of proof is on the taxpayer. Facts govern.
3. Should the IRS disallow a portion of corporate compensation, the disallowance will be taxed twice—once when the corporate expense is reduced and again as a constructive dividend to the employee-stockholder.

NOTE:

Despite these problems, taxpayers seem to fare rather well at court. Some careful planning, along with good corporate minutes, can frequently provide success. In Home Interiors and Gifts, Inc., 73 TC No. 92, a shareholder-employee and her son were paid salaries, including profit sharing, up to $1.1 million a year. Even though the taxpayer's family owned more than 50 percent of the stock, the Tax Court still ruled that their compensation was not unreasonable, particularly in light of the phenomenal increase in sales—360 percent over a five-year period.

22.2 HOW THE IRS SEES THE ISSUE

The IRS sees *nondeductible* dividends being paid out to controlling corporate owners as *deductible compensation*. Its agents attack the issue by claiming that such salaries are unreasonable and not ordinary and necessary business expenses.

Nor do they stop there. They go looking for the icing on the cake—nonsalary benefits such as contributions to pension and medical plans, life insurance, free use of a company car, etc.—all of which they include in the total compensation figure for purposes of making their evaluation.

22.3 FACTORS WHICH THE IRS CONSIDERS WHEN MAKING ITS AUDIT DECISION

When an auditor appears on the scene, he or she begins to build a complete compensation package as mentioned above. Beginning with "Officers' Salaries" the auditor moves along to

- Other salary accounts, such as "manufacturing salaries," "labor," and the like, looking for split charges.
- Expense accounts which might contain amounts paid for personal use of principal officer-stockholders.
- Split salaries and bonuses between multiple corporations controlled by the same taxpayer or taxpayers. (The aggregate may be excessive.)
- Alleged political contributions, or other such, paid to the taxpayer as a pass-through device but which were actually bonuses to him or her.
- Minutes books (which incidentally seem to carry much weight with our courts. More on this point later.)
- Payroll records and tax returns.

Tests for reasonableness. Once the compensation package is complete, the auditor is then in a position to decide—excessive or not? Each stockholder-employee will be judged separately. Here are most of the criteria which will be used to make the decision:

1. Paramount is the application of Regulation 1.162-7. Does the amount paid approximate that which is being paid by other like businesses to equally qualified employees for similar services?

2. Then come more specific tests concerning the principal:

- Nature of duties.
- Technical background and experience.
- Knowledge of the particular business.
- Size and profitability of the concern, with emphasis on the taxpayer's contributions to that profitability.
- Time devoted.
- General or local economic conditions.
- Character and amount of responsibility.

- *Time of year compensation is determined.
- The interrelationship of salaries of stockholder-officers to their respective stock ownership ratios.
- Difficulty of the work itself.
- Future prospects.
- Number of persons capable of performing the duties of the position being considered.

3. Usually the IRS person will examine the individual tax return of the corporate officer. Reported salaries from other corporations or the conduct of a proprietorship or involvement in a partnership will produce good evidence as to the amount of time available for devotion to the corporation in question.

*4. Timing the compensation decision for year's end carries a connotation that profits are being distributed.

5. If officers' salaries were accrued, the IRS will want to make sure that they were paid before the required 2½ months after the close of the tax year.

6. If salaries do not coincide with Forms 941, the IRS will want to know why not. As mentioned in Regulation 1.162-7, the compensation may actually include payment for other purposes. To quote from the regulation:

> An ostensible salary may be in part payment for property. This may occur, for example, where a partnership sells out to a corporation, the former partners agreeing to continue in the service of the corporation. In such a case it may be found that the salaries of the former partners are not merely for services, but in part constitute payment for the transfer of their business.

7. Large salary increases in one year are closely examined for justification, particularly where dividends were not paid.

22.4 CONSIDERATIONS WHEN PREPARING THE RETURN

Probably the most important ingredient in establishing the compensation deduction is proving that there is an employer obligation to pay. In a closely held corporation this is easily accomplished through the use of good minutes.

Corporate Minutes

Suppose, however, that you are sitting down to prepare a return and there are no minutes. Should you concoct some and back date them? No!

It has been well established at law that corporate authorization for compensation must have been present *during the taxable year* to fix the obligation—but neither the law nor the regulations prescribe any particular method by which this fixing should be accomplished.

IMPORTANT:

A formal resolution of the board of directors, as recorded in the official minutes, is the best proof of an obligation to pay. Courts, however, have frequently accepted informal authorizations and agreements as proof—and have further accepted formal obligations in a following year's minutes as ratification of the informal authorization of the previous year.

TAX TIP:

This, then, is your "out." Surely salaries wouldn't have been paid without some word of an informal agreement between board members. Now, at tax time, prepare currently dated minutes to ratify this previously authorized compensation.

Guidelines for preparing the minutes. When voting the authorization and preparing the minutes, do not simply state the salaries involved. Anticipate the requirements of the law as regards reasonable compensation. State, for example, that the taxpayer's salary was increased because of his or her unusual devotion to duty, additional academic training with resultant increased efficiency, the assumption of additional duties, an appreciable growth in sales as a result of the principal's efforts, etc.

Be careful of bonus clauses. Any that are paid only to stockholder-executives and not to other employees will probably be classed as dividends.

A *"hedge"* agreement is sometimes placed in corporate minutes to eliminate the double taxation should the IRS reduce the compensation. This hedge, which has been approved by the IRS in Rev. Rul. 69-115, commonly reads as follows:

> Salary payments made to an officer of the corporation that shall be disallowed in whole or in part as a deductible expense for federal income tax purposes shall be reimbursed by such officer to the corporation to the full extent of the disallowance. It shall be the duty of the board of directors to enforce payment of each such amount disallowed.

CAUTION:

While most courts recognize this "hedge" as legitimate, some do not. The latter believe that it reflects a preexisting knowledge on the part of the taxpayer that his or her compensation would not be reasonable. In such cases the hedge works against your client.

Using the CPI

Using the Consumer Price Index (CPI) to justify steadily increasing salaries is a justifiable and proper move. The Court of Claims in Giles Industries, Inc., vs U.S. 5-20-81—on its own initiative—used the CPI to adjust reasonable compensation upward to satisfy the increase in cost of living.

Part-Time Executives

Part-time executives frequently cause compensation troubles. As soon as employees—particularly the elderly—begin to slow down a little, the Service wants to reduce their pay, but the courts don't always agree. In Patterson v McWant Cast Iron Pipe Co. 331 F 2d 921, the Fifth Circuit said:

> It is well accepted in the business world that an executive's salary is not dependent upon time spent on the job. An executive may do some of his most creative work relaxing at home.

In Lundy Packing, TC Memo 1979-472, the court refused to hold a stockholder-officer's compensation unreasonable because it kept increasing after he reached 70 and because he took six weeks vacation each year.

In a similar case (Shotmeyer, TC Memo 1980-238) the taxpayer was semiretired and lived in Florida 13 months out of 36. He did however conduct some corporate business from that location and made all major corporate decisions. In light of his extensive experience, the court felt that the time he contributed to the business was more valuable than that of his two fellow officers (sons) who ran the day-to-day operations.

22.5 HANDLING THE AUDIT

Where the issue of excessive compensation has been raised, the taxpayer should be closely questioned, using this chapter as a checklist. All possible strong points should be segregated, enlarged upon, and highlighted. Court cases in point should be located and readied for IRS consideration.

Specifically, use the material in book section 22.3 (Test for Reasonableness).

Like businesses. A showing that the salaries in question are comparable to those in like corporations can take you halfway to success.

The Research Institute of America recently published an industry-by-industry survey of rates of executive pay. Included are tabulations for 12,000 companies analyzed by 63 separate groups and classified according to type of business and sales volume. (Obtainable from RIA, Dept. PW, 589 Fifth Ave., New York, NY 10017.)

Qualifications of taxpayer. Capitalize on every favorable facet of your client's background:

Education	Practical Experience
Professional memberships	Awards
Subscription to Trade Journals	Areas of Expertise Which Are Peculiar to Him or Her

Duties. Point out number of hours worked—at office and at home—performing in more than one capacity—treasurer, sales manager, or whatever!

Remaining profits. Show that all profits were not drained off as salaries. Paying off steady dividends, even if not large, will help.

Timing of compensation. Produce minutes which indicate that the taxpayer's salary was determined at the beginning of the year and so was not dependent on corporate profits.

Salary comparisons. Show that the salaries of nonshareholders with *one-third* the responsibility of your client are *half* as large.

Stock ownership vs. amount of compensation. Point out that there is no relationship between stockholdings and the amount of pay—that they are not in proportion.

Compensation for past services. In instances where past corporate earnings did not warrant an adequate salary, the taxpayer can always argue that present compensation includes payment for past services.

TAX TIP:

> This argument, however, should be used only as a last resort. If the auditor accepts the compensation as reasonable—without the past-services consideration—then the present year base will be higher for future past-services considerations.

Increased sales, through increased effort and use of innovative ideas by management, is always a strong basis for increased compensation. With proper facts and a good presentation, payment of extraordinary salaries *can* be justified and deducted.

22.6 PERTINENT COURT DECISIONS—PRO AND CON

Pro
Journal Box Servicing Corporation v. United States
DC, Ind. (1962) 9 AFTR 2d 798

Findings of Fact

Journal Box was a corporation formed for the purpose of salvaging and reprocessing oil waste from the journal boxes of railroad cars. Its construction work was performed for it by an affiliate corporation, the James E. McNamara Construction Company. This latter corporation also operated a standard-bred horse breeding and racing farm.

The compensation issue arose when the government claimed that salaries paid by the farm to the wife and daughter of the president of the construction company were not reasonable in amount in relation to services rendered. Total salaries involved: $2500 in fiscal year 1953; $3400 in each of years 1954 and 1955.

Opinion

The court found that such salaries were reasonable in amount because the wife entertained prospective buyers of the taxpayer's racing stock, and the daughter assisted in the formulation and design of farm advertising in farm journals.

Con
Perlmutter v. Commissioner of Internal Revenue

Findings of Fact

Ben, the president of Perlmutter, Inc., organized the company (a real estate development corporation) in 1955, was its majority stockholder, made all primary decisions, and was responsible for its success and reputation. The company never paid any dividends.

In the fiscal years 1958, 1959, and 1960 Ben devoted one-half to three-quarters of a day to company affairs. His salary was $30,900, $34,900, and $53,901. For the 1960 year Ben took money from the company by charging such withdrawals to a Loans Receivable account which was closed to officers' salaries by a journal entry at year's end.

In the two years after 1960, Ben's salary was reduced to $14,500 and $17,500 respectively. During these years he admittedly worked less time because of ill health.

The IRS reduced the petitioner's 1960 salary to $34,900.

Opinion

The court upheld the government for the following reasons:

- The taxpayer was in total control of the company.
- He did not bear the burden of proving that his salary was reasonable.
- No dividends had ever been paid.
- Ben's efforts on behalf of the corporation continuously decreased over the years along with a corresponding loss in gross receipts and profits.
- The 1960 salary showed a disproportionate increase.
- The method of determining the salary in question was informal and unusual.
- Although the petitioner claimed that his 1960 salary included compensation for past services, the record contained no evidence of such paying intent on the part of the corporation.

22.7 RELEVANT CODE AND REGULATION SECTIONS, PLUS PUBLICATION

Code

Section	162	Trade or Business Expenses

Regulations

Section	1.162-7	Compensation for Personal Services
	1.162-8	Treatment of Excessive Compensation
	1.162-9	Bonuses to Employees

Publication

Publication 535	Business Expenses and Operating Losses

22.8 APPLICABLE IRS MANUAL REFERENCES (INVESTIGATIVE TECHNIQUES)

Tax Audit Guidelines

MT 4233-16	Section 232.2	Officers' Salaries

Standard Explanations Handbook

MT 428(11)-14 Section 35	Compensation

LEGAL AND PROFESSIONAL FEES

23

(Sections 162 and 212)

23.1 IDENTIFYING THE PROBLEM

Legal (and certain other professional fees) are particularly troublesome in that their application to the Code is nowhere clearly defined. In our presentation we will be primarily concerned with legal fees. The others follow generally the same pattern.

- Some are immediately deductible as ordinary and necessary business expenses under Section 162.

- Others must be capitalized under Section 263, such as when they are applicable to the purchase of assets with a useful life of more than one year or when expended for permanent improvements made to increase the value of property.

- Some are deductible as nonbusiness expenses which are connected with the production of income, or in connection with the determination, collection, or refund of any tax. Section 212.

- Still others are personal expenses and not deductible at all, such as when paid for the preparation of a will. Section 262.

- Occasionally, legal fees consist of a combination of activities—some deductible, some not, some subject to capitalization. This could occur during an estate planning project, for example.

- Preparation of will—not deductible.

- Preparation of gift tax return—deductible.

- Corporate recapitalization—fee must be capitalized.

Origin and character of the fee must be considered. (Supreme Court's "Gilmore" rule—U.S. v. Gilmore (1963), 11 AFTR 2d 758, 372 U.S. 39, 9 L. Ed. 570, 83 SCT 623, OTD 1878, 1963-1 CB 355 rev'g (C+Cl, 7 AFTR 2d 1576, 290 F 2d 942.))

Through the courtesy of Prentice-Hall, Inc., an extensive checklist of deductible and nondeductible legal fees is included in book Section 23.4.

23.2 HOW THE IRS SEES THE ISSUE

The Service is concerned that taxpayers apply the "legal-and-professional-fee" expenditure with too wide a brush—placing such expenses as legal, accounting, engineering, appraisal, surveying, and other such charges in *one account,* and then deducting the whole mass as an ordinary expense, no matter the purpose for which each expenditure was made.

From the remarks in its Audit Manual, the Service also seems concerned with the possibility that legal and professional accounts may have been created for the purpose of developing *slush funds* to cover illegal payments or kickbacks (Chapter 13).

It also suspects chicanery when *leases* are involved. Legal costs in this respect must be capitalized over the life of the lease.

Also suspect are professional expenses in connection with the following:

1. Acquisition or construction of real property
2. Tax-exempt income
3. Expenses of persons or entities other than the taxpayer, e.g., corporate payment of a stockholder's legal expense
4. Hybrid situations where portions of the expense may not be deductible
5. Divorce or separation proceedings
6. Expenses of organizing or reorganizing a business (may be amortized over five years)
7. Defense of a person's character not business connected (not deductible)
8. Dissenting stockholder suits (cost generally must be capitalized)
9. Sale of business property (part of cost of sale)
10. Title acquisition and defense (capitalization required)

23.3 FACTORS WHICH THE IRS CONSIDERS WHEN MAKING ITS AUDIT DECISIONS

The Audit Guideline for examiners cautions its people that legal and professional fees come in all sizes and colors and are subject to a variety of tax treatments. Each deduction, therefore, should be considered individually.

Paid bills should not be allowed as substantiation in situations where a description of the professional services rendered is not given. The examiner should seek clarification.

Wherever expense deductions are based on retainer fees, a determination should be made whether the actual professional services involved included items of a capital or nondeductible nature.

An examiner must be alert for political contributions masquerading as professional expenses.

In searching for illegal slush funds that may be hidden in legal and professional expense accounts, the government really becomes serious and expects its agents to

1. Determine and document in detail the normal accounting procedure for entries to the account suspected from the first moment a charge or adjusted entry is originated until it is finally paid and stated in the tax return.
2. Select a sufficient number of transactions to be a valid statistical sample for audit.

3. Secure all documents, starting with the first request for payment through the cancelled check issued in payment, related to the transactions selected for audit.

4. Review each transaction to determine:

   a. Was the request originated in the normal course of business by persons who normally initiate or authorize that type of expenditure?

   b. Was the request approved by a person normally charged with that responsibility?

   c. Is the vendor on the company's regular approved list of vendors or was the purchase specially approved? If so, get explanation.

   d. Was the purchase order issued in normal manner, i.e., were bids taken, were prices compared, etc.?

   e. Was the performance certified by persons who normally certify similar transactions for payment?

   f. What was evidence of performance, documents, reports, etc.?

   g. Was payment approved in normal manner by a person usually responsible for approval in similar transactions?

   h. What were rates, fees, etc. charged in similar transactions? Secure satisfactory explanation for charges in excess of normal rates.

   i. If the payment is to a new vendor, examine the supporting documentation in detail to determine if this is a duplicate service or, if the rates charged are higher than the charges for like services, secure an explanation for the apparent discrepancy.

   j. That the entity and transaction involved are not a sham. Does the entity exist? Was the transaction consummated?

   k. If the vendor correspondence file contains any notations that may indicate the presence of an intent to establish slush funds.

   l. Is there any irregularity in endorsement or negotiation of cancelled checks?

23.4 CONSIDERATIONS WHEN PREPARING THE RETURN

No billing for legal or professional fees should be accepted by a preparer as documentation for a tax deduction unless it specifically separates charges both as to description of services and cost of each.

All taxpayer expense accounts, whether lumped as one under "legal and professional" or separated into many, should be analyzed and correctly categorized for Code application. Failure to perform this step can cause unnecessary difficulties at audit time, which is usually two or three years after day of entry. Some frequent problem areas are discussed below:

Divorce or Separation

Legal fees in these regards are usually personal expenses and nondeductible. Fees paid by a spouse, however, are deductible to the extent that they are attributable to the production or collection of amounts includible in gross income as alimony payments. (See Chapter 20, Divorce and Alimony).

Determination, Collection, or Refund of Any Tax

Legal fees paid for these purposes are deductible under Section 212(3). They include fees paid for advice, return preparation, obtaining tax refunds, and for contesting income tax deficiencies.

Deductible, also, are amounts paid in the determination of real and personal property taxes, if the assets were held for the production of income.

Under the "ordinary and necessary expense" rule, legal fees are deductible for amounts expended in the determination of estate and gift taxes.

Formation of a Business

Section 248 allows for the amortization of corporate organizational expenses over a period of not less than 60 months.

IMPORTANT:

An election to so amortize must be made in a statement attached to the taxpayer's return for the taxable year in which the business begins operation.

The statement must contain:

■ A description and amount of expenditures involved.

■ Dates of such expenditures.

■ Month in which the corporation began business.

■ The number of months over which the expenditures are to be ratably deducted.

Regulation 1.248-1(b) defines organizational expenses as those which are:

1. Directly incident to the creation of the corporation,

2. Chargeable to the capital account, and

3. Of a character which, if expended incident to the creation of a corporation, having a limited life, would be amortizable over such life.

This definition is interpreted as:

Legal services incident to the organization of the corporation such as drafting of the charter, by-laws, minutes; terms of original stock certificates, and the like; necessary accounting services; expenses of temporary directors and of organizational meetings of directors or stockholders; and fees paid to the state of incorporation.

NOTE:

Expenditures connected with issuing or selling shares of stock or other securities are not considered organizational expenditures.

Partnerships may also use the 60-month amortization rule, but under Section 709.

Recently enacted Section 195 allows for the same type of amortization for *start-up expenditures*. Under prior law, costs incurred in locating and investigating new businesses were neither deductible nor amortizable.

Corporate reorganization costs such as legal fees and expenses in connection with mergers and consolidations, recapitalization of existing corporations, and other changes in a company's capital structure are capital expenditures and not deductible.

Litigation.

Legal expenses paid in connection with litigation are deductible under Section 162 where they are directly connected with the taxpayer's trade or business—collection of a debt for example.

TAKE CARE:

The cost of defending or perfecting a title would not be deductible but would have to be capitalized.

Bankruptcy

Normally, when individuals file for voluntary bankruptcy, their legal fees are considered personal expenses—and not deductible. Under the Supreme Court's Gilmore rule (as previously mentioned), however, the origin and character of the fee must be considered.

Such consideration allowed Herbert E. Cox (TC Memo 1981-552) to secure a reversal of the IRS position that his cost of filing for bankruptcy was wholly personal in nature and not deductible. What occurred was this:

Mrs. Cox operated a clothing store which became hopelessly mired in debts. The couple each filed bankruptcy petitions listing $159,000 of store debts out of a total of $163,000. The IRS disallowed the entire legal fee of $1500, claiming that no reasonable allocation could be made between the business and personal portions of the fee.

The court disagreed and allowed a pro rata portion of the $1500 as a deduction.

Legal Fee Checklist

Listed below are capitalizable, deductible, and nondeductible legal fees. They have been excerpted from *Prentice-Hall Tax Ideas:**

Checklist of Capitalizable Fees

• Purchase of securities

• Organization expenditures of a partnership (Partnership organization expenses were not previously subject to the amortization rules of Section 248. However, Section 213(b) of the Tax Reform Act of 1976 added Section 709(b) to the Code. That section allows for amortization of amounts paid or incurred to organize a partnership over a 60-month period. Section 709(b) applies only to amounts paid or incurred in tax years beginning after December 31, 1976).

• Sale of a partnership interest

• Determination of ownership of a partnership interest

• Negotiation and draft of a lease of mineral rights

• Purchase of a patent, copyright, or trademark

• Determination of ownership of a patent, copyright, or trademark

• Research and experimental expenditures not deducted

• Trademark expenditures

• Acquisition of an asset with a useful life of more than one year

• Payment by a mortgage before foreclosing

Checklist of Deductible Fees

• Action to secure or collect alimony

• Tax consequences incident to divorce

• Estate planning (tax or investment advice)

• Will construction contest to determine the amount of annual income payable to taxpayer as a life tenant

- Contest of tax liability
- Tax advice
- Collection of dividends and interest
- Investment counseling (except for fees attributable to tax-exempt income)
- Recovery of income from property taxpayer owns
- Proxy fight if not primarily to benefit individual interests
- Determination of stock voting rights
- Defense of shareholder's derivative suit
- Accounting of partnership income
- Oil and gas unitization and pooling agreements
- Determination of ownership of royalties paid
- Injunction against damage to oil-producing property
- Infringement suit brought by one in the business of buying and selling patents
- Accounting for royalties
- Creation of pension or profit-sharing plan
- Liquidation of a business
- Business casualty
- Debt collection in a business

Deduction for Legal Fees

- Use of business assets owned
- Defending against tort claims arising out of the operation of a business
- Tax investigation
- Tax evasion
- Fraud by a securities broker
- Owner's purchase of heroin for race horses
- Successful defense against charge of attempted bribery of a Revenue Agent who proposed adjustments to business parts of tax return
- Employee business expense
- Collection of prize money
- Preparation of tax returns

Checklist of Nondeductible Fees

- Determination of child support
- Determination of child custody
- Action for divorce or separation
- Will preparation
- Unsuccessful will contest to obtain assets
- Lobbying
- Successful defense against a murder charge

- Successful defense against a shoplifting charge
- Successful defense against an assault and battery charge
- Attempted bribery of Revenue Agent regarding adjustments to personal parts of tax return
- Action to secure release from mental treatment facility
- Action for breach of promise to marry
- Suit to have a trust declared void
- Breach of fiduciary duty for misappropriation of funds

Reproduced from the *Prentice-Hall Tax Ideas* service with the permission of the publisher.

The above areas, of course, should be carefully analyzed in light of the origin test and court and IRS Code applications. Circumstances could alter some of the listed categories.

23.5 HANDLING THE AUDIT

Analyze all accounts which could possibly contain legal and professional fees. Secure "origin and character" of each charge, bearing in mind the "proximate" requirement.

Review all paid bills to substantiate taxpayer's identification. Wherever invoices do not clearly separate each legal or other professional service, contact the payee and request a detailed statement. Be alert for the existence of camouflaged, illegal slush funds. As previously indicated, the auditor will become extremely picky if he or she suspects that one exists.

WARNING:

Should you actually locate such a fund, learn all you can concerning the whys and wherefores of its existence, then attempt to reclassify the items into legitimate deductions. Taxpayers could believe, for example, that certain payments are illegal when in actuality they are not. Some could represent a public relations expense, advertising, a legitimate reimbursement, or other such proper deduction.

Recovery of Legal Fees from the IRS

Until recently the possibility of recovering legal fees incident to adversary proceedings within the IRS—in a district court or the Court of Claims—were slim indeed. (The Tax Court has never been included, although there is a bill currently before Congress to allow recovery of reasonable attorney fees and other costs to taxpayers who win their cases before this tribunal.)

There were two main reasons why recovery proceedings were rarely successful:

1. *The law required that the IRS must have initiated the litigation.* This rarely happened, since proceedings usually began with the taxpayer receiving a statutory notice of deficiency (a formal demand for additional taxes). He or she then either paid the amount demanded and sued for a refund or asked for a hearing before the Tax Court. In either case it was the taxpayer who initiated the action.

2. *Some courts required proof of harassment or bad faith on the part of the investigating agent.* Such evidence cannot be easily acquired.

Enactment of the Equal Access to Justice Act has eliminated both of the above roadblocks. After October 1, 1981, the IRS must bear the burden of proving that its case had a reasonable basis in law and fact. Failing in this endeavor, a winning taxpayer can recover

Legal fees.

Court costs.

Expenses to produce expert witnesses.

Any costs for studies, engineering reports, analyses, etc., which might aid in the defense of his or her position.

NOTE:

This law expires on October 1, 1984, unless extended by Congress.

Expenditure limitations. Reimbursement for legal fees cannot exceed $75 an hour, except under unusual circumstances. All other expenses must be reasonable. (No limit has been placed on accounting fees.)

Recovery rules do not apply to an individual whose net worth exceeds $1,000,000 or a business with a net worth of more than $5,000,000 or with more than 500 employees. The word "business" includes proprietorships, partnerships, and corporations.

How to recover. Within 30 days after disposition of the case the taxpayer must file an application with the appropriate tribunal (either the IRS in adversary proceedings or with the court of hearing) setting forth the amount requested. This should be accompanied by an itemized statement from the attorney showing time utilized and computation of fee—plus documentation for other costs which may have been expended in defense of the taxpayer's positions.

23.6 PERTINENT COURT DECISIONS –PRO AND CON

Pro
William E. Terry (TC Memo 1979-284)

Findings of Fact

Taxpayer was a college professor who additionally operated three other businesses—a washeteria, a realty office, and a tax service.

In 1973 he was indicted for assisting others in the fraudulent preparation of their income tax returns. His first trial resulted in a hung jury, the second in acquittal. The IRS disallowed his legal fees.

Opinion

Legal fees, paid for defense in the criminal action are deductible. The judge referred to case of Tellier v. Comm., 383 U.S. 687 (17 AFTR 2d 633) 1966.

Con
Thomas Kehoe (TC Memo 1968-235)

Findings of Fact

During the taxable year at issue the taxpayer filed a Caveaab0lt to the Last Will and Testament of his uncle, Michael Kehoe. If the caveat had been successful—and the will invalidated—the taxpayer would have become a substantial beneficiary. He deducted the legal costs as a business expense on his income tax return. The IRS objected.

Opinion

"It is clear," said the judge, "that the expenditures of petitioner in connection with the litigation involving Michael's will were made because of petitioner's desire to invalidate the will and inherit Michael's property as his heir-at-law. Since property acquired by inheritance is not includible in gross income, expenditures made by an heir in connection with its acquisition are not deductible by him. See Thomas A. Grabein, 48 TC 750, 752 CG. Sec. 212 IRC of 1954."

23.7 RELEVANT CODE AND REGULATION SECTIONS, PLUS PUBLICATION

Code

Section 162	Trade or Business Expenses
195	Start-up Expenditures
212	Expenses for the Production of Income
248	Organizational Expenditures
262	Personal Living and Family Expenses
263	Capital Expenditures
709	Treatment of Organization and Syndication Fees

Regulations

Section 1.248-1	Election to Amortize Organizational Expenditures
1.248-1(a)	In General
1.248-1(b)	Organizational Expenditures Defined
1.248-1(c)	Time and Manner of Making Election

Publication

535	Business Expenses and Operating Losses

23.8 APPLICABLE IRS MANUAL REFERENCES (INVESTIGATIVE TECHNIQUES)

Audit Guidelines for Examiners

MT 4231-46   Section 5(10)(11)0   Legal and Professional Fees

Specialized Industries Audit Guidelines

MT 4232.8-4   Section 234.3   Legal, Travel, and Other Expenses

In-Depth Examinations

MT 4235-5   Section 7(18)0   Legal Expense, Advertising Expense, Consultant Fees
              7(18)1   Introduction
              7(18)2   Investigative Procedures and Techniques

EVASION OR AVOIDANCE
(Sections 6653 and 7201)

24

24.1 IDENTIFYING THE PROBLEM

Judge Learned Hand, in an oft-quoted statement said, "There is nothing sinister in arranging one's affairs so as to keep taxes as low as possible."

Even the IRS agrees. But the problem is one of balance—how to walk the fence line of avoidance without falling off into the quagmire of evasion. The line is thin and tenuous indeed and, therefore, requires serious preparation before an attempt is made to traverse it.

NOTE CAREFULLY:

Courts use the terms "evasion" and "fraud" interchangeably and treat them accordingly. Conviction on civil fraud charges brings on an ad valorum penalty of 50 percent of the deficiency (Section 6653). After enactment of the Tax Equity and Fiscal Responsibility Act of 1982 (TEFRA) on 9-3-82, the 50 percent penalty also applies to the interest payable on any portion of the underpayment attributable to fraud. (Effective date 9-4-82)

A criminal fraud conviction carries with it a sentence of not more than five years in jail and a fine of not more than $10,000 or both (Section 7201). After TEFRA, however, the fine increases to $100,000 ($500,000 for corporations). AND: Anyone who prepares a false or fraudulent document can now be fined the same $100,000 or $500,000 as the case may be. (Effective date 9-4-82)

So you see, becoming too clever can be dangerous. Certainly "avoidance" schemes should not be attempted or entered into lightly. Plans should be well laid and anchored in good law. The taxpayer should be fully informed of the risks involved, if any exist. Here are definitions of some of the terms at issue:

Fraud is defined by the IRS in its *Audit Techniques Handbook for Internal Revenue Agents* as

1. Deception brought about by misrepresentation of material facts, or silence when good faith requires expression, resulting in material damage to one who relies on it and has the

right to do so. It may be defined more simply as deception with the object of gaining by another's loss.

This manual further declares that "the major difference between civil and criminal fraud is the degree of proof required." The regulations say that the former must be proved by "clear and convincing evidence" —that criminal fraud must be proved "beyond a reasonable doubt."

IMPORTANT:

It's been suggested that criminal fraud becomes civil purely as a matter of government expediency—a means of salvaging a lost criminal case. Clearly, there is little difference between the weight of evidence required to prove criminal fraud and that to prove civil. If the IRS can't prove the former, then neither can it generally prove the latter.

TAX TIP:

In cases where there is insufficient evidence to prove a crime, the IRS drops down one step to a civil fraud charge. If it meets too much opposition there, it goes down still further to the five percent negligence penalty. Certainly a taxpayer should never agree to a civil fraud penalty where the government has abandoned a criminal investigation. All possible appeals should be taken.

"Avoidance of tax," says the IRS Manual, "is not a criminal offense. All taxpayers have the right to reduce, avoid, or minimize their taxes by legitimate means ... one who avoids tax does not conceal or misrepresent, but shapes and pre-plans events to reduce or eliminate liability. Then reports the transactions."

WARNING:

The problem is clear: Stay on track. Be aggressive but make sure that no deception exists. In simplest terms, the courts hold that legal actions are avoidance; illegal actions are evasion.

24.2 HOW THE IRS SEES THE ISSUE

To be blunt, without the "Sword of Damocles" that makes criminal tax fraud a felony, punishable by incarceration, we'd have a poor *voluntary* tax system indeed. Proof that the IRS recognizes this fact lies in the opening statement of their Chapter 900, *Audit Guidelines for Examiners,* MT 4231-46:

The fraud investigation is one of the most important phases in the administration of enforcement of our Internal Revenue Laws. The importance of fraud work can best be measured in terms of its effect on our voluntary compliance system.

ATTENTION:

The Service agrees that the line between evasion and avoidance is fine but insists that it is definite and recognizable. Expect, therefore, that in all gray areas the IRS will take only one position—theirs. This does not mean that only two positions exist— illegal or legal. Most avoidance situations probably will evolve into a conflict over interpretation. This, at least, is the worst spot in which a practitioner should find himself or herself.

Evasion is suspect, according to the IRS Audit Guidelines, where its examiners uncover what they believe to be

Deceit.	Camouflage.
Subterfuge.	Concealment.

Some attempt to color or obscure events, or making things seem other than they are.

Section 913 of MT 4231-46 gives the following example:

(a) Mr. Maple purchased stock in the Oak Corporation on January 2, 1978. Mr. Maple decided on December 3, 1978 to sell the stock which would have resulted in a substantial recognized short-term capital gain.

(b) Upon realizing the benefits to be derived from the long-term capital gain provisions of the IRC, Mr. Maple waited until February 1979 to sell the stock. This is an act of tax avoidance. If Mr. Maple did not realize the benefits which could be gained from the long-term capital gain treatment until after the stock was sold in December 1978, and then altered the date on the purchase statement and reported the sale as a long-term capital gain with a purchase date of November 1977, his acts would be tax evasion.

TAKE NOTE:

As a practical matter, generally the Service will not cry "fraud" unless it can establish that at least a part of the deficiency is due to a false *material* representation of fact by the taxpayer and that he or she *had knowledge* of its falsity and *intended* that it be acted upon or accepted as truth. Mere suspicion or presumption will not—or should not—be sufficient to support fraud penalties.

24.3 FACTORS WHICH THE IRS CONSIDERS WHEN MAKING ITS AUDIT DECISION

Three elements are necessary to prove fraud:

1. An attempt must be made to evade taxes. (Spies v. U.S. 317 U.S. 492)
2. Willfulness must be proved. (Haigler v. U.S. 172 F 2d 986, C.A. 10th)
3. A tax deficiency must exist. (U.S. v. Schneck, 126 F2d 702 C.A. 2d Cert. denied)

The Service recognizes that (2)(a person's state of mind) is most difficult to prove. It cautions its agents, therefore

Bearing in mind that one of the necessary elements of fraud is an "intent to evade tax," it can be appreciated that in many cases the evidence of fraud is more or less circumstantial. *Intent is a mental process.*

The Supreme Court has said, in effect, that the most difficult thing in the world is to know what is going on in the mind of another person.

It, therefore, is necessary to judge a taxpayer's intent by his or her acts.

The badges of fraud. These are factors which the IRS considers in making its "evasion or avoidance" decision. They are well stated in Section 940 of *Audit Guidelines for Examiners* and are reproduced here as Figure 24-1.

940 *(4-23-81)*
Badges of Fraud

(1) The taxpayer who knowingly understates income leaves evidence in the form of identifying earmarks, or so-called "badges" of fraud. Some of the more common "badges" of fraud are as follows.

(a) *Understatement of Income*

1. An understatement of income attributable to specific transactions, and denial by the taxpayer of the receipt of the income or inability to provide a satisfactory explanation for its omission.

    a. Omissions of specific items where similar items are included. Example: Not reporting $1,000 dividend from Company A, while reporting $50 dividend from Company B.

    b. Omissions of entire sources of income. Example: not reporting tip income.

2. An unexplained failure to report substantial amounts of income determined to have been received. This differs from the omission of specific items in that the understatement is determined by use of an income reconstruction method (net worth, bank deposits, personal expenditures, etc.).

    a. Substantial unexplained increases in net worth, especially over a period of years.

    b. Substantial excess of personal expenditures over available resources.

    c. Bank deposits from unexplained sources substantially exceeding reported income.

3. Concealment of bank accounts, brokerage accounts, and other property.

4. Inadequate explanation for dealing in large sums of currency, or the unexplained expenditure of currency.

5. Consistent concealment of unexplained currency, especially when in a business not calling for large amounts of cash.

6. Failure to deposit receipts to business accounts, contrary to normal practices.

7. Failure to file a return, especially for a period of several years although substantial amounts of taxable income were received. Examiners should not solicit delinquent returns where the taxpayer has willfully failed to file. A referral report should be submitted.)

8. Covering up sources of receipts of income by false description of source of disclosed income.

(b) *Claiming Fictitious or Improper Deductions*

1. Substantial overstatement of deductions. For example, deducting $5,000 as travel expense when actually the expense was only $1,000.

2. Substantial amounts of personal expenditure deducted as business expenses. For example, deducting rent paid for personal residence as business rent.

3. Inclusion of obviously unallowable items in unrelated accounts. For example, including political contributions in Purchases.

4. Claiming completely fictitious deductions. For example, claiming a deduction for interest when no interest was paid or incurred.

5. Dependency exemption claimed for nonexistent, deceased, or self-supporting persons.

(c) *Accounting Irregularities*

1. Keeping two sets of books or no books.

2. False entries or alterations made on the books and records, backdated or post dated documents, false invoices or statements, other false documents.

3. Failure to keep adequate records, especially if put on notice by the Service as a result of a prior examination, concealment of records, or refusal to make certain records available.

4. Variance between treatment of questionable items on the return as compared with books.

5. Intentional under or over footing of columns in journal or ledger.

6. Amounts on return not in agreement with amounts in books.

7. Amounts posted to ledger accounts not in agreement with source books or records.

8. Journalizing of questionable items out of correct account. For example: From the Drawing account to an expense account.

(d) *Allocation of Income*

1. Distribution of profits to fictitious partners.

2. Inclusion of income or deductions in the return of a related taxpayer, when difference in tax rates is a factor.

(e) *Acts and Conduct of the Taxpayer*

1. False statement, especially if made under oath, about a material fact involved in the examination. For example, taxpayer submits an affidavit stating that a claimed dependent lived in his household when in fact the individual did not.

2. Attempts to hinder the examination. For example, failure to answer pertinent questions or repeated cancellations of appointments.

3. The taxpayer's knowledge of taxes and business practice where numerous questionable items appear on the returns.

4. Testimony of employees concerning irregular business practices by the taxpayer.

5. Destruction of books and records, especially if just after examination was started.

6. Transfer of assets for purposes of concealment.

(f) *Other Items*

1. Pattern of consistent failure over several years to report income fully.

2. Proof that the return was incorrect to such an extent and in respect to items of such character and magnitude as to compel the conclusion that the falsity was known and deliberate.

(2) The following actions by the taxpayer, standing alone, are usually not sufficient to establish fraud. However, these actions with some of the "badges" listed

above, may be indicative of a willful intent to evade tax:

(a) Refusal to make specific records available. (Examiner should note time and place records were requested.)

(b) Diversion of portion of business income into personal bank account.

(c) File return in different district. (This is weak but should be noted.)

(d) Lack of cooperation by taxpayer. Examiner should cite specific episodes, threats, etc.)

(3) The presence of one or more of these "badges" of fraud does not necessarily mean that the return is fraudulent. However, it should alert the examiner to this possibility and invite further and more probing inquiry.

Figure 24-1

The IRS will not necessarily approach an audit with this checklist in hand but will quickly revert to its use if some overt or suspicious act appears.

24.4 CONSIDERATIONS WHEN PREPARING THE RETURN

From the ominous material which you have just read, you may decide that discretion is the better part of valor—and become overly cautious. Don't do it. You'll be doing your client a disservice.

CAUTION:

This is not to say that you do not bear a heavy burden in this matter. You do; so, despite my suggestion to be aggressive, do not extend your avoidance attempts too dramatically. Always stay in the legal sector. Always keep your client fully informed.

Take any issue that appears to have tax advantages. Research it. Latch onto anything that will support your point of view—regulations, committee reports, court cases. Neither you nor your client will be in any fraud danger as long as you both act in good faith. And stay away from the manufacture of self-serving evidence. (See the section *How to Avoid the Evasion Charge*, which appears below.)

TAKE HOPE:

The Revenue Service is not in the business of "getting you" or your client. It normally will not attempt to stretch a gray-area issue into an evasion classification. On the contrary—experienced Internal Revenue Agents do not enjoy the rigors of fraud work. Most steer clear of it, if they can.

"The Audit Lottery"

Currently, less than two percent of all tax returns are being audited, and many of these are concerned only with special projects such as bartering, outlandish tax shelters, and the UIP (Unreported Income Program). A legitimate, but questionable, tax issue under these conditions certainly carries better odds of winning than does Vegas

CONSIDER THIS:

Here is another situation which seems to have taxpayer possibilities: Suppose that you have a gray-area issue. Why not file return on April 15 to avoid the IRS numbers game? The Service insists that all returns—no matter when filed—are classified for audit potential in the same manner, i.e., by the point system. Each potentially productive item on a return is given a numerical classification—let's say 10 points for a Schedule C loss which could be classed as a hobby; 20 points because of a home office; etc. Once the total reaches a prearranged amount—maybe 150 points—the return pops out for audit. If we presume that the computer assigns these numerical values during the processing of returns when filed, won't the barrel soon be filled with potentially productive audit possibilities?

LET LOGIC LOOSE:

With its limited manpower and emphasis on special projects, after the "for-audit" barrel reaches excessive proportions on April 1—why add more 150's? Logic dictates that further additions would be futile. Removing returns for audit, only to have them returned untouched, makes about as much sense as reclassifying millions of already classified returns. Again, I say, base your issue in good law and take a chance. If you stay away from the fraud stigma—and avoidance fails—only interest charges are the penalty.

How to Avoid the Evasion Charge

Avoiding the evasion charge is not difficult. Consider the following five points:

1. Full disclosure. If you are at all in doubt as to the legality of your position, *make a full disclosure on the tax return*. The courts have long held that such an action obviates fraud. In Jennison v. Comm., (45F2d-5th Cir 1930), for example, a fraud penalty was set aside by the Court of Appeals on the ground, among others, that all relevant matters affecting the transaction had been divulged on the return.
2. Do not use new and untried avoidance devices—not even if your client insists.
3. Stay away from the "badges of fraud."
4. Satisfy yourself that the whole plan bears no relation to evasion and that what you plan is no more dangerous than any other ordinary business risk.
5. In the final analysis—when judging your contemplated avoidance operation—if you are still in doubt, opt in favor of conservatism. Drop the idea or make a full disclosure.

The Statute of Limitations is an important consideration in the planning of an avoidance move.

WARNING:

If the IRS is able to prove the existence of civil fraud, no statute exists. This means that the Service can go back as many years as it likes in making its case (Section 6501(c)).

It can go back six years in making criminal charges (Section 6531). It is therefore unwise to utilize the same borderline avoidance scheme over a long period of time.

DON'T BE LULLED INTO COMPLACENCY:

The IRS has found, in the investigation of thousands of fraud cases, this one continuously reoccurring situation:

Once a taxpayer has established what seems to be a successful evasion scheme (no audits)—he or she continues to dip deeper and deeper into this illegal pot of gold until caught. Don't let this happen to you or your client.

In the absence of fraud the normal three-year statute applies (Section 6501(a)), except that if omitted income exceeds 25 percent of the reported gross income, the statute goes to six years (Section 6501(e)(1)(A)).

Burden of proof. On the issue of fraud, the burden of proof is on the Commissioner (Section 7454). Weight of evidence differs in situations where the fraud is of a civil or criminal nature. Details were discussed under "Identifying the Problem."

Application of the civil fraud penalty. The Commissioner may apply the 50 percent civil fraud penalty to the entire deficiency where any part of the underpayment is due to fraud (Section 6653(b)). At this time, however, there is a bill in committee to allow assessment of the penalty only against the fraudulent portion of the deficiency.

NOTE:

> No penalty exists if there is no underpayment except that such underpayment, for purposes of penalty application, will be computed without benefit of subsequent loss carrybacks. The 50 percent fraud penalty is also assessed in all successful criminal fraud prosecutions, along with jail sentences and fines.

Innocent spouse. At one time the civil fraud penalty attached to both parties who had filed a joint return. Now, under Regulation 301.6653-1(f)

> A taxpayer shall not be subject to the fraud penalty solely by reason of the fraud of a spouse and his filing of a joint return with such spouse.

24.5 HANDLING THE AUDIT

Upon audit, it should be a practitioner's objective, above all else, to recognize the IRS examination for what it is. Does the auditor suspect fraud at the outset, or is he or she only pursuing a routine investigation?

WARNING:

> The answer to this question is vital. If you prepared the return, you can be sure *what's in it*, but you can never be sure *what should have been in it*.

Actions of the examiner can be indicative of his or her intent. IRS *Audit Technique Handbook For Internal Revenue Agents,* Section (10) 90, sets forth instructions to its employees should they discover evidence of fraud. It gives a good insight into what you should expect and is reproduced here as Figure 24-2.

---

(10)90 *(8-30-76)*
Procedure after Discovering
Indications of Fraud

(10)91 *(9-2-80)*
General

(1) IRM 4565.2 provides that if, during an examination, an examiner discovers a firm indication of fraud on the part of the taxpayer, the tax return preparer, or both, the examiners shall suspend his/her activities at the earliest opportunity without disclosing to the taxpayer, his/her representative or employees, the reason for such suspension. He/she will then prepare a report of his/her findings in writing as explained in (10)92. Tle purpose of the referral report is to enable the Criminal Investigation

function to evaluate the criminal potential of the case and decide whether a joint investigation should be initiated. It is important, therefore, that the referral report contain sufficient information to enable the Criminal Investigation function, to make a proper evaluation.

(2) After an examiner discovers the possible existence of fraud he/she must decide when to suspend the examination and prepare a referral report. As stated above, "at the earliest opportunity" does not mean immediately. It means at the earliest point after discovering *firm* indications of fraud. This means more than suspicion. It means the agent has taken steps to perfect the indications of fraud and developed them to the degree necessary to form the basis for a sound referral. This must be done at the first

instance while the books and records are available to the agent, because, later on, they may not be accessible and information contained therein may be impossible to obtain.

(3) On the other hand, if the agent extends his/her examination too far before submitting the referral report he/she may be doing unnecessary work. The special agent who will come into the case later may find it necessary to repeat some of the work previously done in order to document evidence required in a criminal case. Also, the over-extension of the examination may jeopardize criminal prosecution by giving the taxpayer a basis for claiming that the criminal case was substantially built by the examiner under the guise of making an audit for civil tax purposes.

(4) In some instances the presence of a substantial omission of income or unallowable deduction is its own evidence of intent. However, unless the understatement speaks for itself, the taxpayer should be questioned concerning it and the reasons ascertained for treating the suspected items as he/she did. The examiner should ascertain and record the method used in understating the income, and weigh the adequacy and reasonableness of the taxpayer's explanation. These should be evaluated in terms of the nature of the understatement. In this respect

(10)44 will be helpful since it contains many of the identifying earmarks from which intent to defraud can be inferred. At the same time the agent should bear in mind that he/she is not, at this point, building a fraud case against the taxpayer. The examiner should not make a detailed interrogation when questioning the taxpayer, nor should he/she argue about the answers. The examiner should delve into the intent element only as far as necessary to support a finding of an indication of fraud. If the explanations offered are considered inadequate or unreasonable, the agent may properly conclude that the understatement is probably due to fraud and a referral should then be made, and forwarded through proper channels as stated in (1) above.

(5) It is important that potential criminal cases be handled properly by the examiner. The examiner should not discuss the taxpayer's case with Criminal Investigation prior to submission of the referral report. After the referral report is submitted, there should be no further contact with the taxpayer until the referral is either accepted (in which case a special agent should be present) or declined. If contacted by the taxpayer or his/her representative, the examiner should be polite and tactful, without discussing the matter of referral with the taxpayer. The examiner should be sure to document any conversations, showing the date, time and place.

Figure 24-2

IMPORTANT:

It is exceedingly important to note paragraph (2) of Section (10)91 and the reference to *development of evidence of fraud* as quoted below:

...at the first instance while the books and records are available to the agent, because later on, they may not be accessible and information contained therein may be impossible to obtain.

This passage refers to the fact that the government does not attempt to force an individual (by issuance of a summons) to produce his or her records in a criminal matter. To do so would be tantamount to forcing a taxpayer to testify against himself or herself—and thereby ruining the government's case in a constitutional sense.

NOTE ALSO:

Should a *Special Agent* of the Criminal Investigation Division appear with thoughts of criminal fraud on his or her mind, he or she must read the taxpayer a statement of rights in which the taxpayer is advised that the investigation is criminal in nature and that he or she may remain silent and produce no records.
According to Section (10)90 above, an *Internal Revenue Agent* need not state his or her intentions. Such an agent can poke around all he or she wants, collecting criminal evidence at leisure.

IMPORTANT TAX TIP:

For this reason, in instances where the evasion-avoidance issue may possibly arise, I strongly suggest that the taxpayer not be present at audit time and that books and records not be voluntarily produced.

What should be done then? Well, I'd suggest that you have a serious talk with your client, emphatically impressing upon this person that he or she should tell you only the truth at this time. Nothing else will help since neither of you can have knowledge of the type of evidence which the government may already possess.

Run through the Badges of Fraud. If any exist, explore them thoroughly. Possibly, when presented in correct perspective, they can be reclassified as only avoidance items.

After thorough examination of the return and a complete analysis of all facets of the case, you'll have to make a decision. Should you produce the records or not? The intent of the taxpayer should govern.

VERY IMPORTANT:

If he or she admits to concocting an illegal scheme to evade taxes—and you are not a tax attorney—hire one.

If you eventually locate only gray-area items which may be questioned, you produce the records but still do not allow your taxpayer to be questioned. If you are unable to answer the agent's queries, jot them down, discuss them with your client in private, then give the answers—but only if they are not fraudulently damaging.

As the examination progresses and more and more questions pop up, you'll be able to judge what's going on. If all investigative work seems slanted toward fraud possibilities, disengage and wait for the agent's next move.

WARNING:

If the Internal Revenue Agent suddenly ceases to investigate, most certainly disengage. Probably the next person you see will be a Special Agent. Again, if you are not a tax attorney, *hire one*.

BE CAREFUL:

Books have been written concerning the defense of fraud charges. Obviously, there is no space for that here. If you are not an attorney, be careful how deep you delve. The government can force you to testify against your client unless you place yourself under an attorney's umbrella of privilege.

24.6 PERTINENT COURT DECISIONS—PRO AND CON

Pro
Maggie Bailey v Comm. U.S. Ct. of Appeals, 6th Cir No. 20729 (April 27, 1971)

Findings of Fact

Bailey, a bootlegger, kept no records, thereby allowing the IRS to utilize a net worth method for reconstruction of her income. The bootlegger was not able to upset the government's opening net worth position, but the IRS could not prove stock inventory.

Even though the IRS showed that the taxpayer had failed to report some $200,000 over the years 1945 to 1963—had kept no records and had dealt exclusively in cash—the tax court ruled that such deficiencies were insufficient proof of concealment or intent to commit fraud, particularly in view of the fact that the taxpayer was an unsophisticated and uneducated person.

Opinion

The appeals court upheld the tax court's decision.

Con
George C. O'Brien (TC Memo 1976-388)

Findings of Fact

Taxpayer was president and chief stockholder of O'Brien Gear and Machinery Company. Only he and his mother were authorized to sign corporate checks. The accrual method of accounting was utilized on a fiscal-year basis.

The government's investigation determined that accounts receivable for the 1967-1968 period exceeded sales by $150,000, thereby leaving the books with $150,000 more debits than credits.

To correct this imbalance, four entries had been made in the "cash in bank" account which totaled $150,000. Between June and September of 1968, twenty-four checks were prepared by the corporate controller, all made payable to "cash" and totaling $150,000. No entries were made on the corporation's books with respect to these checks. They were removed in reverse numerical order from a check register which was not utilized until 1971.

Mr. O'Brien personally endorsed and cashed eleven of the checks totaling $70,000 and the comptroller an additional eleven, totaling $70,500. It could not be determined who cashed the two remaining checks.

The taxpayer failed to report any income, other than salary, on his pertinent tax return. He disclaimed any knowledge of the understatement of sales or the cashing of checks, claiming that he relied completely on the comptroller for the keeping of books and records and the preparing of checks.

Opinion

The court refused to believe the petitioner's testimony, remarking that as a businessman he most certainly would have questioned the purpose of $150,000 worth of checks, payable to cash and presented to him over a period of three months for his signature.

Furthermore, the petitioner failed to produce any evidence which would explain the use of $70,000 for corporate purposes as obtained from checks which he himself had cashed.

Fraud penalty upheld.

24.7 RELEVANT CODE AND REGULATION SECTIONS

Code

Section 6501(a)	Limitations on Assessment and Collection—General Rule
6501(c)	Limitations on Assessment and Collection—Exceptions
6501(e)(1)A	Limitations on Assessment and Collection—Income Taxes
6531	Periods of Limitation on Criminal Prosecutions
6653	Failure to Pay Tax
6653(b)	Failure to Pay Tax—Fraud

| 7201 | Attempt to Evade or Defeat Tax |
| 7454 | Burden of Proof in Fraud, Foundation Manager, and Transferee Cases |

Regulations

Section 301.6653-1	Failure to Pay Tax
301.6653-1(b)	Failure to Pay Tax—Fraud
301.6653-1(f)	Failure to Pay Tax—Joint Returns

24.8 APPLICABLE IRS MANUAL REFERENCES (INVESTIGATIVE TECHNIQUES)

Audit Technique Handbook for Internal Revenue Agents

MT 4231-37 Section	(10)10	Introduction
	(10)22	Civil and Criminal Cases Distinguished
	(10)31	Definition of Fraud
	(10)32	Avoidance Distinguished from Evasion
	(10)53	Degree of Proof
	(10)60	Tax Evasion Schemes
	(10)90	Procedure After Discovering Indications of Fraud

Audit Guidelines for Examiners

MT 4231-46 Section	912	Definition of Fraud
	913	Avoidance Distinguished from Evasion
	921	Civil and Criminal Fraud Distinguished
	933	Intent to Evade Tax
	940	Badges of Fraud

Collateral Procedures

MT 4500-348 Section	4563.4	Fraud Penalties
	4563.41	Introduction
	4563.42	Criteria for Asserting Civil Penalties

INTEREST EXPENSE
(Section 163)

25

25.1 IDENTIFYING THE PROBLEM

How can there possibly be a problem with interest expense? You pay it and deduct the amount on your business return or as an itemized deduction. Well, like all else in the realm of income taxes, the twisting and turning of law by regulations, court decisions, revenue rulings, etc., have taken a relatively simple issue and made it complicated.

Interest is defined in Section 163(a) as monies "paid or accrued within the taxable year on an indebtedness." The uncomplicated rules for qualification of the deduction are these:

1. Interest must have been paid within the year of the deduction ... or accrued within the year of liability.
2. There must have been a true indebtedness.
3. The interest must have been paid on an obligation of the taxpayer.
4. That individual must have been liable for the interest payment.

Watch for These Snares

Within this simple definition and framework are hidden many snares. The most common are conditionally these:

■ Accrued interest between related parties. (Amount and time of ultimate payment are important.)

■ Interest on funds borrowed to purchase wholly tax-exempt securities. (Not deductible.)

■ Interest on borrowings to buy a life insurance, endowment, or annuity contract if the plan is to systematically borrow part or all of the increases in cash value of the contract. (Not deductible.)

■ Interest paid to carry single-premium life insurance. (Not deductible.)

■ Interest on margin accounts—deductible only where constructively or actually paid. (This can occur only when the broker is paid or when funds in the account become available to the broker through addition of dividends or interest income, or the sale of securities.)

■ Interest that is in reality a dividend. (Not deductible to payor corporation.)

303

■ Interest on certain corporate acquisition indebtedness. (May be part of principal payment.)

■ Carrying charges chargeable to a capital accouunt. (Not deductible.)

■ Investment interest. (Subject to limitations.)

■ "Points" paid in real estate transactions. (For deductibility, it depends who is paying, buyer or seller, and the purpose.)

■ Imputed interest. (Will be imputed by the IRS in cases where it does not exist in installment-sale situations.)

■ IRS interest classed as penalties—and nondeductible. (Can happen.)

■ Interest under the Economic Recovery Act of 1981. (Changes in law. See separate paragraph for details.)

25.2 HOW THE IRS SEES THE ISSUE

The government feels that many principal payments, dividends, loan fees, carrying charges, etc., escape as interest deductions; it feels also that many transactions are shams—not of the arms-length variety but hidden in false shrouds—actually for the purpose of buying tax-exempt securities or life insurance against which the taxpayer intends to systematically borrow part or all of the increases in the cash surrender value. (All tricky and not allowable.)

The Service expects—because of the nature of the deduction—that documentation will exist, and its auditors will ask to examine it.

25.3 FACTORS WHICH THE IRS CONSIDERS WHEN MAKING ITS AUDIT DECISION

The IRS Manual *(Audit Guidelines for Examiners,* MT 4231-47, Section 573) instructs its examiners to approach the interest deduction in the following manner:

(1) Verify amount claimed and determine that the deduction has been taken in the proper year.

(2) Determine whether the payments are for interest or for other items, such as discounts, finance charges, or principal. Finance charges on revolving charge accounts are considered to be interest and are deductible.

(3) Ascertain whether the interest payments are made on a valid, existing debt owed by the taxpayer. If there is a joint and several liability, the entire amount of interest is deductible by the payor. Interest paid as a guarantor does not constitute an interest deduction.

(4) Ascertain whether the debt was incurred to carry or purchase an investment, the income from which is tax-exempt, or was incurred to purchase a single premium life insurance, endowment or annuity contract after March 1, 1954.

(5) Loans from related individuals should be analyzed to determine that the interest rate paid does not exceed the normal rate for available money.

(6) When veryifying an interest deduction, the examiner should inspect the instruments of indebtedness, such as mortgage statements, loan contract, etc. Cancelled checks are not

usually evidence of the liability or payment of interest, and generally should be supported by documentation.

(7) If the taxpayer maintains brokerage accounts, the statements should be analyzed. Interest charged on margin accounts should not be netted against interest or dividend income. It must be claimed as an itemized deduction.

(8) Examiners should verify that the same interest deduction is not claimed twice, i.e., itemized Deductions and Rental Expense.

(9) Examiners should be alert for situations where taxpayers have claimed deductions for accrued interest on existing liabilities and foreclosure proceedings have subsequently occurred. Verify the taxpayer has included the difference between the liability per the books and the liability which was relieved by the foreclosure as income.

(10) If the taxpayer moved during the year under examination, the examiner should check the allocation of interest on the closing statement.

(11) If the taxpayer assumed a mortgage during the year under examination, the examiner must make a proper allocation between the buyer and the seller since the lender will normally issue a statement on total interest paid during the year for that mortgage.

NOTE PARTICULARLY:

"(3) Interest paid as a guarantor does not constitute an interest deduction."

"(7) Interest charged on margin accounts should not be netted against interest or dividend income but must be claimed as an itemized deduction."

Other Manual Sections Add More to the Search Technique

Verification of interest paid to related persons should include a determination that the proceeds of the loan were actually required for business purposes rather than used as a means of siphoning off income by imputing it to the lender in the form of interest paid.

The auditor should be certain that accrual interest payable to related taxpayers is paid within the time limits prescribed by the Code—that all interest, paid or accrued, to related taxpayers is not in excess of prevailing rates in unrelated transactions.

Accrued interest should be checked against the base document to insure that a liability does exist.

If the recipient of the interest is a nonresident alien or other foreign entity, a determination should be made as to whether the proper amount of tax has been withheld.

Interest is not deductible on an insurance loan if it is not paid but added to the amount of the loan.

Split interest—that portion which is deductible against gross income or against adjusted gross income—should be traced to avoid a double deduction, as in the purchase of a car that is used both for business and for pleasure.

Cautious examiners should watch for amounts paid by a home purchaser in connection with the occupancy of a home for a period prior to the date he or she assumed an enforceable liability on the mortage. Any such amounts designated as interest on the mortgage in the settlement papers do not constitute deductible interest but are classed as rent.

If an interest charge is not separately stated on an installment contract, the allowable deduction cannot exceed six percent of the average unpaid balance of the contract or the applicable finance or carrying charge, whichever is smaller.

BE CAREFUL:

The government manual doesn't mention these two, but a good Internal Revenue Agent won't miss them:

1. **Interest on short-term bank loans, which is paid by adding the charge to a replacement note, is not deductible.** Suppose, for example, that the taxpayer borrows $1,000 for 90 days. At the end of that time he or she cannot pay, and the bank allows the borrower to sign a new 90-day note for the $1,000 plus the interst due on the first debt. No deduction is allowed.

2. **Some taxpayers capitalize interest.** Presume that a truck is purchased and financed through a loan. The total cost, including finance charges, is depreciated over the life of the vehicle. A good examiner will look for a possible double deduction through interest and depreciation.

25.4 CONSIDERATIONS WHEN PREPARING THE RETURN

There are a few basic and obvious situations, aside from outright shams, which probably should be mentioned here. Some have been presented previously in this chapter. Others follow.

Capitalization of Construction Period Interest

Prior to TEFRA, construction-period interest was required to be amortized over a period of generally 10 years by individuals, Sub S corporations, and personal holding companies for all realty (excepting low-income housing) which was constructed for use in a trade or business or held for investment.

Now the '82 law applies the same rule to the construction of nonresidential real property by regular corporations.

Investment Interest

The rules for this deduction have changed several times since 1969 but now stand as shown for amounts paid or accrued on or after September 11, 1975.

The deduction for interest on funds borrowed to purchase or carry investment property is limited to $10,000 ($5,000 for married individuals filing separately) plus net investment income (investment income less investment expense).

Example: A married couple incur investment interest expense of $50,000. Their investment income is $20,000 with expenses of $5,000, or net investment income of $15,000. Their deduction, therefore, is limited to $10,000 plus $15,000, or $25,000.

Under Code Section 163(d)(2) the unallowed interest expense of $25,000 may be carried forward until utilized. IRS Form 4952 should be used to compute the deduction.

NOTE:

Only straight-line depreciation is considered when computing investment income and long-term gains are not included.

A *special rule* exists for debts incurred in connection with the acquiring of a 50 percent or more interest of a corporation or partnership. Under the governing section, 163(d)(7), the

$10,000 limitation is increased by the lesser of $15,000 or the amount of interest on the indebtedness, incurred or continued, which is used in the acquisition.

Net Lease

Normally, rents and related deductions will be categorized as business income and will not enter into the investment interest limitation. If, however, the rent and interest is connected with a net lease—and if out-of-pocket expenses exceed lease income—it is possible to increase the interest deduction limitation. See Section 163(d)(4)(A) below:

(4) *Special rules.—*

(A) Property subject to net lease.—For purposes of this subsection, property subject to a lease shall be treated as property held for investment, and not as property used in a trade or business, for a taxable year, if—

(i) for such taxable year the sum of the deductions of the lessor with respect to such property which are allowable solely by reason of section 162 (other than rents and reimbursed amounts with respect to such property) is less than 15 percent of the rental income produced by such property, or

(ii) the lessor is either guaranteed a specified return or is guaranteed in whole or in part against loss of income.

How "Points" Are Treated

"Points" paid by a borrower solely for the use of money are deductible as for prepaid interest (Section 461(j) over the life of the loan, *except* that in the case of a home mortgage, the cost of the points may be deducted in the year of payment, if the following conditions are met:

1. The indebtedness must have been incurred in connection with the purchase or improvement of (and secured by) the taxpayer's principal residence.

2. The charging of points must reflect an established business practice in the geographical area where the loan was made.

3. The deduction allowed can't exceed the number of points generally charged in the area for this type of transaction.

Points, however, are not deductible if paid for specific services by the lender—appraisal fees, cost of preparing mortgage note, settlement charges, etc. These may be capitalized over the life of the mortgage for business property, but must be added to the cost of a residence and used for sale purposes only.

Loan origination or placement fees, such as those charged by the VA and FHA to process mortgages are charges for services rendered and are not deductible as interest.

Points paid by a seller as placement fees for a loan to a buyer—the arranging of financing, for example—are not interest and not deductible. They are considered selling expenses, however, and will reduce the amount realized.

Handling Installment Purchases

Installment purchases, under circumstances where the interest charge is not separately stated, are clearly explained in Section 163(b) which is reproduced here as Figure 25-1.

SEC. 163. INTEREST.
(a) General Rule.—There shall be allowed as a deduction all interest paid or accrued within the taxable year on indebtedness.

(b) Installment Purchases Where Interest Charge Is Not Separately Stated.—
    (1) General rule.—If personal property or educational services are purchased under a contract—
        (A) which provides that payment of part or all of the purchase price is to be made in installments, and
        (b) in which carrying charges are separately stated but the interest charge cannot be ascertained,

then the payments made during the taxable year under the contract shall be treated for purposes of this section as if they included interest equal to 6 percent of the average unpaid balance under the contract during the taxable year. For purposes of the preceding sentence, the average unpaid balance is the sum of the unpaid balance outstanding on the first day of each month beginning during the taxable year, divided by 12. For purposes of this paragraph, the term "educational services" means any service (including lodging) which is purchased from an education organization described in section 170(b)(1)(A)(ii) and which is provided for a student of such organization.

    Prior amendment.—Sec. 163(b)(1) was amended by Sec. 224(c) of Public Law 88-272, Feb. 26, 1964, effective (Sec. 244(d) of P.L. 88-272) for payments made during taxable years beginning after Dec. 31, 1963. Sec. 163(b)(1) as so amended is in P-H Cumulative Changes.

    (2) Limitation.—In the case of any contract to which paragraph (1) applies, the amount treated as interest for any taxable year shall not exceed the aggregate carrying charges which are properly attributable to such taxable year.

Reproduced from the *Prentice-Hall Federal Taxes* service (1983 edition) with the permission of the publisher.

Figure 25-1

Revolving credit accounts, including credit cards. If this type of a credit plan clearly states that a certain percentage, say 1½ percent, of the unpaid balance will be charged each month as interest, then Section 163(a) applies and such charges are deductible. However, if the monthly charge is termed "carrying charges," then Section 163(b) as above comes into play and the allowable interest deduction drops drastically.

Imputed interest. Formerly, in situations concerning deferred or installment sales, taxpayers could save taxes by specifying no—or unreasonably low—amounts of interest. This had the effect of increasing the capital gain and eliminating or reducing fully taxed interest income.

IMPORTANT:
    Recently, under Section 483, the government has insisted on interest charges. It decides whether an amount is unreasonably low by making the following tests:
        Is the stated *simple interest* at least:
        9% for contracts entered into after 6-30-81?
        6% for contracts entered into prior to 7-1-81?
        4% for contracts entered into prior to 7-24-75?

If so, the Service will not impute interest. If not, it will insist on interest charges which are *one percent higher than the above, compounded semiannually.*

In a recent Revenue Ruling (82-124) concerning zero-interest mortgages, the IRS ruled that it will impute interest at the rate of ten percent wherever it finds such mortgages.

How to Compute Unstated Interest

If interest is specified but not stated as a percent, the unstated interest must be determined. This is accomplished by discounting to present values the payments deferred for more than six months. Here's the formula:

1. Find the sum of the sales payments deferred for more than six months. (Do not include any stated interest.)
2. Find the present value of all payments deferred for more than six months using appropriate percentage columns (9%-6%-4%) from tables as included in Regulation 1.483-1. (Include stated interest.) If the amount in (2) is less than the amount in (1), unstated interest exists. Continue to step 3.
3. Locate the present value of payments in (2) by using 10%-7%-5%, as the case may be, in the appropriate table. Deduct this amount from the amount in (1). The difference is unstated interest.

Limitation between family members. Where land is sold or exchanged between family members after 6-30-81, interest will be imputed as seven percent. The limitation does not apply if one of the family members is a nonresident alien, or to the extent that such qualified sales exceed $500,000 in any calendar year.

Changes in The Economic Recovery Tax Act of 1981

For those who are familiar with *straddles* (offsetting investment positions) this new law is bad news.

WATCH THIS ONE:

Under Section 502 of the Act, all interest charges involved with any part of a straddle are no longer deductible but must be capitalized. Effective date: after 6-23-81.

Under prior law, *interest on IRS deficiencies* was established at 90 percent of the prime rate for September, effective on February 1 of the following year—and could not be changed more than once every 23 months.

Under the new law (Section 6621(b)), which was amended by ERTA of 1981, the adjusted prime rate is to be set by October 15 and is based on 100 percent of the September prime. The 23-month requirement has been eliminated and, beginning in 1983, changes will be effective on January 1 of each year.

On 2-1-82, the annual interest rate charged on underpayments and paid on overpayments rose from 12 percent to 20 percent.

"Adjusted prime rate" means the average predominant prime rate quoted by commercial banks to large businesses—as determined by the Board of Governors of the Federal Reserve System.

An imputed interest charge on the sale of land to related persons was explained above.

Enter The Tax Equity and Fiscal Responsibility Act of 1982 (TEFRA)

In computing the new TEFRA alternative minimum tax (beginning in 1983) the following types of interest expense are allowable deductions, except to the extent that they can be carried to another taxable year:

1. Housing interest—mortgage, rehabilitation loans, etc.
2. Other interest to the extent of net investment income included in minimum taxable income.
3. Interest paid on an obligation incurred to purchase a limited partnership interest or Sub Chapter S corporation stock.

*Interest allowable on a safe-harbor sale—leaseback—*cannot now exceed the amount of interest applicable to tax underpayments or overpayments on the date the lease is executed.

Beginning on and after July 1, 1983, TEFRA requires a 10 percent withholding from interest paid in excess of $150 to individuals as well as entities such as partnerships and estates which aren't themselves required to withhold on payments to individuals. Withholdable interest includes most interest paid by other than natural persons. Exempt payments include those made to low-income individuals, the elderly, corporations, governments, security dealers, exempt organizations, and cooperatives.

Interest on tax deficiencies and overpayments (after 1982) will be compounded daily, except as concerns the penalty for underpaying estimated tax. The new law also uses a net method for fixing the rate of interest. Under TEFRA rates will be determined twice a year on the basis of the average adjusted prime rate during the six-month period ending September 30 (effective the following January 1) and March 31 (effective the following July 1).

25.5 HANDLING THE AUDIT

IRS people will expect full documentation for the interest deduction. They rightfully see no reason for a lack of such. Some sort of governing document must, therefore, be produced—a written agreement, a mortgage, a loan contract—something. An outpouring of verbiage won't suffice.

NOTE:

> **An installment sale contract should always be explored thoroughly. Even though interest is not mentioned, the taxpayer-buyer can still take a deduction for imputed interest as detailed in Section 25.4. He or she need not give any consideration to the manner in which the seller is reporting the transaction.**

Underpayment of estimated taxes. Don't get into difficulties over this one. Interest charged on underpaid estimated taxes is computed as interest but not deductible, because it is considered a penalty.

Direct liability, not essential. Despite the fact that an indebtedness should belong to the taxpayer for the interest charge to be deductible, a direct liability is not always required. For example, a real estate owner can take a deduction for interest paid on the mortgage even though he or she is not directly liable (Regulation 1.163-1(b)).

Interest unlimited. Except for usury laws which are applicable in some states, there is no limit to the amount of interest which may be deducted.

TWO EXCEPTIONS:

Investment interest, as previously explained, and interest on safe-harbor leasebacks under TEFRA are the two exemptions to the unlimited rule above.

So don't let a revenue person disallow an interest deduction because it is unreasonable and excessive.

Explore all interest deductions to insure that they were taken in the proper manner:

1. Personal interest as on a home mortgage—itemized deduction on Schedule A.

2. Business interest—Schedule C.

3. Interest expended on property held for the production of rents or royalties—Schedule E.

NOTE:

Classification of interest depends upon the *use* made of borrowed funds—not on the *type* of property used to secure the loan. Some revenue person may try to tell you something different.

See Section 25.3 for additional leads in defensing the audit.

25.6 PERTINENT COURT DECISIONS–PRO AND CON

Pro
Cook et ux v U.S. (DC La 1977) 40 AFTR 2d 77-5486

Findings of Fact

Doctor Avery and his wife made gifts of money to their children and then borrowed the money back with interest. The government disallowed the interest deduction. In his charge to the jury the judge asked that they decide

- Whether bona fide gifts were made since without gifts no loans could exist.
- Whether the plaintiffs were entitled to deduct the amount of interest in controversy.

The court also pointed out that

To be deductible the interest must be paid on an actual, unconditional, enforceable indebtedness. Parents may legitimately deduct interest paid for money borrowed from their minor children. Legal transactions cannot be upset merely because the parties have entered into them for the purpose of minimizing or avoiding taxes which might otherwise accrue.

Opinion

Verdict for the plaintiffs.

Con
Harold W. Wales (TC Memo 1978-125)

Findings of Fact

The petitioner, an attorney, received payments for legal services from a development corporation during 1971, 1972, and 1973. At the same time he worked as a police lieutenant. His parents transferred $4,000 to him in 1968 with the understanding that he would repay them $8,000 in the future. No agreement was made as to any specific interest rate; nor did the parties agree to a specific date for repayment. Mr. Wales was expected to pay the $8,000 when he could afford to or when he received certain fees from Crescent City Development Co. (Crescent City).

At later dates additional funds were transferred from parents to petitioner and were partially repaid with the taxpayer making book entries which indicated that such repayments were part interest and part principal. $4,000 of the above $8,000 was all treated as interest.

Some time prior to 1972, the father died and the mother began living on Social Security. The petitioner made payments to her in 1972 and 1973 of $2,168 and $2,114 respectively, claiming such payments as interest deductions. The IRS disallowed the deductions.

Opinion

With respect to one transfer from the mother, the court ruled that the taxpayer failed to prove that an interest rate had been agreed upon or that the amount he was required to pay in excess of the amount received was interest for use of the money.

With respect to the other transfer, the taxpayer failed to prove that he had a legally enforceable obligation to repay or that the terms of repayment had been agreed upon.

The court further held that the transactions, viewed as a whole, indicated that the petitioner wasn't engaged in a bona fide economic activity—that he undertook to support his parents while claiming an interest deduction for doing so. There was no actual reason for the borrowings; interest rates were astronomical, and the flexible repayment schedule was geared to the parents' income needs.

Held for the government.

25.7 RELEVANT CODE AND REGULATION SECTIONS, PLUS PUBLICATION

Code

Section 163	Interest
163(a)	General Rule
163(b)	Installment Purchases Where Interest Charge Is Not Separately Stated
163(d)	Limitation on Interest on Investment Indebtedness
163(d)(2)	Carryover of Disallowed Investment Interest
163(d)(4)(a)	Special Rules—Property Subject to Net Lease
163(d)(7)	Special Rule Where Taxpayer Owns 50% or More of Enterprise
461(g)	Prepaid Interest
483	Interest on Certain Deferred Payments
6621(b)	Adjustment of Interest Rate

Regulations

Section 1.163-1	Interest Deduction in General
1.483-1	Computation of Interest on Certain Deferred Payments
1.483-1(c)(3)	Total Unstated Interest—Examples

Publication

545   Interest Expense

25.8 APPLICABLE IRS MANUAL REFERENCES (INVESTIGATIVE TECHNIQUES)

Audit Guidelines for Examiners

MT 4231-36   Sec. 742   Interest
MT 4231-47   Sec. 573   Interest

Tax Audit Guidelines, Individuals, Partnerships Estates and Trusts and Corporations

MT 4233-1   Sec. 322.1(10) Interest Expense

Capital Gains and Losses
(Section 1202)

26

26.1 IDENTIFYING THE PROBLEM

While the IRS concentrates a solid portion of its compliance efforts on eliminating questionable tax shelters, the old reliable long-term capital gain keeps rolling along, getting better and better all the time—but only for the informed and careful taxpayer. Manipulation of capital gains and losses can be a dangerous trap for the unwary.

Exceptions of all sorts switch results from good to bad. Long-term gains differ from short term as the clock moves from midnight to 12:01 A.M. Different combinations of each produce varying results. Different types of assets do the same. Mere definition of a capital asset can at times become difficult.

The Economic Recovery Tax Act of 1981 added new requirements and gave additional benefits. The Alternative Minimum Tax for taxpayers other than corporations (Section 55) enters the picture along with the 15 percent add-on minimum tax under Section 56. Sale of property used in a trade or business within the same year as the sale of capital assets can alter tax results.

The Tax Equity and Fiscal Responsibility Act of 1982 removed the requirements of the add-on minimum tax for individuals and gave the alternative minimum tax a "new look" beginning in 1983. The new alternative minimum tax retains the preference for capital gains.

Because of the myriad complexities involved in this issue, we will deal here only with situations that might face an individual taxpayer or his or her proprietorship.

26.2 HOW THE IRS SEES THE ISSUE

The Service sees ordinary income as being converted by taxpayers into long-term capital gains and looks quickly to an individual's profession for manipulations of this sort.

For example: If the taxpayer is a real estate broker, the question arises—was the sold property stock in trade or held as a capital asset? If the taxpayer was a stockbroker, did he or she carry the sold securities in the "for sale" inventory, or as a capital asset held for individual investment?

The Service is also suspicious of lease-purchase arrangements and will ask: Were the sales which gave rise to capital gains really sales—or were they leases, the income from which should have been treated as ordinary income?

What about ordinary losses which should have been treated as capital in nature—as in the case of securities becoming worthless after being held as an investment by an individual proprietorship?

In other words, an IRS agent will see possible additional revenue in everything from an undotted "i" to a wrongfully calculated holding period. Because this type of auditor is usually trained to at least recognize the possibilities inherent in every issue, he or she will utilize the IRS manuals and his or her ingenuity to touch every potential base which might yield "production." The following section (26.3) will provide an insight into just which bases these may be.

26.3 FACTORS WHICH THE IRS CONSIDERS WHEN MAKING ITS AUDIT DECISION

Checklist of Steps an Auditor Will Take

He or she will

■ Make a determination as to the type of asset involved—capital or otherwise.

■ Verify (1) the selling price, (2) expense of sale, (3) adjusted basis of the property, and (4) the holding period.

■ Since the most common capital transactions appearing on nonbusiness returns are sales of securities (processed through brokers), let us follow this audit trail as an example of IRS examination methods.

Using the brokerage slip, the agent will cross-check the dividend and interest income as reported on open returns to determine

1. Whether dividends (for the sold securities) were reported in prior years—and to date of sale in the current year. (Most IRS libraries stock financial publications such as Moody's, Poor's, and Fitch's Dividend Services which carry information as to dividends paid by publicly held corporations.)

WARNING:

If specific dividends or interest were reported for the two prior open years but omitted for the year in question, the agent will want to check for a possible omitted security sale.

2. If a taxpayer leaves his or her securities with a broker in a custody account, the IRS will want to examine the account for credited earnings which may not have been reported.

3. If a margin account was maintained with a broker, the statements will be analyzed to make certain that interest charged was not netted against interest or dividend income but claimed as an itemized deduction, also that no interest was deducted for the carrying of tax-exempt securities.

Other Audit Techniques

■ Where the reported transactions were not made through a broker, the proceeds and expenses of sale will receive closer scrutiny. Disposition of securities in a closely held corporation will be checked for valuation. Gain or loss based only on retained earnings will not be accepted.

■ In the case of capital transactions where no "expense of sale" exists, the auditor will want to be satisfied that legal, accounting, or brokerage fees were not deducted as ordinary expense.

■ Where interest-bearing securities were sold during the year, the auditor will want to make certain that accrued interest was not reported as part of the selling price but, properly, as ordinary income.

■ Where bonds were acquired "flat," i.e., with interest in default, a check will be made to determine that any interest received (which accrued after the purchase date) is reflected in income.

■ If property was sold in prior or current years and a purchase money mortgage or a second mortgage constituted part payment, the government will want to satisfy itself that interest on such indebtedness was correctly reflected.

■ In the case of installment sales, the examining officer's eyes will light up. Was any interest involved? If not, the officer will invoke the imputed interest rule under Section 483. For additional details concerning imputed interest, see Chapter 25 (Interest Expense).

■ The IRS will give particular attention to the adjusted basis of sold properties.

1. Does this basis properly reflect any nonrecognized gain realized from a prior sale?
2. In computing capital improvements, was the value of the taxpayer's labor included?
3. Previous casualty losses should have been deducted from basis with corresponding reconstruction expenses added to the cost. Were they?
4. Where appropriate, the agent will want to review appraisal statements to determine qualification of appraiser and basis upon which value was established.
5. For property acquired by inheritance or gift, corresponding estate or gift tax returns will be requested.

RED FLAG:

Beginning in 1983 the Tax Equity and Fiscal Responsibility Act of 1982 (TEFRA) requires that brokers furnish information statements to the IRS which report gross proceeds from transactions which they carried on for their customers.

The term "brokers" includes dealers, barterers, and others who (for consideration) regularly act as middlemen. Presumably, the term encompasses real estate and securities brokers.

26.4 CONSIDERATIONS WHEN PREPARING THE RETURN

IMPORTANT:

Long before tax time clients should be made to understand the importance of timing in the handling of capital gains and losses.

Example: Taxpayer desires to sell two pieces of property which were used in his business and which may be treated as capital assets under Section 1231. Selling one will result in a gain, the other a loss. If both are sold in the same year, the gain, which is only 40 percent taxable, must be offset by the loss which, by itself, would be 100 percent deductible. Obviously, these assets should be sold in different years.

The next few paragraphs further illustrate the need for client education in the manipulation of the sale of capital assets so that the best possible tax advantage can be obtained.

Calculation of Capital Gains and Losses

The tax treatment of capital gains and losses swings on the holding period. Asset ownership of *one year or less* will result in a short-term capital gain or loss; *longer* than one year will result in a long-term capital transaction.

To compute the manner in which gains and losses will be taxed, first group all sales into short or long-term categories as indicated on Schedule D (Form 1040). This will produce *net* short-term or long-term gains or losses.

Depending upon the following combinations, tax treatment will result as shown:

Combination	Taxed As
Net short-term gain only	Ordinary income
Net long-term gain only	Long Term Capital Gain (LTCG)—40% taxable as ordinary income
Net long-term gain *and* net short-term gain	Computed separately: LTCG—40% taxable Short-term capital gain (STCG)—all ordinary income
Net short-term loss only	Ordinary loss up to $3000 or the taxpayer's taxable income. Unused balance may be carried forward.
Net long-term loss only	50% deductible as ordinary loss up to $3000. (In other words it takes $2 of long-term capital loss to offset $1 of ordinary income.) Unused balance may be carried forward.
Net long-term loss *and* net short-term loss	A combination of the two losses may be used to offset $3000 of ordinary income with the short-term capital loss (STCL) being used first. The LTCL may then be utilized on a 2-to-1 basis as described above. Unused losses may be carried forward but must each retain its own character.
Net short-term gain *and* net long-term loss	Requires computation: First deduct the net long-term loss from the net short-term gain. If the gain exceeds the loss, the full amount of the excess is ordinary income. If the loss exceeds the gain, the excess loss may be used to offset ordinary income up to $3000 on a 2-to-1 basis as described above.
Net long-term gain *and* net short-term loss	Requires computation: First deduct the short-term loss from the long-term gain. If the loss exceeds the gain, the excess is deductible from ordinary income up to $3000 with any unused loss available for carryover as a short-term loss. Should the net long-term gain be greater than the net short-term loss, 40% of the excess is taxed as ordinary income.

COMMENT:

Clearly, with careful planning, most of the above traps can be avoided. The long-term capital gain tax shelter is healthy and available but must be understood and not approached haphazardly, if best results are to be obtained.

Definition of a Capital Asset

Section 1221 defines a capital asset as property held by the taxpayer (whether or not connected with his or her trade or business) but does not include

1. Stock in trade or other property properly included in inventory *or* property held by the taxpayer primarily for sale to customers in the ordinary course of a trade or business.

The latter portion of this exception (after the word *or*) would seem to duplicate the beginning portion in that they both include inventories. The difference, however, lies in the fact that some items held for sale to customers are usually not inventoried—stocks and bonds or building lots, for example.

Where this latter type of property is at issue, the question generally arises as to whether the taxpayer is a dealer or an investor. If he or she is a dealer, then this exception applies and the gain would be ordinary. If the individual is an investor, then any gain or loss would be treated as capital in nature.

NOTE:

This dealer-investor controversy has raged, it seems, forever. Chapter 5 (Dealers vs. Investors) covers the question in depth.

2. The above exception from the definition of capital assets includes property used in a trade or business of a character which is subject to depreciation under Section 167, or real property so used.

Losing the "capital asset" tag in this instance does no harm because of the favored treatment which is allowed by Section 1231 (Property Used in the Trade or Business and Involuntary Conversions). Under this code section—subject to certain limitations—net gain is treated as a long-term capital gain if the property was held for more than one year, while a net loss would be deductible in full.

The same general rule applies to the sale of land held for business use or for production of income.

WARNING:

Loss on the sale of personal capital assets such as boats, cars, vacation homes, and residences are not deductible. Should they be destroyed by casualty, however, some portion of the loss may be recovered under Section 165. (Casualty losses have been fully discussed in Chapter 4.)

3. This third exception applies to copyrights: literary, musical, or artistic composition or memorandum, or similar property held by a taxpayer whose personal efforts created such property.

4. Another exception: Accounts or notes receivable acquired in the ordinary course of a trade or business.

5. The last type of property excepted from the definition of "capital asset" applies to U. S. Government publications received by any taxpayer from the government at no charge or below the price sold to the general public.

Computing the Tax When Capital Gain Exists

The presence of capital gains or losses necessitates consideration of several regulations in addition to Section 1202 (Deduction for Capital Gains):

Code Section 56, Computation of Minimum Tax—Individuals (Form 4625)

Accelerated depreciation and certain amortizations are tax preference items for minimum tax purposes. Their existence, when corresponding capital assets are sold, may cause the 15 percent "add-on" minimum tax to be generated.

Code Section 1231, Supplemental Schedule of Gains and Losses (Form 4797)

This schedule is required in instances where there is a sale of property used in a trade or business or where involuntary conversions occurred from other than casualty or theft.

Code Section 55, Alternative Minimum Tax Computation (Form 6251)

This tax becomes payable only if it exceeds the regular tax liability. Capital gain deductions and adjusted itemized deductions are tax preference items for purposes of this regulation (Section 55), except that itemized deductions were removed as preference items by TEFRA beginning in 1983.

Thanks to the Economic Recovery Tax Act of 1981 the Alternative Minimum Tax rate for tax years beginning with 1982 has been reduced to 10 percent for amounts over $20,000 but not exceeding $60,000—and to 20 percent for amounts above $60,000.

IMPORTANT:

For taxable years before 1979 the Code did not allow income averaging along with the use of the then alternative tax computation. The '81 Tax Act does not appear to make any such objection. Instructions for the 1981 Schedule "G" do, in fact, specifically state, "If you income average you may also use the alternative tax."

Loss from a nonbusiness bad debt is treated as a short-term capital loss and subject to its limitations on deductibility.

Determining the holding period, as previously mentioned, is an important step when making a sale. *Prior planning* is an absolute necessity. Miscalculation by even one day can cause a long-term sale to become short-term, with financial disaster. Short-term losses can be turned into long-term with like results. Here are some general rules which should be followed:

REMEMBER:

To be eligible for long-term treatment, properties (except for some commodity futures) must be held for at least one year *and one day.*

Usually, the holding period begins the day *after* contractual purchase (regardless of later delivery or payment date) and ends on the day of contractual sale.

GOOD NEWS:

In verifying holding periods for security sales, the IRS formerly used the trade date on the brokerage slip, *not* the settlement date. Recently, however, it has decided to allow a taxpayer the right to choose the year in which to report the gain from sales made in the last five days of the year—either the year of sale or the following year. This new decision came about because of the recent changes in installment sale regulations.

In the case of a cash basis taxpayer, the IRS will deem that a loss had been realized on the date of sale, despite the fact that the proceeds were received in a subsequent taxable year. Conversely, the gain on such a transaction will be considered to have occurred upon receipt of the proceeds (IR Manual MT4231-46, Section 529.4), but see GOOD NEWS above.

Wash sales. Be careful of the wash sale. The IRS will be looking for this one. Such a transaction occurs when a stock is sold and quickly bought back, or when an option is acquired to purchase substantially identical securities. Losses from such sales are disallowed if the securities were purchased within 30 days before the sale or repurchased within 30 days after the sale. (Section 1091)

26.5 HANDLING THE AUDIT

One of the most difficult areas in the capital gains arena is the dealer-investor issue. If it exists, there is a good possibility that the IRS will attack it first. Chapter 5 covers the subject in detail. It should be reviewed and evidence collected which may allow the dealer stigma to be eliminated.

NOTE:

This dealer-investor issue is extremely controversial but, in many instances, not hopelessly lost to the taxpayer. Some types of sales, in themselves, give indication that capital gains do rightfully exist. Those listed here should be sought out and exploited for the taxpayer's benefit, along with others that might give rise to the same possibilities: (1) single, isolated transactions, (2) sale under threat of condemnation, (3) sale to raise needed cash, (4) disposal of property because it no longer meets the requirements for which purchased, and (5) property held for a long period of time.

Obviously, these instances tend to show that the properties in question were held for reasons other than for sale to customers in the ordinary operation of a business.

Sale of a personal residence is covered in detail in Chapter 12 of this book.

Sale of a sole proprietorship. The practitioner should make certain that each asset is separately categorized and handled in accordance with its identity, e.g., (1) inventory as ordinary sales, (2) land as Section 1231 property, (3) commercial buildings as Section 1231 property (with any accelerated depreciation correctly recaptured), etc.

Sales to related taxpayers (or those which reflect no gain or loss) are suspect. The former could result in ordinary income to the purchaser. The latter will most certainly be checked for cost or other basis. Rarely do capital transactions emerge even. Review all facets of such capital sales.

At audit time it might be well to do a lot of listening. With a subject as intricate as this one, approaching only those facets which the auditor has in mind would probably be the best policy.

The auditor, for example, might not believe that a "dealer-investor" problem exists. You may immediately be over a giant hurdle without having wasted time. No examiner will be able to think of everything. Find out what he or she wants; then address only these points.

WARNING:

Never broaden this or any other examination by mentioning subjects or details not initiated by the auditor.

Always thoroughly research each suggested IRS audit change. *Know* what you are doing. Rely heavily on Regulations and court cases. They frequently clarify a taxpayer's position to a much sharper degree than does the Code.

26.6 PERTINENT COURT DECISIONS—PRO AND CON

Pro
Thomas N. Melin and Virginia W. Melin, Plaintiffs
v. U. S., Defendant. U. S. Court of Claims,
(No. 53-71, May 11, 1973)

Findings of Fact

Thomas Melin, while employed by the Owens-Parks Lumber Company as a mechanic and equipment operator, invented a lumber-stacking device which he later had patented. He conceived it on his own time but built it at the Owens-Parks plant on their time and with their equipment and parts. The corporation utilized the device for about 16 years without payment to Mr. Melin.

In March of 1964 the taxpayer sold his rights in the device to Owens-Parks. By this time he had become vice-president of the company and a member of the board of directors. The chief executive officer and largest stockholder of the company at the time was Mr. Melin's father, Charles R. Melin. This individual was autocratic and very volatile. He did, in fact, discharge the taxpayer as an officer and employee of Owens-Parks after 1964.

When Thomas Melin claimed a capital gain for the sale of his patent rights, the IRS disagreed claiming that: The taxpayer did not own the patent since it was developed at the Owens plant and should have assigned it to the corporation under the "alter ego" theory as enunciated in Dowse v. Federal Rubber.

Opinion

The court allowed the capital gain, claiming that the corporation had not employed Mr. Melin as an inventor and that it, therefore, could not own his invention—even though it did have "shop rights" because he had built it on their time.

The court further stated that Mr. Melin certainly was not the Owens-Parks alter ego. Clearly, the company was controlled and operated by his father, Charles.

Con
Emmet E. Norton and Frances G. Norton, Plaintiffs
v. U. S., Defendant. U. S. Court of Claims,
(No. 31-75, March 23, 1977)

Statement of Facts

Taxpayer entered into a timber-cutting contract with the U. S. Forest Service. Upon completion of the contract Mr. Norton attempted to claim a capital gain on his profits. The IRS denied the claim.

Opinion

The court upheld the government's position for these reasons:
1. Interest in the contract wasn't realty since the taxpayer didn't get present interest in standing timber on execution of the contract. Title stayed with the U.S. Forest Service until timber was cut and paid for.
2. The contract wasn't a Section 1231 asset since it wasn't depreciable. It wasn't the type of asset that diminished in value as time elapsed. Neither did it have basis or useful life.

26.7 RELEVANT CODE AND REGULATION SECTIONS, PLUS PUBLICATIONS

Code

Section 55	Alternative Minimum Tax for Taxpayers Other Than Corporations
56	Imposition of Tax (Minimum Tax)
165	Losses
167	Depreciation
483	Interest on Certain Deferred Payments
1091	Loss from Wash Sales of Stock or Securities
1202	Deduction for Capital Gains
1212	Capital Loss Carrybacks and Carryovers
1221	Capital Asset Defined
1222	Other Terms Relating to Capital Gains and Losses
1231	Property Used in a Trade or Business and Involuntary Conversions

Regulations

Section 1.1211-1	Limitation on Capital Losses
1.1212-1	Capital Loss Carryovers and Carrybacks
1.1221-1	Meaning of Terms
1.1222-1	Other Terms Relating to Capital Gains and Losses
1.1223-1	Determination of Period for Which Capital Assets Are Held

1.1231-1   Gains and Losses from the Sale or Exchange of Certain Property Used in the Trade or Business

Publications

544   Sales and Other Disposition of Assets

550   Investment Income and Expenses

26.8 APPLICABLE IRS MANUAL REFERENCES (INVESTIGATIVE TECHNIQUES)

Audit Guidelines for Examiners

MT 4231-46 Section 529   Capital Gains and Losses

529.1   Selling Price

529.2   Expense of Sale

529.3   Adjusted Basis of Property

529.4   Holding Period

529.5   Personal Residence

Specialized Industries Audit Guidelines

MT 4232.8-4 Section 480   Capital Gain v. Ordinary Income

Tax Audit Guidelines

MT 4233-16 Section 825   Capital Gains and Losses

The Business
Automobile 27
(Sections 162 and 212)

27.1 IDENTIFYING THE PROBLEM

Deductions for the cost of operating purely business automobiles generally cause few IRS problems. Difficulties arise, however, when the car is used partly for business and partly for personal use. There are two ways to compute car deductions:

1. The actual-expense method or
2. The standard mileage rate as allowed by the IRS.

RECOMMENDATION:

Since the latter is only 20¢ a mile for the first 15,000 business miles and 11¢ a mile thereafter, it is strongly suggested that the actual-expense method be thoroughly tested before the easier standard mileage rate is decided upon. Form 2106 (Employee Business Expenses) can be helpful when making this test.

CAUTION:

If the standard rate is used for a car placed in service after 1980, the taxpayer is considered to have elected to exclude the car from the accelerated cost recovery system (ACRS) for depreciation purposes. (Rev. Proc. 81-54 1981-44 IRB 21) As you will see later, this move can be costly.

Allocation decisions also cause problems. Was the car used 50 percent or 60 percent for business purposes? Only good records will eliminate controversy in this respect.

How can the new ACRS rules best be utilized? What about reimbursed mileage? What are the limitations on use of the standard mileage rate? This chapter is designed to answer these questions and more. There are many tax savings to be had from use of the automobile. Many, which are not readily apparent, will be identified in this chapter.

27.2 HOW THE IRS SEES THE ISSUE

Because of the inherent possibilities of personal pleasure and personal use, the cost of travel and entertainment (T&E) in general is a happy hunting ground for the IRS. See Chapter 18 of this book (Travel and Entertainment) for complete details regarding this issue.

Automobile expenses, specifically, become a part of the T&E audit as a natural progression.

27.3 FACTORS WHICH THE IRS CONSIDERS WHEN MAKING ITS AUDIT DECISION

When examining an automobile deduction, the IRS allows for the cost of business travel (both local and while away from home overnight) but only if such expenses were incurred while carrying on a trade or business (Section 162) or for the production or collection of income (Section 212). According to the *Tax Audit Guidelines for Tax Auditors* (MT 4234-5, Section 774.4) the Service looks first for these business connections.

CAUTION:

Auto deductions will be closely examined to determine that they are not nondeductible commuting expenses. Carrying tools and instruments to and from work does not make such travel business connected. However, if a trailer is rented for the hauling of such tools, the additional cost is deductible. If a truck is required, the difference between normal commuting costs and the cost of the truck operation will be allowed.

If the standard mileage rate was used, the examiner will check to determine that only one vehicle was used at a time and that the car or cars in question were owned by the taxpayer—also that such automobiles were *not*

1. Used for hire, such as a taxi.

2. Used as part of a fleet of cars whereby two or more were operated at the same time.

3. Depreciated by any method other than straight-line.

NOTE:

Wherever the auto has been fully depreciated under the straight-line method or after it has been driven more than 60,000 business miles, the standard mileage rate drops to 11¢ a mile. A taxpayer may switch from using the standard mileage rate for one year to actual cost during the next year and vice versa.

In establishing total mileage driven and the subsequent business portion, the IRS may not be completely satisfied with the Form 2106 (Employee Business Expenses). The auditor will want to examine bills for auto repairs, oil changes, etc., which were paid during the beginning and ending of the year. Possibly the servicing firm entered meter readings on such invoices.

Personal use. Auditors are also advised to look for signatures on gas and oil invoices. If they do not belong to the taxpayer but to his or her spouse or children, this would give indication of personal use.

Insurance policies are sometimes examined to determine whether family members are included as operators of the vehicle in question—and to what extent.

NOTE:

The total cost of gasoline for the year will also be used to estimate total mileage.

In addition, there probably will be an inquiry as to whether the taxpayer owns a second car. Where the answer is negative—and the taxpayer has deducted a substantial portion of operating costs—more and deeper questioning can be expected. What does the family do for entertainment? Do they have any hobbies? How far is it to the nearest grocery store? How do the children get to school? The end result might be a reduction of the business percentage, caused by the large amount of obviously necessary personal travel.

27.4 CONSIDERATIONS WHEN PREPARING THE RETURN

First of all, a decision must be made as to which method should be used to take the car-cost deduction. Because of the new benefits offered by the 1981 Economic Recovery Act (ERTA)—and the inflationary spiral for automobile purchases and operations—a taxpayer should look first to the "actual-cost" method.

NOTE:

A recent Hertz Corporation study showed that the average cost to operate a car ranged from 34¢ per mile, for a subcompact, and upward. The IRS nevertheless refuses to increase its 20¢ standard mileage allowance, basing its decision (it says) on studies conducted with the assistance of an outside consultant.

The Importance of Good Records

Like most tax-saving devices, prior planning is important. Good records are a must if the IRS is to be convinced. The "Car Expenses" and "Mileage Rate" sections of Form 2106 are reproduced below as Figure 27-1. These will give you a good idea as to the material and records which the Service may wish to examine.

TAX TIP:

If you use your car in business, consider using a credit card for gas and oil purchases. This will effortlessly produce automatic documentation of such expenditures.

Computing Depreciation

Computing depreciation under ACRS is a simple procedure. Salvage value is not relevant. Cars or light trucks are considered 3-year recovery property and are depreciated by using the following table:

Recovery Period	Percentage
1st year	25%
2nd year	38%
3rd year	37%

Form **2106** Department of the Treasury Internal Revenue Service (0)	**Employee Business Expenses** (Please use Form 3903 to figure moving expense deduction.) ▶ Attach to Form 1040.	OMB No. 1545-0139 **198_**

Your name	Social security number	Occupation in which expenses were incurred
Employer's name	Employer's address	

Paperwork Reduction Act Notice.—The Paperwork Reduction Act of 1980 says we must tell you why we are collecting this information, how we will use it, and whether you have to give it to us. We ask for the information to carry out the Internal Revenue laws of the United States. We need it to ensure that you are complying with these laws and to allow us to figure and collect the right amount of tax. You are required to give us this information.

Instructions

Use this form to show your business expenses as an employee during 1981. Include amounts:

● You paid as an employee;
● You charged to your employer (such as by credit card);
● You received as an advance, allowance, or repayment.

Several publications available from IRS give more information about business expenses:
Publication 463, *Travel, Entertainment, and Gift Expenses.*
Publication 529, *Miscellaneous Deductions.*
Publication 587, *Business Use of Your Home.*
Publication 508, *Educational Expenses.*

Part I.—You can deduct some business expenses even if you do not itemize your deductions on Schedule A (Form 1040). Examples are expenses for travel (except commuting to and from work), meals, or lodging. List these expenses in Part I and use them in figuring your adjusted gross income on Form 1040, line 31.

Line 2.—You can deduct meals and lodging costs if you were on a business trip away from your main place of work. Do not deduct the cost of meals you ate on one-day trips when you did not need sleep or rest.

Line 3.—If you use a car you own in your work, you can deduct the cost of the business use. Enter the cost here after figuring it in Part IV. You can take either the cost of your actual

expenses (such as gas, oil, repairs, depreciation, etc.) or you can use the standard mileage rate.

The mileage rate is 20 cents a mile up to 15,000 miles. After that, or for all business mileage on a fully depreciated car, the rate is 11 cents a mile. If you use the standard mileage rate to figure the cost of business use, the car is considered to have a useful life of 60,000 miles of business use at the maximum standard mileage rate. After 60,000 miles of business use at the maximum rate, the car is considered to be fully depreciated. (For details, see Publication 463.)

Caution: You cannot use the mileage rate for a leased vehicle.

Figure your mileage rate amount and add it to the business part of what you spent on the car for parking fees, tolls, interest, and State and local taxes (except gasoline tax).

Line 4.—If you were an outside salesperson with other business expenses, list them on line 4. Examples are selling expenses or expenses for stationery and stamps. An outside salesperson does all selling outside the employer's place of business. A driver-salesperson whose main duties are service and delivery, such as delivering bread or milk, is not an outside salesperson. (For details, see Publication 463.)

Line 5.—Show other business expenses on line 5 if your employer repaid you for them. If you were repaid for part of them, show here the amount you were repaid. Show the rest in Part II.

Part II.—You can deduct other business expenses only if (a) your employer did not repay you, and (b) you itemize your deductions on Schedule A (Form 1040). Report these expenses here and under Miscellaneous Deductions on Schedule A. (For details, see Publication 529.)

You can deduct expenses for business use of the part of your home that you exclusively and consistently use for your work. If you are not self-employed, your working at home must be for your employer's convenience. (For business use of home, see Publication 587.)

If you show education expenses in Part I or Part II, you must fill out Part III.

Part III.—You can deduct the cost of education that helps you keep or improve your skills for the job you have now. This includes education that your employer, the law, or regulations require you to get in order to keep your job or your salary. Do not deduct the cost of study that helps you meet the basic requirements for your job or helps you get a new job. (For education expenses, see Publication 508.)

Part IV, line 8—Depreciation

Cars placed in service before 1/1/81:
You must continue to use either the standard mileage rate or the method of depreciation you used in earlier years. You cannot change to either of the new methods available in 1981.

Cars placed in service after 12/31/80:
If you placed a car in service in 1981 and you do not use the standard mileage rate, you must use the new Accelerated Cost Recovery System (ACRS). One method lets you deduct the following percentages of your cost basis regardless of what month you placed the car in service:

1981—25%
1982—38%
1983—37%

Example: You bought a new car, without a trade-in, for $10,000 in September 1981, and used it 60% for business. Your basis for depreciation is $6,000 ($10,000 × 60%). For 1981 your depreciation deduction is $1,500 ($6,000 × 25%). If your percentage of business use changes in 1982, you must refigure your basis for depreciation.

There is also an alternate ACRS method under which you may use a straight-line method over a recovery period of 3, 5, or 12 years.
Note: *If you use the mileage rate, you are considered to have made an election to exclude this vehicle from ACRS.*
You do not have to consider salvage value in either of these methods. Please see Publication 463 for details on how to figure the deduction under either method.

PART I.—Employee Business Expenses Deductible in Figuring Adjusted Gross Income on Form 1040, Line 31

1 Fares for airplane, boat, bus, taxicab, train, etc. . . . .
2 Meals and lodging . . . .
3 Car expenses (from Part IV, line 21) . . . .
4 Outside salesperson's expenses (see Part I instructions above) ▶

5 Other (see Part I instructions above) ▶

6 Add lines 1 through 5 . . . .
7 Employer's payments for these expenses if not included on Form W–2 . . . .
8 Deductible business expenses (subtract line 7 from line 6). Enter here and include on Form 1040, line 23 .
9 Income from excess business expense payments (subtract line 6 from line 7). Enter here and include on Form 1040, line 20 . . . .

PART II.—Employee Business Expenses that are Deductible Only if You Itemize Deductions on Schedule A (Form 1040)

1 Business expenses not included above (list expense and amount) ▶

2 Total. Deduct under Miscellaneous Deductions, Schedule A (Form 1040) . . . .

Form **2106** (1981)

PART IV.—Car Expenses (Use either your actual expenses or the mileage rate.)

	Car 1	Car 2	Car 3
A. Number of months you used car for business during 1981 . .	_____ months	_____ months	_____ months
B. Total mileage for months in line A	_____ miles	_____ miles	_____ miles
C. Business part of line B mileage	_____ miles	_____ miles	_____ miles

Actual Expenses (Include expenses on lines 1–5 for only the months shown in line A, above.)

	Car 1	Car 2	Car 3
1 Gasoline, oil, lubrication, etc.			
2 Repairs			
3 Tires, supplies, etc.			
4 Other: (a) Insurance			
(b) Taxes			
(c) Tags and licenses			
(d) Interest			
(e) Miscellaneous			
5 Total (add lines 1 through 4(e))			
6 Business percentage of car use (divide line C by line B, above)	%	%	%
7 Business part of car expense (multiply line 5 by line 6) . . .			
8 Depreciation (see instructions on front) . . . . Caution: *If you use ACRS, skip line 9 and enter the amount from line 8 on line 10.*			
9 Divide line 8 by 12 months			
10 Multiply line 9 by line A, above			
11 Total (add line 7 and line 10; then skip to line 19)			

Mileage Rate

12 Enter the smaller of (a) 15,000 miles or (b) the combined mileages from line C, above	_____ miles
13 Multiply line 12 by 20¢ (11¢ if car is fully depreciated) and enter here	
14 Enter any combined mileage from line C that is over 15,000 miles	_____ miles ////////
15 Multiply line 14 by 11¢ and enter here	
16 Total mileage expense (add lines 13 and 15)	
17 Business part of car interest and State and local taxes (except gasoline tax)	
18 Total (add lines 16 and 17)	

Figure 27-1

Thus, if your vehicle was purchased any time in 1981 or thereafter, your depreciation allowance would be 25 percent of the unadjusted basis (usually cost) for the first year. No depreciation is allowed in the year of disposition.

If you desire, you may elect an optional recovery period for cars and light trucks of 3, 5, or 12 years on a straight-line basis. Using this basis, you may, however, recover only a half year of depreciation in the first year that the property is placed in service. Under the accelerated method (ACRS) the half-year depreciation convention is built into the tables. Investment credits will apply under both accelerated and optional methods.

Expensing in lieu of depreciation. Under ACRS you may also elect to treat a portion of the cost of your vehicle as a currently deductible expense, if the property was placed in service after 1981. For tax years beginning 1982 and 1983 the allowable expense deduction is $5,000. For years thereafter until 1985 this figure increases until it reaches $10,000. (One-half for married taxpayers filing separately.)

No additional first year depreciation is allowed, nor is any investment credit for that portion of the cost which is allowed as a deduction under this expensing provision.

WARNING:

Upon disposition, the expensed amount will be treated as depreciation for recapture purposes, producing ordinary income to the extent of the amount expensed, plus depreciation taken.

Taking the Standard Mileage Allowance

Taking the standard mileage allowance is proper for self-employed taxpayers or employees. Without the necessity of proving actual costs, these individuals may currently deduct 20¢ a mile for the first 15,000 miles of business travel and 11¢ per mile thereafter (plus the cost of parking fees and tolls).

LOOK:

In instances where a taxpayer is reimbursed by his employer, he or she may continue to receive the 20¢ per mile no matter how many miles are driven—*and without tax consequences, but the reimbursement must be included in income.*

DON'T FORGET:

A proportionate share of the business v. personal investment credit may be taken whether the actual cost or standard mileage allowance method is used.

Should You Sell Your Car or Trade It In?

The answer lies in the existent circumstances. Selling a car at a profit before the ACRS 3 years of ownership are consummated does three things:

1. It produces a taxable gain.
2. It triggers investment credit recapture.
3. If applicable, the $5,000 "expensing" amount will have to be recaptured as depreciation, thus increasing the taxable gain.

Trading the car for an amount that exceeds basis is a tax-free transaction. But the basis of the new car and the consequent investment credit will both be reduced.

Example: After two years of ownership under ACRS, "A" purchased a new car for $15,000. Gain on trade was $3,000, making the new basis $12,000. Depreciation without the basis reduction would have been $3,750 (25% of $15,000)—with the reduction, it would have been $3,000.

Investment credit (using the $15,000 basis) would have been $900 (6 percent of $15,000). With the reduced basis, it would have been $720. Had "A" sold the car, he would have had a taxable gain of $3,000 and an investment credit recapture of 2 percent of the purchase price of his old car ($10,000) or $200 (car held 2 instead of required 3 years). If the taxpayer was in the 50 percent bracket, the tax consequences would have been the following:

Old Car Is Sold

Taxable Gain	<u>$3,000</u>
Income tax due (50% of $3000)	1,500
Investment credit recapture (2% of $10,000)	200
Less increase in depreciation because basis of new car is not reduced ($750 × 50%)	(375)

Less increase in investment credit because basis of new car is not reduced ($900 less $720)   <u>(180)</u>

Out-of-pocket cost   <u>$1,145</u>

Old Car Is Traded

Income tax due	$-0-
Investment credit recapture	-0-
Plus loss of depreciation because basis of new car is reduced ($3750 less $3000 x 50%)	375
Plus loss of investment credit because basis of new car is reduced ($900 less $720)	<u>180</u>
Out-of-pocket cost	<u>$555</u>

Obviously, the thing to do is trade.

27.5 HANDLING THE AUDIT

Even though today's chance of audit is slim (less than two percent), a favorite IRS hunting ground still remains in the fertile fields of Travel and Entertainment. These, of course, include automobiles used for business.

How to Maintain an Expense Log

Ideally, a taxpayer who travels frequently on business should maintain an automobile-expense log somewhat as follows:

Travel Log

Meter reading 1-1-8x   14,789   12-31-8x   34,000

Mileage

Date	From	To	Beginning	Ending	Expenses	
1-2-8x	Office	Troy, NY	14,789	14,980	Gas	$13
	In and around Troy		14,980	15,000	Tolls	2
	Troy	Office	15,000	15,191	Park.	3

With this information at hand, most IRS personnel will rarely be dissatisfied. All the necessary ingredients are here to fully complete the Form 2106 (Employee Business Expenses).

SUGGESTION:

If the standard mileage allowance is to be used, omit the "Expenses" column. After all, there's little to be gained in even suggesting that a profit was realized from employer reimbursement. The code doesn't require proof of reimbursed travel; so don't provide it unless the actual-cost method is to be utilized.

This same type of log should be maintained for automobiles that are used 100 percent for business.

After being advised of an impending audit of this issue, if such a log is not available, an attempt should be made to construct one. Use paid invoices, toll tickets, parking slips, customer invoices, employer reports, etc.

WARNING:

Do not attempt to mislead the IRS agent by claiming that this record was prepared on the spot as the travel occurred. State the truth—that it was reconstructed through use of other data.

Proof of automobile expenses. Under Section 274 (Disallowance of Certain Entertainment, etc., Expenses) the Service holds the taxpayer strictly responsible for good substantiation of travel expenses. The section reads in part:

No deduction shall be allowed—

(1) Under Section 162 or 212 for any traveling expense (including meals and lodging while away from home) ... unless the taxpayer substantiates by adequate records ... the amount of such expense, time and place of travel...

VERY IMPORTANT:

The stern substantiation requirements of Section 274 do *not* apply to local travel. In the absence of exact records, both the IRS and the courts have allowed an approximation or close estimate based on the now famous "Cohan Rule" (Cohan v. Comm. 2nd Cir; 1930, 39 F 2d 540, 8 AFTR 10552). The approximation, however, must have some foundation and must represent an effort to arrive at the correct figure. It cannot be based on an unsupported guess. Therefore, if the taxpayer is totally devoid of substantiation, a strong effort should be made to collect as much as possible. Such material will then allow invocation of the "Cohan Rule."

Allocation of Personal Portion of Car Expense

Where the automobile was used for both business and personal travel, make sure that only the personal portion of the following are used as itemized deductions where applicable:

- State and local personal property taxes
- State and local general sales and compensating use taxes
- Interest on any existing car loan
- Certain casualty and theft losses

Allowable Deductions from Personal Portion of Car Expenses

Do not overlook the following which may be taken as itemized deductions—use of car for: charitable purposes, medical travel, job-related moves.

The IRS allowance is currently at 9¢ per mile for this type of travel. If any of these deductions were omitted on the return being audited, now would be the time to claim them. Possibly, they can be used to offset other IRS changes.

NOTE:

The IRS, in recent Letter Ruling #8326089, stated that medical expenses *do not* include actual car expenses which encompass amounts paid for general repairs or maintenance, insurance, or depreciation.

27.6 PERTINENT COURT DECISIONS—PRO AND CON

Pro
The Lang Chevrolet Company et al
(TC Memo 1967-212)

Findings of Fact

This case involves two Lang corporations which operated Chevrolet and Oldsmobile dealerships. Fred Lang and his son Richard were president and general manager, respectively, of each of the Lang corporations, and majority stockholders.

During the years at issue the corporations furnished automobiles for the free and unlimited use of Fred and Richard.

The IRS disallowed the cost of such use to the corporations, asserting that these expenses were incurred solely for the benefit of the taxpayers as shareholders and so constituted constructive dividends to them rather than deductible business expenses.

Opinion

In upholding the taxpayers' position the court made three important observations:

1. The use of corporate automobiles was not a benefit restricted to stockholders. All corporate officers and supervisory personnel received the same fringe benefit.
2. Allowing employees the free use of corporate automobiles was normal in the automotive sales industry.
3. Fringe benefits of this kind are generally expenses incurred by a business to promote employee good will. Since Richard and Fred were both shareholders and employees, the beneficial use of automobiles accruing to them could have been received in either capacity.

In approaching the constructive dividend issue, the court looked to Section 301 which defines a dividend as: "a distribution of property made by a corporation to a shareholder *with respect to its stock...*" (Emphasis added)

The court then held that, since the use of automobiles was a benefit Fred and Richard received in their capacities as employees—not as shareholders—such benefits did not qualify as dividends ... nor as a "distribution of property ... made by a corporation ... with respect to its stock..."

Con
John M. Lee and Marianne G. Lee
(TC Memo 1980-348)

Findings of Fact

John M. Lee was a union representative. His wife Marianne was a college instructor who contributed three days a month to a charitable organization. In this latter capacity, she used her personal automobile to travel approximately 870 miles for the year in question.

John's W-2 showed that he received a mileage allowance of $1350. On their joint tax return, the taxpayers claimed $5880 as automobile expenses. The IRS allowed $2927 which represented (for the most part) the cost of leasing an automobile.

Opinion

The court, after granting a calendar change and setting the hearing for 4:00 P.M., was not pleased when John did not appear.

Mrs. Lee testified as to various expenses which her husband could have incurred while running for reelection as a union representative but did not produce any evidence to this effect. She admitted that she did not have any receipts. She did, however, convince the judge that she had driven the 870 charitable miles as claimed.

In all other respects the court sustained the government determination because of the petitioner's failure of proof.

27.7 RELEVANT CODE AND REGULATION SECTIONS

Code

Section 38	Investment in Certain Depreciable Property
162	Trade or Business Expenses
167	Depreciation
168	Accelerated Cost Recovery System
212	Expenses for Production of Income
274	Disallowance of Certain Entertainment, etc., Expense

Regulations

Section 1.162-1	Business Expenses
1.162-2	Travel Expenses

Publications

463	Travel, Entertainment, and Gift Expenses
534	Depreciation
572	Investment Credit

27.8 APPLICABLE IRS MANUAL REFERENCES (INVESTIGATIVE TECHNIQUES)

Audit Guidelines for Examiners

MT 4231-46 Section 5(10)(16)0	Travel and Entertainment
547.1	Employee Business Expenses—General
6(14)2.5	Automobile

Residential Rental Property

(Sections 61 and 212)

28

28.1 IDENTIFYING THE PROBLEM

Problems abound, but so do benefits. To encourage the construction of residential rental properties, Congress purposely produced one of the finest shelters still alive in our tax system today.

Along the way it added the Economic Recovery Tax Act of 1981 (ERTA) which provides even greater investment incentive in the form of the accelerated cost recovery system (ACRS).

This depreciation system allows for conversion of ordinary income (in the form of ACRS deductions) into capital gains upon sale of a residential rental property, but this is where the problems begin.

WARNING:

The property must be held for the entire ACRS period of 15 years or depreciation recapture will intervene. Use of straight-line depreciation will not trigger such recapture.

Identification of "rental income" can cause other difficulties. It brings into play such terms as: advance rentals, lease cancellations, expenditures by the lessee, lease with option to purchase, etc. Are payments made under such circumstances classed as rental income or something else? Answers are sometimes difficult to arrive at.

Establishing property as "rental" in nature is extremely important because it allows for more favorable depreciation treatment than does commercial property—an apartment building, for example, as against a motel.

Rental of vacation homes and condominiums can produce unfavorable results if not handled correctly.

Investment in low-income housing can yield excellent tax benefits, but only if the correct bases are touched.

Structuring a rental investment property is also important. If not well planned, the venture can emerge as a trade or business and become subject to self-employment tax and the "commercial" stigma for depreciation recapture purposes.

28.2 HOW THE IRS SEES THE ISSUE

With the emergence of ERTA and ACRS most depreciation issues would appear to have been eliminated. Where there is a sale of property, however, with a lack of recapture, the IRS will want to know why.

Where a residence is partially rented, the IRS suspects that allocations of expenses are slanted to benefit the owner. Possibly, renovation of the taxpayer's quarters were charged as a rental expense.

Of prime importance, too, is the possibility of unreported income. Within this category, the Service sees omitted receipts from sources such as advance payments, bonuses to acquire leases, occupancy rates which are shown in records as less than actual, and lease cancellation payments.

Large losses from rental activities conjure up IRS visions of contrivance. Maybe the owner's mother-in-law is in residence and paying exhorbitantly low rent. Maybe *all* expenses of a partially rented residence have been deducted. Maybe the cost of land is being depreciated.

Losses from the rental of vacation homes are always suspect. Agreements in the form of leases may be actual sales contracts which allow the purchaser to write off all or part of capital expenditures as ordinary expenses.

28.3 FACTORS WHICH THE IRS CONSIDERS WHEN MAKING ITS AUDIT DECISION

Because of favorable depreciation recapture rules, government auditors will want to satisfy themselves that the rental property is actually "residential" in nature. Section 167(j)2(B) defines residential rental property as a building or structure which derives at least 80 percent of its annual gross rental income from dwelling units.

IMPORTANT:

In meeting the 80 percent test—If any portion of the building is occupied by the taxpayer, the gross rental income from such building shall include the rental value of the portion so occupied.

WARNING:

The Service will consider rentals from that portion of a lessee's residence which is used for business purposes as *not* income from a dwelling unit; e.g., a real estate broker who as a lessee used 50 percent of his apartment as a sales office.

Specific audit steps. In general an IRS auditor is instructed to approach the subject of rental income in a manner as described in the audit manual (MT 4231-46, Sec. 542.1) which is reproduced below as Figure 28-1.

Rental Income

(1) Scrutinize transactions with related taxpayers and controlled entities. Look for such features as: shifting income, renting for an inadequate consideration to owner, etc.

(a) Verify the net loss from rentals is not attributable to the fact that the property was rented to a relative or friend for an amount less than the fair market rental value of the property.

(b) Determine if the rental loss involves a vacation home used part of the time by the taxpayer.

(2) Determine whether there may have been income from sources for which no corresponding asset is recorded.

(3) Be alert to possible rental contracts which may be conditional sales.

(4) Depreciation, repairs, and other expenses should be analyzed.

(5) Be alert to prepaid rent or lease deposit items that may not be included in income.

(a) Question the taxpayer directly about the weekly or monthly rent received for each unit and periods of vacancy, if any.

(b) Where rents are received in advance on either the cash or the accrual basis and there is no substantial limitation on disposition, they constititute taxable income when received (constructive receipt). Verify these amounts have been included in income.

(c) A bonus paid by the lessee to the lessor upon execution of the lease constitutes income, as does a lump sum amount paid by the lessee in consideration for the cancellation of a lease. Verify that these amounts have been included in income.

(d) Question the taxpayer about tenants providing services in lieu of rental payments. Verify that the taxpayer has reported the value of the services as income if a deduction has been taken for the value of such services.

(6) Determine whether the taxpayer has coin-operated laundry machines located at the rental units and has reported the income.

(7) Look for fictitious rental income for taxpayer's occupancy. Taxpayer may be attempting to make all expenses deductible without apportionment.

Figure 28-1

More Key Audit Considerations

Usually, in the case of a closely held corporation, the IRS examiner will ask to review the minutes book. Should the examiner notice mention of a lease, he or she will expect to find rental income on the return.

Where the taxpayer uses an accrual method of accounting, a good auditor will go looking for rental income which should have been accrued but was not—particularly in situations where rents are not fixed but based, for example, on sales, earnings, or production by the lessee.

In cases where a net lease exists—and the lessor makes the mortgage payments and pays the real estate taxes—the auditor will want to make certain that such payments were reported as income on the lessor's return.

Damage deposits will also be on the mind of the examiner. If not repaid, were they reported as income? If utilized to make repairs, were the repairs deducted and the deposit not reported?

28.4 CONSIDERATIONS WHEN PREPARING THE RETURN

When you are confronted with newly acquired rental property, a decision must be made concerning the length of time over which the taxpayer intends to retain ownership.

Handling Depreciation

ERTA depreciation changes. Under ACRS the taxpayer may no longer choose from a variety of depreciation methods as listed in Section 167. He or she must now utilize straight-line or ACRS percentages. Most real property is now deemed to have a 15-year useful life (Section 168).

If ACRS percentages are used for depreciation purposes—and the residential property is sold before 15 years expire—depreciation deductions will have to be recaptured as ordinary income to the extent that they exceed straight-line deductions which would have been allowed using 15-year useful life.

Substantial improvements may be depreciated through use of separate elections. Such improvements are considered separate items of property. They are defined below:

1. Amounts are added to a building's capital account during any 12-month period totaling at least 25 percent of the building's adjusted basis (before depreciation) as of the first day of the test period.

2. The improvement is made at least three years after the building is placed in service.

Investment credits do not generally apply to personal property held in conjunction with rental real property, i.e., appliances furnished for tenants' convenience. Motels and hotels may, however, treat such appliances as Section 38 (Investment in Certain Depreciable Property)—and apply the investment credit—because they function as a business and provide "temporary" quarters for transients, generally of less than 30 days' duration.

Lease with Option to Purchase

Whether an agreement in the form of a lease is in reality a conditional sales contract depends upon the intent of the parties. In making this determination, the government does not depend upon any single test but rather attempts to make its decision by using all of the particular facts in the case.

Generally, however, the IRS examining officer will consider that an agreement represents a purchase and sale rather than a rental lease if the following conditions are present:

1. Portions of the periodic payments are specifically applicable to an equity to be acquired by the lessee.

2. The lessee will acquire title upon the payment of a stated amount of rental which, under the contract, is required to be paid.

3. The total amount which the lessee is required to pay for a relatively short period of use constitutes an inordinately large proportion of the full amount required to be paid before title is passed.

4. The agreed rental payments materially exceed current fair rental value.

5. The property may be acquired under a purchase option at a price which is nominal in relation to the value of the property at the time when the option may be exercised—as determined at the time of entering into the original agreement—or which is a relatively small amount when compared with the total payments which are required to be made.

Low-income housing is described in Regulation 1.1039.1(c).

Briefly, the term means that dwelling units will qualify if they are held for occupancy on a rental basis for individuals and families of low or moderate income.

The occupants are considered in this category if their adjusted gross income (anticipated total annual income) is not more than 80 percent of the median income for the area. This is the median income determined, with adjustments for smaller and larger families, by the Secretary of Housing and Urban Development (HUD)

NOTE:

HUD's median generally turns out to be surprisingly high.

The cost of qualified low-income housing may be depreciated under ACRS more rapidly over the first six years than ordinary real property. Rehabilitation of such qualified housing also produces excellent tax benefits—good leverage with quick amortization.

Rehabilitation of low-income housing. Expenditures to rehabilitate low-income housing made after July 24, 1969, and before 1984 may be amortized over a 60-month period. The maximum costs available for amortization are limited to $20,000 per unit except that under ERTA—and if certain conditions are met—the limitation can be increased to $40,000 per unit.

Electing the 60-month amortization requires the attachment of a statement to this effect to the first tax return filed with the use of this stepped-up amortization. Ten items of information must be included in the statement. IRS Publication 534 (Depreciation) furnishes complete details.

Rental of Vacation Homes

Rental of vacation homes is covered in detail in Chapter 25 of this book.

Rental of Condominiums and Cooperatives

If a taxpayer has a condo arrangement, he or she owns outright a dwelling unit in a multiunit building. If the unit is rented, the lessor may deduct all reasonable expenses as for a separate dwelling, plus assessments for the care of common areas of the structure.

Cooperative housing arrangements, however, require different treatment. The lessor, under this arrangement, generally owns shares of stock in a corporation. Determination of deductible expenses may be arrived at by dividing the number of shares owned by the lessor by the total number of shares outstanding—and then multiplying the resultant percentage by each corporate expense, such as interest, taxes, depreciation, repairs, etc.

The cooperative, however, must meet four conditions before expenses may be deducted. They are set forth in IRS Publication 527 (Rental Property).

28.5 HANDLING THE AUDIT

From Section 28.3 of this chapter, locate the general steps that an auditor will take in conducting his or her examination. Review each one. Wherever possible, prepare material that will legally render each seemingly clear government issue impotent.

Where a lease with option to purchase exists, establish the *intent* of each party as evidenced by the contract. In Hendrick v. Comm., for example, amounts received by the lessor over the period of a 68-year lease (at the end of which the lessee was to acquire the property for $10) were sales proceeds rather than rentals. The "intent" was clearly to purchase.

As with many tax issues, it is much more difficult to restructure than to structure correctly in the first place. But what's done is done, and you must do what you can to present the facts in as favorable a light as possible.

Allocation of expenses and depreciation, in the case of a residence which is partially rented, should be carefully reevaluated. Two-family houses with equal square footage generally cause little trouble. The split is 50-50. In other situations, allocation by number of rooms rented, as against number of rooms used for personal living, is possible; comparison by square footage, or even cubic footage, can be equitable. Why cubic footage? Well, possibly one apartment has cathedral ceilings and the other does not.

Be careful of peculiar leases—one, for example, in which the lessee is required to reimburse the lessor for income taxes which he or she must pay on the rental receipts. A pyramiding action can be involved. See Connecticut Railway and Lighting Company v. U. S. (1956) 135 Ct Cl, 650, 142 F. Supp. 907, 49 AFTR 1902.

Rental was $10,000. The tax rate was 40 percent. The lessee was forced to class as rental income an extra $4,000 (40 percent of $10,000) in tax reimbursement, the tax on the reimbursement in the amount of $1,600, the tax on the $1,600 which was $640, then the $640 at the end.

NEW CONSTRUCTION:

Don't agree with any Revenue person who claims that excavating, grading, and soil removal must be added to the cost of the land and become nondepreciable. Such costs, if they have a direct association with the construction of buildings and roads, may be amortized. See Rev. Rul. 68-193, 1968-1 CB 79.

Related parties. Be prepared to substantiate rental losses where tenants are related parties. Make a showing that rents in the general location of the leased property are substantially the same as those charged by the taxpayer.

Depreciation. If the property at issue is classed as "residential rental property" but is partially leased for business purposes, collect sufficient data to prove the previously mentioned 80 percent rule. Otherwise, the building may be placed in the commercial class, thereby creating a climate for recapture problems.

If investment credit has been taken, prepare to show that the rental units in question were regularly rented for periods of less than 30 days. Failure here will eliminate the investment credit.

28.6 PERTINENT COURT DECISIONS—PRO AND CON

Pro
J. V. and Hattie Keenon (TC Memo 1982-144)

Findings of Fact

The Keenons, owners of a two-family dwelling, rented one apartment to their daughter.

While so doing, they deducted rental expense and depreciation in excess of the rental charged. The IRS objected.

Opinion

The court decided in favor of the taxpayers, ruling that the rental payments were reasonable considering the location of the house and certainty of payments. Additionally, it felt that appreciation expectations showed a profit motive; renting to strangers probably would not have increased the rental income and might have led to greater losses.

Con
(Rev. Ruling 75-14)

Findings of Fact

Advice was requested as to whether expenses incurred by an individual when renting to his brother at less than fair market value were deductible.

Opinion

Using Section 183 (Actvities Not Engaged in for Profit) the IRS ruled that the taxpayer did not possess the necessary profit motive to take deductions that exceeded rental income. It was ruled further, that the taxpayer was neither engaged in a trade or business under Section 162 nor holding the property for the production of income under Sec. 212.

It did rule, however, that the taxpayer could deduct expenses under Regulation 1.183-1(b)(1) in the following order and to the following extent:

1. Interest and taxes are deductible in full as itemized deductions under Sections 163 and 164 of the Code.
2. Operating expenses are deductible to the extent that the gross income from rents exceeds the interest and taxes.
3. Depreciation is deductible to the extent that the gross income from rental of the house exceeds the interest, taxes, and operating expenses.

28.7 RELEVANT CODE AND REGULATION SECTIONS, PLUS IRS PUBLICATIONS

Code

Section 38	Investment in Certain Depreciable Property
61	Gross Income Defined
162	Trade or Business
167	Depreciation
168	Accelerated Cost Recovery System
183	Activities Not Engaged in for Profit

212   Expenses for the Production of Income
1039   Certain Sales of Low-Income Housing Projects

Regulations

Section 1.161-8   Rents and Royalties
1.1039   Certain Sales of Low-Income Housing Projects
1.1039-1(c)   Definition—Qualified Housing Project

Publications

527   Rental Property
534   Depreciation
572   Investment Credit
588   Condominiums, Cooperative Apartments and Homeowners Associations

28.8 APPLICABLE IRS MANUAL REFERENCES (INVESTIGATIVE TECHNIQUES)

Audit Guidelines for Examiners

MT 4231-46   Section 529.6   Multiple Dwellings
              542.1   Rental Income

Standard Explanations Handbook

MT 428(11)15 Section 16   Rental Income

Deductions for Taxes   29
(Section 164)

29.1 IDENTIFYING THE PROBLEM

In general, qualifying taxes are deductible either as itemized deductions—reasonable expenses of a trade or business — or expenses incurred for the production of income. The deductibility swings on their purpose.

In some instances, as when property is sold, only portions of the real estate taxes are deductible. A proration, using length of ownership during the year of sale, decides what the portion will be.

WARNING:

If the buyer agrees to pay taxes that were owed by the seller, the taxes paid are not deductible but must be treated as part of the cost of the property. If the buyer reimburses the seller for part of the real estate taxes which he or she has already paid, then this portion is usually deductible by the buyer.

All sorts of applicable taxes (unemployment, social security, sales) may be capitalized while real property is in the process of being developed or improved.

Contested taxes many times affect deductibilty. No deduction may be taken until the contest has been decided, but there are exceptions.

The great multiplicity of taxes (state, local, federal, and foreign) in themselves cause difficulties. Changes in the law over the years have added confusion.

Federal taxes are generally not deductible at all unless they are part of a cost of operating a trade or business or incurred for the production of income—the state gasoline tax, for example.

In the case of some foreign taxes, a choice is available; they may be deducted under Code Section 164 or a credit may be taken for them under Section 901 (Taxes of Foreign Countries and of Possessions of the U.S.)

Real estate taxes in the form of assessments for municipal improvements frequently need clarification. The cost of installing new sidewalks, for instance, may not be deducted as taxes but must be added to the basis of the property involved.

LOOK:

Local benefit taxes are deductible if they are paid for maintenance or repair, or for interest charges related to such benefits.

A frequent, unattended problem in the tax-deduction area is advance planning. A few words in the right spot in a building contract can cause all sales taxes for building materials to become deductible to the buyer. Without these words, such taxes simply become part of the cost of the building.

29.2 HOW THE IRS SEES THE ISSUE

The Service is generally well satisfied with its approach to the identification of taxes as itemized deductions. There are, after all, but four prevalent categories:

1. State, local, or foreign income taxes

2. State, local, or foreign real property taxes

3. State or local personal property taxes

4. State or local general sales taxes

It sees additional revenue possibilities, however, in tax deductions that were prepaid by accrual basis taxpayers. Possibly the date from which the accrual was computed was not in accordance with local or state laws—thereby causing the tax deduction to be overstated.

Additionally, the IRS feels that

■ Many real estate tax deductions should have been capitalized.

■ Portions of others should not have been deducted at all, since they actually represented (as part of the real estate tax) assessments for trash removal, or some such item.

■ Sales tax deductions, which exceed the optional state sales tax tables amount, may have been padded.

■ Taxpayers sometimes include in income only the actual amount of state income tax refund received and not the refund figure as shown on the state return. This may happen because the taxpayer believes that the difference becomes a wash when expenses of an equal amount are included on the return.

■ Real estate taxes placed in escrow through mortgage payments may have been deducted as taxes paid. Only the amount paid by the bank to the municipality is deductible.

■ In the case of foreign income tax, the taxpayer may have utilized both the deduction and the statutory credit options to reduce the U.S. income tax.

WARNING:

A foreign tax credit, or deduction claimed, is an immediate flag to an examiner that income from foreign sources should also be reflected on the return. Where all foreign income is exempt from gross income, no credit or deduction for foreign taxes is allowed.

■ Duplicate tax deductions may have been claimed (1) on Schedule A as an itemized deduction and (2) on Schedule E as a rental expense.

29.3 FACTORS WHICH THE IRS CONSIDERS WHEN MAKING ITS AUDIT DECISION

In addition to checking out the above suspicions, an IRS agent will probably perform the following audit functions:

1. Verify amounts claimed.
2. Determine that the deduction had been taken in the proper year and by the proper individual.
3. Determine whether the tax is of the type deductible in accordance with rules and regulations.
4. Make certain that employment taxes paid on the wages of domestic workers were not deducted.
5. Determine that deductions were not taken for taxes which were being contested and were of an unsettled nature.
6. Check year-end accruals of significant amounts to determine if they are proper.
7. Determine if there are any taxes on the purchase of capital assets that should have been capitalized.
8. Verify that there are no double deductions for social security taxes (FICA) paid. A deduction for such taxes paid on an employee's salary should not include the employee's share of the tax if this amount is included in the salary and wage expense deduction.
9. Verify that both federal and state income taxes and FICA tax withheld were not claimed as business expenses and also included in the gross wage figure.

NOTE:

Some small businesses deduct *all* amounts paid to the IRS as tax expense, but then show as wages only the net amounts to employees. In such cases the total expense will be correct, only the allocation will be improper.

10. Recompute proration of current real estate taxes in year of sale or purchase to determine correctness.
11. Verify that a credit has not been taken for excess tax payments which would be refunded by a foreign country with which the U.S. has a tax treaty if a claim were filed.

29.4 CONSIDERATIONS WHEN PREPARING THE RETURN

Two basic, simple sentences should be kept in mind when considering the tax deduction. They are these:

1. Qualifying taxes are deductible if paid or accrued during the tax year by the person upon whom they are imposed.
2. A tax that is deductible as an expense is deductible by the person incurring such an expense.

There are exceptions, of course, just as for most income tax rules and regulations.

Cooperative housing corporation. Tenant-stockholders may take a deduction for amounts paid to the corporation that represents taxes on property owned and maintained by the coop. For definition of a cooperative housing corporation, see Chapter 28 (Rental Property).

Double tax deductions may sometimes properly occur. A gasoline retailer may deduct a state gasoline tax as a tax, and the consumer may deduct it as a business-related expense.

Reservation of term of years. The owner of a reserved term of years may deduct tax on real property even though another holds title to it (Rev. Rul. 67-21, 1967-1 CB 45).

Owners of condominiums may deduct real estate taxes paid on their apartments (Rev. Rul. 64-31, 1964-1 (Part 1) CB 300).

Election to ratably accrue. An accrual method taxpayer may elect to accrue and deduct real property taxes over the period for which the tax is imposed instead of taking the deduction based on the accrual date (Regulation 1.461-1(c).

NOTE:

The accrual date is usually the lien date or the date the owner becomes personally liable.

An election to ratably accrue may be made by the taxpayer for each separate trade or business and for nonbusiness activities if accounted for separately. If the election is made for the first year in which real property taxes are incurred, the election may be made without the Commissioner's consent by attaching a statement to the income tax return for that year. (The return must be filed by the regular due date, including extensions.)

The statement should indicate

1. The trade or business or nonbusiness activity to which the election is to apply, and the method of accounting used.

2. The period of time to which the taxes are related.

3. The computation of the deduction for real property taxes for the first year of the election (or a summary of each computation).

After the first year in which the taxes were incurred, the taxpayer may elect *with the consent of the Commissioner* to accrue real property taxes ratably. Permission can be obtained by submitting to the Commissioner a request which includes the following:

1. Name and address of the taxpayer

2. The trade or business or nonbusiness activity to which the election is to apply and the method of accounting used

3. The taxable year to which the election first applies

4. The period to which the real property taxes relate

5. The computation of the deduction for real property taxes for the first year of election (or a summary of such computation)

6. An adequate description of the manner in which all real property taxes were deducted in the year prior to the year of election

NOTE:

The written request must be submitted within 90 days after the beginning of the taxable year to which the election is first applicable.

For property under construction. Prior to the advent of TEFRA, individuals, Sub S Corporations, and personal holding companies were required to capitalize interest and property taxes attributable to the construction period (other than low-income housing) which was to be used in a trade or business or held for investment. The amortization period was generally set at 10 years.

After TEFRA (effective 1-1-83) a similar rule applies to the construction of nonresidential realty by a regular corporation.

Applicable taxes include state and federal unemployment taxes, state and local sales taxes, and social security taxes on the wages of employees who are engaged in the development or construction work.

General sales taxes. A general sales tax is one that is charged at one rate on the retail sales of a broad class of items. This type of sales tax is deductible. A selective sales tax that does not apply to a broad range of items is not a general sales tax and is not deductible.

A taxpayer may deduct the actual amount of general sales taxes paid or may use the optional state sales tax table (based on adjusted gross income) to arrive at the deductible amount. If the table is used, all income (taxable or nontaxable) can be considered, e.g., social security payments and the untaxed portion of capital gains.

Some sales taxes may be added to the table amount but only if they are expended while buying the following items:

1. A car, motorcycle, motor home, or truck but only up to the percentage rate charged as general sales taxes.

2. A boat, plane, home (including mobile or prefabricated) *or materials to build a new home if:*
   a. The tax rate was the same as the general sales tax rate, and
   b. The sales receipt or contract shows the amount paid.

IMPORTANT:

When planning the construction of a home, a taxpayer should arrange the building contract to cause himself or herself to become the purchaser of the required construction materials. Through use of this maneuver, the taxpayer obtains the resultant sales tax deduction. Otherwise, the tax would become nondeductible as part of the cost of the residence.

A tax-deduction checklist is reproduced below for quick reference.

Noncorporate Application of Tax Deductions	Itemized Deduction on Schedule A	Trade or Business or for Production of Income	Not Deducted by Individual Taxpayers
Income Tax (State, Local, or Foreign)	X		
Real Property Tax (State, Local, or Foreign)	X	X	
Personal Property Tax (State, or Local)	X	X	
General Sales Tax (State or Local)	X	X	
Gasoline Tax (State or Local)		*X	X

*Included in cost of gas and deductible as an expense of doing business

Noncorporate Application of Tax Deductions	Itemized Deduction on Schedule A	Trade or Business or for Production of Income	Not Deducted by Individual Taxpayers
Highway Use Tax		X	X
Social Security (FICA)		X	X
Railroad Retirement		X	X
Unemployment (FUTA)		X	X
Federal Income Tax			**X
Self-Employment Tax (Part of Federal Income Tax)			**X
Estate, Inheritance, Legacy, Succession, and Gift Taxes			**X
Wagering Taxes	X		
Cigarette and Tobacco Taxes (State and Local)		X	X
Tax on Alcoholic Beverages State and Local		X	X
Admission Taxes (State and Local)		X	X
Registration or Licensing of Motor Vehicles (State and Local)		X	X
Transfer (Stamp) Taxes (State and Local)		X	X
Occupancy Taxes		X	X
Poll Taxes		X	X
Taxes for Improvement to Property (Assessments for streets or sidewalks, etc.)		***X	***X
Federal Excise Taxes, such as the Civil Aircraft Tax, Tax on Communications, and Customs Duties		X	X

29.5 HANDLING THE AUDIT

Occasionally the deduction of *compensating use taxes,* as imposed by various states, becomes an IRS issue. Such taxes *are* deductible when the general sales tax for the item would be deductible.

Federal taxes, such as import duties, excise taxes, and social security, may also raise IRS problems. These *are* deductible if incurred in a trade or business or in a nonbusiness activity under Code Sections 162 and 212 respectively.

Taxes paid for another are usually not deductible, but in "Theodore Bernstein" the court held that they were, because the taxpayer held all the incidents of ownership except for the bare title.

  **Not deductible at all
***Increases basis of property

When renting a residence, the taxpayer may not deduct real estate taxes paid to or for the landlord. But he or she may do so if the tax, by state law, is assessed against the tenant.

Where property changes hands, allocation of taxes is usually closely scrutinized by the Service.

REMEMBER THESE POINTS:

The portion of the tax allocable to the portion of the property tax "preceding" the sale is considered imposed on the seller and is deductible by him or her. The portion allocable to the part of the property tax year "beginning" on the date of the sale is considered imposed on the buyer and is deductible by him or her.

This rule applies whether or not the seller and the buyer apportion the tax between them (Regulation 1.164-6).

IMPORTANT:

In figuring gain or loss, the part of the tax *paid by the buyer and treated as imposed on the seller* is considered part of the amount realized by the seller and represents an additional cost of the property (Regulation 1.1001-1(b)).

Conversely, the tax treated as imposed on the seller is not considered part of the selling price, but the *part paid by the seller and treated as imposed on the buyer* reduces both the amount realized by the seller and the basis of the property to the buyer.

Exceptions to the general rule setting year of deduction. Should the IRS auditor claim, in the case of a cash basis taxpayer, that the tax deduction can be taken only if paid, note the following exceptions: The tax will be considered paid

1. By the buyer in the year of purchase if the seller is liable.
2. By the seller in year of sale, if the buyer is liable or if the seller is liable and the tax is payable after date of sale.

NOTE:

In either of the above two situations, if the tax (or an amount representing the tax) is paid in a tax year after the year of sale, the deduction may be taken in the year of payment *or* in the year of sale (Regulations 1.164-6(d)(1), (2)).

Contested taxes. Generally, in the case of accrual basis taxpayers, a deduction for taxes is postponed until the claim has been adjudicated and settled. This rule is well established in Regulation 1.461-1(a)(3). However, if an IRS person insists on this narrow version of the law,

KNOW THIS:

Under Regulation 1.461-2, the deduction may be taken if the disputed amount has been paid. Putting the amount in escrow qualifies.

Where the taxpayer had admitted liability for a portion of the contested amount, deduction may be taken for the admitted portion.

State and local income tax refunds. An IRS Agent will certainly check to determine whether the refund of state and local income taxes (deducted in the prior year) was reported as income in the year at audit.

WATCH THIS ONE:

> Government examiners are sometimes overenthusiastic in picking up this type of additional income.
>
> Only that portion of the refund *which caused a decrease in tax* in the prior year need be declared as income in the current year—not the entire rebate.

29.6 PERTINENT COURT DECISIONS—PRO AND CON

Pro
C. David and Bernice S. Pettit
(TC Memo 1980-396)

Findings of Fact

Mr. Pettit, during 1977, acted as his own contractor in building a home. He purchased the materials relating to this construction and deducted from his tax return $400 in sales taxes. These were in addition to the amount allowed by the sales tax table. The IRS disallowed the entire $400 deduction.

Opinion

The court recognized that the sales taxes in question were deductible—in addition to the table allowance—if the taxpayer could adequately substantiate his claim for the additional amount.

The petitioner produced a number of cancelled checks and receipts which purported to represent purchases of building materials.

In its decision, the court accepted a sufficient amount of this documentation to allow Mr. Pettit a sales tax deduction of $236.86. It further held that he had failed to carry his burden of proof for the allowance of any greater amount.

Con
(Rev. Rul. 77-29)

Findings of Fact

Advice was requested whether certain fees imposed by a county on real property were deductible as real estate taxes under Section 164 of the Code.

The county imposed an annual fee upon all real property for the collection and disposal of refuse. The assessed value of the property determined the amount of the fee.

Under the state law, the fees are deemed assessments against the property served and, as such, are enforced in the same manner and to the same extent as county ad valorem taxes and are also collected in the same manner.

Opinion

Taxes are not payments for some special privilege granted or service rendered and are, therefore, distinguishable from various other charges imposed for particular purposes under particular powers or functions of government.

Ordinarily, when amounts are paid into a specific fund or earmarked for a specific purpose, they are treated as imposed as a regulatory measure or as a charge for a privilege or service rendered. See Rev. Ruls. 61-152 and 71-49.

Accordingly, the sanitation fees are not deductible as real property taxes under Section 164 of the Code.

29.7 RELEVANT CODE AND REGULATION SECTIONS, PLUS PUBLICATION

Code

Section 162	Trade or Business Expenses
164	Taxes
212	Expenses for the Production of Income
266	Carrying Charges
275	Certain Taxes
461	General Rule for Taxable Year of Deduction
901	Taxes of Foreign Countries and of Possessions of the U. S.

Regulations

Section 1.164-6	Apportionment of Taxes on Real Property Between Seller and Purchaser
1.164-6(d)(1)	Seller Using Cash Receipts and Disbursements Method of Accounting
1.164-6(d)(2)	Purchaser Using the Cash Receipts and Disbursements Method of Accounting
1.164-6(d)(3)	Persons Considered Liable for Tax
1.266-1	Taxes and Carrying Charges Chargeable to Capital Account and Treated as Capital Items
1.461	Statutory Provisions: General Rule for Taxable Year of Deduction
1.461-1(a)(2)	Taxpayers Using an Accrual Method
1.461-1(a)(3)	Other Factors Which Determine When Deductions May Be Taken
1.461-1(c)	Accrual of Real Property Taxes
1.461-2	Timing of Deductions in Certain Cases Where Asserted Liabilities Are Contested
1.1001-1	Computation of Gain or Loss
1.1001-1(b)	Real Estate Taxes as Amounts Received

Publication

535	Business Expenses and Operating Losses

29.8 APPLICABLE IRS MANUAL REFERENCES (INVESTIGATIVE TECHNIQUES)

Audit Guidelines for Examiners

MT 4231-46 Section 526	State Tax Refunds
564	Foreign Tax Credit

MT 4231-46   5(10)(15)0   Taxes
MT 4231-47   572   Taxes

Techniques Handbook for In-Depth Examinations

MT 4235-5   Section 7(11)3   Kinds of Excise Taxes

Sick Pay and Disability Income
(Sections 104 and 105)

30

30.1 IDENTIFYING THE PROBLEM

Despite years of litigation and congressional changes in the covering law, many tax problems still exist regarding health and accident benefits. Some of the major mysteries are listed below in the form of questions which will eventually be answered before this chapter is completed:

- How is sick pay different from disability benefits?
- Is sick pay taxable as income? Is it subject to Social Security and Railroad Retirement taxes?
- Are disability benefits taxable as income—and under what circumstances?
- Does anyone qualify for a total exclusion of disability income? If so, to what extent—and under what conditions?
- What is a qualified health or accident plan and how does it control tax law?
- Does the identity of the finanacier of this plan affect anything?
- Do we, here again as in much tax law, have allocation problems?
- How does Workmen's Compensation enter the picture? Can other like compensation be substituted for it at law?
- Should an incapacitated taxpayer treat his or her benefits as disability income or as a pension subject to retirement benefits?

30.2 HOW THE IRS SEES THE ISSUE

Sick pay is any payment received from an employer-financed plan (in place of wages) while the employee is temporarily absent from work because of sickness or injury.

Before the 1976 Tax Reform Act, an employee who was temporarily absent from work was not subject on tax on sick pay (with dollar limits). Now, however, such pay is taxable

353

unless (1) the employee is permanently and totally disabled or (2) the sick pay was received from an accident or health insurance policy which the employee purchased with his or her own funds. The IRS suspects that the requirements of one or both of these exceptions may not have been satisfied.

If sick pay is received from an employer-financed plan, such benefits are entirely taxable to the recipient. If the plan is partially financed by each, the employer and the employee, then only a corresponding pro rata portion of the sick pay is taxable to the employee. The portion which represents his or her financing of the plan is nontaxable. Wherever this joint financing situation exists, the IRS suspects that a false allocation may exist.

In the case of disability pensions, the Service is wary of three possibilities which would be unfavorable to the U.S.

1. The taxpayer may have taken the disability exclusion without including the income.

2. He or she may not have met the qualifications for exclusion (described later in section 30.4 of this chapter).

3. The recipient may have elected at some previous time to treat his or her disability benefits as pension or annuity income.

WARNING:

Once this election is made, it cannot be revoked.

30.3 FACTORS WHICH THE IRS CONSIDERS WHEN MAKING ITS AUDIT DECISION

An examiner's audit plan will contain procedures to locate the above noncompliance possibilities. It will also specifically search out and seize upon adjustments which may result from the following findings:

■ That Form 2440 (Disability Income Exclusion) was not correctly prepared.

NOTE PARTICULARLY:

The "Physician's Statement of Permanent and Total Disability" located on the bottom of the Form 2440 *must* be completed or the document will not be considered valid.

■ That payments for accrued vacation time were treated as disability benefits, because the taxpayer resigned as the result of injury or illness before reaching the normal retirement age. (Such vacation pay is not excludible as disability income.)

■ That guaranteed payments by a partnership to a partner who was absent because of a permanent illness do not qualify as disability benefits. (The recipient must have been an "employee.")

■ That the taxpayer reached age 65 before January 1 of the taxable year. Exclusion disallowed.

NOTE:

For purposes of Section 105 (Amounts Received Under Accident and Health Plans) an individual reaches age 65 on the day of his or her 65th birthday anniversary.

■ That the taxpayer was not totally and permanently disabled, because he or she was working part time in a competitive work situation and was being paid at least the minimum wage.

■ That, having been injured on the job, the taxpayer received Workmen's Compensation. This he turned over to his employer who continued to pay the taxpayer's full salary. The difference between the Workmen's Compensation and the total salary is taxable income.

Effect of Social Security and Railroad Retirement laws. Under Public law 97-123, sections of the Code (3121(a)(2) and 3231(e)) were amended to cause the first six months of sick pay to become subject to Social Security and Railroad Retirement taxes beginning January 1, 1982.

The IRS will be backtracking at audit time to determine whether these payroll taxes were withheld and paid over.

NOTE, HOWEVER:

The six-month calendar period need not begin running on January 1, 1982. In the case of an employee who was not working and who was receiving sick pay for six months or longer by December 31, 1981, his or her remuneration will *not* be taxed during the first six months of 1982.

30.4 CONSIDERATIONS WHEN PREPARING THE RETURN

Sick pay and disability payments are defined in roughly the same terms except that, in the case of the former, the employee is *temporarily* incapacitated, in the latter, he or she is *permanently and totally* disabled.

A person is considered to be permanently and totally disabled when

1. He or she cannot engage in any substantial gainful activity because of a physical or mental condition; and
2. A physician determines that the condition (1) has lasted or can be expected to last continuously for at least a year, or (b) can be expected to lead to death.

Taxability of Sick Pay

The taxability of sick pay hinges to a great degree upon its source. Amounts received from an accident or health plan, which is paid for by an employer are taxable. Benefits received from a plan paid for by an employee are not taxable. Workmen's Compensation is not taxable. Proceeds of an insurance policy which reimburses the insured for certain business overhead expenses during prolonged periods of sickness or disability are taxable.

How Disability Benefits Are Taxed

This sort of remuneration can be excluded in its entirety, excluded partially or be totally taxable. An exclusion results if ALL of the following tests are met:

1. The taxpayer received disability pay.

NOTE:

To qualify for this test, the disability pay must have been made under a health or accident plan of an employer.

2. The taxpayer was not yet 65 years of age when his or her tax year ended.

IMPORTANT:

Disability benefits received after age 65 are treated as normal pensions or annuities.

3. The taxpayer retired on disability and was permanently and totally disabled at that time.
4. The retired individual, on the first day of the taxable year, had not yet reached the age at which his or her employer's retirement program would have required the taxpayer to retire.
5. The taxpayer did not elect to treat the disability income as a pension.
6. If married on the last day of the year, the taxpayer must have filed a joint return.*

NOTE:

*This rule does not apply if the taxpayer did not live with his or her spouse at any time during the tax year in question.

When does the disability exclusion end? The exclusion will be allowed to continue until the earliest of the following dates is reached:

1. The first day of the tax year in which the taxpayer turns 65.
2. The first day of the tax year for which the taxpayer chooses to treat his or her disability as a pension.
3. The day the taxpayer reaches the age at which his or her employer's retirement program would have required retirement.

Form 2440 (Disability Income Exclusion) should be used to make the exclusion computation.

NOTE:

There is a limitation on the exclusion. The maximum disability payment that can be excluded is $100 per week or $5200 annually. This maximum exclusion is reduced dollar for dollar for adjusted gross income (including disability income) above $15,000. Therefore, there can be no exclusion for anyone with an adjusted gross income of $20,200 or higher ($15,000 plus $5,200).

The Importance of a Qualified Health and Accident Plan

Whether the taxpayer is the majority stockholder and employee of a closely held corporation or an employer who wishes to provide an excellent fringe benefit for his or her employees, the construction of a proper plan is exceedingly important. As you have seen, without such a plan, qualification tests for the disability exclusion cannot even get started.

A formal, legal contract is not necessary but, since the advent of the Employee Retirement Income Security Act of 1974, the plan must be in writing. It also should be known to employees. In addition, benefits provided in contributory pension or profit-sharing plans will be considered as having been made from employer contributions unless the plan expressly provides otherwise.

SUGGESTION:

To make the plan as foolproof as possible (1) put it in writing, (2) distribute copies to all employees, and (3) ask the recipients to sign for each copy.

Group plans. In the case of a group policy where contributions are made jointly by employer and employees, the employer's contributions are proportionate to the net premiums paid by the employer for the last three calendar years of receipt that the policy was in force.

The three-year period begins with the first year for which the net premium is known on the first day of such calendar year. If the policy has not been in force for three years, then the period it has been in force will be used.

Regulation 1.105-5 covers Accident and Health Plans. It is reproduced below as Figure 30-1.

0—§1.105-5 (T.D. 6169, filed 4-13-56; republished in T.D. 6500, filed 11-25-60; amended by T.D. 6722, filed 4-13-64.) **Accident and health plans.**

(a) *In general,* Sections 104(a)(3) and 105(b), (c) and (d) exclude from gross income certain amounts received through accident or health insurance. Section 105(e) provides that for purposes of sections 104 and 105 amounts received through an accident or health plan for employees, and amounts received from a sickness and disability fund for employees maintained under the law of a State, a Territory, or the District of Columbia, shall be treated as amounts received through accident or health insurance. In general, an accident or health plan is an arrangement for the payment of amounts to employees in the event of personal injuries or sickness. A plan may cover one or more employees, and there may be different plans for different employees or classes of employees. An accident or health plan may be either insured or noninsured, and it is not necessary that the plan be in writing or that the employee's rights to benefits under the plan be enforceable. However, if the employee's rights are not enforceable, an amount will be deemed to be received under a plan only if, on the date the employee became sick or injured, the employee was covered by a plan (or a program, policy, or custom having the effect of a plan) providing for the payment of amounts to the employees in the event of personal injuries or sickness, and notice or knowledge of such plan was reasonably available to the employee. It is immaterial who makes payment for the benefits provided by the plan. For example, payment may be made by the employer, a welfare fund, a State sickness or disability benefits fund, an association of employers or employees, or by an insurance company.

(b) *Self-employed individuals.* Under section 105(g), a self-employed individual is not treated as an employee for purposes of section 105. Therefore, for example, benefits paid under an accident or health plan as referred to in section 105(e) to or on behalf of an individual who is self-employed in the business with respect to which the plan is established will not be treated as received through accident and health insurance for purposes of sections 104(a)(3) and 105.

Figure 30-1

Self-employed individuals. Benefits paid to self-employed individuals under a self-employed retirement plan are taxable.

Disability or Pension—A Vital Consideration

Instead of treating disability benefits as disability income, a taxpayer may choose to treat them as a pension or annuity. This may be done at any time before the individual reaches 65. After that date, the disability income must be treated as a pension or annuity.

Making the disability-pension test. A taxpayer may benefit from making the switch to pension treatment

1. If his or her adjusted gross income reduces the taxpayer's disability income exclusion as explained above under heading *Form 2440.*

2. If the taxpayer believes that he or she will not live long enough to recover the pension or annuity cost, tax free without making the switch.

3. If the person has reached minimum retirement age and can take the credit for the elderly.

To make the choice a taxpayer must attach a statement to his or her Form 1040 which declares that he or she

1. Qualifies to claim the disability income exclusion.
2. Chooses to treat the disability benefits as a pension or annuity.
3. Will not claim a disability income exclusion in the year of the choice or any later year.

A physician's statement must also be attached, if one has not previously been submitted.

30.5 HANDLING THE AUDIT

It would seem important, when handling an audit of this issue, that the taxpayer or practitioner be prepared to point out exceptions to the general rules—variances with which the IRS examiner might not be immediately familiar.

Federal Employees' Compensation Act (FECA). Under this act payments for personal injuries or sickness, including payments to beneficiaries in case of death, are not taxable.

NOTE, HOWEVER:

"Continuation pay" for up to 45 days, while a claim is being decided, is taxable. Also, pay for sick leave, while a claim is being processed, is taxable.

Black lung payments are considered to be Workmen's Compensation and as such are not taxed.

Miscellaneous compensation which is not taxed is listed below:

• Damages received by suit or agreement for personal injuries or or sickness.
• Basic Medicare benefits received under Social Security payments.
• Payments received by firemen and police on pension for total permanent disability caused by or arising out of their duties, because they are in the nature of Workmen's Compensation.
• Benefits from state sickness or disability funds financed with employee contributions.
• Disability benefits received for loss of income or earning capacity as a result of injuries sustained under a "no fault" car insurance policy.
• A compensation for permanent loss, or loss of use, of a part or function of the body, or for permanent disfigurement.

IMPORTANT:

Such benefits are not taxed even though the employer paid for the accident and health plan that provided the compensation.

WARNING:

Benefits attributable to medical deductions allowed for an earlier year are not excludible income.

Mandatory retirement age. Don't allow an Internal Revenue person to claim that the mandatory retirement age is 65. For most employees it is probably now 70. In any case, the law says that the mandatory retirement age is the age at which the taxpayer would have been required to retire under the employer's retirement program, had the taxpayer not become disabled.

Penalties for failure to withhold FICA. If the taxpayer-employer failed to comply with Public Law 97-123 (which demands that Social Security be withheld from the first six months of sick pay after 1-1-82), he or she should resist any attempt by the IRS to assess a penalty for this dereliction if such failure was due to reasonable cause, and not willful neglect, and the FICA taxes were paid on or before June 30, 1982.

30.6 PERTINENT COURT DECISIONS—PRO AND CON

Pro
(Rev. Rul. 73-347)

Findings of Fact

Advice was requested as to the consequences of the following arrangement under which the taxpayer received payments when he was absent from work because of illness.

The taxpayer is a member of a union local whose members are employed on a piecework basis by an employer who does not provide a sick pay plan.

When the taxpayer became ill, he received benefit payments pursuant to the rules of his union local. Under these rules, a member who is absent from work on a particular day because of sickness receives a specified percentage of the wages earned on that day by the group of employees with whom he works.

The benefit payments take the form of checks issued by the employer's payroll officer from amounts retained from earnings of the members actually working on that day.

The question presented is whether these payments are amounts received under a *wage continuation plan* subject to the provisions of Section 105(d) of the Code, or amounts received under an *employees' accident and health plan* subject to the provisions of Section 104(a)(3).

Opinion

In the instant case, the employer pays only for piecework actually produced and bears no portion of the cost of the plan. Since Section 105(d) applies only to amounts received by an employee that are attributable to *employer* contributions or amounts paid by the *employer,* the payments described are not subject to the provisions of 105(d) as amounts received under a wage continuation plan—and accordingly are excluded from gross income under Section 104(a)(3) of the Code.

MY WARNING:

The court, however, ruled that each participating worker must include in his or her gross income the entire amount of his or her earnings, including the portion of wages paid over to the employer for the benefit of the ill member.

(AND FURTHER:

That such amounts are not deductible as medical expenses under the provisions of Section 213).

Con
(Rev. Rul. 78-416)

Findings of Fact

Advice was sought as to whether payments received as "continuation of pay" by a federal employer pursuant to Section 11 of the Federal Employees' Compensation Act (FECA) were excludible from gross income under Section 104(a)(1) or Section 105(d) of the Code as compensation for personal injuries or sickness.

PL 93-416 (1974) amended the FECA to provide payment of "continuation pay" for certain employees who had filed claims for a period of wage loss due to a traumatic injury. Compensation for disability does not begin until termination of the "continuation pay" or use of annual leave or sick leave ends.

Opinion

Amounts received as "continuation of pay" are not received as compensation for personal injuries or sickness. Such amounts are, therefore, not excludible from gross income under either Section 104(a)(1) or Section 105(d) of the Code.

30.7 RELEVANT CODE AND REGULATION SECTIONS, PLUS PUBLICATIONS

Code

Section 72	Annuities; Certain Proceeds of Endowment and Life Insurance Contracts
104	Compensation for Injuries or Sickness
105	Amounts Received Under Accident and Health Plans
106	Contributions by Employer to Accident and Health Plans
213	Medical, Dental, etc., Expenses
3121	Definitions (Employment Taxes)
3231(e)	Compensation

Regulations

Section 1.72-15	Applicability of Sec. 72 to Accident or Health Plans
1.104	Statutory Provisions; Compensation for Injuries or Sickness
1.105	Statutory Provisions; Amounts Received Under Accident and Health Plans
1.105-1	Amounts Attributable to Employer Contributions
1.105-5	Accident and Health Plans

Publications

522	Disability Payments
524	Credit for the Elderly
575	Pension and Annuity Income
907	Tax Information for Handicapped and Disabled Individuals

30.8 APPLICABLE IRS MANUAL REFERENCES (INVESTIGATIVE TECHNIQUES)

Audit Guidelines for Examiners

MT 4231-46   Section 533   Disability Income Exclusion

Standard Explanations Handbook

MT 428(11)-14   Section 26   Sick Pay Exclusion and Disability Income Exclusion

INCOME TAX ACRONYMS

The following is an alphabetical listing of acronyms and abbreviations and their meanings commonly used in government publications.

AAA	Agriculture Adjustment Act
ABA	American Bar Association
ACQS	Acquiescence
ACRS	Accelerated Cost Recovery System
ADP	Automatic Data Processing
ADR	Asset Depreciation Range
AET	Accumulated Earnings Tax
AFDC	Aid for Dependent Children
AFRA	Average Freight Rate Assessments
AFTR	American Federal Tax Reports, First Series
AFTR 2d	American Federal Tax Reports, Second Series
AGI	Adjusted Gross Income
AICPA	American Institute of Certified Public Accountants
AIMS	Audit Information Management System
AMA	American Medical Association
ANEPT	Activities Not Engaged in For Profit Test
AODs	Actions on Decisions
APA	Administrative Procedure Act
ARC	Assistant Regional Commissioner
ARM	Appeals and Review Memoranda
ARR	Appeals and Review Recommendations
ASE	American Stock Exchange
AUO	Administratively Uncontrollable Overtime
BEP	Barter Exchange Project
BMF	Business Master File
BTA	Board of Tax Appeals
CA	Court of Appeals
CAAP	Computer-Assisted Audit Program
CADC	Court of Appeals of the District of Columbia
CAF	Centralized Authorization File
CAG	Case Assignment Guide
CASs	Computed Audit Specialists
CB	Cumulative Bulletin
CCA	Chief Counsel Announcement

CCA	Circuit Court of Appeals
CCPA	Consumer Credit Protection Act
CD	Certificate of Deposit
CEP	Coordinated Examination Program
CERT	Certiorari
CERT DEN	Certiorari Denied
CETA	Comprehensive Employment and Training Act
CFR	Code of Federal Regulations
CHAMT	Changes in Accounts Methods Text
CID	Criminal Investigation Division
CLADR	Class Life Asset Depreciation Range
COD	Cash on Delivery
COF	Collection Office Function
COMM	Commissioner of Internal Revenue
CPI	Consumer Price Index
CQRS	Collection Quality Review System
CRO	Commissioner's Reorganization Orders
CSAs	Computer Systems Analysts
CSB	Centralized Services Branch
CSO	Child Support Obligation
CT CLs	Court of Claims
CT Ds	Court Decisions
CTF	Common Trust Funds
CTR	Currency Transaction Report
DAIP	Delinquent Account Inventory Profile
DB	Declining Balance (Depreciation)
DC	District Court
DCAA	Defense Contract Audit Agency
DD	District Director
DDB	Double Declining Balance (Depreciation)
DEA	Drug Enforcement Administration
Den	Denied
DIF	Discriminant Function Selection Process
DISC	Domestic International Sales Corporation
DIIP	Delinquent Investigation Inventory Profile
DLN	Document Location Number
DOL	Department of Labor
DPA	Defense Production Administration
DRA	Disaster Relief Act of 1974
DRC	Delinquent Return Code
EACS	EP/EO Application Control System
EDP	Electronic Data Processing
EEO	Equal Employment Opportunity
EEOC	Equal Employment Opportunity Commission
EIC	Earned Income Credit

EIN	Employer's Identification Number
EOMF	Exempt Organization Master File
EPA	Environmental Protection Agency
EP/EO	Employee Plans/Exempt Organizations
EPMF	Employee Plan Master File
ER	Enforcement Resolution
ERISA	Employment Retirement Income Security Act (of 1974)
ERP	Equipment Replacement Program (by the IRS)
ERTA	Economic Recovery Tax Act (of 1981)
ESOP	Employee Stock Ownership Plan
FAC	Full Absorption Inventory Costing
FCC	Federal Communications Commission
FDA	Food and Drug Administration
FDIC	Federal Deposit Insurance Corporation
FECA	Federal Employees' Compensation Act
FHA	Federal Housing Administration
FHLBB	Federal Home Loan Bank Board
FIC	Foreign Investment Companies
FICA	Federal Insurance Contribution Act
FIFO	First In First Out (Inventories)
FMV	Fair Market Value
FNMA	Federal National Mortgage Association
FOIA	Freedom of Information Act
FRB	Federal Reserve Bank
FRC	Filing Requirement Code
FRD	Federal Rules Division
FRV	Fair Rental Value
F. Supp.	Federal Supplement
FTD	Federal Tax Deposit
FUTA	Federal Unemployment Tax Act
FY	Fiscal Year
GAAP	Generally Accepted Accounting Principles
GAO	General Accounting Office
GCMs	General Counsel's Memoranda
GPM	Graduated Payment Mortgage
GPO	Government Printing Office
GSA	General Services Administration
HCI	Highly Compensated Individual
HSRRA	Hazardous Substance Response Revenue Act
HOLC	Home Owners Loan Corporation
HR	House of Representatives
HUD	Housing and Urban Development
HUT	Highway Use Tax
ICC	Interstate Commerce Commission
IDC	Intangible Drilling Cost

IDIF	Interim Discriminant Function System
IDM	Information Document Match Program
IDP	Individual Development Plan
IDRS	Integrated Data Retrieval System
IMF	Individual Master File
IND	Investigational New Drug
IRA	Individual Retirement Account
IRB	Internal Revenue Bulletin
IRC	Internal Revenue Code
IRM	Internal Revenue Manual
IRP	Information Returns Program
IRS	Internal Revenue Service
IRSS	Information Returns Selection System
ISO	Incentive Stock Option
ITC	Investment Tax Credit
ITU	Income Tax Unit Order
LEM	Law Enforcement Manual
LIFO	Last In First Out (Inventories)
LO	Law Opinions
LRAs	Legal Research Assistants
LTCG	Long Term Capital Gain
LTEX	Lifetime Exclusion of Gain on Sale of Personal Residence
Ltr. Rul.	Letter ruling
LVI	Litigating Vehicle Issues
MIS	Management Information Systems
MS	Manual Supplement
MT	Manual Transmittal
NACI	National Agency Check & Inquiry
NAR	No Activity Report
NCA	National Coordinated Audit
NCIC	National Crime Information Center
NDA	New Drug Application
NEC	Non-Employee Compensation
NHA	National Housing Act
NLPI	National List of Prime Issues
NLRB	National Labor Relations Board
NMF	Non-Master File
NOL	Net Operating Loss
NOLD	Net Operating Loss Deduction
NORP	National Office Review Program
NPCC	Narcotics Project Controlled Cases
NRA	National Industrial Recovery Act
NRSA	National Research Service Awards
NYSE	New York Stock Exchange
OD	Office Decisions

ODT	Office of Defense Transportation
OICs	Offers in Compromise
OIO	Office of International Operations
OMB	Office of Management and Budget
OPN	Office of Personnel Management
PAC	Political Activity Cases
PAL	Programmed Audit Library
PBGC	Pension Benefit Guaranty Corp.
PHC	Personal Holding Company
PIF	Preparer Inventory File
PIL	Preparer's Inventory List
PL	Public Law
PLR	Private Letter Ruling
POA	Power of Attorney
PRO	Problem Resolution Officer
PRP	Problem Resolution Program
PS	Policy Statement
PSROs	Professional Standards Review Organizations
QR	Quality Reviewer
QRDT	Questionable Refund Detection Team
QRE	Quality Review Element
QRP	Questionable Refund Program
Q/TIP	Qualified Terminable Interest Property
R&D	Research and Development
R&E	Research & Experimentation
RCA	Regional Coordinated Audit
RCP	Returns Compliance Program
Regs	Regulations
REIT	Real Estate Investment Trust
Rev.Proc.	Revenue Procedure
RFC	Regulated Futures Contract
RFIF	Refund Information File
RIC	Regulated Investment Companies
ROEP	Regional Office Evaluative Program
ROTC	Reserve Officers Training Corps
RPC	Returns Preparer's Coordinator
RPM	Returns Program Manager
RPS	Remittance Processing System
RR	Revenue Release
RRA	Railroad Retirement Act
RRBP	Retirement-Replacement-Betterment Property
RRNS	Related Returns Notification System
RRTA	Railroad Retirement Tax Act
RSDP	Refund Scheme Detection Program
RSI	Regular Shelter Issues

S&L	Savings and Loan
SAR	Stock Appreciation Right
SAT	Systems Acceptability Testing
SCRIP	Systems for Controlling Returns in Inventory and Production
SEP	Simplified Employee Pension
SEP	Special Enforcement Programs
SEH	Standard Explanations Handbook
SEC	Securities and Exchange Commission
SERFE	Selection of Exempt Returns to Examination System
SESA	State Employment Security Agency
SET	Self-Employment Tax Program
SITR	State Income Tax Refund
SL	Straight Line (Depreciation)
SOI	Statistics of Income
SOP	Settlement Option Procedure
SPD	Standard Position Description
SPf	Special Procedures Function
SPS	Special Procedures Staff
SR	Solicitor's Recommendations
SRC	Secured Return Code
SRP	Special Reliance Procedure
STCG	Short Term Capital Gain
SUB	Supplemental Unemployment Benefits
SUB S	Subchapter S Corporation
SVI	Settlement Vehicle Issues
T&E	Travel and Entertainment
TAM	Technical Advice Memorandum
TBM	Tax Board Memorandum
TBR	Tax Board Recommendation
TC	Tax Court
TCA	Tobacco Control Act
TCE	Tax Counseling for the Elderly
TCM	Tax Court Memorandum
TCMP	Taxpayer Compliance Measurement Program
TD	Treasury Decision
TDA	Taxpayer Delinquency Account
TDO	Treasury Department Orders
TDI	Taxpayer Delinquency Investigation
TEA	Trade Expansion Act
TECS	Treasury Enforcement Communications System
TEFRA	The Tax Equity and Fiscal Responsibility Act of 1982
TGR	Total Gross Receipts
TIN	Taxpayer Indentification Number
TIR	Technical Information Release
TJTC	Targeted Jobs Tax Credit

TMs	Technical Memoranda
TPI	Total Positive Income
TRA of 1976	Tax Reform Act of 1976
TRA of 1978	Tax Reform Act of 1978
TSR	Taxpayer Service Representative
TSS	Taxpayer Service Specialists
TVA	Tennessee Valley Authority
UIP	Unreported Income Program
USC	United States Code
USCA	United States Code Annotated
USCA	United States Court of Appeals
USDA	Uniform Simultaneous Death Act
USDC	United States District Court
USO	United Service Organizations
USHA	United States Housing Authority
VA	Veterans' Administration
VEBA	Voluntary Employees' Beneficiary Association
VISTA	Volunteers In Service To America
VITA	Volunteer Income Tax Assistance
WAAC	Women's Army Auxiliary Corps
WACS	Women's Army Corps
WAVES	Women in the United States Navy
WCAB	War Contracts Adjustment Board
WCV	Weighted Call Value
WFC	War Finance Corporation
WHTC	Western Hemisphere Trade Corporation
WIMS	Walk-In Management System
WIN	Work Incentive Program
WLB	War Labor Board
WMC	War Manpower Commission
WPT	Windfall Profit Tax
WSB	Wage Stabilization Board
WSP	Wheat Stabilization Program
WT	Withholding Tax
ZBA	Zero Bracket Amount

INDEX

A

Abandonment, of property. *See also* Abandonment and demolition losses.
  definition, 248
  sale vs., 249-50
Abandonment and demolition losses, 245-54
  audit guide for taxpayer, 251-52
  code and regulation sections, 253-54
  court decisions, 252-53
  factors considered by IRS, 246-47
  IRS manual references, 254
  problem areas, 245-46
Accelerated cost recovery system (ACRS)
  automobile, business use, 325, 327, 329
  repairs vs. capital expenditures, 34
  residential rental property, 335, 336, 337-38
Activity not engaged in for profit
  hobby losses, 21
  vacation homes, 97
Adjusted prime rate, 309
Alimony, 259-60. *See also* Divorce; Divorce and alimony; Divorced parents.
  lump-sum settlement, 259
  periodic payments, 259
Attorney fees. *See* Legal fees.
Automobile, business use, 325-34
  actual-expense method of deduction, 325, 327
  audit guide for taxpayer, 331-32
  code and regulation sections, 334
  court decisions, 333-34
  depreciation, 325, 327, 329
  expensing in lieu of depreciation, 329-30
  factors considered by IRS, 326
  IRS manual references, 334
  vs. personal use, 326-27, 332
  problem areas, 325
  sale vs. trade in, 330-31
  standard mileage allowance, 236, 325, 326, 330

B

Bad debts, 205-15
  audit guide for taxpayer, 213
  Black Motor Co. Formula, 211-12, 213
  business vs. nonbusiness, 208-9
  code and regulation sections, 215

Bad debts *(cont'd.)*
  court decisions, 214
  factors considered by IRS, 207-8
  IRS manual references, 215
  loan guarantees, 213
  problem areas, 205
  reasonable addition to a reserve, 210-12
  recoveries, 212-13
  reserve method of deduction, 210
  specific write-off method of deduction, 210
Bank deposit method of determining income, 222, 226-27
Bankruptcy, and legal fees, 285
Barter Exchange Project, 265, 266
Bartering, 265-71
  audit guide for taxpayer, 269-71
  code and regulation sections, 271
  court decisions, 271
  factors considered by IRS, 266-67
  IRS manual references, 271
  legitimate swaps, 269
  problem areas, 265
  types of, 268-69
Blindness, as a tax exemption, 195-96
Bookkeeping. *See* Records, inadequate.
Bribery questionnaire, IRS, 172-73, 175
Bribes. *See* Kickbacks.
Broker, 70, 71, 317
Business automobile. *See* Automobile, business use.

C

Capital asset, 67-69
  as charitable contribution, 122
  definition, 319-20
Capital expenditures
  definition, 30
  depreciation, 32
  as medical deductions, 89-90
Capital gains. *See also* Capital gains and losses; **Dealers** vs. investors.
  factors characteristic of, 67
  limitations on, 78
  vs. ordinary income, 69-70
Capital gains and losses, 315-24
  audit guide for taxpayer, 321-22
  calculation, 318-19
  code and regulation sections, 323-24

Captial gains and losses *(cont'd.)*
  court decisions, 322-23
  factors considered by IRS, 316-17
  IRS manual references, 324
  problem areas, 315
Capital improvements. *See* Capital expenditures; Repairs
  vs. capital expenditures.
Casualty losses, 53-65
  audit guide for taxpayer, 61-62
  business and income-producing property, 60-61
  code and regulation sections, 64-65
  computation, 56-57, 59
  court decisions, 62-64
  definition, 53
  disaster area losses, 61
  factors considered by IRS, 55-58
  insurance recovery, 59
  IRS manual references, 65
  $125,000 exclusion, 60
  other casualties, 53, 55
  owner of a property, 57-58
  problem areas, 53-54
  10 percent-of-adjusted gross income (AGI) rule, 54, 55,
    56
  time of loss, 54
  valuation determination, 55-56
  year of deduction, 58
Charitable contributions, 115-28
  "as if" rule, 124
  audit guide for taxpayer, 125-26
  "available cash" test, 116
  code and regulation sections, 128
  corporations, 120-21, 124-25
  court decisions, 126-27
  expenses incident to personal services, 121
  factors considered by IRS, 117-18
  IRS manual references, 128
  limitations on, 115, 118, 119, 120-21
  problem areas, 115-16
  property as, 121-24
  qualified donee, 115, 117, 118-19
  qualified donor, 118-19
  real estate, 122-23
Child and disabled dependent care, 139-51
  audit guide for taxpayer, 148-49
  code and regulation sections, 150
  court decisions, 149-50
  dependent, definition, 145-46
  employment-related expenses, 147-48
  factors considered by IRS, 143-44
  IRS manual references, 150-51
  limitations on amount of credit, 147-48
  problem areas, 139, 142
  qualifying individuals, 145
Child support, 256. *See also* Alimony; Child and
  dependent care expenses; Divorce and alimony.
Cohan Rule
  moving expenses, 137
  travel and entertainment expenses, 240-41, 332

Common law employee, 40-43, 48
Compensation, 273-79
  audit guide for taxpayer, 277-78
  code and regulation sections, 279
  Consumer Price Index (CPI), 276
  corporate minutes, 275-76
  court decisions, 278-79
  factors considered by IRS, 274-75
  IRS manual references, 279
  part-time executives, 276-77
  problem areas, 273
  tests of reasonableness, 274-75
Contributions. *See* Charitable contributions.
Corporations
  charitable contributions, 120-21, 124-25
  compensation, 273-79
  corporate minutes and compensation deductions, 275-76
  nondeductible dividends as deductible compensation, 274
  officers' salaries, 274-75
Cosmetic surgery, 85, 87

D

Day care services, 139
  use of home for, 106-7
Dealers vs. investors, 67-83, 321-22
  audit guide for taxpayer, 78-80
  code and regulation sections, 82-83
  court decisions, 80-82
  factors considered by IRS, 71-74
  held primarily for sale to customers, definition, 74-75
  IRS manual references, 83
  problem areas, 67-69
  real estate holdings, 75
  securities, 70-71, 72-74
Demolition. *See also* Abandonment and demolition losses.
  allowable deductions, 250
  buildings rented prior to, 251
  historic structures, 251
  intent, 246, 247, 250-51
Dental deductions. *See* Medical and dental deductions.
Dependent care expenses. *See* Child and dependent care
  expenses.
Dependents, related, 196-97. *See also* Exemptions and
  dependents.
Depreciation. *See also* Accelerated cost recovery system
  (ACRS).
  computing for automobile, 325, 327, 329
  residential rental property, 337-38, 340
Disability benefits. *See also* Sick pay; Sick pay and
  disability income.
  pension vs., 357-58
  taxation of, 355-56
Disabled dependent care. *See* Child and disabled dependent
  care.
Disaster area losses, 61
Disaster Relief Act of 1974, 61
Discriminate Function System (DIF), 267

Divorce, 258-59. *See also* Alimony; Divorce and alimony; Divorced parents.
    foreign, 257
Divorce and alimony, 255-64. *See also* Alimony; Divorce; Divorced parents.
    audit guide for taxpayer, 262
    code and regulation sections, 264
    court decisions, 263-64
    factors considered by IRS, 257-58
    IRS manual references, 264
    legal fees, 261-62
    problem areas, 255-56
    residential expenses, 261
Divorced parents. *See also* Alimony; Divorce; Divorce and alimony.
    children of, 197, 257
    definition, 197
Documentation. *See* Records, inadequate.
Dwelling units, 97-103. *See also* Home office; Sale of a residence; Vacation homes.

E

Economic Recovery Tax Act of 1981 (ERTA)
    automobile deduction, 327
    capital gains and losses, 315, 320
    charitable contributions, 120
    dependent care assistance, 148
    interest expense, 309
    repairs vs. capital expenditures, 29
    residential rental property, 335
Educational assistance programs, 183-84
Educational expenses, 181-88
    audit guide for taxpayer, 186-87
    code and regulation sections, 188
    court decisions, 187-88
    definition, 181
    factors considered by IRS, 183
    IRS manual references, 188
    nondeductible types, 185
    problem areas, 181-82
    travel, 185-86
Employee, definition, 40
Employee vs. independent contractor, 39-52
    audit guide for taxpayer, 49-50
    code and regulation sections, 52
    court decisions, 50-51
    factors considered by IRS, 44-48
    Form 1099 NEC, 43
    IRS manual references, 52
    payroll taxes, 39, 48
    problem areas, 39
    reasonable basis in worker's employment status, 43
    Safe Haven laws, 43
    tax return preparation checklist, 48-49
Employer, definition, 42
Employment Retirement Income Security Act of 1974, 356

Entertainment expenses. *See also* Travel and entertainment expenses.
    club dues, 232, 238
    gifts, 232, 238
    quiet meals rule, 232, 238
Exemptions and dependents, 189-203
    audit guide for taxpayer, 198-99, 200-201
    code and regulation sections, 202
    court decisions, 199, 201-2
    factors considered by IRS, 192-95
    IRS manual references, 203
    problem areas, 189
    tests for, 192-94
    unqualified dependents, 192
Exemption tests, 192-94

F

Fair market value (FMV)
    bartering, 268-69
    gifts of property, 122-26
Fair rental value (FRV), of dwelling unit, 97-98
Federal Employees' Compensation Act (FECA), 358
Federal taxes, as deductions, 343, 348
Federal Unemployment Tax Act (FUTA), 134
Foreign Corrupt Policies Act (1977), 174
Form 1099 NEC (Non-Employee Compensation), 168, 169
Form 2038 (Questionnaire—Exemption Claimed for Dependent), 189, 190-91, 195, 198
Form 2106 (Employee Business Expense), 186, 233, 237, 325, 326, 328-29
Form 2119 (Sale or Exchange of Principal Residence), 154, 156, 160, 161-62
Form 2441 (Credit for Child and Dependent Care Expenses), 139, 140-41, 142, 143, 147-48
Fraud. *See* Tax fraud.

G

General sales taxes, as deductions, 347
Gifts, 238
Gross income, definition, 265

H

Health and accident plans, 356-57. *See also* Sick pay and disability income.
Hobby losses, 21-28
    audit guide for taxpayer, 25
    burden of proof, 24
    code and regulation sections, 27
    court decisions, 25-27
    factors considered by IRS, 22-24
    financial status of taxpayer, 21, 23
    IRS manual references, 28

Hobby losses *(cont'd.)*
  postponement of determination, 25
  problem areas, 21
Home office, 105-13
  audit.guide for taxpayer, 109-11
  code and regulation sections, 112
  court decisions, 111-12
  for day care services, 106-7
  exclusive use, 105, 107, 109
  factors considered by IRS, 107
  IRS manual references, 112-13
  principal place of business, 105-7
  regular basis, 105, 109
  sale of residence, 159-60
  as storage unit, 107
Husband and wife, definition, 255

                        I

Illegal payments. *See* Kickbacks.
Incentive grants. *See* Kickbacks.
Independent contractor. *See* Employee vs. independent
    contractor.
Indexing, exemptions and dependents, 189, 195
Insurance premiums
  medical and dental deductions, 86, 90, 91, 93
Interest expense, 303-13
  audit guide for taxpayer, 310-11
  capitalization of, 306
  code and regulation sections, 312
  court decisions, 311-12
  factors considered by IRS, 304-6
  installment purchases, 307-9
  interest, definition, 303
  IRS manual references, 313
  investment interest, 306-7
  net lease, 307
  "points," 307
  problem areas, 303-4
  unstated interest, computation of, 309
Investor, 67, 71. *See also* Dealers vs. investors.

                        K

Kickbacks, 167-79
  audit guide for taxpayer, 174-75
  audit techniques by IRS, 176-77
  burden of proof, 175
  code and regulation sections, 178
  court decisions, 177-78
  factors considered by IRS, 171-73
  to foreign officials, 174
  to government employees, 168, 174
  IRS bribery questionnaire, 172-73, 175
  IRS manual references, 179
  under medicare and medicaid, 169, 174
  to persons other than public employees, 173-74
  problem areas, 167-69

                        L

Legal and professional fees, 281-90
  audit guide for taxpayer, 287-88
  bankruptcy, 285
  business, formation of, 284
  casualty losses, 59
  checklist, 285-87
  code and regulation sections, 289
  court decisions, 289-90
  divorce, 256, 261-62, 283
  factors considered by IRS, 282-83
  income tax preparation, 283
  IRS manual references, 289-90
  litigation, 284-85
  problem areas, 281
  recovery of, from IRS, 287-88
Local taxes, as deductions, 344, 349-50

                        M

Medical and dental deductions, 85-96
  audit guide for taxpayer, 92-93
  broad interpretation by courts, 87
  checklist, 88-89
  code and regulation sections, 95
  computation of, 90
  court decisions, 94
  double deductions, 86
  insurance, 86, 90, 93
  IRS manual references, 95-96
  medical care, definition, 88
  nursing care, 89
  nursing homes, 89
  problem areas, 85-86
  special education and training, 89
  time of payment, 88
Moving expenses, 129-38
  audit guide for taxpayer, 134, 136-37
  checklist, 134-35
  code and regulation sections, 138
  court decisions, 137-38
  deduction limitations, 131
  definition, 130-31
  direct vs. indirect, 132
  distance test, 131
  employer handling of, 134
  factors considered by IRS, 130
  foreign moves, 131, 132
  IRS manual references, 138
  one-year rule, 132
  problem areas, 129-30
  time test, 131

                        N

Net worth method of determining income, 222, 226-28
Noncash transactions. *See* Bartering.

O

Office in the home. *See* Home office.
Ordinary and necessary expense rule, 233, 234, 284
Other casualties, 53, 55, 64

P

Professional fees. *See* Legal and professional fees.
Property taxes, as deductions, 349

R

Railroad retirement taxes, 355
Real estate
   capital gains vs. ordinary income, 69-70
   dealer vs. investor distinction, 71-72
   held by a dealer, 75
   "points" as interest expense, 307
Real estate taxes, as deductions, 343, 344
Real property subdivided for sale, 75-77
Rebates. *See* Kickbacks.
Records, inadequate, 217-30
   audit guide for taxpayer, 223-28
   code and regulation sections, 229-30
   court decisions, 228-29
   definition, 219
   factors considered by IRS, 219-22
   IRS manual references, 230
   notice of, from IRS, 219-21
   problem areas, 217-18
   taxpayer's responsibility, 218
Repair, definition, 30
Repairs vs. capital expenditures, 29-37
   audit guide for taxpayer, 34-35
   code and regulation sections, 37
   court decisions, 35-37
   factors considered by IRS, 30-32
   general plan of improvement, 33
   for handicapped and elderly, 33
   IRS manual references, 37
   problem areas, 29
   replacement of worn equipment, 33
   restoration of rundown property, 33
   timing of, 32-33
Residence, sale of. *See* Sale of a residence.
Residential rental property, 335-42
   audit guide for taxpayer, 339-40
   code and regulation sections, 341-42
   condominiums and cooperatives, 339
   court decisions, 340-41
   definition, 336
   factors considered by IRS, 336-37
   IRS manual references, 342
   lease with option to purchase, 338-39
   losses, 336
   low-income housing, 338-39
   problem areas, 335-36
Revenue Act of 1978, educational benefits, 183

S

Safe Haven laws, 43
Sale of a residence, 153-65
   audit guide for taxpayer, 160-63
   code and regulation sections, 164-65
   computation of gain, 160-62
   court decisions, 163-64
   deferral of gain, 153-54
   factors considered by IRS, 155-57
   IRS manual references, 165
   older homes, 162-63
   $125,000 exclusion of gain, 153-57, 159, 162
   principal residence, definition, 158
   problem areas, 153-55
   statute of limitations, 160
Sales tax, as deduction, 344, 347
Securities, dealer vs. investor distinction, 70-71, 72-74
Self-employed individuals. *See also* Employee vs.
   independent contractor.
   noncompliance in paying taxes, 42-43
   types of, 41
Sick pay. *See also* Sick pay and disability income.
   definition, 353
   taxability of, 355
Sick pay and disability income, 353-61. *See also* Sick pay.
   audit guide for taxpayer, 358-59
   code and regulation sections, 360
   court decisions, 359-60
   distinction between, 355
   factors considered by IRS, 354-55
   IRS manual references, 361
   problem areas, 353
Slush funds, 171-72, 179, 282
Social Security taxes
   employee vs. independent contractor controversy, 39-51
   moving expenses, 134
   sick pay, 355, 359
State taxes, as deductions, 344, 349-50
Straddles, 309

T

Tax audit, probability of, 295-96
Tax avoidance. *See* Tax fraud.
Tax Equity and Fiscal Responsibility Act of 1982 (TEFRA)
   bartering, 268
   capital gains and losses, 315, 317
   casualty losses, 54
   common law employee, 40-41
   and Form 1099 NEC, 43
   interest expenses, 310, 311
   medical deductions, 91
Taxes, deductions for, 343-52
   audit guide for taxpayer, 348-50
   checklist, 347-48
   code and regulation sections, 351
   court decisions, 350-51
   factors considered by IRS, 345

Taxes, deductions for *(cont'd.)*
  IRS manual references, 351-52
  problem areas, 343-44
Tax evasion. *See* Tax fraud.
Tax fraud, 291-301
  audit guide for taxpayer, 297-99
  burden of proof, 297
  civil fraud penalty, 297
  code and regulation sections, 300-301
  court decisions, 299-300
  criminal vs. civil, 292, 298-99
  definition, 291-92
  factors considered by IRS, 293-95
  innocent spouse, 297
  IRS manual references, 301
  problem areas, 291-92
Tax Reform Act of 1976
  child and disabled dependent care, 142
  home office, 105
  sick pay and disability income, 353-54
  vacation homes, 97, 98, 101
Tax Reform Act of 1978, dwelling units, 101
Trading. *See* Bartering.
Travel expenses. *See also* Travel and entertainment
     expenses.
  car expenses, 236
  for medical care, 90
  mileage allowances, 236
  per diem allowances, 237
  transportation, 234, 235-36
Travel and entertainment expenses, 231-43. *See also*
     Entertainment expenses; Travel expenses.
  audit guide for taxpayer, 239-41
  code and regulation sections, 242
  conventions, 235

Travel and entertainment expenses *(cont'd.)*
  court decisions, 241-42
  diary, 239
  factors considered by IRS, 233
  guidelines for substantiation of, 238-39
  IRS manual references, 243
  ordinary and necessary test, 233, 234
  problem areas, 231-32
  reimbursed expenses, 236-37
  spouse and, 234-35

U

Uncollectibles. See *Bad debts*.

V

Vacation homes, 97-103. *See also* Sale of a residence.
  audit guide for taxpayer, 101-2
  code sections, 103
  computation of gain or loss, 100-101
  court decisions, 102-3
  factors considered by IRS, 98-99
  15 day/10 percent rule, 97-101
  IRS manual references, 103
  personal use, 97, 101
Volume discounts. *See* Kickbacks.

W

Wash sales, of stock, 321